Lucene in Action

Lucene in Action

OTIS GOSPODNETIĆ
ERIK HATCHER

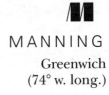

MANNING

Greenwich
(74° w. long.)

For online information and ordering of this and other Manning books, please go to www.manning.com. The publisher offers discounts on this book when ordered in quantity. For more information, please contact:

    Special Sales Department
    Manning Publications Co.
    209 Bruce Park Avenue   Fax: (203) 661-9018
    Greenwich, CT 06830   email: orders@manning.com

Manning Publications Co.   Copyeditor: Tiffany Taylor
209 Bruce Park Avenue   Typesetter: Denis Dalinnik
Greenwich, CT 06830   Cover designer: Leslie Haimes

ISBN 1-932394-28-1

Printed in the United States of America
2 3 4 5 6 7 8 9 10 – VHG – 08 07 06 05

To Ethan, Jakob, and Carole
                                        –E.H.

To the Lucene community, chichimichi, and Saviotlama
                                        –O.G.

brief contents

contents

foreword

Lucene started as a self-serving project. In late 1997, my job uncertain, I sought something of my own to market. Java was the hot new programming language, and I needed an excuse to learn it. I already knew how to write search software, and thought I might fill a niche by writing search software in Java. So I wrote Lucene.

A few years later, in 2000, I realized that I didn't like to market stuff. I had no interest in negotiating licenses and contracts, and I didn't want to hire people and build a company. I liked writing software, not selling it. So I tossed Lucene up on SourceForge, to see if open source might let me keep doing what I liked.

A few folks started using Lucene right away. Around a year later, in 2001, folks at Apache offered to adopt Lucene. The number of daily messages on the Lucene mailing lists grew steadily. Code contributions started to trickle in. Most were additions around the edges of Lucene: I was still the only active developer who fully grokked its core. Still, Lucene was on the road to becoming a real collaborative project.

Now, in 2004, Lucene has a pool of active developers with deep understandings of its core. I'm no longer involved in most day-to-day development; substantial additions and improvements are regularly made by this strong team.

Through the years, Lucene has been translated into several other programming languages, including C++, C#, Perl, and Python. In the original Java, and in these other incarnations, Lucene is used much more widely than I ever would have dreamed. It powers search in diverse applications like discussion groups at Fortune 100 companies, commercial bug trackers, email search supplied by Microsoft, and a web search engine that scales to billions of pages. When, at industry events, I am introduced to someone as the "Lucene guy," more often than not folks tell me how they've used Lucene in a project. I still figure I've only heard about a small fraction of all Lucene applications.

Lucene is much more widely used than it ever would have been if I had tried to sell it. Application developers seem to prefer open source. Instead of having to contact technical support when they have a problem (and then wait for an answer, hoping they were correctly understood), they can frequently just look at the source code to diagnose their problems. If that's not enough, the free support provided by peers on the mailing lists is better than most commercial support. A functioning open-source project like Lucene makes application developers more efficient and productive.

Lucene, through open source, has become something much greater than I ever imagined it would. I set it going, but it took the combined efforts of the Lucene community to make it thrive.

So what's next for Lucene? I can't tell you. Armed with this book, you are now a member of the Lucene community, and it's up to you to take Lucene to new places. Bon voyage!

DOUG CUTTING
Creator of Lucene and Nutch

preface

From Erik Hatcher

I've been intrigued with searching and indexing from the early days of the Internet. I have fond memories (circa 1991) of managing an email list using majordomo, MUSH (Mail User's Shell), and a handful of Perl, awk, and shell scripts. I implemented a CGI web interface to allow users to search the list archives and other users' profiles using grep tricks under the covers. Then along came Yahoo!, AltaVista, and Excite, all which I visited regularly.

After my first child, Jakob, was born, my digital photo archive began growing rapidly. I was intrigued with the idea of developing a system to manage the pictures so that I could attach meta-data to each picture, such as keywords and date taken, and, of course, locate the pictures easily in any dimension I chose. In the late 1990s, I prototyped a filesystem-based approach using Microsoft technologies, including Microsoft Index Server, Active Server Pages, and a third COM component for image manipulation. At the time, my professional life was consumed with these same technologies. I was able to cobble together a compelling application in a couple of days of spare-time hacking.

My professional life shifted toward Java technologies, and my computing life consisted of less and less Microsoft Windows. In an effort to reimplement my personal photo archive and search engine in Java technologies in an operating system–agnostic way, I came across Lucene. Lucene's ease of use far exceeded my expectations—I had experienced numerous other open-source libraries and tools that were far simpler conceptually yet far more complex to use.

In 2001, Steve Loughran and I began writing *Java Development with Ant* (Manning). We took the idea of an image search engine application and generalized it as a document search engine. This application example is used throughout the Ant book and can be customized as an image search engine. The tie to Ant comes not only from a simple compile-and-package build process but also from a custom Ant task, `<index>`, we created that indexes files during the build process using Lucene. This Ant task now lives in Lucene's Sandbox and is described in section 8.4 of this book.

This Ant task is in production use for my custom blogging system, which I call BlogScene (http://www.blogscene.org/erik). I run an Ant build process, after creating a blog entry, which indexes new entries and uploads them to my server. My blog server consists of a servlet, some Velocity templates, and a Lucene index, allowing for rich queries, even syndication of queries. Compared to other blogging systems, BlogScene is vastly inferior in features and finesse, but the full-text search capabilities are very powerful.

I'm now working with the Applied Research in Patacriticism group at the University of Virginia (http://www.patacriticism.org), where I'm putting my text analysis, indexing, and searching expertise to the test and stretching my mind with discussions of how quantum physics relates to literature. "Poets are the unacknowledged engineers of the world."

From Otis Gospodnetić

My interest in and passion for information retrieval and management began during my student years at Middlebury College. At that time, I discovered an immense source of information known as the Web. Although the Web was still in its infancy, the long-term need for gathering, analyzing, indexing, and searching was evident. I became obsessed with creating repositories of information pulled from the Web, began writing web crawlers, and dreamed of ways to search the collected information. I viewed search as the killer application in a largely uncharted territory. With that in the back of my mind, I began the first in my series of projects that share a common denominator: gathering and searching information.

In 1995, fellow student Marshall Levin and I created WebPh, an open-source program used for collecting and retrieving personal contact information. In essence, it was a simple electronic phone book with a web interface (CGI), one of the first of its kind at that time. (In fact, it was cited as an example of prior art in a court case in the late 1990s!) Universities and government institutions around the world have been the primary adopters of this program, and many are still using it. In 1997, armed with my WebPh experience, I proceeded to create Populus, a popular white pages at the time. Even though the technology (similar to that of WebPh) was rudimentary, Populus carried its weight and was a comparable match to the big players such as WhoWhere, Bigfoot, and Infospace.

After two projects that focused on personal contact information, it was time to explore new territory. I began my next venture, Infojump, which involved culling high-quality information from online newsletters, journals, newspapers, and magazines. In addition to my own software, which consisted of large sets of Perl modules and scripts, Infojump utilized a web crawler called Webinator and a full-text search product called Texis. The service provided by Infojump in 1998 was much like that of FindArticles.com today.

Although WebPh, Populus, and Infojump served their purposes and were fully functional, they all had technical limitations. The missing piece in each of them was a powerful information-retrieval library that would allow full-text searches backed by inverted indexes. Instead of trying to reinvent the wheel, I started looking for a solution that I suspected was out there. In early 2000, I found Lucene, the missing piece I'd been looking for, and I fell in love with it.

I joined the Lucene project early on when it still lived at SourceForge and, later, at the Apache Software Foundation when Lucene migrated there in 2002. My devotion to Lucene stems from its being a core component of many ideas that had queued up in my mind over the years. One of those ideas was Simpy, my latest pet project. Simpy is a feature-rich personal web service that lets users tag, index, search, and share information found online. It makes heavy use of Lucene, with thousands of its indexes, and is powered by Nutch, another project of Doug Cutting's (see chapter 10). My active participation in the Lucene project resulted in an offer from Manning to co-author *Lucene in Action* with Erik Hatcher.

Lucene in Action is the most comprehensive source of information about Lucene. The information contained in the next 10 chapters encompasses all the knowledge you need to create sophisticated applications built on top of Lucene. It's the result of a very smooth and agile collaboration process, much like that within the Lucene community. Lucene and *Lucene in Action* exemplify what people can achieve when they have similar interests, the willingness to be flexible, and the desire to contribute to the global knowledge pool, despite the fact that they have yet to meet in person.

acknowledgments

First and foremost, we thank our spouses, Carole (Erik) and Margaret (Otis), for enduring the authoring of this book. Without their support, this book would never have materialized. Erik thanks his two sons, Ethan and Jakob, for their patience and understanding when Dad worked on this book instead of playing with them.

We are sincerely and humbly indebted to Doug Cutting. Without Doug's generosity to the world, there would be no Lucene. Without the other Lucene committers, Lucene would have far fewer features, more bugs, and a much tougher time thriving with the growing adoption of Lucene. Many thanks to all the committers including Peter Carlson, Tal Dayan, Scott Ganyo, Eugene Gluzberg, Brian Goetz, Christoph Goller, Mark Harwood, Tim Jones, Daniel Naber, Andrew C. Oliver, Dmitry Serebrennikov, Kelvin Tan, and Matt Tucker. Similarly, we thank all those who contributed the case studies that appear in chapter 10: Dion Almaer, Michael Cafarella, Bob Carpenter, Karsten Konrad, Terence Parr, Robert Selvaraj, Ralf Steinbach, Holger Stenzhorn, and Craig Walls.

Our thanks to the staff at Manning, including Marjan Bace, Lianna Wlasuik, Karen Tegtmeyer, Susannah Pfalzer, Mary Piergies, Leslie Haimes, David Roberson, Lee Fitzpatrick, Ann Navarro, Clay Andres, Tiffany Taylor, Denis Dalinnik, and Susan Forsyth.

Manning rounded up a great set of reviewers, whom we thank for improving our drafts into what you now read. The reviewers include Doug Warren, Scott Ganyo, Bill Fly, Oliver Zeigermann, Jack Hagan, Michael Oliver, Brian Goetz, Ryan Cox, John D. Mitchell, and Norman Richards. Terry Steichen provided informal feedback, helping clear up some rough spots. Extra-special thanks go to Brian Goetz for his technical editing.

Erik Hatcher

I personally thank Otis for his efforts with this book. Although we've yet to meet in person, Otis has been a joy to work with. He and I have gotten along well and have agreed on the structure and content on this book throughout.

Thanks to Java Java in Charlottesville, Virginia for keeping me wired and wireless; thanks, also, to Greenberry's for staying open later than Java Java and keeping me out of trouble by not having Internet access (update: they now have wi-fi, much to the dismay of my productivity).

The people I've surrounded myself with enrich my life more than anything. David Smith has been a life-long mentor, and his brilliance continues to challenge me; he gave me lots of food for thought regarding Lucene visualization (most of which I'm still struggling to fully grasp, and I apologize that it didn't make it into this manuscript). Jay Zimmerman and the No Fluff, Just Stuff symposium circuit have been dramatically influential for me. The regular NFJS speakers, including Dave Thomas, Stuart Halloway, James Duncan Davidson, Jason Hunter, Ted Neward, Ben Galbraith, Glenn Vanderburg, Venkat Subramaniam, Craig Walls, and Bruce Tate have all been a great source of support and friendship. Rick Hightower and Nick Lesiecki deserve special mention—they both were instrumental in pushing me beyond the limits of my technical and communication abilities. Words do little to express the tireless enthusiasm and encouragement Mike Clark has given me throughout writing *Lucene in Action*. Technically, Mike contributed the JUnitPerf performance-testing examples, but his energy, ambition, and friendship were far more pivotal.

I extend gratitude to Darden Solutions for working with me through my tiring book and travel schedule and allowing me to keep a low-stress part-time day job. A Darden co-worker, Dave Engler, provided the CellPhone skeleton Swing application that I've demonstrated at NFJS sessions and JavaOne and that is included in section 8.6.3; thanks, Dave! Other Darden coworkers, Andrew Shannon and Nick Skriloff, gave us insight into Verity, a competitive solution to using Lucene. Amy Moore provided graphical insight. My great friend Davie Murray patiently created figure 4.4, enduring several revision requests. Daniel Steinberg is a personal friend and mentor, and he allowed me to air Lucene ideas as articles at java.net. Simon Galbraith, a great friend and now a search guru, and I had fun bouncing search ideas around in email.

Otis Gospodnetić

Writing *Lucene in Action* was a big effort for me, not only because of the technical content it contains, but also because I had to fit it in with a full-time day job, side pet projects, and of course my personal life. Somebody needs to figure out how to extend days to at least 48 hours. Working with Erik was a pleasure: His agile development skills are impressive, his flexibility and compassion admirable.

I hate cheesy acknowledgements, but I really can't thank Margaret enough for being so supportive and patient with me. I owe her a lifetime supply of tea and rice. My parents Sanja and Vito opened my eyes early in my childhood by showing me as much of the world as they could, and that made a world of difference. They were also the ones who suggested I write my first book, which eliminated the fear of book-writing early in my life.

I also thank John Stewart and the rest of Wireless Generation, Inc., my employer, for being patient with me over the last year. If you buy a copy of the book, I'll thank you, too!

about this book

Lucene in Action delivers details, best practices, caveats, tips, and tricks for using the best open-source Java search engine available.

This book assumes the reader is familiar with basic Java programming. Lucene itself is a single Java Archive (JAR) file and integrates into the simplest Java stand-alone console program as well as the most sophisticated enterprise application.

Roadmap

We organized part 1 of this book to cover the core Lucene Application Programming Interface (API) in the order you're likely to encounter it as you integrate Lucene into your applications:

- In chapter 1, you meet Lucene. We introduce some basic information-retrieval terminology, and we note Lucene's primary competition. Without wasting any time, we immediately build simple indexing and searching applications that you can put right to use or adapt to your needs. This example application opens the door for exploring the rest of Lucene's capabilities.

- Chapter 2 familiarizes you with Lucene's basic indexing operations. We describe the various field types and techniques for indexing numbers and dates. Tuning the indexing process, optimizing an index, and how to deal with thread-safety are covered.

- Chapter 3 takes you through basic searching, including details of how Lucene ranks documents based on a query. We discuss the fundamental query types as well as how they can be created through human-entered query expressions.

- Chapter 4 delves deep into the heart of Lucene's indexing magic, the analysis process. We cover the analyzer building blocks including tokens, token streams, and token filters. Each of the built-in analyzers gets its share of attention and detail. We build several custom analyzers, showcasing synonym injection and metaphone (like soundex) replacement. Analysis of non-English languages is given attention, with specific examples of analyzing Chinese text.

- Chapter 5 picks up where the searching chapter left off, with analysis now in mind. We cover several advanced searching features, including sorting, filtering, and leveraging term vectors. The advanced query types make their appearance, including the spectacular SpanQuery family. Finally, we cover Lucene's built-in support for query multiple indexes, even in parallel and remotely.

- Chapter 6 goes well beyond advanced searching, showing you how to extend Lucene's searching capabilities. You'll learn how to customize search results sorting, extend query expression parsing, implement hit collecting, and tune query performance. Whew!

Part 2 goes beyond Lucene's built-in facilities and shows you what can be done around and above Lucene:

- In chapter 7, we create a reusable and extensible framework for parsing documents in Word, HTML, XML, PDF, and other formats.

- Chapter 8 includes a smorgasbord of extensions and tools around Lucene. We describe several Lucene index viewing and developer tools as well as the many interesting toys in Lucene's Sandbox. Highlighting search terms is one such Sandbox extension that you'll likely need, along with other goodies like building an index from an Ant build process, using noncore analyzers, and leveraging the WordNet synonym index.

- Chapter 9 demonstrates the ports of Lucene to various languages, such as C++, C#, Perl, and Python.

- Chapter 10 brings all the technical details of Lucene back into focus with many wonderful case studies contributed by those who have built interesting, fast, and scalable applications with Lucene at their core.

Who should read this book?

Developers who need powerful search capabilities embedded in their applications should read this book. *Lucene in Action* is also suitable for developers who are curious about Lucene or indexing and search techniques, but who may not have an immediate need to use it. Adding Lucene know-how to your toolbox is valuable for future projects—search is a hot topic and will continue to be in the future.

This book primarily uses the Java version of Lucene (from Apache Jakarta), and the majority of the code examples use the Java language. Readers familiar with Java will be right at home. Java expertise will be helpful; however, Lucene has been ported to a number of other languages including C++, C#, Python, and Perl. The concepts, techniques, and even the API itself are comparable between the Java and other language versions of Lucene.

Code examples

The source code for this book is available from Manning's website at http://www.manning.com/hatcher2. Instructions for using this code are provided in the README file included with the source-code package.

The majority of the code shown in this book was written by us and is included in the source-code package. Some code (particularly the case-study code) isn't provided in our source-code package; the code snippets shown there are owned by the contributors and are donated as is. In a couple of cases, we have included a small snippet of code from Lucene's codebase, which is licensed under the Apache Software License (http://www.apache.org/licenses/LICENSE-2.0).

Code examples don't include package and import statements, to conserve space; refer to the actual source code for these details.

Why JUnit?

We believe code examples in books should be top-notch quality and real-world applicable. The typical "hello world" examples often insult our intelligence and generally do little to help readers see how to really adapt to their environment.

We've taken a unique approach to the code examples in *Lucene in Action*. Many of our examples are actual JUnit test cases (http://www.junit.org). JUnit, the de facto Java unit-testing framework, easily allows code to assert that a particular assumption works as expected in a repeatable fashion. Automating JUnit test cases through an IDE or Ant allows one-step (or no steps with continuous integration) confidence building. We chose to use JUnit in this book because we use it daily in our other projects and want you to see how we really code. Test Driven Development (TDD) is a development practice we strongly espouse.

If you're unfamiliar with JUnit, please read the following primer. We also suggest that you read *Pragmatic Unit Testing in Java with JUnit* by Dave Thomas and Andy Hunt, followed by Manning's *JUnit in Action* by Vincent Massol and Ted Husted.

JUnit primer

This section is a quick and admittedly incomplete introduction to JUnit. We'll provide the basics needed to understand our code examples. First, our JUnit test cases extend `junit.framework.TestCase` and many extend it indirectly through our custom `LiaTestCase` base class. Our concrete test classes adhere to a naming convention: we suffix class names with *Test*. For example, our `QueryParser` tests are in `QueryParserTest.java`.

JUnit runners automatically execute all methods with the signature `public void testXXX()`, where *XXX* is an arbitrary but meaningful name. JUnit test methods should be concise and clear, keeping good software design in mind (such as not repeating yourself, creating reusable functionality, and so on).

Assertions

JUnit is built around a set of `assert` statements, freeing you to code tests clearly and letting the JUnit framework handle failed assumptions and reporting the details. The most frequently used `assert` statement is `assertEquals`; there are a number of overloaded variants of the `assertEquals` method signature for various data types. An example test method looks like this:

```
public void testExample() {
  SomeObject obj = new SomeObject();
  assertEquals(10, obj.someMethod());
}
```

The `assert` methods throw a runtime exception if the expected value (10, in this example) isn't equal to the actual value (the result of calling `someMethod` on `obj`, in this example). Besides `assertEquals`, there are several other `assert` methods for convenience. We also use `assertTrue(expression)`, `assertFalse(expression)`, and `assertNull(expression)` statements. These test whether the expression is true, false, and null, respectively.

The `assert` statements have overloaded signatures that take an additional `String` parameter as the first argument. This `String` argument is used entirely for reporting purposes, giving the developer more information when a test fails. We use this `String` message argument to be more descriptive (or sometimes comical).

By coding our assumptions and expectations in JUnit test cases in this manner, we free ourselves from the complexity of the large systems we build and can focus on fewer details at a time. With a critical mass of test cases in place, we can remain confident and agile. This confidence comes from knowing that changing code, such as optimizing algorithms, won't break other parts of the system, because if it did, our automated test suite would let us know long before the code made it to production. Agility comes from being able to keep the codebase clean through refactoring. Refactoring is the art (or is it a science?) of changing the internal structure of the code so that it accommodates evolving requirements without affecting the external interface of a system.

JUnit in context

Let's take what we've said so far about JUnit and frame it within the context of this book. JUnit test cases ultimately extend from `junit.framework.TestCase`, and test methods have the `public void testXXX()` signature. One of our test cases (from chapter 3) is shown here:

```
public class BasicSearchingTest extends LiaTestCase {          ◁─┐ LiaTestCase extends
                                                                  junit.framework.
  public void testTerm() throws Exception {                       TestCase
    IndexSearcher searcher = new IndexSearcher(directory);   ◁─┐ directory comes
    Term t = new Term("subject", "ant");                        from LiaTestCase
    Query query = new TermQuery(t);
    Hits hits = searcher.search(query);
    assertEquals("JDwA", 1, hits.length());   ◁─┐ One hit expected for
                                                  search for "ant"
    t = new Term("subject", "junit");
    hits = searcher.search(new TermQuery(t));
    assertEquals(2, hits.length());   ◁─┐ Two hits expected
                                          for "junit"
    searcher.close();
  }
}
```

Of course, we'll explain the Lucene API used in this test case later. Here we'll focus on the JUnit details. A variable used in `testTerm`, `directory`, isn't defined in this class. JUnit provides an initialization hook that executes prior to every test method; this hook is a method with the `public void setUp()` signature. Our `LiaTestCase` base class implements `setUp` in this manner:

```
public abstract class LiaTestCase extends TestCase {
  private String indexDir = System.getProperty("index.dir");
  protected Directory directory;

  protected void setUp() throws Exception {
    directory = FSDirectory.getDirectory(indexDir, false);
  }
}
```

If our first `assert` in `testTerm` fails, we see an exception like this:

```
junit.framework.AssertionFailedError: JDwA expected:<1> but was:<0>
    at lia.searching.BasicSearchingTest.
⇒    testTerm(BasicSearchingTest.java:20)
```

This failure indicates our test data is different than what we expect.

Testing Lucene

The majority of the tests in this book test Lucene itself. In practice, is this realistic? Isn't the idea to write test cases that test our own code, not the libraries themselves? There is an interesting twist to Test Driven Development used for learning an API: Test Driven Learning. It's immensely helpful to write tests directly to a new API in order to learn how it works and what you can expect from it. This is precisely what we've done in most of our code examples, so that tests are testing Lucene itself. Don't throw these learning tests away, though. Keep them around to ensure your expectations of the API hold true when you upgrade to a new version of the API, and refactor them when the inevitable API change is made.

Mock objects

In a couple of cases, we use mock objects for testing purposes. Mock objects are used as probes sent into real business logic in order to assert that the business logic is working properly. For example, in chapter 4, we have a `SynonymEngine` interface (see section 4.6). The real business logic that uses this interface is an analyzer. When we want to test the analyzer itself, it's unimportant what type of `SynonymEngine` is used, but we want to use one that has well defined and predictable behavior. We created a `MockSynonymEngine`, allowing us to reliably and predictably test our analyzer. Mock objects help simplify test cases such that they test only a single facet of a system at a time rather than having intertwined dependencies that lead to complexity in troubleshooting what really went wrong when a test fails. A nice effect of using mock objects comes from the design changes it leads us to, such as separation of concerns and designing using interfaces instead of direct concrete implementations.

Our test data

Most of our book revolves around a common set of example data to provide consistency and avoid having to grok an entirely new set of data for each section. This example data consists of book details. Table 1 shows the data so that you can reference it and make sense of our examples.

Table 1   Sample data used throughout this book

Title / Author	Category	Subject
A Modern Art of Education Rudolf Steiner	/education/pedagogy	education philosophy psychology practice Waldorf
Imperial Secrets of Health and Longevity Bob Flaws	/health/alternative/Chinese	diet chinese medicine qi gong health herbs
Tao Te Ching 道德經 Stephen Mitchell	/philosophy/eastern	taoism
Gödel, Escher, Bach: an Eternal Golden Braid Douglas Hofstadter	/technology/computers/ai	artificial intelligence number theory mathematics music
Mindstorms Seymour Papert	/technology/computers/programming/education	children computers powerful ideas LOGO education
Java Development with Ant Erik Hatcher, Steve Loughran	/technology/computers/programming	apache jakarta ant build tool junit java development
JUnit in Action Vincent Massol, Ted Husted	/technology/computers/programming	junit unit testing mock objects
Lucene in Action Otis Gospodnetić, Erik Hatcher	/technology/computers/programming	lucene search
Extreme Programming Explained Kent Beck	/technology/computers/programming/methodology	extreme programming agile test driven development methodology
Tapestry in Action Howard Lewis-Ship	/technology/computers/programming	tapestry web user interface components
The Pragmatic Programmer Dave Thomas, Andy Hunt	/technology/computers/programming	pragmatic agile methodology developer tools

The data, besides the fields shown in the table, includes fields for ISBN, URL, and publication month. The fields for category and subject are our own subjective values, but the other information is objectively factual about the books.

Code conventions and downloads

Source code in listings or in text is in a fixed width font to separate it from ordinary text. Java method names, within text, generally won't include the full method signature.

In order to accommodate the available page space, code has been formatted with a limited width, including line continuation markers where appropriate.

We don't include import statements and rarely refer to fully qualified class names—this gets in the way and takes up valuable space. Refer to Lucene's Java-docs for this information. All decent IDEs have excellent support for automatically adding import statements; Erik blissfully codes without knowing fully qualified classnames using IDEA IntelliJ, and Otis does the same with XEmacs. Add the Lucene JAR to your project's classpath, and you're all set. Also on the classpath issue (which is a notorious nuisance), we assume that the Lucene JAR and any other necessary JARs are available in the classpath and don't show it explicitly.

We've created a lot of examples for this book that are freely available to you. A .zip file of all the code is available from Manning's web site for *Lucene in Action*: http://www.manning.com/hatcher2. Detailed instructions on running the sample code are provided in the main directory of the expanded archive as a README file.

Author online

The purchase of *Lucene in Action* includes free access to a private web forum run by Manning Publications, where you can discuss the book with the authors and other readers. To access the forum and subscribe to it, point your web browser to http://www.manning.com/hatcher2. This page provides information on how to get on the forum once you are registered, what kind of help is available, and the rules of conduct on the forum.

About the authors

Erik Hatcher codes, writes, and speaks on technical topics that he finds fun and challenging. He has written software for a number of diverse industries using many different technologies and languages. Erik coauthored *Java Development with Ant* (Manning, 2002) with Steve Loughran, a book that has received wonderful industry acclaim. Since the release of Erik's first book, he has spoken at numerous venues including the No Fluff, Just Stuff symposium circuit, JavaOne,

O'Reilly's Open Source Convention, the Open Source Content Management Conference, and many Java User Group meetings. As an Apache Software Foundation member, he is an active contributor and committer on several Apache projects including Lucene, Ant, and Tapestry. Erik currently works at the University of Virginia's Humanities department supporting Applied Research in Patacriticism. He lives in Charlottesville, Virginia with his beautiful wife, Carole, and two astounding sons, Ethan and Jakob.

Otis Gospodnetić has been an active Lucene developer for four years and maintains the jGuru Lucene FAQ. He is a Software Engineer at Wireless Generation, a company that develops technology solutions for educational assessments of students and teachers. In his spare time, he develops Simpy, a Personal Web service that uses Lucene, which he created out of his passion for knowledge, information retrieval, and management. Previous technical publications include several articles about Lucene, published by O'Reilly Network and IBM developerWorks. Otis also wrote *To Choose and Be Chosen: Pursuing Education in America*, a guidebook for foreigners wishing to study in the United States; it's based on his own experience. Otis is from Croatia and currently lives in New York City.

About the title

By combining introductions, overviews, and how-to examples, the *In Action* books are designed to help learning *and* remembering. According to research in cognitive science, the things people remember are things they discover during self-motivated exploration.

Although no one at Manning is a cognitive scientist, we are convinced that for learning to become permanent it must pass through stages of exploration, play, and, interestingly, re-telling of what is being learned. People understand and remember new things, which is to say they master them, only after actively exploring them. Humans learn *in action*. An essential part of an *In Action* guide is that it is example-driven. It encourages the reader to try things out, to play with new code, and explore new ideas.

There is another, more mundane, reason for the title of this book: our readers are busy. They use books to do a job or solve a problem. They need books that allow them to jump in and jump out easily and learn just what they want just when they want it. They need books that aid them *in action*. The books in this series are designed for such readers.

About the cover illustration

The figure on the cover of *Lucene in Action* is "An inhabitant of the coast of Syria."
The illustration is taken from a collection of costumes of the Ottoman Empire
published on January 1, 1802, by William Miller of Old Bond Street, London.
The title page is missing from the collection and we have been unable to track it
down to date. The book's table of contents identifies the figures in both English
and French, and each illustration bears the names of two artists who worked on
it, both of whom would no doubt be surprised to find their art gracing the front
cover of a computer programming book…two hundred years later.

The collection was purchased by a Manning editor at an antiquarian flea market in the "Garage" on West 26th Street in Manhattan. The seller was an American based in Ankara, Turkey, and the transaction took place just as he was
packing up his stand for the day. The Manning editor did not have on his person
the substantial amount of cash that was required for the purchase and a credit
card and check were both politely turned down.

With the seller flying back to Ankara that evening the situation was getting
hopeless. What was the solution? It turned out to be nothing more than an old-
fashioned verbal agreement sealed with a handshake. The seller simply pro-
posed that the money be transferred to him by wire and the editor walked out
with the seller's bank information on a piece of paper and the portfolio of
images under his arm. Needless to say, we transferred the funds the next day,
and we remain grateful and impressed by this unknown person's trust in one of
us. It recalls something that might have happened a long time ago.

The pictures from the Ottoman collection, like the other illustrations that
appear on our covers, bring to life the richness and variety of dress customs of
two centuries ago. They recall the sense of isolation and distance of that
period—and of every other historic period except our own hyperkinetic present.

Dress codes have changed since then and the diversity by region, so rich at
the time, has faded away. It is now often hard to tell the inhabitant of one conti-
nent from another. Perhaps, trying to view it optimistically, we have traded a cul-
tural and visual diversity for a more varied personal life. Or a more varied and
interesting intellectual and technical life.

We at Manning celebrate the inventiveness, the initiative, and, yes, the fun of
the computer business with book covers based on the rich diversity of regional
life of two centuries ago, brought back to life by the pictures from this collection.

Part 1

Core Lucene

The first half of this book covers out-of-the-box (errr... out of the JAR) Lucene. You'll "Meet Lucene" with a general overview and develop a complete indexing and searching application. Each successive chapter systematically delves into specific areas. "Indexing" data and documents and subsequently "Searching" for them are the first steps to using Lucene. Returning to a glossed-over indexing process, "Analysis," will fill in your understanding of what happens to the text indexed with Lucene. Searching is where Lucene really shines: This section concludes with "Advanced searching" techniques using only the built-in features, and "Extending search" showcasing Lucene's extensibility for custom purposes.

Meet Lucene

This chapter covers
- Understanding Lucene
- Using the basic indexing API
- Working with the search API
- Considering alternative products

One of the key factors behind Lucene's popularity and success is its simplicity. The careful exposure of its indexing and searching API is a sign of the well-designed software. Consequently, you don't need in-depth knowledge about how Lucene's information indexing and retrieval work in order to start using it. Moreover, Lucene's straightforward API requires you to learn how to use only a handful of its classes.

In this chapter, we show you how to perform basic indexing and searching with Lucene with ready-to-use code examples. We then briefly introduce all the core elements you need to know for both of these processes. We also provide brief reviews of competing Java/non-Java, free, and commercial products.

1.1 Evolution of information organization and access

In order to make sense of the perceived complexity of the world, humans have invented categorizations, classifications, genuses, species, and other types of hierarchical organizational schemes. The Dewey decimal system for categorizing items in a library collection is a classic example of a hierarchical categorization scheme. The explosion of the Internet and electronic data repositories has brought large amounts of information within our reach. Some companies, such as Yahoo!, have made organization and classification of online data their business. With time, however, the amount of data available has become so vast that we needed alternate, more dynamic ways of finding information. Although we can classify data, trawling through hundreds or thousands of categories and subcategories of data is no longer an efficient method for finding information.

The need to quickly locate information in the sea of data isn't limited to the Internet realm—desktop computers can store increasingly more data. Changing directories and expanding and collapsing hierarchies of folders isn't an effective way to access stored documents. Furthermore, we no longer use computers just for their raw computing abilities: They also serve as multimedia players and media storage devices. Those uses for computers require the ability to quickly find a specific piece of data; what's more, we need to make rich media—such as images, video, and audio files in various formats—easy to locate.

With this abundance of information, and with time being one of the most precious commodities for most people, we need to be able to make flexible, free-form, ad-hoc queries that can quickly cut across rigid category boundaries and find exactly what we're after while requiring the least effort possible.

To illustrate the pervasiveness of searching across the Internet and the desktop, figure 1.1 shows a search for *lucene* at Google. The figure includes a context

Figure 1.1   Convergence of Internet searching with Google and the web browser.

menu that lets us use Google to search for the highlighted text. Figure 1.2 shows the Apple Mac OS X Finder (the counterpart to Microsoft's Explorer on Windows) and the search feature embedded at upper right. The Mac OS X music player, iTunes, also has embedded search capabilities, as shown in figure 1.3.

Search functionality is everywhere! All major operating systems have embedded searching. The most recent innovation is the Spotlight feature (http://www.apple.com/macosx/tiger/spotlighttech.html) announced by Steve Jobs in the

Figure 1.2   Mac OS X Finder with its embedded search capability.

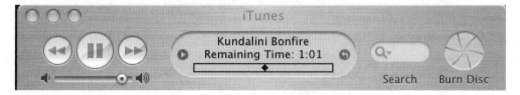

Figure 1.3   Apple's iTunes intuitively embeds search functionality.

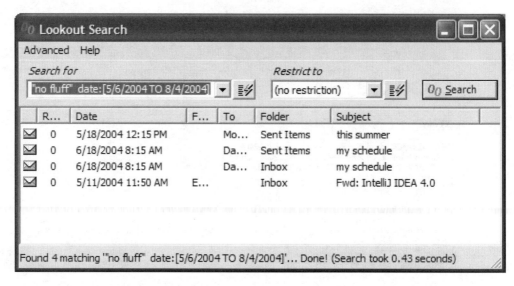

Figure 1.4   Microsoft's newly acquired Lookout product, using Lucene.Net underneath.

next version of Mac OS X (nicknamed *Tiger*); it integrates indexing and searching across all file types including rich metadata specific to each type of file, such as emails, contacts, and more.[1]

Google has gone IPO. Microsoft has released a beta version of its MSN search engine; on a potentially related note, Microsoft acquired Lookout, a product leveraging the Lucene.Net port of Lucene to index and search Microsoft Outlook email and personal folders (as shown in figure 1.4). Yahoo! purchased Overture and is beefing up its custom search capabilities.

To understand what role Lucene plays in search, let's start from the basics and learn about what Lucene is and how it can help you with your search needs.

1.2 *Understanding Lucene*

Different people are fighting the same problem—information overload—using different approaches. Some have been working on novel user interfaces, some on intelligent agents, and others on developing sophisticated search tools like Lucene. Before we jump into action with code samples later in this chapter, we'll give you a high-level picture of what Lucene is, what it is not, and how it came to be.

---

[1]   Erik freely admits to his fondness of all things Apple.

1.2.1 *What Lucene is*

Lucene is a high performance, scalable Information Retrieval (IR) library. It lets you add indexing and searching capabilities to your applications. Lucene is a mature, free, open-source project implemented in Java; it's a member of the popular Apache Jakarta family of projects, licensed under the liberal Apache Software License. As such, Lucene is currently, and has been for a few years, the most popular free Java IR library.

> **NOTE**   Throughout the book, we'll use the term Information Retrieval (IR) to describe search tools like Lucene. People often refer to IR libraries as *search engines*, but you shouldn't confuse IR libraries with web search engines.

As you'll soon discover, Lucene provides a simple yet powerful core API that requires minimal understanding of full-text indexing and searching. You need to learn about only a handful of its classes in order to start integrating Lucene into an application. Because Lucene is a Java library, it doesn't make assumptions about what it indexes and searches, which gives it an advantage over a number of other search applications.

People new to Lucene often mistake it for a ready-to-use application like a file-search program, a web crawler, or a web site search engine. That isn't what Lucene is: Lucene is a software library, a toolkit if you will, not a full-featured search application. It concerns itself with text indexing and searching, and it does those things very well. Lucene lets your application deal with business rules specific to its problem domain while hiding the complexity of indexing and searching implementation behind a simple-to-use API. You can think of Lucene as a layer that applications sit on top of, as depicted in figure 1.5.

A number of full-featured search applications have been built on top of Lucene. If you're looking for something prebuilt or a framework for crawling, document handling, and searching, consult the Lucene Wiki "powered by" page (http://wiki.apache.org/jakarta-lucene/PoweredBy) for many options: Zilverline, SearchBlox, Nutch, LARM, and jSearch, to name a few. Case studies of both Nutch and SearchBlox are included in chapter 10.

1.2.2 *What Lucene can do for you*

Lucene allows you to add indexing and searching capabilities to your applications (these functions are described in section 1.3). Lucene can index and make searchable any data that can be converted to a textual format. As you can see in figure 1.5,

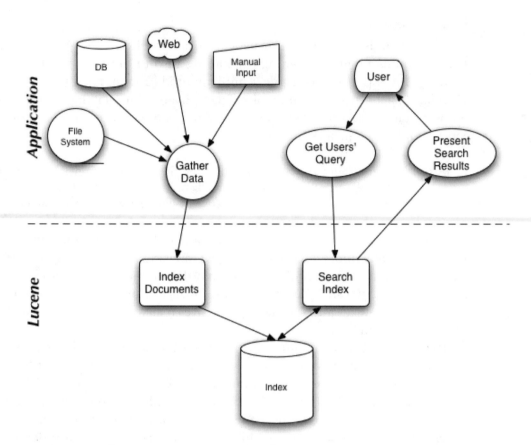

Figure 1.5   A typical application integration with Lucene

Lucene doesn't care about the source of the data, its format, or even its language, as long as you can convert it to text. This means you can use Lucene to index and search data stored in files: web pages on remote web servers, documents stored in local file systems, simple text files, Microsoft Word documents, HTML or PDF files, or any other format from which you can extract textual information.

Similarly, with Lucene's help you can index data stored in your databases, giving your users full-text search capabilities that many databases don't provide. Once you integrate Lucene, users of your applications can make searches such as `+George +Rice -eat -pudding`, `Apple -pie +Tiger`, `animal:monkey AND food:banana`, and so on. With Lucene, you can index and search email messages, mailing-list archives, instant messenger chats, your Wiki pages ... the list goes on.

1.2.3 *History of Lucene*

Lucene was originally written by Doug Cutting;[2] it was initially available for download from its home at the SourceForge web site. It joined the Apache Software Foundation's Jakarta family of high-quality open source Java products in September 2001. With each release since then, the project has enjoyed increased visibility, attracting more users and developers. As of July 2004, Lucene version 1.4 has been released, with a bug fix 1.4.2 release in early October. Table 1.1 shows Lucene's release history.

Table 1.1   Lucene's release history

Version	Release date	Milestones
0.01	March 2000	First open source release (SourceForge)
1.0	October 2000	
1.01b	July 2001	Last SourceForge release
1.2	June 2002	First Apache Jakarta release
1.3	December 2003	Compound index format, QueryParser enhancements, remote searching, token positioning, extensible scoring API
1.4	July 2004	Sorting, span queries, term vectors
1.4.1	August 2004	Bug fix for sorting performance
1.4.2	October 2004	IndexSearcher optimization and misc. fixes
1.4.3	Winter 2004	Misc. fixes

NOTE   Lucene's creator, Doug Cutting, has significant theoretical and practical experience in the field of IR. He's published a number of research papers on various IR topics and has worked for companies such as Excite, Apple, and Grand Central. Most recently, worried about the decreasing number of web search engines and a potential monopoly in that realm, he created Nutch, the first open-source World-Wide Web search engine (http://www.nutch.org); it's designed to handle crawling, indexing, and searching of several billion frequently updated web pages. Not surprisingly, Lucene is at the core of Nutch; section 10.1 includes a case study of how Nutch leverages Lucene.

---

[2] *Lucene* is Doug's wife's middle name; it's also her maternal grandmother's first name.

Doug Cutting remains the main force behind Lucene, but more bright minds have joined the project since Lucene's move under the Apache Jakarta umbrella. At the time of this writing, Lucene's core team includes about half a dozen active developers, two of whom are authors of this book. In addition to the official project developers, Lucene has a fairly large and active technical user community that frequently contributes patches, bug fixes, and new features.

1.2.4   Who uses Lucene

Who doesn't? In addition to those organizations mentioned on the Powered by Lucene page on Lucene's Wiki, a number of other large, well-known, multinational organizations are using Lucene. It provides searching capabilities for the Eclipse IDE, the Encyclopedia Britannica CD-ROM/DVD, FedEx, the Mayo Clinic, Hewlett-Packard, *New Scientist* magazine, Epiphany, MIT's OpenCourseware and DSpace, Akamai's EdgeComputing platform, and so on. Your name will be on this list soon, too.

1.2.5   Lucene ports: Perl, Python, C++, .NET, Ruby

One way to judge the success of open source software is by the number of times it's been ported to other programming languages. Using this metric, Lucene is quite a success! Although the original Lucene is written in Java, as of this writing Lucene has been ported to Perl, Python, C++, and .NET, and some groundwork has been done to port it to Ruby. This is excellent news for developers who need to access Lucene indices from applications written in different languages. You can learn more about some of these ports in chapter 9.

1.3   Indexing and searching

At the heart of all search engines is the concept of *indexing*: processing the original data into a highly efficient cross-reference lookup in order to facilitate rapid searching. Let's take a quick high-level look at both the indexing and searching processes.

1.3.1   What is indexing, and why is it important?

Suppose you needed to search a large number of files, and you wanted to be able to find files that contained a certain word or a phrase. How would you go about writing a program to do this? A naïve approach would be to sequentially scan each file for the given word or phrase. This approach has a number of flaws, the most obvious of which is that it doesn't scale to larger file sets or cases where files are very large. This is where indexing comes in: To search large amounts of text quickly, you must first index that text and convert it into a format that will let you search it rapidly, eliminating the slow sequential scanning process. This conversion process is called *indexing*, and its output is called an *index*.

You can think of an index as a data structure that allows fast random access to words stored inside it. The concept behind it is analogous to an index at the end of a book, which lets you quickly locate pages that discuss certain topics. In the case of Lucene, an index is a specially designed data structure, typically stored on the file system as a set of index files. We cover the structure of index files in detail in appendix B, but for now just think of a Lucene index as a tool that allows quick word lookup.

1.3.2 *What is searching?*

Searching is the process of looking up words in an index to find documents where they appear. The quality of a search is typically described using *precision* and *recall* metrics. Recall measures how well the search system finds relevant documents, whereas precision measures how well the system filters out the irrelevant documents. However, you must consider a number of other factors when thinking about searching. We already mentioned speed and the ability to quickly search large quantities of text. Support for single and multiterm queries, phrase queries, wildcards, result ranking, and sorting are also important, as is a friendly syntax for entering those queries. Lucene's powerful software library offers a number of search features, bells, and whistles—so many that we had to spread our search coverage over three chapters (chapters 3, 5, and 6).

1.4 *Lucene in action: a sample application*

Let's see Lucene in action. To do that, recall the problem of indexing and searching files, which we described in section 1.3.1. Furthermore, suppose you need to index and search files stored in a directory tree, not just in a single directory. To show you Lucene's indexing and searching capabilities, we'll use a pair of command-line applications: Indexer and Searcher. First we'll index a directory tree containing text files; then we'll search the created index.

These example applications will familiarize you with Lucene's API, its ease of use, and its power. The code listings are complete, ready-to-use command-line programs. If file indexing/searching is the problem you need to solve, then you can copy the code listings and tweak them to suit your needs. In the chapters that follow, we'll describe each aspect of Lucene's use in much greater detail.

Before we can search with Lucene, we need to build an index, so we start with our `Indexer` application.

1.4.1 Creating an index

In this section you'll see a single class called `Indexer` and its four static methods; together, they recursively traverse file system directories and index all files with a .txt extension. When `Indexer` completes execution it leaves behind a Lucene index for its sibling, `Searcher` (presented in section 1.4.2).

We don't expect you to be familiar with the few Lucene classes and methods used in this example—we'll explain them shortly. After the annotated code listing, we show you how to use `Indexer`; if it helps you to learn how `Indexer` is used before you see how it's coded, go directly to the usage discussion that follows the code.

Using Indexer to index text files

Listing 1.1 shows the `Indexer` command-line program. It takes two arguments:

- A path to a directory where we store the Lucene index
- A path to a directory that contains the files we want to index

Listing 1.1 `Indexer`: traverses a file system and indexes .txt files

```
/**
 * This code was originally written for
 * Erik's Lucene intro java.net article
 */
public class Indexer {

  public static void main(String[] args) throws Exception {
    if (args.length != 2) {
      throw new Exception("Usage: java " + Indexer.class.getName()
        + " <index dir> <data dir>");
    }
    File indexDir = new File(args[0]);        ← Create Lucene index in this directory
    File dataDir = new File(args[1]);         ← Index files in this directory

    long start = new Date().getTime();
    int numIndexed = index(indexDir, dataDir);
    long end = new Date().getTime();

    System.out.println("Indexing " + numIndexed + " files took "
      + (end - start) + " milliseconds");
  }

  // open an index and start file directory traversal
  public static int index(File indexDir, File dataDir)
    throws IOException {
```

```
  if (!dataDir.exists() || !dataDir.isDirectory()) {
    throw new IOException(dataDir
      + " does not exist or is not a directory");
  }

  IndexWriter writer = new IndexWriter(indexDir,        ❶ Create
    new StandardAnalyzer(), true);                        Lucene index
  writer.setUseCompoundFile(false);

  indexDirectory(writer, dataDir);

  int numIndexed = writer.docCount();
  writer.optimize();
  writer.close();          ◁──┐ Close
  return numIndexed;           │ index
}

// recursive method that calls itself when it finds a directory
private static void indexDirectory(IndexWriter writer, File dir)
  throws IOException {

  File[] files = dir.listFiles();

  for (int i = 0; i < files.length; i++) {
    File f = files[i];
    if (f.isDirectory()) {
      indexDirectory(writer, f);        ❷ Recurse
    } else if (f.getName().endsWith(".txt")) {    ◁──┐ Index .txt
      indexFile(writer, f);                          │ files only
    }
  }
}

// method to actually index a file using Lucene
private static void indexFile(IndexWriter writer, File f)
  throws IOException {

  if (f.isHidden() || !f.exists() || !f.canRead()) {
    return;
  }

  System.out.println("Indexing " + f.getCanonicalPath());

  Document doc = new Document();
  doc.add(Field.Text("contents", new FileReader(f)));   ❸ Index file
                                                           content
  doc.add(Field.Keyword("filename", f.getCanonicalPath()));   ❹ Index
  writer.addDocument(doc);        ❺ Add document               filename
}                                   to Lucene index
}
```

Interestingly, the bulk of the code performs recursive directory traversal (❷). Only the creation and closing of the IndexWriter (❶) and four lines in the indexFile method (❸ ❹ ❺) of Indexer involve the Lucene API—effectively six lines of code.

This example intentionally focuses on text files with .txt extensions to keep things simple while demonstrating Lucene's usage and power. In chapter 7, we'll show you how to handle nontext files, and we'll develop a small ready-to-use framework capable of parsing and indexing documents in several common formats.

Running Indexer

From the command line, we ran Indexer against a local working directory including Lucene's own source code. We instructed Indexer to index files under the /lucene directory and store the Lucene index in the build/index directory:

```
% java lia.meetlucene.Indexer build/index/lucene

Indexing /lucene/build/test/TestDoc/test.txt
Indexing /lucene/build/test/TestDoc/test2.txt
Indexing /lucene/BUILD.txt
Indexing /lucene/CHANGES.txt
Indexing /lucene/LICENSE.txt
Indexing /lucene/README.txt
Indexing /lucene/src/jsp/README.txt
Indexing /lucene/src/test/org/apache/lucene/analysis/ru/
⇒   stemsUnicode.txt
Indexing /lucene/src/test/org/apache/lucene/analysis/ru/test1251.txt
Indexing /lucene/src/test/org/apache/lucene/analysis/ru/testKOI8.txt
Indexing /lucene/src/test/org/apache/lucene/analysis/ru/
⇒   testUnicode.txt
Indexing /lucene/src/test/org/apache/lucene/analysis/ru/
⇒   wordsUnicode.txt
Indexing /lucene/todo.txt
Indexing 13 files took 2205 milliseconds
```

Indexer prints out the names of files it indexes, so you can see that it indexes only files with the .txt extension.

> **NOTE** If you're running this application on a Windows platform command shell, you need to adjust the command line's directory and path separators. The Windows command line is java build/index c:\lucene.

When it completes indexing, Indexer prints out the number of files it indexed and the time it took to do so. Because the reported time includes both file-directory traversal and indexing, you shouldn't consider it an official performance measure.

In our example, each of the indexed files was small, but roughly two seconds to index a handful of text files is reasonably impressive.

Indexing speed is a concern, and we cover it in chapter 2. But generally, searching is of even greater importance.

1.4.2 Searching an index

Searching in Lucene is as fast and simple as indexing; the power of this functionality is astonishing, as chapters 3 and 5 will show you. For now, let's look at Searcher, a command-line program that we'll use to search the index created by Indexer. (Keep in mind that our Searcher serves the purpose of demonstrating the use of Lucene's search API. Your search application could also take a form of a web or desktop application with a GUI, an EJB, and so on.)

In the previous section, we indexed a directory of text files. The index, in this example, resides in a directory of its own on the file system. We instructed Indexer to create a Lucene index in a build/index directory, relative to the directory from which we invoked Indexer. As you saw in listing 1.1, this index contains the indexed files and their absolute paths. Now we need to use Lucene to search that index in order to find files that contain a specific piece of text. For instance, we may want to find all files that contain the keyword *java* or *lucene*, or we may want to find files that include the phrase "system requirements".

Using Searcher to implement a search

The Searcher program complements Indexer and provides command-line searching capability. Listing 1.2 shows Searcher in its entirety. It takes two command-line arguments:

- The path to the index created with Indexer
- A query to use to search the index

> **Listing 1.2** **Searcher**: searches a Lucene index for a query passed as an argument

```
/**
 * This code was originally written for
 * Erik's Lucene intro java.net article
 */
public class Searcher {

  public static void main(String[] args) throws Exception {
    if (args.length != 2) {
      throw new Exception("Usage: java " + Searcher.class.getName()
        + " <index dir> <query>");
    }
```

```
                                              | Index directory
    File indexDir = new File(args[0]);   <─┘  created by Indexer
    String q = args[1];     <─ Query string

    if (!indexDir.exists() || !indexDir.isDirectory()) {
      throw new Exception(indexDir +
        " does not exist or is not a directory.");
    }

    search(indexDir, q);
  }

  public static void search(File indexDir, String q)
    throws Exception {
    Directory fsDir = FSDirectory.getDirectory(indexDir, false);
    IndexSearcher is = new IndexSearcher(fsDir);        ❶ Open index

    Query query = QueryParser.parse(q, "contents",      ❷ Parse query
      new StandardAnalyzer());
    long start = new Date().getTime();
    Hits hits = is.search(query);        ❸ Search index
    long end = new Date().getTime();

    System.err.println("Found " + hits.length() +    <─┐ Write search
      " document(s) (in " + (end - start) +            | stats
      " milliseconds) that matched query '" +
        q + "':");

    for (int i = 0; i < hits.length(); i++) {
      Document doc = hits.doc(i);               ❹ Retrieve matching document
      System.out.println(doc.get("filename"));  <─┐ Display
    }                                              | filename
  }
}
```

Searcher, like its Indexer sibling, has only a few lines of code dealing with
Lucene. A couple of special things occur in the search method,

❶ We use Lucene's IndexSearcher and FSDirectory classes to open our index for
searching.

❷ We use QueryParser to parse a human-readable query into Lucene's Query class.

❸ Searching returns hits in the form of a Hits object.

❹ Note that the Hits object contains only references to the underlying documents.
In other words, instead of being loaded immediately upon search, matches are
loaded from the index in a lazy fashion—only when requested with the hits.
doc(int) call.

Running Searcher

Let's run `Searcher` and find some documents in our index using the query `'lucene'`:

```
%java lia.meetlucene.Searcher build/index 'lucene'

Found 6 document(s) (in 66 milliseconds) that matched
⇒   query 'lucene':
/lucene/README.txt
/lucene/src/jsp/README.txt
/lucene/BUILD.txt
/lucene/todo.txt
/lucene/LICENSE.txt
/lucene/CHANGES.txt
```

The output shows that 6 of the 13 documents we indexed with `Indexer` contain the word *lucene* and that the search took a meager 66 milliseconds. Because `Indexer` stores files' absolute paths in the index, `Searcher` can print them out. It's worth noting that storing the file path as a field was our decision and appropriate in this case, but from Lucene's perspective it's arbitrary meta-data attached to indexed documents.

Of course, you can use more sophisticated queries, such as `'lucene AND doug'` or `'lucene AND NOT slow'` or `'+lucene +book'`, and so on. Chapters 3, 5, and 6 cover all different aspects of searching, including Lucene's query syntax.

Using the xargs utility

The `Searcher` class is a simplistic demo of Lucene's search features. As such, it only dumps matches to the standard output. However, `Searcher` has one more trick up its sleeve. Imagine that you need to find files that contain a certain keyword or phrase, and then you want to process the matching files in some way. To keep things simple, let's imagine that you want to list each matching file using the `ls` UNIX command, perhaps to see the file size, permission bits, or owner. By having matching document paths written unadorned to the standard output, and having the statistical output written to standard error, you can use the nifty UNIX `xargs` utility to process the matched files, as shown here:

```
% java lia.meetlucene.Searcher build/index
⇒   'lucene AND NOT slow' | xargs ls -l

Found 6 document(s) (in 131 milliseconds) that
⇒   matched query 'lucene AND NOT slow':
-rw-r--r--  1 erik   staff    4215 10 Sep 21:51 /lucene/BUILD.txt
-rw-r--r--  1 erik   staff   17889 28 Dec 10:53 /lucene/CHANGES.txt
-rw-r--r--  1 erik   staff    2670  4 Nov 2001 /lucene/LICENSE.txt
```

```
-rw-r--r--   1 erik   staff     683  4 Nov  2001 /lucene/README.txt
-rw-r--r--   1 erik   staff     370 26 Jan  2002 /lucene/src/jsp/
⇒  README.txt
-rw-r--r--   1 erik   staff     943 18 Sep 21:27 /lucene/todo.txt
```

In this example, we chose the Boolean query `'lucene AND NOT slow'`, which finds all files that contain the word *lucene* and don't contain the word *slow*. This query took 131 milliseconds and found 6 matching files. We piped `Searcher`'s output to the `xargs` command, which in turn used the `ls -l` command to list each matching file. In a similar fashion, the matched files could be copied, concatenated, emailed, or dumped to standard output.[3]

Our example indexing and searching applications demonstrate Lucene in a lot of its glory. Its API usage is simple and unobtrusive. The bulk of the code (and this applies to all applications interacting with Lucene) is plumbing relating to the business purpose—in this case, `Indexer`'s file system crawler that looks for text files and `Searcher`'s code that prints matched filenames based on a query to the standard output. But don't let this fact, or the conciseness of the examples, tempt you into complacence: There is a lot going on under the covers of Lucene, and we've used quite a few best practices that come from experience. To effectively leverage Lucene, it's important to understand more about how it works and how to extend it when the need arises. The remainder of this book is dedicated to giving you these missing pieces.

1.5 *Understanding the core indexing classes*

As you saw in our `Indexer` class, you need the following classes to perform the simplest indexing procedure:

- `IndexWriter`
- `Directory`
- `Analyzer`
- `Document`
- `Field`

What follows is a brief overview of these classes, to give you a rough idea about their role in Lucene. We'll use these classes throughout this book.

---

[3] Neal Stephenson details this process nicely in "In the Beginning Was the Command Line": http://www.cryptonomicon.com/beginning.html.

1.5.1 *IndexWriter*

IndexWriter is the central component of the indexing process. This class creates a new index and adds documents to an existing index. You can think of Index-Writer as an object that gives you write access to the index but doesn't let you read or search it. Despite its name, IndexWriter isn't the only class that's used to modify an index; section 2.2 describes how to use the Lucene API to modify an index.

1.5.2 *Directory*

The Directory class represents the location of a Lucene index. It's an abstract class that allows its subclasses (two of which are included in Lucene) to store the index as they see fit. In our Indexer example, we used a path to an actual file system directory to obtain an instance of Directory, which we passed to IndexWriter's constructor. IndexWriter then used one of the concrete Directory implementations, FSDirectory, and created our index in a directory in the file system.

In your applications, you will most likely be storing a Lucene index on a disk. To do so, use FSDirectory, a Directory subclass that maintains a list of real files in the file system, as we did in Indexer.

The other implementation of Directory is a class called RAMDirectory. Although it exposes an interface identical to that of FSDirectory, RAMDirectory holds all its data in memory. This implementation is therefore useful for smaller indices that can be fully loaded in memory and can be destroyed upon the termination of an application. Because all data is held in the fast-access memory and not on a slower hard disk, RAMDirectory is suitable for situations where you need very quick access to the index, whether during indexing or searching. For instance, Lucene's developers make extensive use of RAMDirectory in all their unit tests: When a test runs, a fast in-memory index is created or searched; and when a test completes, the index is automatically destroyed, leaving no residuals on the disk. Of course, the performance difference between RAMDirectory and FSDirectory is less visible when Lucene is used on operating systems that cache files in memory. You'll see both Directory implementations used in code snippets in this book.

1.5.3 *Analyzer*

Before text is indexed, it's passed through an Analyzer. The Analyzer, specified in the IndexWriter constructor, is in charge of extracting tokens out of text to be indexed and eliminating the rest. If the content to be indexed isn't plain text, it should first be converted to it, as depicted in figure 2.1. Chapter 7 shows how to extract text from the most common rich-media document formats. `Analyzer` is an abstract class, but Lucene comes with several implementations of it. Some of them deal with skipping *stop words* (frequently used words that don't help distinguish one document from the other, such as *a, an, the, in,* and *on*); some deal with conversion of tokens to lowercase letters, so that searches aren't case-sensitive; and so on. `Analyzer`s are an important part of Lucene and can be used for much more than simple input filtering. For a developer integrating Lucene into an application, the choice of analyzer(s) is a critical element of application design. You'll learn much more about them in chapter 4.

1.5.4 Document

A `Document` represents a collection of fields. You can think of it as a virtual document—a chunk of data, such as a web page, an email message, or a text file—that you want to make retrievable at a later time. Fields of a document represent the document or meta-data associated with that document. The original source (such as a database record, a Word document, a chapter from a book, and so on) of document data is irrelevant to Lucene. The meta-data such as author, title, subject, date modified, and so on, are indexed and stored separately as fields of a document.

> **NOTE** When we refer to a document in this book, we mean a Microsoft Word, RTF, PDF, or other type of a document; we aren't talking about Lucene's `Document` class. Note the distinction in the case and font.

Lucene only deals with text. Lucene's core does not itself handle anything but `java.lang.String` and `java.io.Reader`. Although various types of documents can be indexed and made searchable, processing them isn't as straightforward as processing purely textual content that can easily be converted to a `String` or `Reader` Java type. You'll learn more about handling nontext documents in chapter 7.

In our `Indexer`, we're concerned with indexing text files. So, for each text file we find, we create a new instance of the `Document` class, populate it with `Field`s (described next), and add that `Document` to the index, effectively indexing the file.

1.5.5 Field

Each `Document` in an index contains one or more named fields, embodied in a class called `Field`. Each field corresponds to a piece of data that is either queried against or retrieved from the index during search.

Lucene offers four different types of fields from which you can choose:

- `Keyword`—Isn't analyzed, but is indexed and stored in the index verbatim. This type is suitable for fields whose original value should be preserved in its entirety, such as URLs, file system paths, dates, personal names, Social Security numbers, telephone numbers, and so on. For example, we used the file system path in `Indexer` (listing 1.1) as a `Keyword` field.

- `UnIndexed`—Is neither analyzed nor indexed, but its value is stored in the index as is. This type is suitable for fields that you need to display with search results (such as a URL or database primary key), but whose values you'll never search directly. Since the original value of a field of this type is stored in the index, this type isn't suitable for storing fields with very large values, if index size is an issue.

- `UnStored`—The opposite of `UnIndexed`. This field type is analyzed and indexed but isn't stored in the index. It's suitable for indexing a large amount of text that doesn't need to be retrieved in its original form, such as bodies of web pages, or any other type of text document.

- `Text`—Is analyzed, and is indexed. This implies that fields of this type can be searched against, but be cautious about the field size. If the data indexed is a `String`, it's also stored; but if the data (as in our `Indexer` example) is from a `Reader`, it isn't stored. This is often a source of confusion, so take note of this difference when using `Field.Text`.

All fields consist of a name and value pair. Which field type you should use depends on how you want to use that field and its values. Strictly speaking, Lucene has a single `Field` type: Fields are distinguished from each other based on their characteristics. Some are analyzed, but others aren't; some are indexed, whereas others are stored verbatim; and so on.

Table 1.2 provides a summary of different field characteristics, showing you how fields are created, along with common usage examples.

Table 1.2   An overview of different field types, their characteristics, and their usage

Field method/type	Analyzed	Indexed	Stored	Example usage
Field.Keyword(String, String)		✔	✔	Telephone and Social Security numbers, URLs, personal names
Field.Keyword(String, Date)				Dates
Field.UnIndexed(String, String)			✔	Document type (PDF, HTML, and so on), if not used as a search criteria

continued on next page

Table 1.2   An overview of different field types, their characteristics, and their usage *(continued)*

Field method/type	Analyzed	Indexed	Stored	Example usage
Field.UnStored(String, String)	✔	✔		Document titles and content
Field.Text(String, String)	✔	✔	✔	Document titles and content
Field.Text(String, Reader)	✔	✔		Document titles and content

Notice that all field types can be constructed with two `Strings` that represent the field's name and its value. In addition, a `Keyword` field can be passed both a `String` and a `Date` object, and the `Text` field accepts a `Reader` object in addition to the `String`. In all cases, the value is converted to a `Reader` before indexing; these additional methods exist to provide a friendlier API.

> **NOTE** Note the distinction between `Field.Text(String, String)` and `Field.Text(String, Reader)`. The `String` variant *stores* the field data, whereas the `Reader` variant does not. To index a `String`, but not store it, use `Field.UnStored(String, String)`.

Finally, `UnStored` and `Text` fields can be used to create *term vectors* (an advanced topic, covered in section 5.7). To instruct Lucene to create term vectors for a given `UnStored` or `Text` field, you can use `Field.UnStored(String, String, true)`, `Field.Text(String, String, true)`, or `Field.Text(String, Reader, true)`.

You'll apply this handful of classes most often when using Lucene for indexing. In order to implement basic search functionality, you need to be familiar with an equally small and simple set of Lucene search classes.

1.6 *Understanding the core searching classes*

The basic search interface that Lucene provides is as straightforward as the one for indexing. Only a few classes are needed to perform the basic search operation:

- `IndexSearcher`
- `Term`
- `Query`
- `TermQuery`
- `Hits`

The following sections provide a brief introduction to these classes. We'll expand on these explanations in the chapters that follow, before we dive into more advanced topics.

1.6.1 *IndexSearcher*

IndexSearcher is to searching what IndexWriter is to indexing: the central link to the index that exposes several search methods. You can think of IndexSearcher as a class that opens an index in a read-only mode. It offers a number of search methods, some of which are implemented in its abstract parent class Searcher; the simplest takes a single Query object as a parameter and returns a Hits object. A typical use of this method looks like this:

```
IndexSearcher is = new IndexSearcher(
                 FSDirectory.getDirectory("/tmp/index", false));
Query q = new TermQuery(new Term("contents", "lucene"));
Hits hits = is.search(q);
```

We cover the details of IndexSearcher in chapter 3, along with more advanced information in chapters 5 and 6.

1.6.2 *Term*

A Term is the basic unit for searching. Similar to the Field object, it consists of a pair of string elements: the name of the field and the value of that field. Note that Term objects are also involved in the indexing process. However, they're created by Lucene's internals, so you typically don't need to think about them while indexing. During searching, you may construct Term objects and use them together with TermQuery:

```
Query q = new TermQuery(new Term("contents", "lucene"));
Hits hits = is.search(q);
```

This code instructs Lucene to find all documents that contain the word *lucene* in a field named contents. Because the TermQuery object is derived from the abstract parent class Query, you can use the Query type on the left side of the statement.

1.6.3 *Query*

Lucene comes with a number of concrete Query subclasses. So far in this chapter we've mentioned only the most basic Lucene Query: TermQuery. Other Query types are BooleanQuery, PhraseQuery, PrefixQuery, PhrasePrefixQuery, RangeQuery, FilteredQuery, and SpanQuery. All of these are covered in chapter 3. Query is the common, abstract parent class. It contains several utility methods, the most interesting of which is setBoost(float), described in section 3.5.9.

1.6.4 *TermQuery*

`TermQuery` is the most basic type of query supported by Lucene, and it's one of the primitive query types. It's used for matching documents that contain fields with specific values, as you've seen in the last few paragraphs.

1.6.5 *Hits*

The `Hits` class is a simple container of pointers to ranked search results—documents that match a given query. For performance reasons, `Hits` instances don't load from the index all documents that match a query, but only a small portion of them at a time. Chapter 3 describes this in more detail.

1.7 *Review of alternate search products*

Before you select Lucene as your IR library of choice, you may want to review other solutions in the same domain. We did some research into alternate products that you may want to consider and evaluate; this section summarizes our findings. We group these products in two major categories:

- Information Retrieval libraries
- Indexing and searching applications

The first group is smaller; it consists of full-text indexing and searching libraries similar to Lucene. Products in this group let you embed them in your application, as shown earlier in figure 1.5.

The second, larger group is made up of ready-to-use indexing and searching software. This software is typically designed to index and search a particular type of data, such as web pages, and is less flexible than software in the former group. However, some of these products also expose their lower-level API, so you can sometimes use them as IR libraries as well.

1.7.1 *IR libraries*

In our research for this chapter, we found two IR libraries—Egothor and Xapian—that offer a comparable set of features and are aimed at roughly the same audience: developers. We also found MG4J, which isn't an IR library but is rather a set of tools useful for building an IR library; we think developers working with IR ought to know about it. Here are our reviews of all three products.

Egothor

A full-text indexing and searching Java library, Egothor uses core algorithms that are very similar to those used by Lucene. It has been in existence for several years and has a small but active developer and user community. The lead developer is Czech developer Leo Galambos, a PhD student with a solid academic background in the field of IR. He sometimes participates in Lucene's user and developer mailing list discussions.

Egothor supports an extended Boolean model, which allows it to function as both pure Boolean model and the Vector model. You can tune which model to use via a simple query-time parameter. This software features a number of different query types, supports similar search syntax, and allows multithreaded querying, which can come in handy if you're working on a multi-CPU computer or searching remote indices.

The Egothor distribution comes with several ready-to-use applications, such as a web crawler called Capek, a file indexer with a Swing GUI, and more. It also provides parsers for several rich-text document formats, such as PDF and Microsoft Word documents. As such, Egothor and Capek are comparable to the Lucene/Nutch combination, and Egother's file indexer and document parsers are similar to the small document parsing and indexing framework presented in chapter 7 of this book.

Free, open source, and released under a BSD-like license, the Egothor project is comparable to Lucene in most aspects. If you have yet to choose a full-text indexing and searching library, you may want to evaluate Egothor in addition to Lucene. Egothor's home page is at http://www.egothor.org/; as of this writing, it features a demo of its web crawler and search functionality.

Xapian

Xapian is a Probabilistic Information Retrieval library written in C++ and released under GPL. This project (or, rather, its predecessors) has an interesting history: The company that developed and owned it went through more than half a dozen acquisitions, name changes, shifts in focus, and such.

Xapian is actively developed software. It's currently at version 0.8.3, but it has a long history behind it and is based on decades of experience in the IR field. Its web site, http://www.xapian.org/, shows that it has a rich set of features, much like Lucene. It supports a wide range of queries and has a query parser that supports human-friendly search syntax; stemmers based on Dr. Martin Porter's Snowball project; parsers for a several rich-document types; bindings for Perl, Python, PHP, and (soon) Java; remote index searching; and so on.

In addition to providing an IR library, Xapian comes with a web site search application called Omega, which you can download separately.

MG4J

Although MG4J (Managing Gigabytes for Java) isn't an IR library like Lucene, Egothor, and Xapian, we believe that every software engineer reading this book should be aware of it because it provides low-level support for building Java IR libraries. MG4J is named after a popular IR book, *Managing Gigabytes: Compressing and Indexing Documents and Images*, written by Ian H. Witten, Alistair Moffat, and Timothy C. Bell. After collecting large amounts of web data with their distributed, fault-tolerant web crawler called UbiCrawler, its authors needed software capable of analyzing the collected data; out of that need, MG4J was born.

The library provides optimized classes for manipulating I/O, inverted index compression, and more. The project home page is at http://mg4j.dsi.unimi.it/; the library is free, open source, released under LGPL, and currently at version 0.8.2.

1.7.2 Indexing and searching applications

The other group of available software, both free and commercial, is assembled into prepackaged products. Such software usually doesn't expose a lot of its API and doesn't require you to build a custom application on top of it. Most of this software exposes a mechanism that lets you control a limited set of parameters but not enough to use the software in a way that's drastically different from its assumed use. (To be fair, there are notable exceptions to this rule.)

As such, we can't compare this software to Lucene directly. However, some of these products may be sufficient for your needs and let you get running quickly, even if Lucene or some other IR library turns out to be a better choice in the long run. Here's a short list of several popular products in this category:

- *SWISH, SWISH-E, and SWISH++*—http://homepage.mac.com/pauljlucas/software/swish/, http://swish-e.org/
- *Glimpse and Webglimpse*—http://webglimpse.net/
- *Namazu*—http://www.namazu.org/
- *ht://Dig*—http://www.htdig.org/
- *Harvest and Harvest-NG*—http://www.sourceforge.net/projects/harvest/, http://webharvest.sourceforge.net/ng/
- *Microsoft Index Server*—http://www.microsoft.com/NTServer/techresources/webserv/IndxServ.asp
- *Verity*—http://www.verity.com/

1.7.3 *Online resources*

The previous sections provide only brief overviews of the related products. Several resources will help you find other IR libraries and products beyond those we've mentioned:

- *DMOZ*—At the DMOZ Open Directory Project (ODP), you'll find http://dmoz.org/Computers/Software/Information_Retrieval/ and all its subcategories very informative.
- *Google*—Although Google Directory is based on the Open Directory's data, the two directories do differ. So, you should also visit http://directory.google.com/Top/Computers/Software/Information_Retrieval/.
- *Searchtools*—There is a web site dedicated to search tools at http://www.searchtools.com/. This web site isn't always up to date, but it has been around for years and is fairly comprehensive. Software is categorized by operating system, programming language, licenses, and so on. If you're interested only in search software written in Java, visit http://www.searchtools.com/tools/tools-java.html.

We've provided positive reviews of some alternatives to Lucene, but we're confident that your requisite homework will lead you to Lucene as the best choice!

1.8 Summary

In this chapter, you've gained some basic Lucene knowledge. You now know that Lucene is an Information Retrieval library, not a ready-to-use product, and that it most certainly is not a web crawler, as people new to Lucene sometimes think. You've also learned a bit about how Lucene came to be and about the key people and the organization behind it.

In the spirit of Manning's *in Action* books, we quickly got to the point by showing you two standalone applications, `Indexer` and `Searcher`, which are capable of indexing and searching text files stored in a file system. We then briefly described each of the Lucene classes used in these two applications. Finally, we presented our research findings for some products similar to Lucene.

Search is everywhere, and chances are that if you're reading this book, you're interested in search being an integral part of your applications. Depending on your needs, integrating Lucene may be trivial, or it may involve architectural considerations

We've organized the next couple of chapters as we did this chapter. The first thing we need to do is index some documents; we discuss this process in detail in chapter 2.

Indexing 2

This chapter covers

- Performing basic index operations
- Boosting Documents and Fields during indexing
- Indexing dates, numbers, and Fields for use in sorting search results
- Using parameters that affect Lucene's indexing performance and resource consumption
- Optimizing indexes
- Understanding concurrency, multithreading, and locking issues in the context of indexing

So you want to search files stored on your hard disk, or perhaps search your email, web pages, or even data stored in a database. Lucene can help you do that. However, before you can search something, you have to index it, and that's what you'll learn to do in this chapter.

In chapter 1, you saw a simple indexing example. This chapter goes further and teaches you about index updates, parameters you can use to tune the indexing process, and more advanced indexing techniques that will help you get the most out of Lucene. Here you'll also find information about the structure of a Lucene index, important issues to keep in mind when accessing a Lucene index with multiple threads and processes, and the locking mechanism that Lucene employs to prevent concurrent index modification.

2.1 *Understanding the indexing process*

As you saw in the chapter 1, only a few methods of Lucene's public API need to be called in order to index a document. As a result, from the outside, indexing with Lucene looks like a deceptively simple and monolithic operation. However, behind the simple API lies an interesting and relatively complex set of operations that we can break down into three major and functionally distinct groups, as described in the following sections and depicted in figure 2.1.

2.1.1 *Conversion to text*

To index data with Lucene, you must first convert it to a stream of plain-text tokens, the format that Lucene can digest. In chapter 1, we limited our examples to indexing and searching .txt files, which allowed us to slurp their content and use it to populate `Field` instances. However, things aren't always that simple.

Suppose you need to index a set of manuals in PDF format. To prepare these manuals for indexing, you must first find a way to extract the textual information from the PDF documents and use that extracted data to create Lucene `Documents` and their `Fields`. If you look back at table 1.2, page 21, you'll see that `Field` methods always take `String` values and, in some cases, `Date` and `Reader` values. No methods would accept a PDF Java type, even if such a type existed. You face the same situation if you want to index Microsoft Word documents or any document format other than plain text. Even when you're dealing with XML or HTML documents, which use plain-text characters, you still need to be smart about preparing the data for indexing, to avoid indexing things like XML elements or HTML tags, and index the real data in those documents.

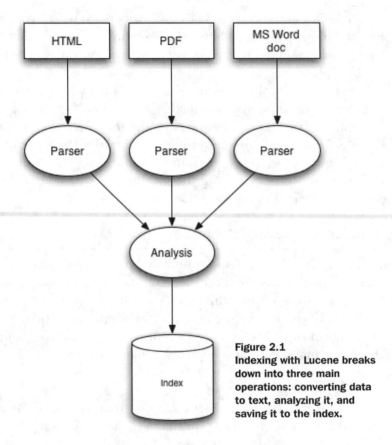

**Figure 2.1
Indexing with Lucene breaks
down into three main
operations: converting data
to text, analyzing it, and
saving it to the index.**

The details of text extraction are in chapter 7 where we build a small but complete framework for indexing all document formats depicted in figure 2.1 plus a few others. As a matter of fact, you'll notice that figure 2.1 and figure 7.3 resemble each other.

2.1.2 *Analysis*

Once you've prepared the data for indexing and created Lucene Documents populated with Fields, you can call IndexWriter's addDocument(Document) method and hand your data off to Lucene to index. When you do that, Lucene first analyzes the data to make it more suitable for indexing. To do so, it splits the textual data into chunks, or *tokens*, and performs a number of optional operations on them. For instance, the tokens could be lowercased before indexing, to make searches case-insensitive. Typically it's also desirable to remove all frequent but meaningless tokens from the input, such as stop words (*a, an, the, in, on,* and so on) in English text. Similarly, it's common to analyze input tokens and reduce them to their roots.

This very important step is called *analysis*. The input to Lucene can be analyzed in so many interesting and useful ways that we cover this process in detail in chapter 4. For now, think of this step as a type of a filter.

2.1.3 Index writing

After the input has been analyzed, it's ready to be added to the index. Lucene stores the input in a data structure known as an *inverted index*. This data structure makes efficient use of disk space while allowing quick keyword lookups. What makes this structure inverted is that it uses tokens extracted from input documents as lookup keys instead of treating documents as the central entities. In other words, instead of trying to answer the question "what words are contained in this document?" this structure is optimized for providing quick answers to "which documents contain word X?"

If you think about your favorite web search engine and the format of your typical query, you'll see that this is exactly the query that you want to be as quick as possible. The core of all of today's web search engines are inverted indexes. What makes each search engine different is a set of closely guarded tricks used to improve the structure by adding more parameters, such as Google's well-known PageRank factor. Lucene, too, has its own set of tricks; you can learn about some of them in appendix B.

2.2 Basic index operations

In chapter 1, you saw how to add documents to an index. But we'll summarize the process here, along with descriptions of delete and update operations, to provide you with a convenient single reference point.

2.2.1 Adding documents to an index

To summarize what you already know, let's look at the code snippet that serves as the base class for unit tests in this chapter. The code in listing 2.1 creates a compound index imaginatively named *index-dir*, stored in the system's temporary directory: /tmp on UNIX, or C:\TEMP on computers using Windows. (Compound indexes are covered in appendix B.) We use `SimpleAnalyzer` to analyze the input text, and we then index two simple `Documents`, each containing all four types of `Fields`: `Keyword`, `UnIndexed`, `UnStored`, and `Text`.

Listing 2.1 Preparing a new index before each test in a base test case class

```
public abstract class BaseIndexingTestCase extends TestCase {
  protected String[] keywords = {"1", "2"};
  protected String[] unindexed = {"Netherlands", "Italy"};
  protected String[] unstored = {"Amsterdam has lots of bridges",
                                 "Venice has lots of canals"};
  protected String[] text = {"Amsterdam", "Venice"};
  protected Directory dir;
                                                   Run before
                                                   every test
  protected void setUp() throws IOException {   ◄┘
    String indexDir =
      System.getProperty("java.io.tmpdir", "tmp") +
      System.getProperty("file.separator") + "index-dir";
    dir = FSDirectory.getDirectory(indexDir, true);
    addDocuments(dir);
  }

  protected void addDocuments(Directory dir)
    throws IOException {
    IndexWriter writer = new IndexWriter(dir, getAnalyzer(),
      true);
    writer.setUseCompoundFile(isCompound());
    for (int i = 0; i < keywords.length; i++) {
      Document doc = new Document();
      doc.add(Field.Keyword("id", keywords[i]));
      doc.add(Field.UnIndexed("country", unindexed[i]));
      doc.add(Field.UnStored("contents", unstored[i]));
      doc.add(Field.Text("city", text[i]));
      writer.addDocument(doc);
    }
    writer.optimize();
    writer.close();
  }

  protected Analyzer getAnalyzer() {     ◄┐  Default
    return new SimpleAnalyzer();            │  Analyzer
  }

  protected boolean isCompound() {
    return true;
  }
}
```

Since this BaseIndexingTestCase class will be extended by other unit test classes
in this chapter, we'll point out a few important details. BaseIndexingTestCase
creates the same index every time its setUp() method is called. Since setUp() is
called before a test is executed, each test runs against a freshly created index.

Although the base class uses `SimpleAnalyzer`, the subclasses can override the `get-Analyzer()` method to return a different type of `Analyzer`.

Heterogeneous Documents

One handy feature of Lucene is that it allows `Documents` with different sets of `Fields` to coexist in the same index. This means you can use a single index to hold `Documents` that represent different entities. For instance, you could have `Documents` that represent retail products with `Fields` such as *name* and *price*, and `Documents` that represent people with `Fields` such as name, age, and gender.

Appendable Fields

Suppose you have an application that generates an array of synonyms for a given word, and you want to use Lucene to index the base word plus all its synonyms. One way to do it would be to loop through all the synonyms and append them to a single `String`, which you could then use to create a Lucene `Field`. Another, perhaps more elegant way to index all the synonyms along with the base word is to just keep adding the same `Field` with different values, like this:

```
String baseWord = "fast";
String synonyms[] = String {"quick", "rapid", "speedy"};
Document doc = new Document();
doc.add(Field.Text("word", baseWord));
for (int i = 0; i < synonyms.length; i++) {
  doc.add(Field.Text("word", synonyms[i]));
}
```

Internally, Lucene appends all the words together and index them in a single `Field` called word, allowing you to use any of the given words when searching.

2.2.2 Removing Documents from an index

Although most applications are more concerned with getting `Documents` into a Lucene index, some also need to remove them. For instance, a newspaper publisher may want to keep only the last week's worth of news in its searchable indexes. Other applications may want to remove all `Documents` that contain a certain term.

`Document` deletion is done using a class that is somewhat inappropriately called `IndexReader`. This class doesn't delete `Documents` from the index immediately. Instead, it marks them as deleted, waiting for the actual `Document` deletion until `IndexReader`'s `close()` method is called. With this in mind, let's look at Listing 2.2: It inherits `BaseIndexingTestCase` class, which means that before each test method is run, the base class re-creates the two-`Document` index, as described in section 2.2.1.

Listing 2.2   Removing Documents from a Lucene index by internal Document number

```
public class DocumentDeleteTest extends BaseIndexingTestCase {

    public void testDeleteBeforeIndexMerge() throws IOException {
        IndexReader reader = IndexReader.open(dir);
        assertEquals(2, reader.maxDoc());              ❶ Next Document number is 2
        assertEquals(2, reader.numDocs());             ❷ 2 Documents in index
        reader.delete(1);          ❸ Delete Document with id 1

        assertTrue(reader.isDeleted(1));          ❹ Document deleted
        assertTrue(reader.hasDeletions());        ❺ Index contains deletions
        assertEquals(2, reader.maxDoc());
        assertEquals(1, reader.numDocs());
                                                  ❻ 1 indexed Document;
                                                     next Document
        reader.close();                              number is 2

        reader = IndexReader.open(dir);

        assertEquals(2, reader.maxDoc());         ❼ Next Document
        assertEquals(1, reader.numDocs());           number is 2, after
                                                     IndexReader reopened
        reader.close();
    }

    public void testDeleteAfterIndexMerge() throws IOException {
        IndexReader reader = IndexReader.open(dir);
        assertEquals(2, reader.maxDoc());
        assertEquals(2, reader.numDocs());
        reader.delete(1);
        reader.close();

        IndexWriter writer = new IndexWriter(dir, getAnalyzer(),
            false);
        writer.optimize();
        writer.close();

        reader = IndexReader.open(dir);

        assertFalse(reader.isDeleted(1));         ❽ Optimizing
        assertFalse(reader.hasDeletions());          renumbers
        assertEquals(1, reader.maxDoc());            Documents
        assertEquals(1, reader.numDocs());

        reader.close();
    }
```

❶❷❸ The code in listing 2.2 shows how to delete a Document by specifying its internal Document number. It also shows the difference between two IndexReader methods that are often mixed up: maxDoc() and numDocs(). The former returns the next available internal Document number, and the latter returns the number of Documents in an index. Because our index contains only two Documents, numDocs() returns 2; and since Document numbers start from zero, maxDoc() returns 2 as well.

> **NOTE** Each Lucene Document has a unique internal number. These number assignments aren't permanent, because Lucene renumbers Documents internally when index segments are merged. Hence, you shouldn't assume that a given Document will always have the same Document number.

4 5 The unit test in the testDeleteBeforeIndexMerge() method also demonstrates the use of IndexReader's hasDeletions() method to check if an index contains any Documents marked for deletion and the isDeleted(int) method to check the status of a Document specified by its Document number.

6 7 As you can see, numDocs() is aware of Document deletion immediately, whereas maxDoc() isn't.

8 Furthermore, in the method testDeleteAfterIndexMerge() we close the IndexReader and force Lucene to merge index segments by optimizing the index. When we subsequently open the index with IndexReader, the maxDoc() method returns 1 rather than 2, because after a delete and merge, Lucene renumbered the remaining Documents. Only one Document remains in the index, so the next available Document number is 1.

In addition to deleting a single Document by specifying its Document number, as we've done, you can delete several Documents by using IndexReader's delete(Term) method. Using this deletion method lets you delete all Documents that contain the specified term. For instance, to remove a Document that contains the word *Amsterdam* in a city field, you can use IndexReader like so:

```
IndexReader reader = IndexReader.open(dir);
reader.delete(new Term("city", "Amsterdam"));
reader.close();
```

You should be extra careful when using this approach, because specifying a term present in all indexed Documents will wipe out a whole index. The usage of this method is similar to the Document number-based deletion method; you can see it in section 2.2.4.

You may wonder why Lucene performs Document deletion from IndexReader and not IndexWriter instances. That question is asked in the Lucene community every few months, probably due to imperfect and perhaps misleading class names. Lucene users often think that IndexWriter is the only class that can modify an index and that `IndexReader` accesses an index in a read-only fashion. In reality, `IndexWriter` touches only the list of index segments and a small subset of index files when segments are merged. On the other hand, `IndexReader` knows how to parse all index files and make sense out of them. When a `Document` is deleted, `IndexReader` first needs to locate the segment containing the specified `Document` before it can mark it as deleted. There are currently no plans to change either the names or behavior of these two Lucene classes.

2.2.3 *Undeleting Documents*

Because `Document` deletion is deferred until the closing of the `IndexReader` instance, Lucene allows an application to change its mind and undelete `Document`s that have been marked as deleted. A call to `IndexReader`'s `undeleteAll()` method undeletes all deleted `Document`s by removing all .del files from the index directory. Subsequently closing the `IndexReader` instance therefore leaves all `Document`s in the index. `Document`s can be undeleted only if the call to `undeleteAll()` was done using the same instance of `IndexReader` that was used to delete the `Document`s in the first place.

2.2.4 *Updating Documents in an index*

"How do I update a document in an index?" is a frequently asked question on the Lucene user mailing list. Lucene doesn't offer an `update(Document)` method; instead, a `Document` must first be deleted from an index and then re-added to it, as shown in listing 2.3.

Listing 2.3 Updating indexed `Document`s by first deleting them and then re-adding them

```
public class DocumentUpdateTest extends BaseIndexingTestCase {

  public void testUpdate() throws IOException {

    assertEquals(1, getHitCount("city", "Amsterdam"));

    IndexReader reader = IndexReader.open(dir);                  ⟵ Delete Documents
    reader.delete(new Term("city", "Amsterdam"));                  with "Amsterdam"
    reader.close();                                                in city field

    assertEquals(0, getHitCount("city", "Amsterdam"));           ⟵ Verify Document
                                                                   removal
    IndexWriter writer = new IndexWriter(dir, getAnalyzer(),
      false);                              Re-add Document
    Document doc = new Document();         with new city
    doc.add(Field.Keyword("id", "1"));     name: "Haag"
```

```
    doc.add(Field.UnIndexed("country", "Netherlands"));      ⌐ᐃ
    doc.add(Field.UnStored("contents",                          Re-add Document
      "Amsterdam has lots of bridges"));                        with new city
    doc.add(Field.Text("city", "Haag"));                        name: "Haag"
    writer.addDocument(doc);
    writer.optimize();
    writer.close();

    assertEquals(1, getHitCount("city", "Haag"));      ◁┐ Verify Document
  }                                                       │ update

  protected Analyzer getAnalyzer() {
    return new WhitespaceAnalyzer();
  }

  private int getHitCount(String fieldName, String searchString)
    throws IOException {
    IndexSearcher searcher = new IndexSearcher(dir);
    Term t = new Term(fieldName, searchString);
    Query query = new TermQuery(t);
    Hits hits = searcher.search(query);
    int hitCount = hits.length();
    searcher.close();
    return hitCount;
  }
}
```

We first remove all Documents whose city Field contains the term *Amsterdam*; then we add a new Document whose Fields are the same as those of the removed Document, except for a new value in the city Field. Instead of the *Amsterdam*, the new Document has *Haag* in its city Field. We have effectively updated one of the Documents in the index.

Updating by batching deletions

Our example deletes and re-adds a single Document. If you need to delete and add multiple Documents, it's best to do so in batches. Follow these steps:

1 Open IndexReader.
2 Delete all the Documents you need to delete.
3 Close IndexReader.
4 Open IndexWriter.
5 Add all the Documents you need to add.
6 Close IndexWriter.

This is important to remember: Batching `Document` deletion and indexing will always be faster than interleaving delete and add operations.

With add, update, and delete operations under your belt, let's discuss how to fine-tune the performance of indexing and make the best use of available hardware resources.

> **TIP**   When deleting and adding `Documents`, do it in batches. This will always be faster than interleaving delete and add operations.

2.3 *Boosting Documents and Fields*

Not all `Documents` and `Fields` are created equal—or at least you can make sure that's the case by selectively boosting `Documents` or `Fields`. Imagine you have to write an application that indexes and searches corporate email. Perhaps the requirement is to give company employees' emails more importance than other email messages. How would you go about doing this?

`Document` *boosting* is a feature that makes such a requirement simple to implement. By default, all `Documents` have no boost—or, rather, they all have the same boost factor of 1.0. By changing a `Document`'s boost factor, you can instruct Lucene to consider it more or less important with respect to other `Documents` in the index. The API for doing this consists of a single method, `setBoost(float)`, which can be used as follows:

```
public static final String COMPANY_DOMAIN = "example.com";
public static final String BAD_DOMAIN = "yucky-domain.com";

Document doc = new Document();
String senderEmail = getSenderEmail();
String senderName = getSenderName();
String subject = getSubject();
String body = getBody();
doc.add(Field.Keyword("senderEmail", senderEmail));
doc.add(Field.Text("senderName", senderName));
doc.add(Field.Text("subject", subject));
doc.add(Field.UnStored("body", body));
if (getSenderDomain().endsWithIgnoreCase(COMPANY_DOMAIN)) {
  doc.setBoost(1.5);        ❶ Employee boost factor: 1.5
}
else if (getSenderDomain().endsWithIgnoreCase(BAD_DOMAIN)) {
  doc.setBoost(0.1);        ❷ Bad domain boost factor: 0.1
}
writer.addDocument(doc);
```

In this example, we check the domain name of the email message sender to determine whether the sender is a company employee.

❶ When we index messages sent by the company's employees, we set their boost factor to 1.5, which is greater than the default factor of 1.0.

❷ When we encounter messages from a sender associated with a fictional bad domain, we label them as nearly insignificant by lowering their boost factor to 0.1.

Just as you can boost Documents, you can also boost individual Fields. When you boost a Document, Lucene internally uses the same boost factor to boost each of its Fields. Imagine that another requirement for the email-indexing application is to consider the subject Field more important than the Field with a sender's name. In other words, search matches made in the subject Field should be more valuable than equivalent matches in the senderName Field in our earlier example. To achieve this behavior, we use the setBoost(float) method of the Field class:

```
Field senderNameField = Field.Text("senderName", senderName);
Field subjectField = Field.Text("subject", subject);
subjectField.setBoost(1.2);
```

In this example, we arbitrarily picked a boost factor of 1.2, just as we arbitrarily picked Document boost factors of 1.5 and 0.1 earlier. The boost factor values you should use depend on what you're trying to achieve; you may need to do a bit of experimentation and tuning to achieve the desired effect.

It's worth noting that shorter Fields have an implicit boost associated with them, due to the way Lucene's scoring algorithm works. Boosting is, in general, an advanced feature that many applications can work very well without.

Document and Field boosting comes into play at search time, as you'll learn in section 3.5.9. Lucene's search results are ranked according to how closely each Document matches the query, and each matching Document is assigned a score. Lucene's scoring formula consists of a number of factors, and the boost factor is one of them.

2.4 *Indexing dates*

Email messages include sent and received dates, files have several timestamps associated with them, and HTTP responses have a Last-Modified header that includes the date of the requested page's last modification. Chances are, like many other Lucene users, you'll need to index dates. Lucene comes equipped with a Field.Keyword(String, Date) method, as well as a DateField class, which make date indexing easy. For example, to index today's date, you can do this:

```
Document doc = new Document();
doc.add(Field.Keyword("indexDate", new Date()));
```

Internally, Lucene uses the `DateField` class to convert the given date to a `String` suitable for indexing. Handling dates this way is simple, but you must be careful when using this method: Dates converted to indexable `Strings` by `DateField` include all the date parts, down to the millisecond. As you'll read in section 6.5, this can cause performance problems for certain types of queries. In practice, you rarely need dates that are precise down to the millisecond, at least to query on. Generally, you can round dates to an hour or even to a day.

Since all `Field` values are eventually turned into text, you may very well index dates as `Strings`. For instance, if you can round the date to a day, index dates as YYYYMMDD `Strings` using the `Field.Keyword(String, String)` method. Another good reason for taking this approach is that you'll be able to index dates before the Unix Epoch (Jan 1, 1970), which `DateField` can't handle. Although several workarounds and patches for solving this limitation have been contributed over the past few years, none of them were sufficiently elegant. As a consequence, they can still be found in Lucene's patch queue, but they aren't included in Lucene. Judging by how often Lucene users bring up this limitation, not being able to index dates prior to 1970 usually isn't a problem.

> **NOTE**   If you only need the date for searching, and not the timestamp, index as `Field.Keyword("date", "YYYYMMDD")`. If the full timestamp needs to be preserved for retrieval, index a second `Field` as `Field.Keyword ("timestamp", <java.util.Date>)`.

If you choose to format dates or times in some other manner, take great care that the `String` representation is lexicographically orderable; doing so allows for sensible date-range queries. A benefit of indexing dates in YYYYMMDD format is the ability to query by year only, by year and month, or by exact year, month, and day. To query by year only, use a `PrefixQuery` for YYYY, for example. We discuss `PrefixQuery` further in section 3.4.3.

2.5 *Indexing numbers*

There are two common scenarios in which number indexing is important. In one scenario, numbers are embedded in the text to be indexed, and you want to make sure those numbers are indexed so that you can use them later in searches. For instance, your documents may contain sentences like "Mt. Everest is 8848 meters tall": You want to be able to search for the number 8848 just like you can search for the word *Everest* and retrieve the document that contains the sentence.

In the other scenario, you have Fields that contain only numeric values, and you want to be able to index them and use them for searching. Moreover, you may want to perform range queries using such Fields. For example, if you're indexing email messages, one of the possible index Fields could hold the message size, and you may want to be able to find all messages of a given size; or, you may want to use range queries to find all messages whose size is in a certain range. You may also have to sort results by size.

Lucene can index numeric values by treating them as strings internally. If you need to index numbers that appear in free-form text, the first thing you should do is pick the Analyzer that doesn't discard numbers. As we discuss in section 4.3, WhitespaceAnalyzer and StandardAnalyzer are two possible candidates. If you feed them a sentence such as "Mt. Everest is 8848 meters tall," they extract 8848 as a token and pass it on for indexing, allowing you to later search for 8848. On the other hand, SimpleAnalyzer and StopAnalyzer throw numbers out of the token stream, which means the search for 8848 won't match any documents.

Fields whose sole value is a number don't need to be analyzed, so they should be indexed as Field.Keyword. However, before just adding their raw values to the index, you need to manipulate them a bit, in order for range queries to work as expected. When performing range queries, Lucene uses lexicographical values of Fields for ordering. Consider three numeric Fields whose values are 7, 71, and 20. Although their natural order is 7, 20, 71, their lexicographical order is 20, 7, 71. A simple and common trick for solving this inconsistency is to prepad numeric Fields with zeros, like this: 007, 020, 071. Notice that the natural and the lexicographical order of the numbers is now consistent. For more details about searching numeric Fields, see section 6.3.3.

NOTE   When you index Fields with numeric values, pad them if you want to use them for range queries

2.6 *Indexing Fields used for sorting*

When returning search hits, Lucene orders them by their score by default. Sometimes, however, you need to order results using some other criteria. For instance, if you're searching email messages, you may want to order results by sent or received date, or perhaps by message size. If you want to be able to sort results by a Field value, you must add it as a Field that is indexed but not tokenized (for example, `Field.Keyword`). `Fields` used for sorting must be convertible to `Integers`, `Floats`, or `Strings`:

```
Field.Keyword("size", "4096");
Field.Keyword("price", "10.99");
Field.Keyword("author", "Arthur C. Clark");
```

Although we've indexed numeric values as `Strings`, you can specify the correct `Field` type (such as `Integer` or `Long`) at sort time, as described in section 5.1.7.

NOTE   `Fields` used for sorting have to be indexed and must not be tokenized.

2.7 Controlling the indexing process

Indexing small and midsized document collections works well with the default Lucene setup. However, if your application deals with very large indexes, you'll probably want some control over Lucene's indexing process to ensure optimal indexing performance. For instance, you may be indexing several million documents and want to speed up the process so it takes minutes instead of hours. Your computer may have spare RAM, but you need to know how to let Lucene make more use of it. Lucene has several parameters that allow you to control its performance and resource use during indexing.

2.7.1 Tuning indexing performance

In a typical indexing application, the bottleneck is the process of writing index files onto a disk. If you were to profile an indexing application, you'd see that most of the time is spent in code sections that manipulate index files. Therefore, you need to instruct Lucene to be smart about indexing new `Documents` and modifying existing index files.

As shown in figure 2.2, when new `Documents` are added to a Lucene index, they're initially buffered in memory instead of being immediately written to the disk.

This buffering is done for performance reasons; and luckily, the `IndexWriter` class exposes several instance variables that allow you to adjust the size of this buffer and the frequency of disk writes. These variables are summarized in table 2.1.

Table 2.1   Parameters for indexing performance tuning

IndexWriter variable	System property	Default value	Description
mergeFactor	org.apache.lucene.mergeFactor	10	Controls segment merge frequency and size

continued on next page

Table 2.1   Parameters for indexing performance tuning *(continued)*

IndexWriter variable	System property	Default value	Description
maxMergeDocs	org.apache.lucene.maxMergeDocs	Integer.MAX_VALUE	Limits the number of documents per segement
minMergeDocs	org.apache.lucene.minMergeDocs	10	Controls the amount of RAM used when indexing

IndexWriter's mergeFactor lets you control how many Documents to store in memory before writing them to the disk, as well as how often to merge multiple index segments together. (Index segments are covered in appendix B.) With the default value of 10, Lucene stores 10 Documents in memory before writing them to a single segment on the disk. The mergeFactor value of 10 also means that once the number of segments on the disk has reached the power of 10, Lucene merges these segments into a single segment.

For instance, if you set mergeFactor to 10, a new segment is created on the disk for every 10 Documents added to the index. When the tenth segment of size 10 is added, all 10 are merged into a single segment of size 100. When 10 such segments of size 100 have been added, they're merged into a single segment containing 1,000 Documents, and so on. Therefore, at any time, there are no more than 9 segments in the index, and the size of each merged segment is the power of 10.

There is a small exception to this rule that has to do with maxMergeDocs, another IndexWriter instance variable: While merging segments, Lucene ensures

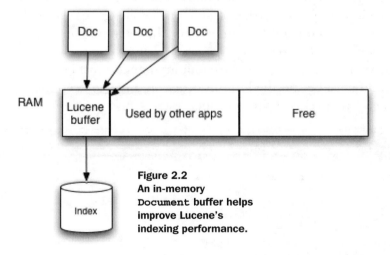

**Figure 2.2
An in-memory
Document buffer helps
improve Lucene's
indexing performance.**

that no segment with more than `maxMergeDocs` Documents is created. For instance, suppose you set `maxMergeDocs` to 1,000. When you add the ten-thousandth Document, instead of merging multiple segments into a single segment of size 10,000, Lucene creates the tenth segment of size 1,000 and keeps adding new segments of size 1,000 for every 1,000 Documents added.

Now that you've seen how `mergeFactor` and `maxMergeDocs` work, you can deduce that using a higher value for `mergeFactor` causes Lucene to use more RAM but let it write data to disk less frequently, consequently speeding up the indexing process. A lower `mergeFactor` uses less memory and causes the index to be updated more frequently, which makes it more up to date but also slows down the indexing process. Similarly, a higher `maxMergeDocs` is better suited for batch indexing, and a lower `maxMergeDocs` is better for more interactive indexing. Be aware that because a higher `mergeFactor` means less frequent merges, it results in an index with more index files. Although this doesn't affect indexing performance, it may slow searching, because Lucene will need to open, read, and process more index files.

`minMergeDocs` is another `IndexWriter` instance variable that affects indexing performance. Its value controls how many Documents have to be buffered before they're merged to a segment. The `minMergeDocs` parameter lets you trade in more of your RAM for faster indexing. Unlike `mergeFactor`, this parameter doesn't affect the size of index segments on disk.

Example: IndexTuningDemo

To get a better feel for how different values of `mergeFactor`, `maxMergeDocs` and `minMergeDocs` affect indexing speed, look at the `IndexTuningDemo` class in listing 2.4. This class takes four command-line arguments: the total number of Documents to add to the index, the value to use for `mergeFactor`, the value to use for `maxMergeDocs`, and the value for `minMergeDocs`. All four arguments must be specified, must be integers, and must be specified in this order. In order to keep the code short and clean, there are no checks for improper usage.

Listing 2.4 Demonstration of using `mergeFactor`, `maxMergeDocs`, and `minMergeDocs`

```
public class IndexTuningDemo {

  public static void main(String[] args) throws Exception {
    int docsInIndex  = Integer.parseInt(args[0]);

    // create an index called 'index-dir' in a temp directory
    Directory dir = FSDirectory.getDirectory(
```

```
        System.getProperty("java.io.tmpdir", "tmp") +
        System.getProperty("file.separator") + "index-dir", true);
    Analyzer analyzer = new SimpleAnalyzer ();
    IndexWriter writer = new IndexWriter(dir, analyzer, true);

    // set variables that affect speed of indexing
    writer.mergeFactor   = Integer.parseInt(args[1]);
    writer.maxMergeDocs  = Integer.parseInt(args[2]);
    writer.minMergeDocs  = Integer.parseInt(args[3]);
    writer.infoStream    = System.out;
    System.out.println("Merge factor:    " + writer.mergeFactor);
    System.out.println("Max merge docs: " + writer.maxMergeDocs);
    System.out.println("Min merge docs: " + writer.minMergeDocs);

    long start = System.currentTimeMillis();
    for (int i = 0; i < docsInIndex; i++) {
      Document doc = new Document();
      doc.add(Field.Text("fieldname", "Bibamus"));
      writer.addDocument(doc);
    }
    writer.close();
    long stop = System.currentTimeMillis();
    System.out.println("Time: " + (stop - start) + " ms");
  }
}
```

Adjust settings that affect indexing performance

❷ **Tell IndexWriter to print info to System.out**

The first argument represents the number of Documents to add to the index; the second argument is the value to use for the mergeFactor, followed by maxMergeDocs value; and the last argument is the value to use for the minMergeDocs parameter:

```
% java lia.indexing.IndexTuningDemo 100000 10 9999999 10


Merge factor:    10
Max merge docs: 9999999
Min merge docs: 10
Time: 74136 ms


% java lia.indexing.IndexTuningDemo 100000 100 9999999 10
Merge factor:    100
Max merge docs: 9999999
Min merge docs: 10
Time: 68307 ms
```

Both invocations create an index with 100,000 Documents, but the first one takes longer to complete (74,136 ms versus 68,307 ms). That's because the first invocation uses the default mergeFactor of 10, which causes Lucene to write Documents to the disk more often than the second invocation (`mergeFactor` of 100). Let's look at a few more runs with different parameter values:

```
% java lia.indexing.IndexTuningDemo 100000 10 9999999 100

Merge factor:    10
Max merge docs: 9999999
Min merge docs: 100
Time: 54050 ms

% java lia.indexing.IndexTuningDemo 100000 100 9999999 100

Merge factor:    100
Max merge docs: 9999999
Min merge docs: 100
Time: 47831 ms

% java lia.indexing.IndexTuningDemo 100000 100 9999999 1000

Merge factor:    100
Max merge docs: 9999999
Min merge docs: 1000
Time: 44235 ms

% java lia.indexing.IndexTuningDemo 100000 1000 9999999 1000

Merge factor:    1000
Max merge docs: 9999999
Min merge docs: 1000
Time: 44223 ms

% java -server -Xms128m -Xmx256m
⇒   lia.indexing.IndexTuningDemo 100000 1000 9999999 1000

Merge factor:    1000
Max merge docs: 9999999
Min merge docs: 1000
Time: 36335 ms

% java lia.indexing.IndexTuningDemo 100000 1000 9999999 10000
Exception in thread "main" java.lang.OutOfMemoryError
```

Indexing speed improves as we increase `mergeFactor` and `minMergeDocs`, and when we give the JVM a larger start and maximum heap. Note how using 10,000 for `minMergeDocs` resulted in an `OutOfMemoryError`; this can also happen if you choose too large a `mergeFactor` value.

NOTE   Increasing `mergeFactor` and `minMergeDocs` improves indexing speed, but only to a point. Higher values also use more RAM and may cause your indexing process to run out of memory, if they're set too high.

Keep in mind that the `IndexTuningDemo` is, as its name implies, only a demonstration of the use and effect of `mergeFactor`, `maxMergeDocs`, and `minMergeDocs`. In this class, we add `Documents` with a single `Field` consisting of a single word. Consequently, we can use a very high `mergeFactor`. In practice, applications that use Lucene tend to work with indexes whose documents have several `Fields` and whose `Fields` contain larger chunks of text. Those applications won't be able to use `mergeFactor` and `minMergeDocs` values as high as those we used here unless they run on computers with very large amounts of RAM—which is the factor that limits `mergeFactor` and `minMergeDocs` for a given index. If you choose to run `IndexTuningDemo`, keep in mind the effect that the operating system's and file system's cache can have on its performance. Be sure to warm up the caches and run each configuration several times, ideally on the otherwise idle computer. Furthermore, create a large enough index to minimize the effect of these caches. Finally, it's worth repeating that using a higher `mergeFactor` will affect search performance—increase its value with caution.

NOTE   Don't forget that giving your JVM a larger memory heap may improve indexing performance. This is often done with a combination of `-Xms` and `-Xmx` command-line arguments to the Java interpreter. Giving the JVM a larger heap also lets you increase the values of the `mergeFactor` and `minMergeDocs` parameters. Making sure that the HotSpot, JIT, or similar JVM option is enabled also has positive effects.

Changing the maximum open files limit under UNIX
Note that although these three variables can help improve indexing performance, they also affect the number of file descriptors that Lucene uses and can therefore cause the "Too many open files" exception when used with multifile indexes. (Multifile indexes and compound indexes are covered in appendix B.) If you get this error, you should first check the contents of your index directory. If it contains multiple segments, you should optimize the index using `IndexWriter`'s `optimize()` method, as described in section 2.8; optimization helps indexes that contain more than one segment by merging them into a single index segment. If optimizing the index doesn't solve the problem, or if your index already has only a single segment, you can try increasing the maximum number of open files allowed on your computer. This is usually done at the operating-system level and

varies from OS to OS. If you're using Lucene on a computer that uses a flavor of
the UNIX OS, you can see the maximum number of open files allowed from the
command line.

Under bash, you can see the current settings with the built-in ulimit command:

```
% ulimit -n
```

Under tcsh, the equivalent is

```
% limit descriptors
```

To change the value under bash, use this command:

```
% ulimit -n <max number of open files here>
```

Under tcsh, use the following:

```
% limit descriptors <max number of open files here>
```

To estimate a setting for the maximum number of open files used while indexing, keep in mind that the maximum number of files Lucene will open at any
one time during indexing is

```
(1 + mergeFactor) * FilesPerSegment
```

For instance, with a default mergeFactor of 10, while creating an index with
1 million Documents, Lucene will require at the most 88 open files on an unoptimized multifile index with a single indexed field. We get to this number by using
the following formula:

```
11 segments/index * (7 files/segment + 1 file for indexed field)
```

If even this doesn't eliminate the problem of too many simultaneously open files,
and you're using a multifile index structure, you should consider converting your
index to the compound structure. As described in appendix B, doing so will further reduce the number of files Lucene needs to open when accessing your index.

> **NOTE**   If your computer is running out of available file descriptors, and your
> index isn't optimized, consider optimizing it.

2.7.2 *In-memory indexing: RAMDirectory*

In the previous section, we mentioned that Lucene does internal buffering by
holding newly added documents in memory prior to writing them to the disk.
This is done automatically and transparently when you use FSDirectory, a file-
based Directory implementation. But perhaps you want to have more control

over indexing, its memory use, and the frequency of flushing the in-memory buffer to disk. You can use RAMDirectory as a form of in-memory buffer.

RAMDirectory versus FSDirectory

Everything that FSDirectory does on disk, RAMDirectory performs in memory, and is thus much faster. The code in listing 2.5 creates two indexes: one backed by an FSDirectory and the other by RAMDirectory. Except for this difference, they're identical—each contains 1,000 Documents with identical content.

Listing 2.5   RAMDirectory always out-performs FSDirectory

```
public class FSversusRAMDirectoryTest extends TestCase {

  private Directory fsDir;
  private Directory ramDir;
  private Collection docs = loadDocuments(3000, 5);

  protected void setUp() throws Exception {
    String fsIndexDir =
      System.getProperty("java.io.tmpdir", "tmp") +
      System.getProperty("file.separator") + "fs-index";

    ramDir = new RAMDirectory();
    fsDir = FSDirectory.getDirectory(fsIndexDir, true);
  }

  public void testTiming() throws IOException {
    long ramTiming = timeIndexWriter(ramDir);
    long fsTiming = timeIndexWriter(fsDir);

    assertTrue(fsTiming > ramTiming);

    System.out.println("RAMDirectory Time: " + (ramTiming) + " ms");
    System.out.println("FSDirectory Time : " + (fsTiming) + " ms");
  }

  private long timeIndexWriter(Directory dir) throws IOException {
    long start = System.currentTimeMillis();
    addDocuments(dir);
    long stop = System.currentTimeMillis();
    return (stop - start);
  }

  private void addDocuments(Directory dir) throws IOException {
    IndexWriter writer = new IndexWriter(dir, new SimpleAnalyzer(),
      true);

    /**
```

Create Directory whose content is held in RAM

Create Directory whose content is stored on disk

RAMDirectory is faster than FSDirectory

```
   // change to adjust performance of indexing with FSDirectory
   writer.mergeFactor = writer.mergeFactor;           Parameters that
   writer.maxMergeDocs = writer.maxMergeDocs;         affect performance
   writer.minMergeDocs = writer.minMergeDocs;         of FSDirectory
   */

   for (Iterator iter = docs.iterator(); iter.hasNext();) {
      Document doc = new Document();
      String word = (String) iter.next();
      doc.add(Field.Keyword("keyword", word));
      doc.add(Field.UnIndexed("unindexed", word));
      doc.add(Field.UnStored("unstored", word));
      doc.add(Field.Text("text", word));
      writer.addDocument(doc);
   }
   writer.optimize();
   writer.close();
}

private Collection loadDocuments(int numDocs, int wordsPerDoc) {
   Collection docs = new ArrayList(numDocs);
   for (int i = 0; i < numDocs; i++) {
      StringBuffer doc = new StringBuffer(wordsPerDoc);
      for (int j = 0; j < wordsPerDoc; j++) {
         doc.append("Bibamus ");
      }
      docs.add(doc.toString());
   }
   return docs;
}
}
```

Although there are better ways to construct benchmarks (see section 6.5 for an example of how you can use JUnitPerf to measure performance of index searching), this benchmark is sufficient for illustrating the performance advantage that RAMDirectory has over FSDirectory. If you run the test from listing 2.5 and gradually increase the value of mergeFactor or minMergeDocs, you'll notice that the FSDirectory-based indexing starts to approach the speed of the RAMDirectory-based one. However, you'll also notice that no matter what combination of parameters you use, the FSDirectory-based index never outperforms its RAM-based cousin.

Even though you can use indexing parameters to instruct Lucene to merge segments on disk less frequently, FSDirectory-based indexing has to write them to the disk eventually; that is the source of the performance difference between the two Directory implementations. RAMDirectory simply never writes anything on disk. Of course, this means that once your indexing application exits, your RAMDirectory-based index is gone.

Batch indexing by using RAMDirectory as a buffer

Suppose you want to improve indexing performance with Lucene, and manipulating IndexWriter's mergeFactor, maxMergeDocs, and minMergeDocs proves insufficient. You have the option of taking control in your own hands by using RAMDirectory to buffer writing to an FSDirectory-based index yourself. Here's a simple recipe for doing that:

1   Create an FSDirectory-based index.

2   Create a RAMDirectory-based index.

3   Add Documents to the RAMDirectory-based index.

4   Every so often, flush everything buffered in RAMDirectory into FSDirectory.

5   Go to step 3. (Who says GOTO is dead?)

We can translate this recipe to the following mixture of pseudocode and the actual Lucene API use:

```
FSDirectory fsDir = FSDirectory.getDirectory("/tmp/index",
  true);
RAMDirectory ramDir = new RAMDirectory();

IndexWriter fsWriter = IndexWriter(fsDir,
  new SimpleAnalyzer(), true);
IndexWriter ramWriter = new IndexWriter(ramDir,
  new SimpleAnalyzer(), true);

while (there are documents to index) {
  ... create Document ...
  ramWriter.addDocument(doc);

  if (condition for flushing memory to disk has been met) {
    fsWriter.addIndexes(Directory[] {ramDir});    <─┐  Merge in-memory RAMDirectory
    ramWriter.close();                               │  with on-disk FSDirectory
    ramWriter = new IndexWriter(ramDir, new SimpleAnalyzer(),  <─┐
      true);                                         Create new in-memory
  }                                                  RAMDirectory buffer
}
```

This approach gives you the freedom to flush Documents buffered in RAM onto disk whenever you choose. For instance, you could use a counter that triggers flushing after every *N* Documents added to a RAMDirectory-based index. Similarly, you could have a timer that periodically forces the flush regardless of the number of `Documents` added. A more sophisticated approach would involve keeping track of `RAMDirectory`'s memory consumption, in order to prevent `RAMDirectory` from growing too large.

Whichever logic you choose, eventually you'll use `IndexWriter`'s `addIndexes` `(Directory[])` method to merge your `RAMDirectory`-based index with the one on disk. This method takes an array of `Directory`s of any type and merges them all into a single `Directory` whose location is specified in the `IndexWriter` constructor.

Parallelizing indexing by working with multiple indexes

The idea of using `RAMDirectory` as a buffer can be taken even further, as shown in figure 2.3. You could create a multithreaded indexing application that uses multiple `RAMDirectory`-based indexes in parallel, one in each thread, and merges them into a single index on the disk using `IndexWriter`'s `addIndexes(Directory[])` method.

Again, when and how you choose to synchronize your threads and merge their `RAMDirectory`s to a single index on disk is up to you. Of course, if you have

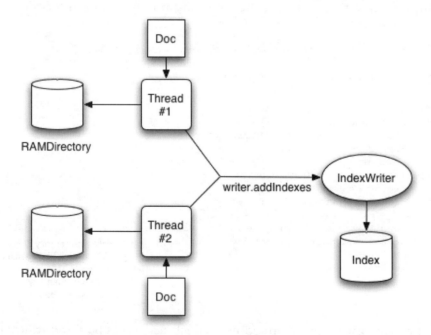

Figure 2.3   A multithreaded application that uses multiple `RAMDirectory` instances for parallel indexing.

multiple hard disks, you could also parallelize the disk-based indexes, since the two disks can operate independently.

And what if you have multiple computers connected with a fast network, such as Fiber Channel? That, too, can be exploited by using a set of computers as an indexing cluster. A sophisticated indexing application could create in-memory or file system-based indexes on multiple computers in parallel and periodically send their index to a centralized server, where all indexes are merged into one large index.

The architecture in figure 2.4 has two obvious flaws: the centralized index represents a single point of failure and is bound to become a bottleneck when the number of indexing nodes increases. Regardless, this should give you some ideas. When you learn how to use Lucene to perform searches over multiple indexes in parallel and even do it remotely (see section 5.6), you'll see that Lucene lets you create very large distributed indexing and searching clusters.

By now, you can clearly see a few patterns. RAM is faster than disk: If you need to squeeze more out of Lucene, use RAMDirectory to do most of your indexing in faster RAM. Minimize index merges. If you have sufficient resources, such as multiple CPUs, disks, or even computers, parallelize indexing and use the addIndexes(Directory[]) method to write to a single index, which you should eventually build and search. To make full use of this approach, you need to ensure that the thread or computer that performs the indexing on the disk is never idle, because idleness translates to wasted time.

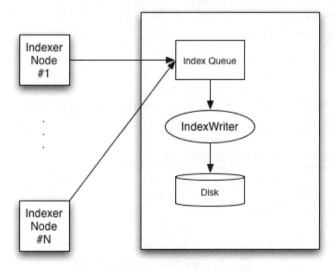

Figure 2.4
A cluster of indexer nodes that send their small indexes to a large centralized indexing server.

In section 3.2.3, we discuss the move in the opposite direction: how to get an existing index stored on the file system into RAM. This topic is reserved for the chapter on searching because searching is the most appropriate reason to bring a file system index into RAM.

2.7.3   *Limiting Field sizes: maxFieldLength*

Some applications index documents whose sizes aren't known in advance. To control the amount of RAM and hard-disk memory used, they need to limit the amount of input they index. Other applications deal with documents of known size but want to index only a portion of each document. For example, you may want to index only the first 200 words of each document. Lucene's IndexWriter exposes maxFieldLength, an instance variable that lets you programmatically truncate very large document Fields. With a default value of 10,000, Lucene indexes only the first 10,000 terms in each Document Field. This effectively means that only the first 10,000 terms are relevant for searches, and any text beyond the ten-thousandth term isn't indexed.

To limit Field sizes to 1,000 terms, an application sets maxFieldLength to 1,000; to virtually eliminate the limit, an application should set maxFieldLength to Integer.MAX_VALUE. The value of maxFieldLength can be changed at any time during indexing, and the change takes effect for all subsequently added documents. The change isn't retroactive, so any fields already truncated due to a lower maxFieldLength will remain truncated. Listing 2.6 shows a concrete example.

Listing 2.6   Controlling field size with maxFieldLength

```
public class FieldLengthTest extends TestCase {

  private Directory dir;
  private String[] keywords = {"1", "2"};
  private String[] unindexed = {"Netherlands", "Italy"};
  private String[] unstored = {"Amsterdam has lots of bridges",
                               "Venice has lots of canals"};
  private String[] text = {"Amsterdam", "Venice"};

  protected void setUp() throws IOException {
    String indexDir =
      System.getProperty("java.io.tmpdir", "tmp") +
      System.getProperty("file.separator") + "index-dir";
    dir = FSDirectory.getDirectory(indexDir, true);
  }

  public void testFieldSize() throws IOException {
    addDocuments(dir, 10);        ❶ Index first 10 terms of each Field
```

```
        assertEquals(1, getHitCount("contents", "bridges"));     ❷ Term bridges
                                                                    was indexed
        addDocuments(dir, 1);    ❸ Index first term of each Field
        assertEquals(0, getHitCount("contents", "bridges"));     ❹ Term bridges
    }                                                               wasn't indexed

    private int getHitCount(String fieldName, String searchString)
        throws IOException {
        IndexSearcher searcher = new IndexSearcher(dir);
        Term t = new Term(fieldName, searchString);
        Query query = new TermQuery(t);
        Hits hits = searcher.search(query);
        int hitCount = hits.length();
        searcher.close();
        return hitCount;
    }

    private void addDocuments(Directory dir, int maxFieldLength)
        throws IOException {
        IndexWriter writer = new IndexWriter(dir, new SimpleAnalyzer(),
            true);
        writer.maxFieldLength = maxFieldLength;          ❺ Set number of
        for (int i = 0; i < keywords.length; i++) {         terms to index
            Document doc = new Document();
            doc.add(Field.Keyword("id", keywords[i]));
            doc.add(Field.UnIndexed("country", unindexed[i]));
            doc.add(Field.UnStored("contents", unstored[i]));
            doc.add(Field.Text("city", text[i]));
            writer.addDocument(doc);
        }
        writer.optimize();
        writer.close();
    }
}
```

From this listing, you see how we can limit the number of Document terms we index:

❶ ❺ First we instruct IndexWriter to index the first 10 terms.

❷ After the first Document is added, we're able to find a match for the term *bridges* because it's the fifth term in the document containing the text "Amsterdam has lots of bridges".

❸ We reindex this Document, instructing IndexWriter to index only the first term.

❹ Now we're unable to find a Document that contained the term *bridges* because Lucene indexed only the first term, *Amsterdam*. The rest of the terms, including *bridges*, were ignored.

2.8 *Optimizing an index*

Index *optimization* is the process that merges multiple index files together in order to reduce their number and thus minimize the time it takes to read in the index at search time. Recall from section 2.7 that while it's adding new Documents to an index, Lucene buffers several Documents in memory before combining them into a segment that it writes onto a disk, optionally merging this new segment with previously created segments. Although you can control the segment-merging process with mergeFactor, maxMergeDocs, and minMergeDocs, when indexing is done you could still be left with several segments in the index.

Searching an index made up of multiple segments works properly, but Lucene's API lets you further optimize the index and thereby reduce Lucene's resource consumption and improve search performance. Index optimization merges all index segments into a single segment. You can optimize an index with a single call to IndexWriter's optimize() method. (You may have noticed such calls in previous code listings, so we'll omit a separate listing here.) Index optimization involves a lot of disk IO, so use it judiciously.

Figures 2.5 and 2.6 show the difference in index structure between an unoptimized and an optimized multifile index, respectively.

It's important to emphasize that *optimizing an index only affects the speed of searches against that index, and doesn't affect the speed of indexing.* Adding new Documents to an unoptimized index is as fast as adding them to an optimized index. The increase in search performance comes from the fact that with an optimized index, Lucene needs to open and process fewer files than when running a search against an unoptimized index. If you take another look at figures 2.5 and 2.6, you can see that the optimized index has far fewer index files.

Optimizing disk space requirements

It's worthwhile to mention that while optimizing an index, Lucene merges existing segments by creating a brand-new segment whose content in the end represents the content of all old segments combined. Thus, while the optimization is in progress, disk space usage progressively increases. When it finishes creating the new segment, Lucene discards all old segments by removing their index files. Consequently, just before the old segments are removed, the disk space usage of an index doubles because both the combined new unified segment and all the old segments are present in the index. After optimization, the indexes disk usage falls back to the same level as before optimization. Keep in mind that the rules of index optimization hold for both multifile and compound indexes.

```
-rw-rw-r--    1 otis    otis         1000 Aug 25 12:45 _1pp.f1
-rw-rw-r--    1 otis    otis         1000 Aug 25 12:45 _1pp.f2
-rw-rw-r--    1 otis    otis         1000 Aug 25 12:45 _1pp.f3
-rw-rw-r--    1 otis    otis       130000 Aug 25 12:45 _1pp.fdt
-rw-rw-r--    1 otis    otis         8000 Aug 25 12:45 _1pp.fdx
-rw-rw-r--    1 otis    otis           39 Aug 25 12:45 _1pp.fnm
-rw-rw-r--    1 otis    otis         5558 Aug 25 12:45 _1pp.frq
-rw-rw-r--    1 otis    otis        11000 Aug 25 12:45 _1pp.prx
-rw-rw-r--    1 otis    otis           19 Aug 25 12:45 _1pp.tii
-rw-rw-r--    1 otis    otis           98 Aug 25 12:45 _1pp.tis
-rw-rw-r--    1 otis    otis         1000 Aug 25 12:45 _2kk.f1
-rw-rw-r--    1 otis    otis         1000 Aug 25 12:45 _2kk.f2
-rw-rw-r--    1 otis    otis         1000 Aug 25 12:45 _2kk.f3
-rw-rw-r--    1 otis    otis       130000 Aug 25 12:45 _2kk.fdt
-rw-rw-r--    1 otis    otis         8000 Aug 25 12:45 _2kk.fdx
-rw-rw-r--    1 otis    otis           39 Aug 25 12:45 _2kk.fnm
-rw-rw-r--    1 otis    otis         5558 Aug 25 12:45 _2kk.frq
-rw-rw-r--    1 otis    otis        11000 Aug 25 12:45 _2kk.prx
-rw-rw-r--    1 otis    otis           19 Aug 25 12:45 _2kk.tii
-rw-rw-r--    1 otis    otis           98 Aug 25 12:45 _2kk.tis
-rw-rw-r--    1 otis    otis            4 Aug 25 12:45 deletable
-rw-rw-r--    1 otis    otis           42 Aug 25 12:45 segments
```

Figure 2.5 Index structure of an unoptimized multifile index showing multiple segments in an index directory

Why optimize?

Although fully unoptimized indexes perform flawlessly for most applications, applications that handle large indexes will benefit from working with optimized indexes. Environments that keep references to multiple indexes open for searching will especially benefit, because their use of fully optimized indexes will require fewer open file descriptors.

Suppose you're writing a server application that will ultimately result in every user having their own index to which new documents will slowly be added over time. As documents are added to each index, the number of segments in each index will grow, too. This means that while searching such unoptimized indexes, Lucene will have to keep references to a large number of open files; it will eventually reach the limit set by your operating system. To aid the situation, you

-rw-rw-r--	1 otis	otis	3000	Aug	25	12:43	_2kl.f1
-rw-rw-r--	1 otis	otis	3000	Aug	25	12:43	_2kl.f2
-rw-rw-r--	1 otis	otis	3000	Aug	25	12:43	_2kl.f3
-rw-rw-r--	1 otis	otis	390000	Aug	25	12:43	_2kl.fdt
-rw-rw-r--	1 otis	otis	24000	Aug	25	12:43	_2kl.fdx
-rw-rw-r--	1 otis	otis	39	Aug	25	12:43	_2kl.fnm
-rw-rw-r--	1 otis	otis	16683	Aug	25	12:43	_2kl.frq
-rw-rw-r--	1 otis	otis	33000	Aug	25	12:43	_2kl.prx
-rw-rw-r--	1 otis	otis	19	Aug	25	12:43	_2kl.tii
-rw-rw-r--	1 otis	otis	98	Aug	25	12:43	_2kl.tis
-rw-rw-r--	1 otis	otis	4	Aug	25	12:43	deletable
-rw-rw-r--	1 otis	otis	25	Aug	25	12:43	segments

Figure 2.6 Index structure of a fully optimized multifile index showing a single segment in an index directory

should develop a system that allows for a periodic index optimization. The mechanism can be as simple as having a standalone application that periodically iterates over all your users' indexes and runs the following:

```
IndexWriter writer = new IndexWriter("/path/to/index",
  analyzer, false);
writer.optimize();
writer.close();
```

Of course, if this is run from a standalone application, you must be careful about concurrent index modification. An index should be modified by only a single operating system process at a time. In other words, only a single process should open index with IndexWriter at a time. As you'll see in the remaining sections of this chapter, Lucene uses a file-based locking mechanism to try to prevent this type of concurrent index modification.

When to optimize

Although an index can be optimized by a single process at any point during indexing, and doing so won't damage the index or make it unavailable for searches, optimizing an index while performing indexing operation isn't recommended. It's best to optimize an index only at the very end, when you know that the index will remain unchanged for a while. Optimizing during indexing will only make indexing take longer.

NOTE Contrary to a popular belief, optimizing an index doesn't improve indexing speed. Optimizing an index improves only the speed of searching by minimizing the number of index files that need to be opened, processed, and searched. Optimize an index only at the end of the indexing process, when you know the index will remain unmodified for a while.

2.9 *Concurrency, thread-safety, and locking issues*

In this section, we cover three closely related topics: concurrent index access, thread-safety of `IndexReader` and `IndexWriter`, and the locking mechanism that Lucene uses to prevent index corruption. These issues are often misunderstood by users new to Lucene. Understanding these topics is important, because it will eliminate surprises that can result when your indexing application starts serving multiple users simultaneously or when it has to deal with a sudden need to scale by parallelizing some of its operations.

2.9.1 *Concurrency rules*

Lucene provides several operations that can modify an index, such as document indexing, updating, and deletion; when using them, you need to follow certain rules to avoid index corruption. These issues raise their heads frequently in web applications, where multiple requests are typically handled simultaneously. Lucene's concurrency rules are simple but should be strictly followed:

- Any number of read-only operations may be executed concurrently. For instance, multiple threads or processes may search the same index in parallel.
- Any number of read-only operations may be executed while an index is being modified. For example, users can search an index while it's being optimized or while new documents are being added to the index, updated, or deleted from the index.
- Only a single index-modifying operation may execute at a time. An index should be opened by a single `IndexWriter` or a single `IndexReader` at a time.

Based on these concurrency rules, we can create a more comprehensive set of examples, shown in table 2.2. These rules represent the allowed and disallowed concurrent operations on a single index.

Table 2.2   Examples of allowed and disallowed concurrent operations performed on a single Lucene index

Operation	Allowed or disallowed
Running multiple concurrent searches against the same index	Allowed
Running multiple concurrent searches against an index that is being built, optimized, or merged with another index, or whose documents are being deleted or updated	Allowed
Adding or updating documents in the same index using multiple instances of `IndexWriter`	Disallowed
Failing to close the `IndexReader` that was used to delete documents from an index before opening a new `IndexWriter` to add more documents to the same index	Disallowed
Failing to close the `IndexWriter` that was used to add documents to an index before opening a new `IndexReader` to delete or update documents from the same index	Disallowed

NOTE   When you're running operations that modify an index, always keep in mind that only one index-modifying operation should be run on the same index at a time.

2.9.2 Thread-safety

It's important to know that although making simultaneous index modifications with multiple instances of `IndexWriter` or `IndexReader` isn't allowed, as shown in table 2.2, both of these classes are thread-safe. Therefore, a *single instance* of either class *can be shared among multiple threads*, and all calls to its index-modifying methods will be properly synchronized so that index modifications are executed one after the other. Figure 2.7 depicts such a scenario.

Additional external synchronization is unnecessary. Despite the fact that both classes are thread-safe, an application using Lucene must ensure that index-modifying operations of these two classes don't overlap. That is to say, before adding new documents to an index, you must close all `IndexReader` instances that have deleted `Documents` from the same index. Similarly, before deleting or updating documents in an index, you must close the `IndexWriter` instance that opened that same index before.

The concurrency matrix in the table 2.3 gives an overview of operations that can or can't be executed simultaneously. It assumes that a single instance of `IndexWriter` or a single instance of `IndexReader` is used. Note that we don't list

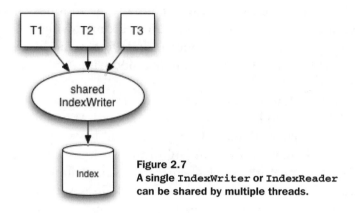

Figure 2.7
A single `IndexWriter` or `IndexReader` can be shared by multiple threads.

updating as a separate operation because an update is really a delete operation followed by an add operation, as you saw in section 2.2.4

Table 2.3 Concurrency matrix when the same instance of `IndexWriter` or `IndexReader` is used. Marked intersections signify operations that can't be executed simultaneously.

	Query	Read document	Add	Delete	Optimize	Merge
Query						
Read document						
Add				X		
Delete			X		X	X
Optimize				X		
Merge				X		

This matrix can be summarized as follows:

- A document can't be added (`IndexWriter`) while a document is being deleted (`IndexReader`).
- A document can't be deleted (`IndexReader`) while the index is being optimized (`IndexWriter`).
- A document can't be deleted (`IndexReader`) while the index is being merged (`IndexWriter`).

From the matrix and its summary, you can see a pattern: an index-modifying `IndexReader` operation can't be executed while an index-modifying `IndexWriter` operation is in progress. This rule is symmetrical: An index-modifying `Index-Writer` operation can't be executed while an index-modifying `IndexReader` operation is in progress.

You can think of these Lucene concurrency rules as analogous to the rules of good manners and proper and legal conduct in our society. Although these rules don't have to be strictly followed, not following them can have repercussions. In real life, breaking a rule may land you in jail; in the world of Lucene, it could corrupt your index. Lucene anticipates misuse and even misunderstanding of concurrency issues, so it uses a locking mechanism to do its best to prevent inadvertent index corruption. Lucene's index-locking mechanism is described in the next section.

2.9.3 *Index locking*

Related to the concurrency issues in Lucene is the topic of locking. To prevent index corruption from misuse of its API, Lucene creates file-based locks around all code segments that need to be executed by a single process at a time. Each index has its own set of lock files; by default, all lock files are created in a computer's temporary directory as specified by Java's `java.io.tmpdir` system property.

If you look at that directory while indexing documents, you'll see Lucene's write.lock file; if you catch Lucene while it's merging segments, you'll notice the commit.lock file, too. You can change the lock directory by setting the `org.apache.lucene.lockDir` system property to the desired directory. This system property can be set programmatically using a Java API, or it can be set from the command line using `-Dorg.apache.lucene.lockDir=/path/to/lock/dir` syntax. If you have multiple computers that need to access the same index stored on a shared disk, you should set the lock directory explicitly so that applications on different computers see each other's locks. Because of known issues with lock files and NFS, choose a directory that doesn't reside on an NFS volume. Here's what both locks may look like:

```
% ls -1 /tmp/lucene*.lock

lucene-de61b2c77401967646cf8916982a09a0-write.lock
lucene-de61b2c77401967646cf8916982a09a0-commit.lock
```

The write.lock file is used to keep processes from concurrently attempting to modify an index. More precisely, the write.lock is obtained by `IndexWriter` when `IndexWriter` is instantiated and kept until it's closed. The same lock file is also obtained by `IndexReader` when it's used for deleting `Documents`, undeleting them, or setting `Field` norms. As such, write.lock tends to lock the index for writing for longer periods of time.

The commit.lock is used whenever segments are being read or merged. It's obtained by an `IndexReader` before it reads the segments file, which names all index segments, and it's released only after `IndexReader` has opened and read all the referenced segments. `IndexWriter` also obtains the commit.lock right before it creates a new segments file and keeps it until it removes the index files that have been made obsolete by operations such as segment merges. Thus, the commit.lock may be created more frequently than the write.lock, but it should never lock the index for long since during its existence index files are only opened or deleted and only a small segments file is written to disk. Table 2.4 summarizes all spots in the Lucene API that lock an index.

Table 2.4   A summary of all Lucene locks and operations that create and release them

Lock File	Class	Obtained in	Released in	Description
write.lock	IndexWriter	Constructor	close()	Lock released when `IndexWriter` is closed
write.lock	IndexReader	delete(int)	close()	Lock released when `IndexReader` is closed
write.lock	IndexReader	undeleteAll(int)	close()	Lock released when `IndexReader` is closed
write.lock	IndexReader	setNorms (int, String, byte)	close()	Lock released when `IndexReader` is closed
commit.lock	IndexWriter	Constructor	Constructor	Lock released as soon as segment information is read or written
commit.lock	IndexWriter	addIndexes (IndexReader[])	addIndexes (IndexReader[])	Lock obtained while the new segment is written
commit.lock	IndexWriter	addIndexes (Directory[])	addIndexes (Directory[])	Lock obtained while the new segment is written
commit.lock	IndexWriter	mergeSegments (int)	mergeSegments (int)	Lock obtained while the new segment is written
commit.lock	IndexReader	open(Directory)	open(Directory)	Lock obtained until all segments are read

continued on next page

Table 2.4 A summary of all Lucene locks and operations that create and release them *(continued)*

Lock File	Class	Obtained in	Released in	Description
commit.lock	SegmentReader	doClose()	doClose()	Lock obtained while the segment's file is written or rewritten
commit.lock	SegmentReader	undeleteAll()	undeleteAll()	Lock obtained while the segment's .del file is removed

You should be aware of two additional methods related to locking:

- IndexReader's isLocked(Directory)—Tells you whether the index specified in its argument is locked. This method can be handy when an application needs to check whether the index is locked before attempting one of the index-modifying operations.

- IndexReader's unlock(Directory)—Does exactly what its name implies. Although this method gives you power to unlock any Lucene index at any time, using it is dangerous. Lucene creates locks for a good reason, and unlocking an index while it's being modified can result in a corrupt and unusable index.

Although you now know which lock files Lucene uses, when it uses them, why it uses them, and where they're stored in the file system, you should resist touching them. Furthermore, you should always rely on Lucene's API to manipulate them. If you don't, your code may break if Lucene starts using a different locking mechanism in the future, or even if it changes the name or location of its lock files.

Locking in action

To demonstrate locking, listing 2.7 provides an example of a situation where Lucene uses locks to prevent multiple index-modifying operations from running against the same index simultaneously. In the testWriteLock() method, Lucene blocks the second IndexWriter from opening an index that has already been opened by another IndexWriter. This is an example of write.lock in action.

Listing 2.7 Using file-based locks to prevent index corruption

```
public class LockTest extends TestCase {

  private Directory dir;

  protected void setUp() throws IOException {
```

```
    String indexDir =
      System.getProperty("java.io.tmpdir", "tmp") +
      System.getProperty("file.separator") + "index";
    dir = FSDirectory.getDirectory(indexDir, true);
  }

  public void testWriteLock() throws IOException {
    IndexWriter writer1 = null;
    IndexWriter writer2 = null;

    try {
      writer1 = new IndexWriter(dir, new SimpleAnalyzer(), true);
      writer2 = new IndexWriter(dir, new SimpleAnalyzer(), true);

      fail("We should never reach this point");
    }
    catch (IOException e) {
      e.printStackTrace();            <─┐  Expected exception:
    }                                     only one IndexWriter
    finally {                             allowed on single index
      writer1.close();
      assertNull(writer2);
    }
  }

  public void testCommitLock() throws IOException {
    IndexReader reader1 = null;
    IndexReader reader2 = null;

    try {
      IndexWriter writer = new IndexWriter(dir, new SimpleAnalyzer(),
        true);
      writer.close();
      reader1 = IndexReader.open(dir);
      reader2 = IndexReader.open(dir);
    }
    finally {
      reader1.close();
      reader2.close();
    }
  }
}
```

The testCommitLock() method demonstrates the use of a commit.lock that is obtained in IndexReader's open(Directory) method and released by the same method as soon as all index segments have been read. Because the lock is released by the same method that obtained it, we're able to access the same directory with the second IndexReader even before the first one has been closed. (You may wonder about the IndexWriter you see in this method: Its sole purpose is to seed the index by creating the required segments file, which contains information about all existing index segments. Without the segments file IndexReader would be lost, because it wouldn't know which segments to read from the index directory.)

When we run this code we see an exception stack trace caused by the locked index, which resembles the following stack trace:

```
java.io.IOException: Lock obtain timed out
        at org.apache.lucene.store.Lock.obtain(Lock.java:97)
        at
org.apache.lucene.index.IndexWriter.<init>(IndexWriter.java:173)
        at lia.indexing.LockTest.testWriteLock(LockTest.java:34)
```

As we mentioned earlier, new users of Lucene sometimes don't have a good understanding of the concurrency issues described in this section and consequently run into locking issues, such as the one show in the previous stack trace. If you see similar exceptions in your applications, please don't disregard them if the consistency of your indexes is at all important to you. Lock-related exceptions are typically a sign of a misuse of the Lucene API; if they occur in your application, you should resolve them promptly.

2.9.4 *Disabling index locking*

We strongly discourage meddling with Lucene's locking mechanism and disregarding the lock-related exception. However, in some situations you may want to disable locking in Lucene, and doing so won't corrupt your index. For instance, your application may need to access a Lucene index stored on a CD-ROM. A CD is a read-only medium, which means your application will be operating in a read-only mode, too. In other words, your application will be using Lucene only to search the index and won't modify the index in any way. Although Lucene already stores its lock files in the system's temporary directory—a directory usually open for writing by any user of the system—you can disable both write.lock and commit.lock by setting the disableLuceneLocks system property to the string "true".

2.10 *Debugging indexing*

Let's discuss one final, fairly unknown Lucene feature (if we may so call it). If you ever need to debug Lucene's index-writing process, remember that you can get Lucene to output information about its indexing operations by setting IndexWriter's public instance variable infoStream to one of the OutputStreams, such as System.out:

```
IndexWriter writer = new IndexWriter(dir, new SimpleAnalyzer(),
  true);
writer.infoStream = System.out;
...
```

This reveals information about segment merges, as shown here, and may help you tune indexing parameters described earlier in the chapter:

```
merging segments _0 (1 docs) _1 (1 docs) _2 (1 docs)
_3 (1 docs) _4 (1 docs) _5 (1 docs) _6 (1 docs)
_7 (1 docs) _8 (1 docs)_9 (1 docs) into _a (10 docs)
merging segments _b (1 docs) _c (1 docs) _d (1 docs)
_e (1 docs) _f (1 docs) _g (1 docs) _h (1 docs)
_i (1 docs) _j (1 docs) k (1 docs) into _l (10 docs)
merging segments _m (1 docs) _n (1 docs) _o (1 docs)
_p (1 docs) _q (1 docs) _r (1 docs) _s (1 docs)
_t (1 docs) _u (1 docs) _v (1 docs) into _w (10 docs)
```

In addition, if you need to peek inside your index once it's built, you can use Luke: a handy third-party tool that we discuss in section 8.2, page 269.

2.11 *Summary*

This chapter has given you a solid understanding of how a Lucene index operates. In addition to adding Documents to an index, you should now be able to remove and update indexed Documents as well as manipulate a couple of indexing factors to fine-tune several aspects of indexing to meet your needs. The knowledge about concurrency, thread-safety, and locking is essential if you're using Lucene in a multithreaded application or a multiprocess system. By now you should be dying to learn how to search with Lucene, and that's what you'll read about in the next chapter.

3

Adding search to your application

This chapter covers

- Querying a Lucene index
- Working with search results
- Understanding Lucene scoring
- Parsing human-entered query expressions

If we can't find it, it effectively doesn't exist. Even if we have indexed documents, our effort is wasted unless it pays off by providing a reliable and fast way to find those documents. For example, consider this scenario:

> Give me a list of all books published in the last 12 months on the subject of "Java" where "open source" or "Jakarta" is mentioned in the contents. Restrict the results to only books that are on special. Oh, and under the covers, also ensure that books mentioning "Apache" are picked up, because we explicitly specified "Jakarta". And make it snappy, on the order of milliseconds for response time.[1]

Do you have a repository of hundreds, thousands, or millions of documents that needs similar search capability?

Providing search capability using Lucene's API is straightforward and easy, but lurking under the covers is a sophisticated mechanism that can meet your search requirements such as returning the most relevant documents first and retrieving the results incredibly fast. This chapter covers common ways to search using the Lucene API. The majority of applications using Lucene search can provide a search feature that performs nicely using the techniques shown in this chapter. Chapter 5 delves into more advanced search capabilities, and chapter 6 elaborates on ways to extend Lucene's classes for even greater searching power.

We begin with a simple example showing that the code you write to implement search is generally no more than a few lines long. Next we illustrate the scoring formula, providing a deep look into one of Lucene's most special attributes. With this example and a high-level understanding of how Lucene ranks search results, we'll then explore the various types of search queries Lucene handles natively.

3.1 *Implementing a simple search feature*

Suppose you're tasked with adding search to an application. You've tackled getting the data indexed, but now it's time to expose the full-text searching to the end users. It's hard to imagine that adding search could be any simpler than it is with Lucene. Obtaining search results requires only a few lines of code, literally. Lucene provides easy and highly efficient access to those search results, too, freeing you to focus your application logic and user interface around those results.

---

[1] We cover all the pieces to make this happen with Lucene, including a specials filter in chapter 6, synonym injection in chapter 4, and the Boolean logic in this chapter.

In this chapter, we'll limit our discussion to the primary classes in Lucene's API that you'll typically use for search integration (shown in table 3.1). Sure, there is more to the story, and we go beyond the basics in chapters 5 and 6. In this chapter, we'll cover the details you'll need for the majority of your applications.

Table 3.1 Lucene's primary searching API

Class	Purpose
IndexSearcher	Gateway to searching an index. All searches come through an IndexSearcher instance using any of the several overloaded search methods.
Query (and subclasses)	Concrete subclasses encapsulate logic for a particular query type. Instances of Query are passed to an IndexSearcher's search method.
QueryParser	Processes a human-entered (and readable) expression into a concrete Query object.
Hits	Provides access to search results. Hits is returned from IndexSearcher's search method.

When you're *querying* a Lucene index, an ordered collection of *hits* is returned. The hits collection is ordered by *score* by default.[2] Lucene computes a score (a numeric value of relevance) for each document, given a query. The hits themselves aren't the actual matching documents, but rather are references to the documents matched. In most applications that display search results, users access only the first few documents, so it isn't necessary to retrieve the actual documents for all results; you need to retrieve only the documents that will be presented to the user. For large indexes, it wouldn't even be possible to collect all matching documents into available physical computer memory.

In the next section, we put IndexSearcher, Query, and Hits to work with some basic term searches.

3.1.1 *Searching for a specific term*

IndexSearcher is the central class used to search for documents in an index. It has several overloaded search methods. You can search for a specific *term* using the most commonly used search method. A term is a value that is paired with its containing field name—in this case, subject.

---

[2] The word *collection* in this sense does *not* refer to java.util.Collection.

NOTE   Important: The original text may have been normalized into terms by the analyzer, which may eliminate terms (such as stop words), convert terms to lowercase, convert terms to base word forms (*stemming*), or insert additional terms (*synonym processing*). It's crucial that the terms passed to IndexSearcher be consistent with the terms produced by analysis of the source documents. Chapter 4 discusses the analysis process in detail.

Using our example book data index, we'll query for the words *ant* and *junit*, which are words we know were indexed. Listing 3.1 performs a term query and asserts that the single document expected is found. Lucene provides several built-in Query types (see section 3.4), TermQuery being the most basic.

Listing 3.1   SearchingTest: Demonstrates the simplicity of searching using a TermQuery

```
public class SearchingTest extends LiaTestCase {

  public void testTerm() throws Exception {
    IndexSearcher searcher = new IndexSearcher(directory);
    Term t = new Term("subject", "ant");
    Query query = new TermQuery(t);
    Hits hits = searcher.search(query);
    assertEquals("JDwA", 1, hits.length());

    t = new Term("subject", "junit");
    hits = searcher.search(new TermQuery(t));
    assertEquals(2, hits.length());

    searcher.close();
  }
}
```

A Hits object is returned from our search. We'll discuss this object in section 3.2, but for now just note that the Hits object encapsulates access to the underlying Documents. This encapsulation makes sense for efficient access to documents. Full documents aren't immediately returned; they're fetched on demand. In this example we didn't concern ourselves with the actual documents associated with the hits returned because we were only interested in asserting that the proper number of documents were found.

Next, we discuss how to transform a user-entered query expression into a Query object.

3.1.2 *Parsing a user-entered query expression: QueryParser*

Two more features round out what the majority of searching applications require: sophisticated query expression parsing and access to the documents returned. Lucene's search methods require a Query object. *Parsing* a query expression is the act of turning a user-entered query such as "mock OR junit" into an appropriate Query object instance;[3] in this case, the Query object would be an instance of BooleanQuery with two nonrequired clauses, one for each term. The following code parses two query expressions and asserts that they worked as expected. After returning the hits, we retrieve the title from the first document found:

```
public void testQueryParser() throws Exception {
   IndexSearcher searcher = new IndexSearcher(directory);

   Query query = QueryParser.parse("+JUNIT +ANT -MOCK",
                                   "contents",
                                   new SimpleAnalyzer());
   Hits hits = searcher.search(query);
   assertEquals(1, hits.length());
   Document d = hits.doc(0);
   assertEquals("Java Development with Ant", d.get("title"));

   query = QueryParser.parse("mock OR junit",
                             "contents",
                             new SimpleAnalyzer());
   hits = searcher.search(query);
   assertEquals("JDwA and JIA", 2, hits.length());
}
```

Lucene includes an interesting feature that parses query expressions through the QueryParser class. It parses rich expressions such as the two shown ("+JUNIT +ANT -MOCK" and "mock OR junit") into one of the Query implementations. Dealing with human-entered queries is the primary purpose of the QueryParser.

QueryParser requires an *analyzer* to break pieces of the query into terms. In the first expression, the query was entirely uppercased. The terms of the contents field, however, were lowercased when indexed. QueryParser, in this example, uses SimpleAnalyzer, which lowercases the terms before constructing a Query object. (Analysis is covered in great detail in the next chapter, but it's intimately intertwined with indexing text and searching with QueryParser.) The main point regarding analysis to consider in this chapter is that you need to be sure to query on the actual terms indexed. QueryParser is the only searching piece that uses an

---

[3] Query expressions are similar to SQL expressions used to query a database in that the expression must be parsed into something at a lower level that the database server can understand directly.

analyzer. Querying through the API using `TermQuery` and the others discussed in section 3.4 doesn't use an analyzer but does rely on matching terms to what was indexed. In section 4.1.2, we talk more about the interactions of `QueryParser` and the analysis process.

Equipped with the examples shown thus far, you're more than ready to begin searching your indexes. There are, of course, many more details to know about searching. In particular, `QueryParser` requires additional explanation. Next is an overview of how to use `QueryParser`, which we return to in greater detail later in this chapter.

Using QueryParser

Before diving into the details of `QueryParser` (which we do in section 3.5), let's first look at how it's used in a general sense. `QueryParser` has a static `parse()` method to allow for the simplest use. Its signature is

```
static public Query
    parse(String query, String field, Analyzer analyzer)
        throws ParseException
```

The `query` `String` is the expression to be parsed, such as "+cat +dog". The second parameter, `field`, is the name of the default field to associate with terms in the expression (more on this in section 3.5.4). The final argument is an `Analyzer` instance. (We discuss analyzers in detail in the next chapter and then cover the interactions between `QueryParser` and the analyzer in section 4.1.2.) The `testQueryParser()` method shown in section 3.1.2 demonstrates using the static `parse()` method.

If the expression fails to parse, a `ParseException` is thrown, a condition that your application should handle in a graceful manner. `ParseException`'s message gives a reasonable indication of why the parsing failed; however, this description may be too technical for end users.

The static `parse()` method is quick and convenient to use, but it may not be sufficient. Under the covers, the static method instantiates an instance of `Query-Parser` and invokes the instance `parse()` method. You can do the same thing yourself, which gives you a finer level of control. There are various settings that can be controlled on a `QueryParser` instance, such as the default operator (which defaults to OR). These settings also include locale (for date parsing), default phrase slop, and whether to lowercase wildcard queries. The `QueryParser` constructor takes the default field and analyzer. The instance `parse()` method is passed the expression to parse. See section 3.5.6 for an example.

Handling basic query expressions with QueryParser

QueryParser translates query expressions into one of Lucene's built-in query types. We'll cover each query type in section 3.4; for now, take in the bigger picture provided by table 3.2, which shows some examples of expressions and their translation.

Table 3.2 Expression examples that QueryParser handles

Query expression	Matches documents that...
java	Contain the term *java* in the default field
java junit java OR junit	Contain the term *java* or *junit*, or both, in the default field[a]
+java +junit java AND junit	Contain both *java* and *junit* in the default field
title:ant	Contain the term *ant* in the title field
title:extreme -subject:sports title:extreme AND NOT subject:sports	Have *extreme* in the title field and don't have *sports* in the subject field
(agile OR extreme) AND methodology	Contain *methodology* and must also contain *agile* and/or *extreme*, all in the default field
title:"junit in action"	Contain the exact phrase *"junit in action"* in the title field
title:"junit action"~5	Contain the terms *junit* and *action* within five positions of one another
java*	Contain terms that begin with *java*, like *javaspaces*, *javaserver*, and *java.net*
java~	Contain terms that are close to the word *java*, such as *lava*
lastmodified: [1/1/04 TO 12/31/04]	Have lastmodified field values between the dates January 1, 2004 and December 31, 2004

[a] *The default operator is OR. It can be set to AND (see section 3.5.2).*

With this broad picture of Lucene's search capabilities, you're ready to dive into details. We'll revisit QueryParser in section 3.5, after we cover the more foundational pieces.

3.2 *Using IndexSearcher*

Let's take a closer look at Lucene's `IndexSearcher` class. Like the rest of Lucene's primary API, it's simple to use. Searches are done using an instance of `Index-Searcher`. Typically, you'll use one of the following approaches to construct an `IndexSearcher`:

- By `Directory`
- By a file system path

We recommend using the `Directory` constructor—it's better to decouple searching from where the index resides, allowing your searching code to be agnostic to whether the index being searched is on the file system, in RAM, or elsewhere. Our base test case, `LiaTestCase`, provides `directory`, a `Directory` implementation. Its actual implementation is an `FSDirectory` loaded from a file system index. Our `setUp()` method opens an index using the static `FSDirectory.get-Directory()` method, with the index path defined from a JVM system property:

```
public abstract class LiaTestCase extends TestCase {
  private String indexDir = System.getProperty("index.dir");
  protected Directory directory;

  protected void setUp() throws Exception {
    directory = FSDirectory.getDirectory(indexDir,false);
  }

  // ...
}
```

The last argument to `FSDirectory.getDirectory()` is `false`, indicating that we want to open an existing index, not construct a new one. An `IndexSearcher` is created using a `Directory` instance, as follows:

```
IndexSearcher searcher = new IndexSearcher(directory);
```

After constructing an `IndexSearcher`, we call one of its `search` methods to perform a search. The three main search method signatures available to an `Index-Searcher` instance are shown in table 3.3. This chapter only deals with `search(Query)` method, and that may be the only one you need to concern yourself with. The other `search` method signatures, including the sorting variants, are covered in chapter 5.

Table 3.3 Primary `IndexSearcher` search methods

`IndexSearcher.search` method signature	When to use
`Hits search(Query query)`	Straightforward searches needing no filtering.
`Hits search(Query query, Filter filter)`	Searches constrained to a subset of available documents, based on filter criteria.
`void search(Query query, HitCollector results)`	Used only when *all* documents found from a search will be needed. Generally, only the top few documents from a search are needed, so using this method could be a performance killer.

An `IndexSearcher` instance searches only the index as it existed at the time the `IndexSearcher` was instantiated. If indexing is occurring concurrently with searching, newer documents indexed won't be visible to searches. In order to see the new documents, you must instantiate a new `IndexSearcher`.

3.2.1 Working with Hits

Now that we've called `search(Query)`, we have a `Hits` object at our disposal. The search results are accessed through `Hits`. Typically, you'll use one of the `search` methods that returns a `Hits` object, as shown in table 3.3. The `Hits` object provides efficient access to search results. Results are ordered by relevance—in other words, by how well each document matches the query (sorting results in other ways is discussed in section 5.1).

There are only four methods on a `Hits` instance; they're listed in table 3.4. The method `Hits.length()` returns the number of *matching documents*. A matching document is one with a score greater than zero, as defined by the scoring formula covered in section 3.3. The hits, by default, are in decreasing score order.

Table 3.4 `Hits` methods for efficiently accessing search results

`Hits` method	Return value
`length()`	Number of documents in the `Hits` collection
`doc(n)`	Document instance of the *n*th top-scoring document
`id(n)`	Document ID of the *n*th top-scoring document
`score(n)`	Normalized score (based on the score of the topmost document) of the *n*th top-scoring document, guaranteed to be greater than 0 and less than or equal to 1

The `Hits` object caches a limited number of documents and maintains a most-recently-used list. The first 100 documents are automatically retrieved and cached initially. The `Hits` collection lends itself to environments where users are presented with only the top few documents and typically don't need more than those because only the best-scoring hits are the desired documents.

The methods `doc(n)`, `id(n)`, and `score(n)` require documents to be loaded from the index when they aren't already cached. This leads us to recommend only calling these methods for documents you truly need to display or access; defer calling them until needed.

3.2.2 Paging through Hits

Presenting search results to end users most often involves displaying only the first 20 or so most relevant documents. Paging through `Hits` is a common need. There are a couple of implementation approaches:

- Keep the original `Hits` and `IndexSearcher` instances available while the user is navigating the search results.
- Requery each time the user navigates to a new page.

It turns out that requerying is most often the best solution. Requerying eliminates the need to store per-user state. In a web application, staying stateless (no HTTP session) is often desirable. Requerying at first glance seems a waste, but Lucene's blazing speed more than compensates.

In order to requery, the original search is reexecuted and the results are displayed beginning on the desired page. How the original query is kept depends on your application architecture. In a web application where the user types in an expression that is parsed with `QueryParser`, the original expression could be made part of the hyperlinks for navigating the pages and reparsed for each request, or the expression could be kept in a hidden HTML field or as a cookie.

Don't prematurely optimize your paging implementations with caching or persistence. First implement your paging feature with a straightforward requery; chances are you'll find this sufficient for your needs.

3.2.3 Reading indexes into memory

Using `RAMDirectory` is suitable for situations requiring only transient indexes, but most applications need to persist their indexes. They will eventually need to use `FSDirectory`, as we've shown in the previous two chapters.

However, in some scenarios, indexes are used in a read-only fashion. Suppose, for instance, that you have a computer whose main memory exceeds the size of a Lucene index stored in the file system. Although it's fine to always search the index stored in the index directory, you could make better use of your hardware resources by loading the index from the slower disk into the faster RAM and then searching that in-memory index. In such cases, `RAMDirectory`'s constructor can be used to read a file system–based index into memory, allowing the application that accesses it to benefit from the superior speed of the RAM:

```
RAMDirectory ramDir = new RAMDirectory(dir);
```

`RAMDirectory` has several overloaded constructors, allowing a `java.io.File`, a path `String`, or another `Directory` to load into RAM. Using an `IndexSearcher` with a `RAMDirectory` is straightforward and no different than using an `FSDirectory`.

3.3 *Understanding Lucene scoring*

We chose to discuss this complex topic early in this chapter so you'll have a general sense of the various factors that go into Lucene scoring as you continue to read. Without further ado, meet Lucene's similarity scoring formula, shown in figure 3.1. The score is computed for each document (d) matching a specific.

> **NOTE** If this equation or the thought of mathematical computations scares you, you may safely skip this section. Lucene scoring is top-notch as is, and a detailed understanding of what makes it tick isn't necessary to take advantage of Lucene's capabilities.

This score is the *raw score*. Scores returned from `Hits` aren't necessarily the raw score, however. If the top-scoring document scores greater than 1.0, all scores are normalized from that score, such that all scores from `Hits` are guaranteed to be 1.0 or less. Table 3.5 describes each of the factors in the scoring formula.

$$\sum_{t\ in\ q} tf\left(t\ in\ d\right)\cdot idf\left(t\right)\cdot boost\left(t.field\ in\ d\right)\cdot lengthNorm\left(t.field\ in\ d\right)$$

Figure 3.1   Lucene uses this formula to determine a document score based on a query.

Table 3.5   Factors in the scoring formula

Factor	Description
`tf(t in d)`	Term frequency factor for the term (`t`) in the document (`d`).
`idf(t)`	Inverse document frequency of the term.
`boost(t.field in d)`	Field boost, as set during indexing.
`lengthNorm(t.field in d)`	Normalization value of a field, given the number of terms within the field. This value is computed during indexing and stored in the index.
`coord(q, d)`	Coordination factor, based on the number of query terms the document contains.
`queryNorm(q)`	Normalization value for a query, given the sum of the squared weights of each of the query terms.

Boost factors are built into the equation to let you affect a query or field's influence on score. Field boosts come in explicitly in the equation as the `boost(t.field in d)` factor, set at indexing time. The default value of field boosts, logically, is 1.0. During indexing, a `Document` can be assigned a boost, too. A `Document` boost factor implicitly sets the starting field boost of all fields to the specified value. Field-specific boosts are multiplied by the starting value, giving the final value of the field boost factor. It's possible to add the same named field to a `Document` multiple times, and in such situations the field boost is computed as all the boosts specified for that field and document multiplied together. Section 2.3 discusses index-time boosting in more detail.

In addition to the explicit factors in this equation, other factors can be computed on a per-query basis as part of the `queryNorm` factor. Queries themselves can have an impact on the document score. Boosting a `Query` instance is sensible only in a multiple-clause query; if only a single term is used for searching, boosting it would boost all matched documents equally. In a multiple-clause boolean query, some documents may match one clause but not another, enabling the boost factor to discriminate between queries. Queries also default to a 1.0 boost factor.

Most of these scoring formula factors are controlled through an implementation of the `Similarity` class. `DefaultSimilarity` is the implementation used unless otherwise specified. More computations are performed under the covers of `DefaultSimilarity`; for example, the term frequency factor is the square root of the actual frequency. Because this is an "in action" book, it's beyond the book's scope to delve into the inner workings of these calculations. In practice, it's extremely rare to need a change in these factors. Should you need to change these factors, please refer to Similarity's Javadocs, and be prepared with a solid understanding of these factors and the effect your changes will have.

It's important to note that a change in index-time boosts or the Similarity methods used during indexing require that the index be rebuilt for all factors to be in sync.

3.3.1 *Lucene, you got a lot of 'splainin' to do!*

Whew! The scoring formula seems daunting—and it is. We're talking about factors that rank one document higher than another based on a query; that in and of itself deserves the sophistication going on. If you want to see how all these factors play out, Lucene provides a feature called Explanation. IndexSearcher has an explain method, which requires a Query and a document ID and returns an Explanation object.

The Explanation object internally contains all the gory details that factor into the score calculation. Each detail can be accessed individually if you like; but generally, dumping out the explanation in its entirety is desired. The .toString() method dumps a nicely formatted text representation of the Explanation. We wrote a simple program to dump Explanations, shown here:

```
public class Explainer {
  public static void main(String[] args) throws Exception {
    if (args.length != 2) {
      System.err.println("Usage: Explainer <index dir> <query>");
      System.exit(1);
    }

    String indexDir = args[0];
    String queryExpression = args[1];

    FSDirectory directory =
        FSDirectory.getDirectory(indexDir, false);

    Query query = QueryParser.parse(queryExpression,
        "contents", new SimpleAnalyzer());

    System.out.println("Query: " + queryExpression);

    IndexSearcher searcher = new IndexSearcher(directory);
    Hits hits = searcher.search(query);

    for (int i = 0; i < hits.length(); i++) {
```

```
Explanation explanation =
                        searcher.explain(query, hits.id(i));      ◁─┐

System.out.println("----------");                      Generate
Document doc = hits.doc(i);                     Explanation of single
System.out.println(doc.get("title"));            Document for query
System.out.println(explanation.toString());   ◁─┐ Output
    }                                              Explanation
  }
}
```

Using the query `junit` against our sample index produced the following output; notice that the most relevant title scored best:

```
Query: junit
----------
JUnit in Action
0.65311843 = fieldWeight(contents:junit in 2), product of:
   1.4142135 = tf(termFreq(contents:junit)=2)     ❶ "junit"
   1.8472979 = idf(docFreq=2)                         appears twice in
   0.25 = fieldNorm(field=contents, doc=2)            contents


----------
Java Development with Ant
0.46182448 = fieldWeight(contents:junit in 1), product of:
   1.0 = tf(termFreq(contents:junit)=1)          ❷ "junit"
   1.8472979 = idf(docFreq=2)                         appears once
   0.25 = fieldNorm(field=contents, doc=1)            in contents
```

❶ *JUnit in Action* has the term *junit* twice in its `contents` field. The `contents` field in our index is an aggregation of the `title` and `subject` fields to allow a single field for searching.

❷ *Java Development with Ant* has the term *junit* only once in its `contents` field.

There is also a `.toHtml()` method that outputs the same hierarchical structure, except as nested HTML `<ul>` elements suitable for outputting in a web browser. In fact, the `Explanation` feature is a core part of the Nutch project (see the case study in section 10.1), allowing for transparent ranking.

`Explanations` are handy to see the inner workings of the score calculation, but they expend the same amount of effort as a query. So, be sure not to use extraneous `Explanation` generation.

3.4 *Creating queries programmatically*

As you saw in section 3.2, querying Lucene ultimately requires a call to `Index-Searcher`'s `search` using an instance of `Query`. `Query` subclasses can be instantiated directly; or, as we discussed in section 3.1.2, a `Query` can be constructed through the use of a parser such as QueryParser. If your application will rely solely on QueryParser to construct Query objects, understanding Lucene's direct API capabilities is still important because QueryParser uses them.

Even if you're using QueryParser, combining a parsed query expression with an API-created Query is a common technique to augment, refine, or constrain a human-entered query. For example, you may want to restrict free-form parsed expressions to a subset of the index, like documents only within a category. Depending on your search's user interface, you may have date pickers to select a date range, drop-downs for selecting a category, and a free-form search box. Each of these clauses can be stitched together using a combination of QueryParser, BooleanQuery, RangeQuery, and a TermQuery. We demonstrate building a similar aggregate query in section 5.5.4.

This section covers each of Lucene's built-in Query types. The QueryParser expression syntax that maps to each Query type is provided.

3.4.1 Searching by term: TermQuery

The most elementary way to search an index is for a specific term. A term is the smallest indexed piece, consisting of a field name and a text-value pair. Listing 3.1 provided an example of searching for a specific term. This code constructs a Term object instance:

```
Term t = new Term("contents", "java");
```

A TermQuery accepts a single Term:

```
Query query = new TermQuery(t);
```

All documents that have the word *java* in a contents field are returned from searches using this TermQuery. Note that the value is case-sensitive, so be sure to match the case of terms indexed; this may not be the exact case in the original document text, because an analyzer (see chapter 5) may have indexed things differently.

TermQuerys are especially useful for retrieving documents by a key. If documents were indexed using Field.Keyword(), the same value can be used to retrieve these documents. For example, given our book test data, the following code retrieves the single document matching the ISBN provided:

```
public void testKeyword() throws Exception {
  IndexSearcher searcher = new IndexSearcher(directory);
  Term t = new Term("isbn", "1930110995");
  Query query = new TermQuery(t);
  Hits hits = searcher.search(query);
  assertEquals("JUnit in Action", 1, hits.length());
}
```

A `Field.Keyword` field doesn't imply that it's unique, though. It's up to you to ensure uniqueness during indexing. In our data, `isbn` is unique among all documents.

TermQuery and QueryParser

A single word in a query expression corresponds to a term. A `TermQuery` is returned from `QueryParser` if the expression consists of a single word. The expression `java` creates a `TermQuery`, just as we did with the API in `testKeyword`.

3.4.2 *Searching within a range: RangeQuery*

Terms are ordered lexicographically within the index, allowing for efficient searching of terms within a range. Lucene's `RangeQuery` facilitates searches from a starting term through an ending term. The beginning and ending terms may either be included or excluded. The following code illustrates range queries inclusive of the begin and end terms:

```
public class RangeQueryTest extends LiaTestCase {
  private Term begin, end;

  protected void setUp() throws Exception {
    begin = new Term("pubmonth","198805");

    // pub date of TTC was October 1988
    end = new Term("pubmonth","198810");

    super.setUp();
  }

  public void testInclusive() throws Exception {
    RangeQuery query = new RangeQuery(begin, end, true);
    IndexSearcher searcher = new IndexSearcher(directory);

    Hits hits = searcher.search(query);
    assertEquals("tao", 1, hits.length());
  }
}
```

Our test data set has only one book, *Tao Te Ching* by Stephen Mitchell, published between May 1988 and October 1988; it was published in October 1988. The third argument to construct a `RangeQuery` is a boolean flag indicating whether the range is inclusive. Using the same data and range, but exclusively, one less book is found:

```
public void testExclusive() throws Exception {
  RangeQuery query = new RangeQuery(begin, end, false);
```

```
IndexSearcher searcher = new IndexSearcher(directory);

Hits hits = searcher.search(query);
assertEquals("there is no tao", 0, hits.length());
}
```

RangeQuery and QueryParser

QueryParser constructs RangeQuerys from the expression [begin TO end] or {begin TO end}. Square brackets denote an inclusive range, and curly brackets denote an exclusive range. If the begin and end terms represent dates (and parse successively as such), then ranges over fields created as dates using DateField or Keyword(String, Date) can be constructed. See section 3.5.5 for more on RangeQuery and QueryParser.

3.4.3 Searching on a string: PrefixQuery

Searching with a PrefixQuery matches documents containing terms beginning with a specified string. It's deceptively handy. The following code demonstrates how you can query a hierarchical structure *recursively* with a simple PrefixQuery. The documents contain a category keyword field representing a hierarchical structure:

```
public class PrefixQueryTest extends LiaTestCase {
  public void testPrefix() throws Exception {
    IndexSearcher searcher = new IndexSearcher(directory);

    Term term = new Term("category",
                "/technology/computers/programming");     Search for
    PrefixQuery query = new PrefixQuery(term);            programming
                                                          books, including
    Hits hits = searcher.search(query);                  subcategories
    int programmingAndBelow = hits.length();

    hits = searcher.search(new TermQuery(term));     Search only for
    int justProgramming = hits.length();            programming books,
                                                    not subcategories
    assertTrue(programmingAndBelow > justProgramming);
  }
}
```

Our PrefixQueryTest demonstrates the difference between a PrefixQuery and a TermQuery. A methodology category exists below the /technology/computers/programming category. Books in this subcategory are found with a PrefixQuery but not with the TermQuery on the parent category.

PrefixQuery and QueryParser

QueryParser creates a PrefixQuery for a term when it ends with an asterisk (*) in query expressions. For example, luc* is converted into a PrefixQuery using *luc* as the term. By default, the prefix text is lowercased by QueryParser. See section 3.5.7 for details on how to control this setting.

3.4.4 *Combining queries: BooleanQuery*

The various query types discussed here can be combined in complex ways using BooleanQuery. BooleanQuery itself is a container of Boolean *clauses*. A clause is a subquery that can be optional, required, or prohibited. These attributes allow for logical AND, OR, and NOT combinations. You add a clause to a BooleanQuery using this API method:

```
public void add(Query query, boolean required, boolean prohibited)
```

A BooleanQuery can be a clause within another BooleanQuery, allowing for sophisticated groupings. Let's look at some examples. First, here's an AND query to find the most recent books on one of our favorite subjects, *search*:

```
public void testAnd() throws Exception {
    TermQuery searchingBooks =
                new TermQuery(new Term("subject","search"));

    RangeQuery currentBooks =
                new RangeQuery(new Term("pubmonth","200401")
                               new Term("pubmonth","200412"),
                               true);

    BooleanQuery currentSearchingBooks = new BooleanQuery();
    currentSearchingBooks.add(searchingBook s, true, false);
    currentSearchingBooks.add(currentBooks, true, false);

    IndexSearcher searcher = new IndexSearcher(directory);
    Hits hits = searcher.search(currentSearchingBooks);

    assertHitsIncludeTitle(hits, "Lucene in Action");
}

// following method from base LiaTestCase class
protected final void assertHitsIncludeTitle(
                                      Hits hits, String title)
    throws IOException {
    for (int i=0; i < hits.length(); i++) {
        Document doc = hits.doc(i);
        if (title.equals(doc.get("title"))) {
            assertTrue(true);
```

① All books with subject "search"

② All books in 2004

③ Combines two queries

④ Custom convenience assert method

```
      return;                ④  Custom
   }                            convenience
}                               assert method

fail("title '" + title + "' not found");
}
```

❶ This query finds all books containing the subject "search".

❷ This query find all books published in 2004. (Note that this could also be done with a "2004" PrefixQuery.)

❸ Here we combine the two queries into a single boolean query with both clauses required (the second argument is true).

❹ This custom convenience assert method allows more readable test cases.

BooleanQuery.add has two overloaded method signatures. One accepts a Boolean-Clause, and the other accepts a Query and two boolean flags. A BooleanClause is a container of a query and the two boolean flags, so we omit coverage of it. The boolean flags are required and prohibited, respectively. There are four logical combinations of these flags, but the case where both are true is an illogical and invalid combination. A required clause means exactly that: Only documents matching that clause are considered. Table 3.6 shows the various combinations and effect of the required and prohibited flags.

Table 3.6 BooleanQuery clause attributes

		required	
		false	**true**
prohibited	**false**	Clause is optional	Clause must match
	true	Clause must not match	Invalid

Performing an OR query only requires setting the required and prohibited flags both to false, as in this example:

```
public void testOr() throws Exception {
  TermQuery methodologyBooks = new TermQuery(
     new Term("category",
        "/technology/computers/programming/methodology"));

  TermQuery easternPhilosophyBooks = new TermQuery(
     new Term("category",
        "/philosophy/eastern"));

  BooleanQuery enlightenmentBooks = new BooleanQuery();
```

```
    enlightenmentBooks.add(methodologyBooks, false, false);
    enlightenmentBooks.add(easternPhilosophyBooks, false, false);

    IndexSearcher searcher = new IndexSearcher(directory);
    Hits hits = searcher.search(enlightenmentBooks);

    assertHitsIncludeTitle(hits, "Extreme Programming Explained");
    assertHitsIncludeTitle(hits,
                        "Tao Te Ching \u9053\u5FB7\u7D93"4);
}
```

`BooleanQuerys` are restricted to a maximum number of clauses; 1,024 is the default. This limitation is in place to prevent queries from adversely affecting performance. A `TooManyClauses` exception is thrown if the maximum is exceeded. It may seem that this is an extreme number and that constructing this number of clauses is unlikely, but under the covers Lucene does some of its own query rewriting for queries like `RangeQuery` and turns them into a `BooleanQuery` with nested optional (not required, not prohibited) `TermQuerys`. Should you ever have the unusual need of increasing the number of clauses allowed, there is a `setMax-ClauseCount(int)` method on `BooleanQuery`.

BooleanQuery and QueryParser

`QueryParser` handily constructs `BooleanQuerys` when multiple terms are specified. Grouping is done with parentheses, and the `prohibited` and `required` flags are set when the –, +, AND, OR, and NOT operators are specified.

3.4.5 Searching by phrase: PhraseQuery

An index contains positional information of terms. `PhraseQuery` uses this information to locate documents where terms are within a certain distance of one another. For example, suppose a field contained the phrase "the quick brown fox jumped over the lazy dog". Without knowing the exact phrase, you can still find this document by searching for documents with fields having *quick* and *fox* near each other. Sure, a plain `TermQuery` would do the trick to locate this document knowing either of those words; but in this case we only want documents that have phrases where the words are either exactly side by side (*quick fox*) or have one word in between (*quick* [irrelevant] *fox*).

The maximum allowable positional distance between terms to be considered a match is called *slop*. *Distance* is the number of positional moves of terms to

---

[4] The \u notation is a Unicode escape sequence. In this case, these are the Chinese characters for *Tao Te Ching*. We use this for our search of Asian characters in section 4.8.3.

reconstruct the phrase in order. Let's take the phrase just mentioned and see how the slop factor plays out. First we need a little test infrastructure, which includes a `setUp()` method to index a single document and a custom `matched (String[], int)` method to construct, execute, and assert a phrase query matched the test document:

```
public class PhraseQueryTest extends TestCase {
  private IndexSearcher searcher;

  protected void setUp() throws IOException {
    // set up sample document
    RAMDirectory directory = new RAMDirectory();
    IndexWriter writer = new IndexWriter(directory,
        new WhitespaceAnalyzer(), true);
    Document doc = new Document();
    doc.add(Field.Text("field",
            "the quick brown fox jumped over the lazy dog"));
    writer.addDocument(doc);
    writer.close();

    searcher = new IndexSearcher(directory);
  }

  private boolean matched(String[] phrase, int slop)
      throws IOException {
    PhraseQuery query = new PhraseQuery();
    query.setSlop(slop);

    for (int i=0; i < phrase.length; i++) {
      query.add(new Term("field", phrase[i]));
    }

    Hits hits = searcher.search(query);
    return hits.length() > 0;
  }
}
```

Because we want to demonstrate several phrase query examples, we wrote the `matched` method to simplify the code. Phrase queries are created by adding terms in the desired order. By default, a `PhraseQuery` has its slop factor set to zero, specifying an exact phrase match. With our `setUp()` and helper `matched` method, our test case succinctly illustrates how `PhraseQuery` behaves. Failing and passing slop factors show the boundaries:

```
public void testSlopComparison() throws Exception {
  String[] phrase = new String[] {"quick", "fox"};

  assertFalse("exact phrase not found", matched(phrase, 0));

  assertTrue("close enough", matched(phrase, 1));
}
```

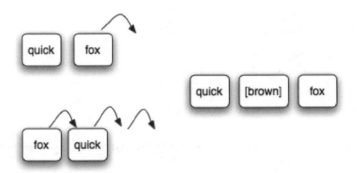

Figure 3.2 Illustrating `PhraseQuery` slop factor: "quick fox" requires a slop of 1 to match, whereas "fox quick" requires a slop of 3 to match.

Terms added to a phrase query don't have to be in the same order found in the field, although order does impact slop-factor considerations. For example, had the terms been reversed in the query (*fox* and then *quick*), the number of moves needed to match the document would be three, not one. To visualize this, consider how many moves it would take to physically move the word *fox* two slots past *quick*; you'll see that it takes one move to move *fox* into the same position as *quick* and then two more to move *fox* beyond *quick* sufficiently to match "quick brown fox".

Figure 3.2 shows how the slop positions work in both of these phrase query scenarios, and this test case shows the match in action:

```
public void testReverse() throws Exception {
   String[] phrase = new String[] {"fox", "quick"};

   assertFalse("hop flop", matched(phrase, 2));
   assertTrue("hop hop slop", matched(phrase, 3));
}
```

Let's now examine how multiple term phrase queries work.

Multiple-term phrases

`PhraseQuery` supports multiple-term phrases. Regardless of how many terms are used for a phrase, the slop factor is the maximum *total* number of moves allowed to put the terms in order. Let's look at an example of a multiple-term phrase query:

```
public void testMultiple() throws Exception {
   assertFalse("not close enough",
      matched(new String[] {"quick", "jumped", "lazy"}, 3));
```

```
        assertTrue("just enough",
            matched(new String[] {"quick", "jumped", "lazy"}, 4));

        assertFalse("almost but not quite",
            matched(new String[] {"lazy", "jumped", "quick"}, 7));

        assertTrue("bingo",
            matched(new String[] {"lazy", "jumped", "quick"}, 8));
    }
```

Now that you've seen how phrase queries match, we turn our attention to how phrase queries affect the score.

Phrase query scoring

Phrase queries are scored based on the edit distance needed to match the phrase. More exact matches count for more weight than sloppier ones. The phrase query factor is shown in figure 3.3. The inverse relationship with distance ensures that greater distances have lower scores.

$$\frac{1}{distance+1}$$

**Figure 3.3
Sloppy phrase
scoring**

NOTE   Terms surrounded by double quotes in QueryParser parsed expressions are translated into a PhraseQuery. The slop factor defaults to zero, but you can adjust the slop factor by adding a tilde (~) followed by an integer. For example, the expression "quick fox"~3 is a PhraseQuery with the terms *quick* and *fox* and a slop factor of 3. There are additional details about PhraseQuery and the slop factor in section 3.5.6. Phrases are analyzed by the analyzer passed to the QueryParser, adding another layer of complexity, as discussed in section 4.1.2.

3.4.6 Searching by wildcard: WildcardQuery

Wildcard queries let you query for terms with missing pieces but still find matches. Two standard wildcard characters are used: * for zero or more characters, and ? for zero or one character. Listing 3.2 demonstrates WildcardQuery in action.

Listing 3.2   Searching on the wild(card) side

```
private void indexSingleFieldDocs(Field[] fields) throws Exception {
  IndexWriter writer = new IndexWriter(directory,
      new WhitespaceAnalyzer(), true);
  for (int i = 0; i < fields.length; i++) {
    Document doc = new Document();
    doc.add(fields[i]);
    writer.addDocument(doc);
  }
```

```
      writer.optimize();
      writer.close();
   }

   public void testWildcard() throws Exception {
      indexSingleFieldDocs(new Field[]
        { Field.Text("contents", "wild"),
          Field.Text("contents", "child"),
          Field.Text("contents", "mild"),
          Field.Text("contents", "mildew") });

      IndexSearcher searcher = new IndexSearcher(directory);
      Query query = new WildcardQuery(
              new Term("contents", "?ild*"));            ◁─┐ Construct
      Hits hits = searcher.search(query);                 │ WildcardQuery
      assertEquals("child no match", 3, hits.length());   │ using Term

      assertEquals("score the same", hits.score(0),
                                     hits.score(1), 0.0);
      assertEquals("score the same", hits.score(1),
                                     hits.score(2), 0.0);

   }
```

Note how the wildcard pattern is created as a `Term` (the pattern to match) even though it isn't explicitly used as an exact term under the covers. Internally, it's used as a pattern to match terms in the index. A `Term` instance is a convenient placeholder to represent a field name and a string.

> **WARNING** Performance degradations can occur when you use `WildcardQuery`. A larger prefix (characters before the first wildcard character) decreases the terms enumerated to find matches. Beginning a pattern with a wildcard query forces the term enumeration to search *all* terms in the index for matches.

Oddly, the closeness of a wildcard match has no affect on scoring. The last two assertions in listing 3.2, where *wild* and *mild* are closer matches to the pattern than *mildew*, demonstrate this.

WildcardQuery and QueryParser

`QueryParser` supports `WildcardQuery` using the same syntax for a term as used by the API. There are a few important differences, though. With `QueryParser`, the first character of a wildcarded term may not be a wildcard character; this restriction prevents users from putting asterisk-prefixed terms into a search expression, incurring an expensive operation of enumerating all the terms. Also, if the only wildcard character in the term is a trailing asterisk, the query is optimized to a `PrefixQuery`. Wildcard terms are lowercased automatically by default, but this can be changed. See section 3.5.7 for more on wildcard queries and `QueryParser`.

3.4.7 Searching for similar terms: FuzzyQuery

The final built-in query is one of the more interesting. Lucene's `FuzzyQuery` matches terms *similar* to a specified term. The *Levenshtein distance* algorithm determines how similar terms in the index are to a specified target term.[5] *Edit distance* is another term for Levenshtein distance; it's a measure of similarity between two strings, where distance is measured as the number of character deletions, insertions, or substitutions required to transform one string to the other string. For example, the edit distance between *three* and *tree* is 1, because only one character deletion is needed.

    Levenshtein distance isn't the same as the distance calculation used in `PhraseQuery` and `PhrasePrefixQuery`. The phrase query distance is the number of term moves to match, whereas Levenshtein distance is an intraterm computation of character moves. The `FuzzyQuery` test demonstrates its usage and behavior:

```
public void testFuzzy() throws Exception {
  indexSingleFieldDocs(new Field[] {
    Field.Text("contents", "fuzzy"),
    Field.Text("contents", "wuzzy")
  });

  IndexSearcher searcher = new IndexSearcher(directory);
  Query query = new FuzzyQuery(new Term("contents", "wuzza"));
  Hits hits = searcher.search(query);
  assertEquals("both close enough", 2, hits.length());

  assertTrue("wuzzy closer than fuzzy",
             hits.score(0) !=  hits.score(1));

  assertEquals("wuzza bear",
               "wuzzy", hits.doc(0).get("contents"));
}
```

This test illustrates a couple of key points. Both documents match; the term searched for (*wuzza*) wasn't indexed but was close enough to match. `FuzzyQuery` uses a *threshold* rather than a pure edit distance. The threshold is a factor of the edit distance divided by the string length.

---

[5] See http://www.merriampark.com/ld.htm for more information about Levenshtein distance.

$$1 - \frac{distance}{min(textlen, targetlen)}$$

Figure 3.4
`FuzzyQuery` distance formula.

Edit distance affects scoring, such that terms with less edit distance are scored higher. Distance is computed using the formula shown in figure 3.4.

> **WARNING** `FuzzyQuery` enumerates all terms in an index to find terms within the allowable threshold. Use this type of query sparingly, or at least with the knowledge of how it works and the effect it may have on performance.

FuzzyQuery and QueryParser

`QueryParser` supports `FuzzyQuery` by suffixing a term with a tilde (~). For example, the `FuzzyQuery` from the previous example would be `wuzza~` in a query expression. Note that the tilde is also used to specify sloppy phrase queries, but the context is different. Double quotes denote a phrase query and aren't used for fuzzy queries.

3.5 *Parsing query expressions: QueryParser*

Although API-created queries can be powerful, it isn't reasonable that all queries should be explicitly written in Java code. Using a human-readable textual query representation, Lucene's `QueryParser` constructs one of the previously mentioned `Query` subclasses. This constructed `Query` instance could be a complex entity, consisting of nested `BooleanQuerys` and a combination of almost all the `Query` types mentioned, but an expression entered by the user could be as readable as this:

```
+pubdate:[20040101 TO 20041231] Java AND (Jakarta OR Apache)
```

This query searches for all books about Java that also include *Jakarta* or *Apache* in their contents and were published in 2004.

> **NOTE** Whenever special characters are used in a query expression, you need to provide an escaping mechanism so that the special characters can be used in a normal fashion. `QueryParser` uses a backslash (\) to escape special characters within terms. The escapable characters are as follows:
>
> ```
> \ + - ! ( ) : ^ ] { } ~ * ?
> ```

The following sections detail the expression syntax, examples of using Query-Parser, and customizing `QueryParser`'s behavior. The discussion of `QueryParser` in this section assumes knowledge of the query types previously discussed in section 3.4. We begin with a handy way to glimpse what `QueryParser` does to expressions.

3.5.1 Query.toString

Seemingly strange things can happen to a query expression as it's parsed with QueryParser. How can you tell what really happened to your expression? Was it translated properly into what you intended? One way to peek at a resultant Query instance is to use the toString() method.

All concrete core Query classes we've discussed in this chapter have a special toString() implementation. They output valid QueryParser parsable strings. The standard Object.toString() method is overridden and delegates to a toString(String field)() method, where field is the name of the default field. Calling the no-arg toString() method uses an empty default field name, causing the output to explicitly use field selector notation for all terms. Here's an example of using the toString() method:

```
public void testToString() throws Exception {
  BooleanQuery query = new BooleanQuery();
  query.add(
    new FuzzyQuery(new Term("field", "kountry6")), true, false);
  query.add(
    new TermQuery(new Term("title", "western")), false, false);

  assertEquals("both kinds",
               "+kountry~ title:western",
               query.toString("field"));
}
```

The toString() methods (particularly the String-arg one) are handy for visual debugging of complex API queries as well as getting a handle on how Query-Parser interprets query expressions. Don't rely on the ability to go back and forth accurately between a Query.toString() representation and a QueryParser-parsed expression, though. It's generally accurate, but an analyzer is involved and may confuse things; this issue is discussed further in section 4.1.2.

3.5.2 Boolean operators

Constructing Boolean queries textually via QueryParser is done using the operators AND, OR, and NOT. Terms listed without an operator specified use an implicit operator, which by default is OR. The query abc xyz will be interpreted as either abc OR xyz or abc AND xyz, based on the implicit operator setting. To switch parsing to use AND, use an instance of QueryParser rather than the static parse method:

---

[6] Misspelled on purpose to illustrate FuzzyQuery.

```
QueryParser parser = new QueryParser("contents", analyzer);
parser.setOperator(QueryParser.DEFAULT_OPERATOR_AND);
```

Placing a NOT in front of a term excludes documents matching the following term. Negating a term must be combined with at least one nonnegated term to return documents; in other words, it isn't possible to use a query like NOT term to find all documents that don't contain a term. Each of the uppercase word operators has shortcut syntax; table 3.7 illustrates various syntax equivalents.

Table 3.7   Boolean query operator shortcuts

Verbose syntax	Shortcut syntax
a AND b	+a +b
a OR b	a b
a AND NOT b	+a −b

3.5.3 *Grouping*

Lucene's BooleanQuery lets you construct complex nested clauses; likewise, QueryParser enables it with query expressions. Let's find all the methodology books that are either about agile or extreme methodologies. We use parentheses to form subqueries, enabling advanced construction of BooleanQerys:

```
public void testGrouping() throws Exception {
    Query query = QueryParser.parse(
        "(agile OR extreme) AND methodology",
        "subject",
        analyzer);
    Hits hits = searcher.search(query);

    assertHitsIncludeTitle(hits, "Extreme Programming Explained");
    assertHitsIncludeTitle(hits, "The Pragmatic Programmer");
}
```

Next, we discuss how a specific field can be selected. Notice that field selection can also leverage parentheses.

3.5.4 *Field selection*

QueryParser needs to know the field name to use when constructing queries, but it would generally be unfriendly to require users to identify the field to search (the end user may not need or want to know the field names). As you've seen, the default field name is provided to the parse method. Parsed queries aren't restricted, however, to searching only the default field. Using field selector notation, you can specify terms in nondefault fields. For example, when HTML documents are indexed with the title and body areas as separate fields, the default field will likely be body. Users can search for title fields using a query such as title:lucene. You can group field selection over several terms using field:(a b c).

3.5.5 *Range searches*

Text or date range queries use bracketed syntax, with TO between the beginning term and ending term. The type of bracket determines whether the range is inclusive (square brackets) or exclusive (curly brackets). Our testRangeQuery() method demonstrates both inclusive and exclusive range queries:

```
public void testRangeQuery() throws Exception {
    Query query = QueryParser.parse(
        "pubmonth:[200401 TO 200412]", "subject", analyzer);    ❶ Inclusive
                                                                    range
    assertTrue(query instanceof RangeQuery);

    Hits hits = searcher.search(query);
    assertHitsIncludeTitle(hits, "Lucene in Action");

    query = QueryParser.parse(
        "{200201 TO 200208}", "pubmonth", analyzer);            ❷ Exclusive
                                                                    range
    hits = searcher.search(query);
    assertEquals("JDwA in 200208", 0, hits.length());           ❸ Demonstrates
}                                                                   exclusion of
                                                                    pubmonth 200208
```

❶ This inclusive range uses a field selector since the default field is subject.

❷ This exclusive range uses the default field pubmonth.

❸ *Java Development with Ant* was published in August 2002, so we've demonstrated that the pubmonth value 200208 is excluded from the range.

> **NOTE** Nondate range queries use the beginning and ending terms as the user entered them, without modification. In other words, the beginning and ending terms are *not* analyzed. Start and end terms must not contain whitespace, or parsing fails. In our example index, the field pubmonth isn't a date field; it's text of the format YYYYMM.

Handling date ranges

When a range query is encountered, the parser code first attempts to convert the start and end terms to dates. If the terms are valid dates, according to DateFormat. SHORT and lenient parsing within the default or specified locale, then the dates are converted to their internal textual representation (see section 2.4 on DateField).

If either of the two terms fails to parse as a valid date, they're both used as is for a textual range.

The Query's toString() output is interesting for date-range queries. Let's parse one to see:

```
Query query = QueryParser.parse("modified:[1/1/04 TO 12/31/04]",
                                "subject", analyzer);
System.out.println(query);
```

This outputs something strange:

```
modified:[0dowcq3k0 TO 0e3dwg0w0]
```

Internally, all terms are text to Lucene, and dates are represented in a lexico-graphically ordered text format. As long as our modified field was indexed properly as a Date, all is well despite this odd-looking output.

Controlling the date-parsing locale

To change the locale used for date parsing, construct a QueryParser instance and call setLocale(). Typically the client's locale would be determined and used, rather than the default locale. For example, in a web application, the HttpServlet-Request object contains the locale set by the client browser. You can use this locale to control the locale used by date parsing in QueryParser, as shown in listing 3.3.

Listing 3.3 Using the client locale in a web application

```
public class SearchServlet extends HttpServlet {
  protected void doGet(HttpServletRequest request,
                       HttpServletResponse response)
     throws ServletException, IOException {

    QueryParser parser = new QueryParser("contents",
       new StandardAnalyzer());

    parser.setLocale(request.getLocale());

    try {
      Query query = parser.parse(request.getParameter("q"));
    } catch (ParseException e) {
     // ... handle exception
    }

    // ... display results ...
  }
}
```

QueryParser's setLocale is one way in which Lucene facilitates internationalization (often abbreviated I18N) concerns. Text analysis is another, more important, place where such concerns are handled. Further I18N issues are discussed in section 4.8.2.

3.5.6 *Phrase queries*

Terms enclosed in double quotes create a PhraseQuery. The text between the quotes is analyzed; thus the resultant PhraseQuery may not be exactly the phrase originally specified. This process has been the subject of some confusion. For example, the query "This is Some Phrase*", when analyzed by the Standard-Analyzer, parses to a PhraseQuery using the phrase "some phrase". The StandardAnalyzer removes the words *this* and *is* because they match the default stop word list (more in section 4.3.2 on StandardAnalyzer). A common question is why the asterisk isn't interpreted as a wildcard query. Keep in mind that surrounding text with double quotes causes the surrounded text to be analyzed and converted into a PhraseQuery. Single-term phrases are optimized to a TermQuery. The following code demonstrates both the effect of analysis on a phrase query expression and the TermQuery optimization:

```
public void testPhraseQuery() throws Exception {
   Query q = QueryParser.parse("\"This is Some Phrase*\"",
      "field", new StandardAnalyzer());
   assertEquals("analyzed",
      "\"some phrase\"", q.toString("field"));

   q = QueryParser.parse("\"term\"", "field", analyzer);
   assertTrue("reduced to TermQuery", q instanceof TermQuery);
}
```

The slop factor is zero unless you specify it using a trailing tilde (~) and the desired integer slop value. Because the implicit analysis of phrases may not match what was indexed, the slop factor can be set to something other than zero automatically if it isn't specified using the tilde notation:

```
public void testSlop() throws Exception {
   Query q = QueryParser.parse(
      "\"exact phrase\"", "field", analyzer);
   assertEquals("zero slop",
      "\"exact phrase\"", q.toString("field"));

   QueryParser qp = new QueryParser("field", analyzer);
   qp.setPhraseSlop(5);
   q = qp.parse("\"sloppy phrase\"");
   assertEquals("sloppy, implicitly",
      "\"sloppy phrase\"~5", q.toString("field"));
}
```

A sloppy `PhraseQuery`, as noted, doesn't require that the terms match in the same order. However, a `SpanNearQuery` (discussed in section 5.4.3) has the ability to guarantee an in-order match. In section 6.3.4, we extend `QueryParser` and substitute a `SpanNearQuery` when phrase queries are parsed, allowing for sloppy in-order phrase matches.

3.5.7 *Wildcard and prefix queries*

If a term contains an asterisk or a question mark, it's considered a `Wildcard-Query`. When the term only contains a trailing asterisk, `QueryParser` optimizes it to a `PrefixQuery` instead. Both prefix and wildcard queries are lowercased by default, but this behavior can be controlled:

```
public void testLowercasing() throws Exception {
   Query q = QueryParser.parse("PrefixQuery*", "field",
                   analyzer);
   assertEquals("lowercased",
       "prefixquery*", q.toString("field"));

   QueryParser qp = new QueryParser("field", analyzer);
   qp.setLowercaseWildcardTerms(false);
   q = qp.parse("PrefixQuery*");
   assertEquals("not lowercased",
       "PrefixQuery*", q.toString("field"));
}
```

To turn off the automatic lowercasing, you must construct your own instance of `QueryParser` rather than use the static parse method.

Wildcards at the beginning of a term are prohibited using `QueryParser`, but an API-coded `WildcardQuery` may use leading wildcards (at the expense of performance). Section 3.4.6 discusses more about the performance issue, and section 6.3.1 provides a way to prohibit `WildcardQuery`s from parsed expressions if you wish.

3.5.8 *Fuzzy queries*

A trailing tilde (~) creates a fuzzy query on the preceding term. The same performance caveats the apply to `WildcardQuery` also apply to fuzzy queries and can be disabled with a customization similar to that discussed in section 6.3.1.

3.5.9 *Boosting queries*

A carat (^) followed by a floating-point number sets the boost factor for the preceding query. Section 3.3 discusses boosting queries in more detail. For example, the query expression `junit^2.0 testing` sets the `junit` `TermQuery` to a boost of 2.0

and leaves the testing TermQuery at the default boost of 1.0. You can apply a boost to any type of query, including parenthetical groups.

3.5.10 *To QueryParse or not to QueryParse?*

QueryParser is a quick and effortless way to give users powerful query construction, but it isn't right for all scenarios. QueryParser can't create every type of query that can be constructed using the API. In chapter 5, we detail a handful of API-only queries that have no QueryParser expression capability. You must keep in mind all the possibilities available when exposing free-form query parsing to an end user; some queries have the potential for performance bottlenecks, and the syntax used by the built-in QueryParser may not be suitable for your needs. You can exert some limited control by subclassing QueryParser (see section 6.3.1).

Should you require different expression syntax or capabilities beyond what QueryParser offers, technologies such as ANTLR[7] and JavaCC[8] are great options. We don't discuss the creation of a custom query parser; however, the source code for Lucene's QueryParser is freely available for you to borrow from.

You can often obtain a happy medium by combining a QueryParser-parsed query with API-created queries as clauses in a BooleanQuery. This approach is demonstrated in section 5.5.4. For example, if users need to constrain searches to a particular category or narrow them to a date range, you can have the user interface separate those selections into a category chooser or separate date-range fields.

3.6 *Summary*

Lucene rapidly provides highly relevant search results to queries. Most applications need only a few Lucene classes and methods to enable searching. The most fundamental things for you to take from this chapter are an understanding of the basic query types (of which TermQuery, RangeQuery, and BooleanQuery are the primary ones) and how to access search results.

Although it can be a bit daunting, Lucene's scoring formula (coupled with the index format discussed in appendix B and the efficient algorithms) provides the magic of returning the most relevant documents first. Lucene's QueryParser parses human-readable query expressions, giving rich full-text search power to end users. QueryParser immediately satisfies most application requirements;

[7] http://www.antlr.org.

[8] http://javacc.dev.java.net.

however, it doesn't come without caveats, so be sure you understand the rough edges. Much of the confusion regarding `QueryParser` stems from unexpected analysis interactions; chapter 4 goes into great detail about analysis, including more on the `QueryParser` issues.

And yes, there is more to searching than we've covered in this chapter, but understanding the groundwork is crucial. Chapter 5 delves into Lucene's more elaborate features, such as constraining (or filtering) the search space of queries and sorting search results by field values; chapter 6 explores the numerous ways you can extend Lucene's searching capabilities for custom sorting and query parsing.

Analysis

4

This chapter covers
- Understanding the analysis process
- Exploring QueryParser issues
- Writing custom analyzers
- Handling foreign languages

Analysis, in Lucene, is the process of converting field text into its most fundamental indexed representation, *terms*. These terms are used to determine what documents match a query during searches. For example, if this sentence were indexed into a field (let's assume type `Field.Text`), the terms might start with *for* and *example*, and so on, as separate terms in sequence. An *analyzer* is an encapsulation of the analysis process. An analyzer tokenizes text by performing any number of operations on it, which could include extracting words, discarding punctuation, removing accents from characters, lowercasing (also called *normalizing*), removing common words, reducing words to a root form (*stemming*), or changing words into the basic form (*lemmatization*). This process is also called *tokenization*, and the chunks of text pulled from a stream of text are called *tokens*. `Tokens`, combined with their associated field name, are terms.

Lucene's primary goal is to facilitate information *retrieval*. The emphasis on retrieval is important. You want to throw gobs of text at Lucene and have them be richly searchable by the individual words within that text. In order for Lucene to know what "words" are, it *analyzes* the text during indexing, extracting it into terms. These terms are the primitive building blocks for searching.

Choosing the right analyzer is a crucial development decision with Lucene. One size doesn't fit all when it comes to choosing an analyzer. Language is one factor in choosing an analyzer, because each has its own unique features. Another factor to consider in choosing an analyzer is the domain of the text being analyzed; different industries have different terminology, acronyms, and abbreviations that may deserve attention. Although we present many of the considerations for choosing analyzers, no single analyzer will suffice for all situations. It's possible that none of the built-in analysis options are adequate for your needs, and you'll need to invest in creating a custom analysis solution; pleasantly, Lucene's building blocks make this quite easy.

One of the best questions you can ask as you contemplate the analysis process is, "What would Google do?" Google's actual algorithms are proprietary and kept relatively secret, but the results from searches give some insight. Searching for the phrase "to be or not to be" with and without the quotes is a fun experiment. Without the quotes, the only word Google considers (at the time of writing) is, surprisingly, *not;*[1] it throws away the others as being too common. However, Google doesn't throw away these *stop words* during indexing, as you can

---

[1] Interestingly, the first result (at the time of writing) for "to be or not to be" (without quotes) at Google is the site "Am I Hot or Not?"—seriously!

see by searching for the phrase with quotes. This is an interesting phenomenon: An astounding number of stop words are being indexed! How does Google accomplish the indexing of every word of every web page on the Internet without running out of storage? A Lucene-based analyzer exists that provides a solution to this issue, as we'll discuss.

In this chapter, we'll cover all aspects of the Lucene analysis process, including how and where to use analyzers, what the built-in analyzers do, and how to write your own custom analyzers using the building blocks provided by the core Lucene API.

4.1 Using analyzers

Before we get into the gory details of what lurks inside an analyzer, let's look at how an analyzer is used within Lucene. Analysis occurs at two spots: during indexing and when using QueryParser. In the following two sections, we detail how an analyzer is used in these scenarios.

Before we begin with any code details, look at listing 4.1 to get a feel for what the analysis process is all about. Two phrases are analyzed, each by four of the built-in analyzers. The phrases are "The quick brown fox jumped over the lazy dogs" and "XY&Z Corporation - xyz@example.com". Each token is shown between square brackets to make the separations apparent. During indexing, the tokens extracted during analysis are the terms indexed. And, most important, the terms indexed are the terms that are searchable!

Listing 4.1   Visualizing analyzer effects

```
Analyzing "The quick brown fox jumped over the lazy dogs"
  WhitespaceAnalyzer:
    [The] [quick] [brown] [fox] [jumped] [over] [the] [lazy] [dogs]

  SimpleAnalyzer:
    [the] [quick] [brown] [fox] [jumped] [over] [the] [lazy] [dogs]

  StopAnalyzer:
    [quick] [brown] [fox] [jumped] [over] [lazy] [dogs]

  StandardAnalyzer:
    [quick] [brown] [fox] [jumped] [over] [lazy] [dogs]

Analyzing "XY&Z Corporation - xyz@example.com"
  WhitespaceAnalyzer:
    [XY&Z] [Corporation] [-] [xyz@example.com]
```

```
SimpleAnalyzer:
  [xy] [z] [corporation] [xyz] [example] [com]

StopAnalyzer:
  [xy] [z] [corporation] [xyz] [example] [com]

StandardAnalyzer:
  [xy&z] [corporation] [xyz@example.com]
```

The code that generated this analyzer output is shown later, in listing 4.2. A few interesting things happen in this example. Look at how the word *the* is treated, and likewise the company name XY&Z and the e-mail address xyz@example.com; look at the special hyphen character (-) and the case of each token. Section 4.2.3 explains more of the details of what happened.

Lucene doesn't make the results of the analysis process visible to the end user. Terms pulled from the original text are indexed and are matched during searching. When searching with QueryParser, the analysis process happens again in order to ensure the best possible matches.

4.1.1 *Indexing analysis*

During indexing, an Analyzer instance is handed to the IndexWriter in this manner:

```
Analyzer analyzer = new StandardAnalyzer();
IndexWriter writer = new IndexWriter(directory, analyzer, true);
```

In this example, we use the built-in StandardAnalyzer, one of the several available within the core Lucene library. Each tokenized field of each document indexed with the IndexWriter instance uses the analyzer specified. Two special Field types are designated to be tokenized: Text and UnStored.

> **NOTE** Field.Text(String, String) creates a tokenized *and* stored field. Rest assured the *original* String value is stored. However, the output of the designated Analyzer dictates what is indexed.

The following code demonstrates indexing of a document with these two field types:

```
Document doc = new Document();
doc.add(Field.Text("title", "This is the title"));
doc.add(Field.UnStored("contents", "...document contents..."));
writer.addDocument(doc);
```

Both `"title"` and `"contents"` are analyzed using the `Analyzer` instance provided to the `IndexWriter`. However, if an individual document has special analysis needs, the analyzer may be specified on a per-document basis, like this:

```
writer.addDocument(doc, analyzer);
```

During indexing, the granularity of analyzer choice is at the `IndexWriter` or per-`Document` level. It would seem that each field may deserve unique analysis and that even this per-`Document` analysis is too course grained. Analyzers have access to the field name being analyzed, so finer-grained, field-specific analysis is possible; we discuss per-field analysis in section 4.4.

Field.`Keyword` indexed fields aren't *tokenized*. A Field.`Keyword` field is indexed as a single term with the value exactly as provided. Once indexed, though, there is no difference in a term from Field.`Keyword` and a term created from an analyzer; both are terms with no knowledge of how they were indexed. This can lead to troublesome behavior when you're using `QueryParser`, as we mention again in the next section.

4.1.2   *QueryParser analysis*

The `Analyzer` is the key to the terms indexed. As you saw in chapter 3, you need to be sure to query on the exact terms indexed in order to find documents (we covered `QueryParser` expression parsing and usage details in sections 3.1.2 and 3.5). When you're using API-created queries such as `TermQuery`, it's the developer's responsibility to ensure that the terms used will match what was indexed.

Presenting users with a free-form option of querying is often what you're asked to implement, and `QueryParser` comes in handy for processing user-entered query expressions. `QueryParser` uses an analyzer to do its best job to match the terms that were indexed. An analyzer is specified on the static `parse` method:

```
Query query = QueryParser.parse(expression, "contents", analyzer);
```

Or, if you're using a `QueryParser` instance, the analyzer is specified on the constructor:

```
QueryParser parser = new QueryParser("contents", analyzer);
query = parser.parse(expression);
```

`QueryParser` analyzes individual pieces of the expression, not the expression as a whole, which may include operators, parenthesis, and other special expression syntax to denote range, wildcard, and fuzzy searches.

QueryParser analyzes all text equally, without knowledge of how it was indexed. This is a particularly thorny issue when you're querying for fields that were indexed as Field.Keyword. We address this situation in section 4.4.

Should you use the same analyzer with QueryParser that you used during indexing? The short, most accurate, answer is, "it depends." If you stick with the basic built-in analyzers, then you'll probably be fine using the same analyzer in both situations. However, when you're using more sophisticated analyzers, quirky cases can come up in which using different analyzers between indexing and Query-Parser is best. We discuss this issue in more detail in section 4.6.

4.1.3 *Parsing versus analysis: when an analyzer isn't appropriate*

An important point about analyzers is that they're used internally for fields flagged to be tokenized. Documents such as HTML, Microsoft Word, XML, and others, contain meta-data such as author, title, last modified date, and potentially much more. When you're indexing rich documents, this meta-data should be separated and indexed as separate fields. Analyzers are used to analyze a specific field at a time and break things into tokens only within that field; creating new fields isn't possible within an analyzer.

Analyzers don't help in field separation because their scope is to deal with a single field at a time. Instead, *parsing* these documents prior to analysis is required. For example, it's a common practice to separate at least the <title> and <body> of HTML documents into separate fields. In these cases, the documents should be parsed, or preprocessed, into separate blocks of text representing each field. Chapter 7 covers several specific document types and provides options for indexing them; it also discusses parsing various document types in detail.

4.2 *Analyzing the analyzer*

In order to fully appreciate and understand how Lucene's textual analysis works, we need to open the hood and tinker around a bit. Because it's possible that you'll be constructing your own analyzers, knowing the architecture and building blocks provided is crucial.

The Analyzer class is the base class. Quite elegantly, it turns text into a stream of tokens, literally a TokenStream. The single required method signature implemented by analyzers is

```
public TokenStream tokenStream(String fieldName, Reader reader)
```

Notice that an analyzer can be used to key off the field name. Because field names are arbitrary and application dependent, all the built-in analyzers ignore the field name. Custom analyzers are free to utilize the field name or, more easily, to use the special `PerFieldAnalyzerWrapper` that delegates the analysis for each field to analyzers you associate with field names (detailed coverage is in section 4.4).

Let's start "simply" with the `SimpleAnalyzer` and see what makes it tick. The following code is copied directly from Lucene's codebase:

```
public final class SimpleAnalyzer extends Analyzer {
  public TokenStream tokenStream(String fieldName, Reader reader) {
    return new LowerCaseTokenizer(reader);
  }
}
```

The `LowerCaseTokenizer` divides text at nonletters (determined by `Character.isLetter`), removing nonletter characters and, true to its name, lowercasing each character. A `TokenStream` is an enumerator-like class that returns successive `Tokens`, returning `null` when the end has been reached (see listing 4.3, where `Analyzer-Utils` enumerates the tokens returned).

In the following sections, we take a detailed look at each of the major players used by analyzers, including `Token` and the `TokenStream` family.

4.2.1 What's in a token?

A stream of tokens is the fundamental output of the analysis process. During indexing, fields designated for tokenization are processed with the specified analyzer, and each token is written to the index as a term. This distinction between tokens and terms may seem confusing at first. Let's see what forms a `Token`; we'll come back to how that translates into a term.

For example, let's analyze the text "the quick brown fox". Each token represents an individual word of that text. A token carries with it a text value (the word itself) as well as some meta-data: the start and end offsets in the original text, a token type, and a position increment. Figure 4.1 shows the details of the token stream analyzing this phrase with the `SimpleAnalyzer`.

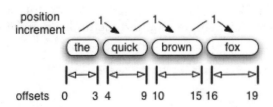

Figure 4.1
Token stream with positional and offset information

The start offset is the character position in the original text where the token text begins, and the end offset is the position just after the last character of the token text. The token type is a `String`, defaulting to `"word"`, that you can control and use in the token-filtering process if desired. As text is tokenized, the position relative to the previous token is recorded as the position increment value. All the built-in tokenizers leave the position increment at the default value of 1, indicating that all tokens are in successive positions, one after the other.

Tokens into terms

After text is analyzed during indexing, each token is posted to the index as a term. The position increment is the *only* additional meta-data associated with the token carried through to the index. Start and end offset as well as token type are discarded—these are only used during the analysis process.

Position increments

The token position increment value relates the current token to the previous one. Generally, position increments are 1, indicating that each word is in a unique and successive position in the field. Position increments factor directly into performing phrase queries (see section 3.4.5) and span queries (see section 5.4), which rely on knowing how far terms are from one another within a field.

Position increments greater than 1 allow for gaps and can be used to indicate where words have been removed. See section 4.7.1 for an example of stop-word removal that leaves gaps using position increments.

A token with a zero position increment places the token in the same position as the previous token. Analyzers that inject word aliases can use a position increment of zero for the aliases. The effect is that phrase queries work regardless of which alias was used in the query. See our `SynonymAnalyzer` in section 4.6 for an example that uses position increments of zero.

4.2.2 *TokenStreams uncensored*

There are two different styles of `TokenStreams`: `Tokenizer` and `TokenFilter`. A good generalization to explain the distinction is that `Tokenizers` deal with individual characters, and `TokenFilters` deal with words. Figure 4.2 shows this architecture graphically.

A `Tokenizer` is a `TokenStream` that tokenizes the input from a `Reader`. When you're indexing a `String` through `Field.Text(String, String)` or `Field.UnStored(String, String)` (that is, the indexed field constructors which accept a `String`), Lucene wraps the `String` in a `StringReader` for tokenization.

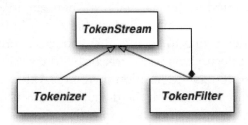

Figure 4.2
`TokenStream` architecture:
`TokenFilters` filter a
`TokenStream`.

The second style of `TokenStream`, `TokenFilter`, lets you chain `TokenStreams` together. This powerful mechanism lives up to its namesake as a stream filter. A `TokenStream` is fed into a `TokenFilter`, giving the filter a chance to add, remove, or change the stream as it passes through.

Figure 4.3 shows the full `TokenStream` inheritance hierarchy within Lucene. Note the composite pattern used by `TokenFilter` to encapsulate another `Token-Stream` (which could, of course, be another `TokenFilter`). Table 4.1 provides detailed descriptions for each of the classes shown in figure 4.3.

Table 4.1   Analyzer building blocks provided in Lucene's core API

Class name	Description
TokenStream	Base class with `next()` and `close()` methods.
Tokenizer	**`TokenStream` whose input is a `Reader`.**
CharTokenizer	Parent class of character-based tokenizers, with abstract `isTokenChar()` method. Emits tokens for contiguous blocks when `isTokenChar == true`. Also provides the capability to normalize (for example, lowercase) characters. `Token`s are limited to a maximum size of 255 characters.
WhitespaceTokenizer	`CharTokenizer` with `isTokenChar()` true for all nonwhitespace characters.
LetterTokenizer	`CharTokenizer` with `isTokenChar()` true when `Character.isLetter` is true.
LowerCaseTokenizer	`LetterTokenizer` that normalizes all characters to lowercase.
StandardTokenizer	Sophisticated grammar-based tokenizer, emitting tokens for high-level types like e-mail addresses (see section 4.3.2 for more details). Each emitted token is tagged with a special type, some of which are handled specially by `StandardFilter`.
TokenFilter	**`TokenStream` whose input is another `TokenStream`.**
LowerCaseFilter	Lowercases token text.

continued on next page

Table 4.1   Analyzer building blocks provided in Lucene's core API *(continued)*

Class name	Description
StopFilter	Removes words that exist in a provided set of words.
PorterStemFilter	Stems each token using the Porter stemming algorithm. For example, *country* and *countries* both stem to *countri*.
StandardFilter	Designed to be fed by a `StandardTokenizer`. Removes dots from acronyms and *'s* (apostrophe followed by *S*) from words with apostrophes.

Taking advantage of the `TokenFilter` chaining pattern, you can build complex analyzers from simple `Tokenizer`/`TokenFilter` building blocks. `Tokenizers` start the analysis process by churning the character input into *tokens* (mostly these correspond to words in the original text). `TokenFilters` then take over the remainder of the analysis, initially wrapping a `Tokenizer` and successively wrapping nested `TokenFilters`. To illustrate this in code, here is the heart of `StopAnalyzer`:

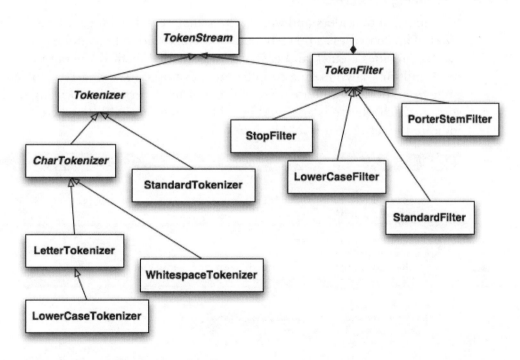

Figure 4.3   `TokenStream` class hierarchy

```
public TokenStream tokenStream(String fieldName, Reader reader) {
  return new StopFilter(
             new LowerCaseTokenizer(reader),
             stopTable);
}
```

In `StopAnalyzer`, a `LowerCaseTokenizer` feeds a `StopFilter`. The `LowerCaseTokenizer` emits tokens that are adjacent letters in the original text, lowercasing each of the characters in the process. Nonletter characters form token boundaries and aren't included in any emitted token. Following this word tokenizer and lowercaser, `StopFilter` removes words in a stop-word list (see section 4.3.1).

Buffering is a feature that's commonly needed in the `TokenStream` implementations. Low-level `Tokenizers` do this to buffer up characters to form tokens at boundaries such as whitespace or nonletter characters. `TokenFilters` that emit additional tokens into the stream they're filtering must queue an incoming token and the additional ones and emit them one at a time; our `SynonymFilter` in section 4.6 is an example of a queuing filter.

4.2.3 *Visualizing analyzers*

It's important to understand what various analyzers do with your text. Seeing the effect of an analyzer is a powerful and immediate aid to this understanding. Listing 4.2 provides a quick and easy way to get visual feedback about the four primary built-in analyzers on a couple of text examples. `AnalyzerDemo` includes two predefined phrases and an array of the four analyzers we're focusing on in this section. Each phrase is analyzed by all the analyzers, with bracketed output to indicate the terms that would be indexed.

Listing 4.2 `AnalyzerDemo`: seeing analysis in action

```
/**
 * Adapted from code which first appeared in a java.net article
 * written by Erik
 */
public class AnalyzerDemo {
  private static final String[] examples = {
    "The quick brown fox jumped over the lazy dogs",
    "XY&Z Corporation - xyz@example.com"
  };

  private static final Analyzer[] analyzers = new Analyzer[] {
    new WhitespaceAnalyzer(),
    new SimpleAnalyzer(),
    new StopAnalyzer(),
    new StandardAnalyzer()
  };
```

```
public static void main(String[] args) throws IOException {
  // Use the embedded example strings, unless
  // command line arguments are specified, then use those.
  String[] strings = examples;
  if (args.length > 0) {
    strings = args;
  }

  for (int i = 0; i < strings.length; i++) {
    analyze(strings[i]);
  }
}

private static void analyze(String text) throws IOException {
  System.out.println("Analyzing \"" + text + "\"");
  for (int i = 0; i < analyzers.length; i++) {
    Analyzer analyzer = analyzers[i];
    String name = analyzer.getClass().getName();
    name = name.substring(name.lastIndexOf(".") + 1);
    System.out.println("  " + name + ":");
    System.out.print("    ");
    AnalyzerUtils.displayTokens(analyzer, text);
    System.out.println("\n");
  }
}
}
```

The real fun happens in `AnalyzerUtils` (listing 4.3), where the analyzer is applied to the text and the tokens are extracted. `AnalyzerUtils` passes text to an analyzer without indexing it and pulls the results in a manner similar to what happens during the indexing process under the covers of `IndexWriter`.

Listing 4.3 `AnalyzerUtils`: delving into an analyzer

```
public class AnalyzerUtils {
  public static Token[] tokensFromAnalysis
            (Analyzer analyzer, String text) throws IOException {
    TokenStream stream =
          analyzer.tokenStream("contents", new StringReader(text));    Invoke analysis
    ArrayList tokenList = new ArrayList();                             process
    while (true) {
      Token token = stream.next();
      if (token == null) break;

      tokenList.add(token);
    }

    return (Token[]) tokenList.toArray(new Token[0]);
  }
```

```
    public static void displayTokens
                (Analyzer analyzer, String text) throws IOException {
      Token[] tokens = tokensFromAnalysis(analyzer, text);

      for (int i = 0; i < tokens.length; i++) {
        Token token = tokens[i];

        System.out.print("[" + token.termText() + "] ");   ◁── Output tokens
      }                                                          surrounded by
    }                                                            brackets

    // ... other methods introduced later ...

  }
```

Generally you wouldn't invoke the analyzer's `tokenStream` method explicitly except for this type of diagnostic or informational purpose (and the field name `contents` is arbitrary in the `tokensFromAnalysis()` method). We do, however, cover one production use of this method for query highlighting in section 8.7, page 300.

`AnalyzerDemo` produced the output shown in listing 4.1. Some key points to note are as follows:

- `WhitespaceAnalyzer` didn't lowercase, left in the dash, and did the bare minimum of tokenizing at whitespace boundaries.

- `SimpleAnalyzer` left in what may be considered irrelevant (stop) words, but it did lowercase and tokenize at nonalphabetic character boundaries.

- Both `SimpleAnalyzer` and `StopAnalyzer` mangled the corporation name by splitting XY&Z and removing the ampersand.

- `StopAnalyzer` and `StandardAnalyzer` threw away occurrences of the word *the*.

- `StandardAnalyzer` kept the corporation name intact and lowercased it, removed the dash, and kept the e-mail address together. No other built-in analyzer is this thorough.

We recommend keeping a utility like this handy to see what tokens emit from your analyzers of choice. In fact, rather than write this yourself, you can use our `AnalyzerUtils` or the `AnalyzerDemo` code for experimentation. The `AnalyzerDemo` application lets you specify one or more strings from the command line to be analyzed instead of the embedded example ones:

```
% java lia.analysis.AnalyzerDemo "No Fluff, Just Stuff"
Analyzing "No Fluff, Just Stuff"
```

```
org.apache.lucene.analysis.WhitespaceAnalyzer:
  [No] [Fluff,] [Just] [Stuff]

org.apache.lucene.analysis.SimpleAnalyzer:
  [no] [fluff] [just] [stuff]

org.apache.lucene.analysis.StopAnalyzer:
  [fluff] [just] [stuff]

org.apache.lucene.analysis.standard.StandardAnalyzer:
  [fluff] [just] [stuff]
```

Let's now look deeper into what makes up a `Token`.

Looking inside tokens

`TokenStream`s can create `Token`s, and `TokenFilter`s may access their meta-data. To demonstrate accessing token meta-data, we added the `displayTokensWithFull-Details` utility method in `AnalyzerUtils`:

```
public static void displayTokensWithFullDetails
    (Analyzer analyzer, String text) throws IOException {
  Token[] tokens = tokensFromAnalysis(analyzer, text);

  int position = 0;

  for (int i = 0; i < tokens.length; i++) {
    Token token = tokens[i];

    int increment = token.getPositionIncrement();

    if (increment > 0) {
      position = position + increment;
      System.out.println();
      System.out.print(position + ": ");
    }

    System.out.print("[" + token.termText() + ":" +
        token.startOffset() + "->" +
        token.endOffset() + ":" +
        token.type() + "] ");
  }
}
```

We display all token information on the example phrase using `SimpleAnalyzer`:

```
public static void main(String[] args) throws IOException {
  displayTokensWithFullDetails(new SimpleAnalyzer(),
      "The quick brown fox....");
}
```

Here's the output:

```
1: [the:0->3:word]
2: [quick:4->9:word]
3: [brown:10->15:word]
4: [fox:16->19:word]
```

Each token is in a successive position relative to the previous one (noted by the incrementing numbers 1, 2, 3, and 4). The word *the* begins at offset 0 and ends before offset 3 in the original text. Each of the tokens has a type of word. We present a similar, but simpler, visualization of token position increments in section 4.6.1, and we provide a visualization of tokens sharing the same position.

What good are start and end offsets?

The start and end offset values aren't used in the core of Lucene. Are they useless? Not entirely. The term highlighter discussed in section 8.7 uses a Token-Stream and the resulting Tokens outside of indexing to determine where in a block of text to begin and end highlighting, allowing words that users search for to stand out in search results.

Token-type usefulness

You can use the token-type value to denote special lexical types for tokens. Under the covers of StandardAnalyzer is a StandardTokenizer that parses the incoming text into different types based on a grammar. Analyzing the phrase "I'll e-mail you at xyz@example.com" with StandardAnalyzer produces this interesting output:

```
1: [i'll:0->4:<APOSTROPHE>]
2: [e:5->6:<ALPHANUM>]
3: [mail:7->11:<ALPHANUM>]
4: [you:12->15:<ALPHANUM>]
5: [xyz@example.com:19->34:<EMAIL>]
```

Notice the token type of each token. The token i'll has an apostrophe, which StandardTokenizer notices in order to keep it together as a unit; and likewise for the e-mail address. We cover the other StandardAnalyzer effects in section 4.3.2. StandardAnalyzer is the only built-in analyzer that leverages the token-type data. Our Metaphone and synonym analyzers, in sections 4.5 and 4.6, provide another example of token type usage.

4.2.4 Filtering order can be important

The order of events can be critically important during analysis. Each step may rely on the work of a previous step. A prime example is that of stop-word removal. StopFilter does a case-sensitive look-up of each token in a set of stop words. It relies on being fed lowercased tokens. As an example, we first write a functionally equivalent StopAnalyzer variant; we'll follow it with a flawed variant that reverses the order of the steps:

```
public class StopAnalyzer2 extends Analyzer {
  private Set stopWords;

  public StopAnalyzer2() {
    stopWords =
      StopFilter.makeStopSet(StopAnalyzer.ENGLISH_STOP_WORDS);
  }

  public StopAnalyzer2(String[] stopWords) {
    this.stopWords = StopFilter.makeStopSet(stopWords);
  }

  public TokenStream tokenStream(String fieldName, Reader reader) {
    return new StopFilter(
      new LowerCaseFilter(new LetterTokenizer(reader)),
        stopWords);
  }
}
```

StopAnalyzer2 uses a LetterTokenizer feeding a LowerCaseFilter, rather than just a LowerCaseTokenizer. A LowerCaseTokenizer, however, has a performance advantage since it lowercases as it tokenizes, rather than dividing the process into two steps. This test case proves that our StopAnalyzer2 works as expected, by using AnalyzerUtils.tokensFromAnalysis and asserting that the stop word the was removed:

```
public void testStopAnalyzer2() throws Exception {
    Token[] tokens =
      AnalyzerUtils.tokensFromAnalysis(
        new StopAnalyzer2(), "The quick brown...");

    assertTrue(
      AnalyzerUtils.tokensEqual(tokens,
                                new String[] {"quick", "brown"}));
}
```

We've added a unit-test helper method to our AnalyzerUtils that asserts tokens match an expected list:

```
public static void assertTokensEqual(
                        Token[] tokens, String[] strings) {
    Assert.assertEquals(strings.length, tokens.length);

    for (int i = 0; i < tokens.length; i++) {
      Assert.assertEquals("index " + i,
```

```
                       strings[i], tokens[i].termText());
   }
  }
```

To illustrate the importance that the order can make with token filtering, we've written a flawed analyzer that swaps the order of the `StopFilter` and the `LowerCaseFilter`:

```
/**
 * Stop words not necessarily removed due to filtering order
 */
public class StopAnalyzerFlawed extends Analyzer {
  private Set stopWords;

  public StopAnalyzerFlawed() {
    stopWords =
        StopFilter.makeStopSet(StopAnalyzer.ENGLISH_STOP_WORDS);
  }

  public StopAnalyzerFlawed(String[] stopWords) {
    this.stopWords = StopFilter.makeStopSet(stopWords);
  }

  /**
   * Ordering mistake here
   */
  public TokenStream tokenStream(String fieldName, Reader reader) {
    return new LowerCaseFilter(
        new StopFilter(new LetterTokenizer(reader),
        stopWords));
  }
}
```

The `StopFilter` presumes all tokens have already been lowercased and does a case-sensitive lookup. Another test case shows that *The* was not removed (it's the first token of the analyzer output), yet it was lowercased:

```
public void testStopAnalyzerFlawed() throws Exception {
  Token[] tokens =
    AnalyzerUtils.tokensFromAnalysis(
      new StopAnalyzerFlawed(), "The quick brown...");

  assertEquals("the", tokens[0].termText());
}
```

Lowercasing is just one example where order may matter. Filters may assume previous processing was done. For example, the `StandardFilter` is designed to be used in conjunction with `StandardTokenizer` and wouldn't make sense with any other `TokenStream` feeding it. There may also be performance considerations when you order the filtering process. Consider an analyzer that removes stop words and also injects synonyms into the token stream—it would be more efficient to remove the stop words first so that the synonym injection filter would have fewer terms to consider (see section 4.6 for a detailed example).

4.3 Using the built-in analyzers

Lucene includes several built-in analyzers. The primary ones are shown in table 4.2. We'll leave discussion of the two language-specific analyzers, RussianAnalyzer and GermanAnalyzer, to section 4.8.2 and the special per-field analyzer wrapper, PerFieldAnalyzerWrapper, to section 4.4.

Table 4.2 Primary analyzers available in Lucene

Analyzer	Steps taken
WhitespaceAnalyzer	Splits tokens at whitespace
SimpleAnalyzer	Divides text at nonletter characters and lowercases
StopAnalyzer	Divides text at nonletter characters, lowercases, and removes stop words
StandardAnalyzer	Tokenizes based on a sophisticated grammar that recognizes e-mail addresses, acronyms, Chinese-Japanese-Korean characters, alphanumerics, and more; lowercases; and removes stop words

The built-in analyzers we discuss in this section—WhitespaceAnalyzer, Simple-Analyzer, StopAnalyzer, and StandardAnalyzer—are designed to work with text in almost any Western (European-based) language. You can see the effect of each of these analyzers in the output in section 4.2.3. WhitespaceAnalyzer and Simple-Analyzer are both trivial and we don't cover them in more detail here. We explore the StopAnalyzer and StandardAnalyzer in more depth because they have non-trivial effects.

4.3.1 StopAnalyzer

StopAnalyzer, beyond doing basic word splitting and lowercasing, also removes stop words. Embedded in StopAnalyzer is a list of common English stop words; this list is used unless otherwise specified:

```
public static final String[] ENGLISH_STOP_WORDS = {
  "a", "an", "and", "are", "as", "at", "be", "but", "by",
  "for", "if", "in", "into", "is", "it",
```

```
    "no", "not", "of", "on", "or", "s", "such",
    "t", "that", "the", "their", "then", "there", "these",
    "they", "this", "to", "was", "will", "with"
  };
```

The `StopAnalyzer` has a second constructor that allows you to pass your own list as a `String[]` instead. Of note are two items in the default list: `"s"` and `"t"`. Contractions are commonly used in English, such as *don't, can't,* and *it's.* Prior to removing stop words, the `StopAnalyzer` keeps successive characters together, splitting at nonletter characters including the apostrophe and leaving the *s* and *t* characters as standalone tokens; since these characters are meaningless on their own, it makes sense to remove them.

Stop word removal brings up another interesting issue: What happened to the holes left by the words removed? Suppose you index "one is not enough". The tokens emitted from `StopAnalyzer` will be `one` and `enough`, with `is` and `not` thrown away. `StopAnalyzer` currently does no accounting for words removed, so the result is exactly as if you indexed "one enough". If you were to use `Query-Parser` along with `StopAnalyzer`, this document would match phrase queries for "one enough", "one is enough", "one but not enough", and the original "one is not enough". Remember, `QueryParser` also analyzes phrases, and each of these reduces to "one enough" and matches the terms indexed. There is a "hole" lot more to this topic, which we cover in section 4.7.3 (after we provide more details about token positions).

Having the stop words removed presents an interesting semantic question. Do you lose some potential meaning? The answer to this question is, "It depends." It depends on your use of Lucene and whether searching on these words is meaningful to your application. We briefly revisit this somewhat rhetorical question later, in section 4.7.3. To emphasize and reiterate an important point, only the tokens emitted from the analyzer (or indexed as `Field.Keyword`) are available for searching.

4.3.2 *StandardAnalyzer*

`StandardAnalyzer` holds the honor as the most generally useful built-in analyzer. A JavaCC-based[2] grammar underlies it, tokenizing with cleverness for the following lexical types: alphanumerics, acronyms, company names, e-mail addresses, computer host names, numbers, words with an interior apostrophe, serial numbers, IP addresses, and CJK (Chinese Japanese Korean) characters. `StandardAnalyzer` also

---

[2] Java Compiler-Compiler (JavaCC) is a sophisticated lexical parser. See http://javacc.dev.java.net.

includes stop-word removal, using the same mechanism as the StopAnalyzer (identical default English list, and an optional String[] constructor to override). StandardAnalyzer makes a great first choice.

Using StandardAnalyzer is no different than using any of the other analyzers, as you can see from its use in section 4.1.1 and AnalyzerDemo (listing 4.2). Its unique effect, though, is apparent in the different treatment of text. For example, look at listing 4.1, and compare the different analyzers on the phrase "XY&Z Corporation - xyz@example.com". StandardAnalyzer is the only one that kept XY&Z together as well as the e-mail address xyz@example.com; both of these showcase the vastly more sophisticated analysis process.

4.4 *Dealing with keyword fields*

It's easy to index a keyword using Field.Keyword, which is a single token added to a field that bypasses tokenization and is indexed exactly as is as a single term. It's also straightforward to query for a term through TermQuery. A dilemma can arise, however, if you expose QueryParser to users and attempt to query on Field.Keyword-created fields. The "keyword"-ness of a field is only known during indexing. There is nothing special about keyword fields once they're indexed; they're just terms.

Let's see the issue exposed with a straightforward test case that indexes a document with a keyword field and then attempts to find that document again:

```
public class KeywordAnalyzerTest extends TestCase {
  RAMDirectory directory;
  private IndexSearcher searcher;

  public void setUp() throws Exception {
    directory = new RAMDirectory();
    IndexWriter writer = new IndexWriter(directory,
                                         new SimpleAnalyzer(),
                                         true);

    Document doc = new Document();                          Field not
    doc.add(Field.Keyword("partnum", "Q36"));        ◁── analyzed
    doc.add(Field.Text("description", "Illidium Space Modulator"));
    writer.addDocument(doc);

    writer.close();

    searcher = new IndexSearcher(directory);
  }

  public void testTermQuery() throws Exception {
```

```
      Query query = new TermQuery(new Term("partnum", "Q36"));        ◁— No analysis
      Hits hits = searcher.search(query);                                here
      assertEquals(1, hits.length());     ◁— Document found
    }                                        as expected
  }
```

So far, so good—we've indexed a document and can retrieve it using a `TermQuery`. But what happens if we generate a query using `QueryParser`?

```
      public void testBasicQueryParser() throws Exception {
        Query query = QueryParser.parse("partnum:Q36 AND SPACE",
                                        "description",
                                        new SimpleAnalyzer());      ❶ QueryParser
                                                                       analyzes each
                                                                       term and phrase
        Hits hits = searcher.search(query);
        assertEquals("note Q36 -> q",
                "+partnum:q +space", query.toString("description"));   ❷
        assertEquals("doc not found :(", 0, hits.length());
      }                                                              toString()
                                                                     method
```

❶ `QueryParser` analyzes each term and phrase of the query expression. Both *Q36* and *SPACE* are analyzed separately. `SimpleAnalyzer` strips nonletter characters and lowercases, so *Q36* becomes *q*. But at indexing time, *Q36* was left as is. Notice, also, that this is the same analyzer used during indexing.

❷ Query has a nice `toString()` method (see section 3.5.1) to return the query as a `QueryParser`-like expression. Notice that *Q36* is gone.

This issue of `QueryParser` analyzing a keyword field emphasizes a key point: *indexing and analysis are intimately tied to searching*. The `testBasicQueryParser` test shows that searching for terms created using `Field.Keyword` when a query expression is analyzed can be problematic. It's problematic because `QueryParser` analyzed the `partnum` field, but it shouldn't have. There are a few possible solutions to this type of dilemma:

- Separate your user interface such that a user selects a part number separately from free-form queries. Generally, users don't want to know (and shouldn't need to know) about the field names in the index.

- Explore the use of field-specific analysis.

- If part numbers or other textual constructs are common lexical occurrences in the text you're analyzing, consider creating a custom domain-specific analyzer that recognizes part numbers, and so on, and leaves them as is.

- Subclass `QueryParser` and override one or both of the `getFieldQuery` methods to provide field-specific handling.

Designing a search user interface is very application dependent; BooleanQuery (section 3.4.4) and filters (section 5.5) provide the support you need to combine query pieces in sophisticated ways. Section 8.5 covers ways to use JavaScript in a web browser for building queries. The information in this chapter provides the foundation for building domain-centric analyzers. We'll delve more deeply into using field-specific analysis for the remainder of this section. We cover subclassing QueryParser in section 6.3; however, there is no advantage to doing so in this scenario over the PerFieldAnalyzerWrapper solution we present here.

An IndexWriter only deals with an analyzer choice on a per-instance or per-Document basis. Internally, though, analyzers can act on the field name being analyzed. The built-in analyzers don't leverage this capability because they're designed for general-purpose use regardless of field name. When you're confronted with a situation requiring unique analysis for different fields, one option is the PerFieldAnalyzerWrapper.

We developed a KeywordAnalyzer that tokenizes the entire stream as a single token, imitating how Field.Keyword is handled during indexing. We only want one field to be "analyzed" in this manner, so we leverage the PerFieldAnalyzerWrapper to apply it only to the partnum field. First let's look at the KeywordAnalyzer in action as it fixes the situation:

```
public void testPerFieldAnalyzer() throws Exception {
    PerFieldAnalyzerWrapper analyzer = new PerFieldAnalyzerWrapper(
                                          new SimpleAnalyzer());
    analyzer.addAnalyzer("partnum", new KeywordAnalyzer());        ❶

    Query query = QueryParser.parse("partnum:Q36 AND SPACE",        Apply
                                    "description",                  KeywordAnalyzer
                                    analyzer);                      only to partnum

    Hits hits = searcher.search(query);
    assertEquals("Q36 kept as-is",
            "+partnum:Q36 +space", query.toString("description"));
    assertEquals("doc found!", 1, hits.length());                  Document
                                                                   is found
}
```

❶ We apply the KeywordAnalyzer only to the partnum field, and we use the Simple-Analyzer for all other fields. This is the same effective result as during indexing.

❷ Note that the query now has the proper term for the partnum field, and the document is found as expected.

The built-in PerFieldAnalyzerWrapper constructor requires the default analyzer as a parameter. To assign a different analyzer to a field, use the addAnalyzer method. During tokenization, the analyzer specific to the field name is used; the default is used if no field-specific analyzer has been assigned.

The internals of KeywordAnalyzer illustrate character buffering. Listing 4.4 shows the entire analyzer implementation.

Listing 4.4 KeywordAnalyzer: emulating Field.Keyword

```
/**
 * "Tokenizes" the entire stream as a single token.
 */
public class KeywordAnalyzer extends Analyzer {
  public TokenStream tokenStream(String fieldName,
                                 final Reader reader) {
    return new TokenStream() {
      private boolean done;
      private final char[] buffer = new char[1024];
      public Token next() throws IOException {
        if (!done) {
          done = true;
          StringBuffer buffer = new StringBuffer();
          int length = 0;
          while (true) {
            length = reader.read(this.buffer);
            if (length == -1) break;

            buffer.append(this.buffer, 0, length);
          }
          String text = buffer.toString();
          return new Token(text, 0, text.length());
        }
        return null;
      }
    };
  }
}
```

Given KeywordAnalyzer, we could streamline our code (in KeywordAnalyzer-Test.setUp) and use the same PerFieldAnalyzerWrapper used in testPerField-Analyzer during indexing. Using a KeywordAnalyzer on special fields during indexing would eliminate the use of Field.Keyword during indexing and replace it with Field.Text. Aesthetically, it may be pleasing to see the same analyzer used during indexing and querying, and using PerFieldAnalyzerWrapper makes this possible.

4.4.1 *Alternate keyword analyzer*

Take note of the `TokenStream` infrastructure (figure 4.2 and table 4.1). A simpler keyword analyzer is possible if you're sure your keywords are 255 characters or less. Subclassing `CharTokenizer` and saying that every character is a token character gives this much cleaner implementation:

```
public class SimpleKeywordAnalyzer extends Analyzer {

    public TokenStream tokenStream(String fieldName,
                                   Reader reader) {
        return new CharTokenizer(reader) {
            protected boolean isTokenChar(char c) {
                return true;
            }
        };
    }

}
```

In our example, we could substitute `KeywordAnalyzer` with `SimpleKeyword-Analyzer` since our part numbers are definitely less than 255 characters. You certainly don't want user-enterable fields to be anywhere near 255 characters in length!

4.5 *"Sounds like" querying*

Have you ever played the game Charades, cupping your hand to your ear to indicate that your next gestures refer to words that "sound like" the real words you're trying to convey? Neither have we. Suppose, though, that a high-paying client has asked you to implement a search engine accessible by J2ME-enabled devices, such as a cell phone, to help during those tough charade matches. In this section, we'll implement an analyzer to convert words to a phonetic root using an implementation of the Metaphone algorithm from the Jakarta Commons Codec project. We chose the Metaphone algorithm as an example, but other algorithms are available, such as Soundex.

Being the test-driven guys we are, we begin with a test to illustrate the high-level goal of our search experience:

```
public void testKoolKat() throws Exception {
    RAMDirectory directory = new RAMDirectory();
    Analyzer analyzer = new MetaphoneReplacementAnalyzer();

    IndexWriter writer = new IndexWriter(directory, analyzer, true);
```

```
Document doc = new Document();
doc.add(Field.Text("contents", "cool cat"));     ◁─┐ Original
writer.addDocument(doc);                              document
writer.close();


IndexSearcher searcher = new IndexSearcher(directory);
Query query = QueryParser.parse("kool kat",       ◁─┐ User typed in
                               "contents",            hip query
                               analyzer);

Hits hits = searcher.search(query);      ◁─┐ Hip query
                                             matches!
assertEquals(1, hits.length());          ◁─┘
assertEquals("cool cat", hits.doc(0).get("contents"));   ◁─┐ Original value
                                                             still available
searcher.close();
}
```

It seems like magic! The user searched for "kool kat". Neither of those terms
were in our original document, yet the search found the desired match. Searches
on the original text would also return the expected matches. The trick lies under
the MetaphoneReplacementAnalyzer:

```
public class MetaphoneReplacementAnalyzer extends Analyzer {
  public TokenStream tokenStream(String fieldName, Reader reader) {
    return new MetaphoneReplacementFilter(
              new LetterTokenizer(reader));
  }
}
```

Because the Metaphone algorithm expects words that only include letters, the
LetterTokenizer is used to feed our metaphone filter. The LetterTokenizer doesn't
lowercase, however. The tokens emitted are *replaced* by their metaphone equivalent, so lowercasing is unnecessary. Let's now dig into the MetaphoneReplacement-
Filter, where the real work is done:

```
public class MetaphoneReplacementFilter extends TokenFilter {
  public static final String METAPHONE = "METAPHONE";

  private Metaphone metaphoner = new Metaphone();       ◁─┐ org.apache.commons
                                                            .codec.language.
  public MetaphoneReplacementFilter(TokenStream input) {    Metaphone
    super(input);
  }

  public Token next() throws IOException {
    Token t = input.next();      ◁─┐ Pull next
                                     token
```

```
    if (t == null) return null;         ⟵┐ When null, end
                                           │ has been reached
    try {
      return new Token(metaphoner.encode(t.termText()),
                       t.startOffset(),
                       t.endOffset(),
                       METAPHONE);    ⟵ Set token type
    } catch (EncoderException e) {
      // if cannot encode, simply return original token
      return t;
    }

  }
}
```

                                              ⟶ Convert token
                                                to Metaphone
                                                encoding;
                                                leave position
                                                info as is

The token emitted by our MetaphoneReplacementFilter, as its name implies, literally replaces the incoming token (unless for some reason the encoding failed, and the original is emitted). This new token is set with the same position offsets as the original, because it's a replacement in the same position. The last argument to the Token constructor indicates the *token type*. Each token can be associated with a String indicating its type, giving meta-data to later filtering in the analysis process. The StandardTokenizer, as discussed in "Token type usefulness" under section 4.2.3, tags tokens with a type that is later used by the StandardFilter. The METAPHONE type isn't used in our examples, but it demonstrates that a later filter could be Metaphone-token aware by calling Token's type() method.

> **NOTE** Token types, such as the METAPHONE type used in MetaphoneReplacement-Analyzer, are carried through the analysis phase but aren't encoded into the index. Unless specified otherwise, the type word is used for tokens by default. Section 4.2.3 discusses token types further.

As always, it's good to view what an analyzer is doing with text. Using our Analyzer-Utils, two phrases that sound similar yet are spelled completely differently are tokenized and displayed:

```
public static void main(String[] args) throws IOException {
  MetaphoneReplacementAnalyzer analyzer =
                          new MetaphoneReplacementAnalyzer();
  AnalyzerUtils.displayTokens(analyzer,
              "The quick brown fox jumped over the lazy dogs");

  System.out.println("");
  AnalyzerUtils.displayTokens(analyzer,
              "Tha quik brown phox jumpd ovvar tha lazi dogz");
}
```

We get a sample of the Metaphone encoder, shown here:

```
[0] [KK] [BRN] [FKS] [JMPT] [OFR] [0] [LS] [TKS]
[0] [KK] [BRN] [FKS] [JMPT] [OFR] [0] [LS] [TKS]
```

Wow—an exact match!

In practice, it's unlikely you'll want sounds-like matches except in special places; otherwise, far too many undesired matches may be returned.[3] In the "What would Google do?" sense, a sounds-like feature would be great for situations where a user misspelled every word and no documents were found, but alternative words could be suggested. One implementation approach to this idea could be to run all text through a sounds-like analysis and build a cross-reference lookup to consult when a correction is needed.

4.6 *Synonyms, aliases, and words that mean the same*

Our next custom analyzer injects synonyms of words into the outgoing token stream, but places the synonyms in the *same position* as the original word. By adding synonyms during indexing, you make searches find documents that may not contain the original search terms but match the synonyms of those words. Test first, of course:

```
public void testJumps() throws Exception {
  Token[] tokens =
    AnalyzerUtils.tokensFromAnalysis(synonymAnalyzer⁴, "jumps");    ⟵  Analyze one word

  AnalyzerUtils.assertTokensEqual(tokens,
                     new String[] {"jumps", "hops", "leaps"});    ⟵  Three words come out

  // ensure synonyms are in the same position as the original
  assertEquals("jumps", 1, tokens[0].getPositionIncrement());
  assertEquals("hops", 0, tokens[1].getPositionIncrement());
  assertEquals("leaps", 0, tokens[2].getPositionIncrement());
}
```

---

[3] While working on this chapter, Erik asked his brilliant 5-year-old son, Jakob, how he would spell *cool cat*. Jakob replied, "c-o-l c-a-t". What a wonderfully confusing language English is. Erik imagines that a "sounds-like" feature in search engines designed for children would be very useful. Metaphone encodes *cool*, *kool*, and *col* all as KL.

[4] The construction of SynonymAnalyzer is shown shortly.

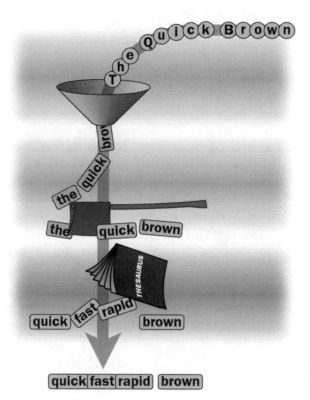

**Figure 4.4
SynonymAnalyzer
visualized as factory
automation**

Notice that our unit test shows not only that synonyms for the word *jumps* are
emitted from the SynonymAnalyzer but also that the synonyms are placed in the
same position (increment of zero) as the original word.

Let's see what the SynonymAnalyzer is doing; then we'll explore the implications
of position increments. Figure 4.4 graphically shows what our SynonymAnalyzer
does to text input, and listing 4.5 is the implementation.

Listing 4.5 SynonymAnalyzer implementation

```
public class SynonymAnalyzer extends Analyzer {
  private SynonymEngine engine;

  public SynonymAnalyzer(SynonymEngine engine) {
    this.engine = engine;
  }

  public TokenStream tokenStream(String fieldName, Reader reader) {
    TokenStream result = new SynonymFilter(
```

```
                        new StopFilter(
                          new LowerCaseFilter(
                            new StandardFilter(
                              new StandardTokenizer(reader)))),
                          StandardAnalyzer.STOP_WORDS),
                        engine
                      );
    return result;
  }
}
```

Once again, the analyzer code is minimal and simply chains a `Tokenizer`
together with a series of `TokenFilters`; in fact, this is the `StandardAnalyzer`
wrapped with an additional filter. (See table 4.1 for more on these basic analyzer
building blocks.) The final `TokenFilter` in the chain is the new `SynonymFilter`
(listing 4.6), which gets to the heart of the current discussion. When you're
injecting terms, buffering is needed. This filter uses a `Stack` as the buffer.

Listing 4.6 `SynonymFilter`: buffering tokens and emitting one at a time

```
public class SynonymFilter extends TokenFilter {
  public static final String TOKEN_TYPE_SYNONYM = "SYNONYM";

  private Stack synonymStack;
  private SynonymEngine engine;

  public SynonymFilter(TokenStream in, SynonymEngine engine) {
    super(in);
    synonymStack = new Stack();        ◁─┐ Synonym
    this.engine = engine;                │ buffer
  }

  public Token next() throws IOException {
    if (synonymStack.size() > 0) {
      return (Token) synonymStack.pop();
    }                                         ❶ Pop buffered
                                                synonyms
    Token token = input.next();     ❷ Read next token
    if (token == null) {
      return null;
    }

    addAliasesToStack(token);       ❸ Push synonyms of current token onto stack

    return token;     ❹ Return current token
  }
```

```
private void addAliasesToStack(Token token) throws IOException {
  String[] synonyms = engine.getSynonyms(token.termText());        ❺
                                                          Retrieve synonyms
  if (synonyms == null) return;

  for (int i = 0; i < synonyms.length; i++) {
    Token synToken = new Token(synonyms[i],
                               token.startOffset(),
                               token.endOffset(),                  ❻
                               TOKEN_TYPE_SYNONYM);          Push synonyms
    synToken.setPositionIncrement(0);   ❼ Set position    onto stack
                                           increment
    synonymStack.push(synToken);         to zero
  }
 }
}
```

❶ The code successively pops the stack of buffered synonyms from the last streamed-in token until it's empty.

❷ After all previous token synonyms have been emitted, we read the next token.

❸ We push all synonyms of the current token onto the stack.

❹ Now we return the current (and original) token before its associated synonyms.

❺ Synonyms are retrieved from the SynonymEngine.

❻ We push each synonym onto the stack.

❼ The position increment is set to zero, allowing synonyms to be virtually in the same place as the original term.

The design of SynonymAnalyzer allows for pluggable SynonymEngine implementations. SynonymEngine is a one-method interface:

```
public interface SynonymEngine {
  String[] getSynonyms(String s) throws IOException;
}
```

Using an interface for this design easily allows mock-object implementations for testing purposes.[5] We leave it as an exercise for you to create production-quality SynonymEngine implementations.[6] For our examples, we use a simple mock that's hard-coded with a few synonyms:

---

[5] If mock objects are new to you, see the "about this book" section at the beginning of the book for a description and references you can consult for more information.

[6] It's cruel to leave you hanging with a mock implementation, isn't it? Actually, we've implemented a powerful SynonymEngine using the WordNet database. It's covered in section 8.6.2.

```
public class MockSynonymEngine implements SynonymEngine {
  private static HashMap map = new HashMap();

  static {
    map.put("quick", new String[] {"fast", "speedy"});
    map.put("jumps", new String[] {"leaps", "hops"});
    map.put("over", new String[] {"above"});
    map.put("lazy", new String[] {"apathetic", "sluggish"});
    map.put("dogs", new String[] {"canines", "pooches"});
  }

  public String[] getSynonyms(String s) {
    return (String[]) map.get(s);
  }
}
```

The synonyms generated by MockSynonymEngine are one-way: For example, *quick* has the synonyms *fast* and *speedy*, but *fast* has no synonyms. This is, by definition, a mock object used for testing in a controlled environment, so we don't need to worry about the one-way nature of this implementation.

Leveraging the position increment seems powerful, and indeed it is. You should only modify increments knowing of some odd cases that arise in searching, though. Since synonyms are indexed just like other terms, TermQuery works as expected. Also, PhraseQuery works as expected when we use a synonym in place of an original word. The SynonymAnalyzerTest test case in listing 4.7 demonstrates things working well using API-created queries.

Listing 4.7 SynonymAnalyzerTest: showing that synonym queries work

```
public class SynonymAnalyzerTest extends TestCase {
  private RAMDirectory directory;
  private IndexSearcher searcher;
  private static SynonymAnalyzer synonymAnalyzer =
                  new SynonymAnalyzer(new MockSynonymEngine());

  public void setUp() throws Exception {
    directory = new RAMDirectory();

    IndexWriter writer = new IndexWriter(directory,
                                         synonymAnalyzer,      ❶
                                         true);
    Document doc = new Document();                             Analyze with
    doc.add(Field.Text("content",                             SynonymAnalyzer
                  "The quick brown fox jumps over the lazy dogs"));  ◁─┐
    writer.addDocument(doc);                                  Index single
    writer.close();                                           document

    searcher = new IndexSearcher(directory);
```

```
      }

      public void tearDown() throws Exception {
        searcher.close();
      }

      public void testSearchByAPI() throws Exception {

        TermQuery tq = new TermQuery(new Term("content", "hops"));   ❷  Search for
        Hits hits = searcher.search(tq);                                 "hops"
        assertEquals(1, hits.length());

        PhraseQuery pq = new PhraseQuery();
        pq.add(new Term("content", "fox"));
        pq.add(new Term("content", "hops"));          ❸  Search for
        hits = searcher.search(pq);                       "fox hops"
        assertEquals(1, hits.length());
      }
    }
```

❶ We perform the analysis with a custom SynonymAnalyzer, using MockSynonym-Engine.

❷ A search for the word *hops* matches the document.

❸ A search for the phrase "fox hops" also matches.

The phrase "…fox jumps…" was indexed, and our SynonymAnalyzer injected *hops* in the same position as *jumps*. A TermQuery for *hops* succeeded, as did an exact PhraseQuery for "fox hops". Excellent!

All is well, until we decide to use QueryParser to create queries instead of doing so directly with the API. Once again, a test points out the oddity explicitly:

```
    public void testWithQueryParser() throws Exception {
      Query query = QueryParser.parse("\"fox jumps\"",
                                      "content",
                                      synonymAnalyzer);
      Hits hits = searcher.search(query);
      assertEquals("!!!! what?!", 0, hits.length());    ◁─  Analyzer can't find
                                                            document using phrase
                                                            from original document
      query = QueryParser.parse("\"fox jumps\"",
                                "content",
                                new StandardAnalyzer());
      hits = searcher.search(query);
      assertEquals("*whew*", 1, hits.length());     ◁─  StandardAnalyzer still
    }                                                   finds document
```

The first part of testWithQueryParser uses the SynonymAnalyzer to also analyze the query string itself. Oddly, the query fails to match, even using the same analyzer used for indexing. But, if we use the StandardAnalyzer (recall that Synonym-Analyzer has the same core, except for injecting the synonyms), the expected match is found. Why is this? One of the first diagnostic steps recommended when using QueryParser is to dump the toString() value of the Query instance:

```
public static void main(String[] args) throws Exception {
  Query query = QueryParser.parse("\"fox jumps\"",
                  "content",
                  synonymAnalyzer);

  System.out.println("\"fox jumps\" parses to " +
                                    query.toString("content"));

  System.out.println("From AnalyzerUtils.tokensFromAnalysis: ");
  AnalyzerUtils.displayTokens(synonymAnalyzer,
                              "\"fox jumps\"");
}
```

Here's the output:

```
"fox jumps" parses to "fox jumps hops leaps"

From AnalyzerUtils.tokensFromAnalysis:
[fox] [jumps] [hops] [leaps]
```

QueryParser works similarly to our AnalyzerUtils.tokensFromAnalysis, meaning it glues all terms from analysis together to form a PhraseQuery and ignores token position increment information. The search for "fox jumps" doesn't work using QueryParser and the SynonymAnalyzer because internally the query is for the phrase "fox jumps hops leaps". By having a slightly different analysis process for QueryParser than for indexing, the problem is solved. There is no need to inject synonyms while querying anyway, since the index already contains the synonyms.

You have another option with synonyms: expanding them into each query rather than indexing. We didn't implement this approach, but the techniques and tools provided in this chapter would be essential to implement it effectively. The awkwardly named PhrasePrefixQuery (see section 5.2) is one option to consider, perhaps created through an overridden QueryParser.getFieldQuery method; this is a possible option to explore if you wish to implement synonym injection at query time.

4.6.1 *Visualizing token positions*

Our AnalyzerUtils.tokensFromAnalysis doesn't show us all the information when dealing with analyzers that set position increments other than 1. In order to get a better view of these types of analyzers, we add an additional utility method, displayTokensWithPositions, to AnalyzerUtils:

```
public static void displayTokensWithPositions
            (Analyzer analyzer, String text) throws IOException {
  Token[] tokens = tokensFromAnalysis(analyzer, text);

  int position = 0;

  for (int i = 0; i < tokens.length; i++) {
    Token token = tokens[i];

    int increment = token.getPositionIncrement();

    if (increment > 0) {
      position = position + increment;
      System.out.println();
      System.out.print(position + ": ");
    }

    System.out.print("[" + token.termText() + "] ");
  }
}
```

We wrote a quick piece of code to see what our SynonymAnalyzer is really doing:

```
public class SynonymAnalyzerViewer {
  public static void main(String[] args) throws IOException {
    AnalyzerUtils.displayTokensWithPositions(
      new SynonymAnalyzer(new MockSynonymEngine()),
      "The quick brown fox jumps over the lazy dogs");
  }
}
```

And we can now visualize the synonyms placed in the same positions as the original words:

```
1: [quick] [speedy] [fast]
2: [brown]
3: [fox]
4: [jumps] [hops] [leaps]
5: [over] [above]
6: [lazy] [sluggish] [apathetic]
7: [dogs] [pooches] [canines]
```

Each number on the left represents the token position. The numbers here are continuous, but they wouldn't be if the analyzer left holes (as you'll see with the next custom analyzer). Multiple terms shown for a single position illustrates where synonyms were added.

4.7 *Stemming analysis*

Our final analyzer pulls out all the stops. It has a ridiculous, yet descriptive name: `PositionalPorterStopAnalyzer`. This analyzer removes stop words, leaving positional holes where words are removed, and also leverages a stemming filter.

The `PorterStemFilter` is shown in figure 4.3, but it isn't used by any built-in analyzer. It *stems* words using the Porter stemming algorithm created by Dr. Martin Porter, and it's best defined in his own words:

> The Porter stemming algorithm (or 'Porter stemmer') is a process for removing the commoner morphological and inflexional endings from words in English. Its main use is as part of a term normalisation process that is usually done when setting up Information Retrieval systems.[7]

In other words, the various forms of a word are reduced to a common root form. For example, the words *breathe*, *breathes*, *breathing*, and *breathed*, via the Porter stemmer, reduce to *breath*.

The Porter stemmer is one of many stemming algorithms. See section 8.3.1, page 283, for coverage of an extension to Lucene that implements the Snowball algorithm (also created by Dr. Porter). KStem is another stemming algorithm that has been adapted to Lucene (search Google for KStem and Lucene).

4.7.1 *Leaving holes*

Gaps are left where stop words are removed by adjusting the position increment of the tokens (see also "Looking inside tokens" in section 4.2.3). This is illustrated from the output of `AnalyzerUtils.displayTokensWithPositions`:

```
2: [quick]
3: [brown]
4: [fox]
5: [jump]
6: [over]
8: [lazi]
9: [dog]
```

Positions 1 and 7 are missing due to the removal of *the*. Stop-word removal that leaves gaps is accomplished using a custom `PositionalStopFilter`:

```
public class PositionalStopFilter extends TokenFilter {
  private Set stopWords;
```

---

[7] From Dr. Porter's website: http://www.tartarus.org/~martin/PorterStemmer/index.html.

```
    public PositionalStopFilter(TokenStream in, Set stopWords) {
      super(in);
      this.stopWords = stopWords;
    }

    public final Token next() throws IOException {
      int increment = 0;
      for (Token token = input.next();
              token != null; token = input.next()) {

        if (!stopWords.contains(token.termText())) {
          token.setPositionIncrement(
              token.getPositionIncrement() + increment);        ◁── Leave gap for
          return token;                                              skipped stop
        }                                                            words

        increment++;
      }

      return null;
    }
}
```

The analyzer, `PositionalPorterStopAnalyzer` (shown in listing 4.8), provides the list of stop words to remove.

4.7.2 *Putting it together*

This custom analyzer uses our custom stop-word removal filter, which is fed from a `LowerCaseTokenizer`. The results of the stop filter are fed to the Porter stemmer. Listing 4.8 shows the full implementation of this sophisticated analyzer. `LowerCaseTokenizer` kicks off the analysis process, feeding tokens through our custom stop-word removal filter and finally stemming the words using the built-in Porter stemmer.

> **Listing 4.8** `PositionalPorterStopAnalyzer`: removes stop words (leaving gaps) and stems words

```
public class PositionalPorterStopAnalyzer extends Analyzer {
  private Set stopWords;

  public PositionalPorterStopAnalyzer() {
    this(StopAnalyzer.ENGLISH_STOP_WORDS);
  }

  public PositionalPorterStopAnalyzer(String[] stopList) {
    stopWords = StopFilter.makeStopSet(stopList);
  }
```

```
public TokenStream tokenStream(String fieldName, Reader reader) {
  return new PorterStemFilter(
          new PositionalStopFilter(
            new LowerCaseTokenizer(reader),
          stopWords)
        );
  }
}
```

Leaving gaps when stop words are removed makes logical sense but introduces new issues that we explore next.

4.7.3 *Hole lot of trouble*

As you saw with the SynonymAnalyzer, messing with token position information can cause trouble during searching. PhraseQuery and QueryParser are the two troublemakers. Exact phrase matches now fail, as illustrated in our test case:

```
public class PositionalPorterStopAnalyzerTest extends TestCase {
  private static PositionalPorterStopAnalyzer porterAnalyzer =
    new PositionalPorterStopAnalyzer();

  private RAMDirectory directory;

  public void setUp() throws Exception {
    directory = new RAMDirectory();
    IndexWriter writer =
        new IndexWriter(directory, porterAnalyzer, true);

    Document doc = new Document();
    doc.add(Field.Text("contents",
                "The quick brown fox jumps over the lazy dogs"));
    writer.addDocument(doc);
    writer.close();
  }

  public void testExactPhrase() throws Exception {
    IndexSearcher searcher = new IndexSearcher(directory);
    Query query = QueryParser.parse("\"over the lazy\"",
                                    "contents",
                                    porterAnalyzer);

    Hits hits = searcher.search(query);
    assertEquals("exact match not found!", 0, hits.length());
  }

}
```

As shown, an exact phrase query didn't match. This is disturbing, of course. Unlike the synonym analyzer situation, using a different analyzer won't solve the problem. The difficulty lies deeper inside PhraseQuery and its current inability to deal with positional gaps. All terms in a PhraseQuery must be side by side, and in our test case, the phrase it's searching for is "over lazi" (stop word removed with remaining words stemmed).

PhraseQuery does allow a little looseness, called *slop*. This is covered in greater detail in section 3.4.5; however, it would be unkind to leave without showing a phrase query working. Setting the slop to 1 allows the query to effectively ignore the gap:

```
public void testWithSlop() throws Exception {
    IndexSearcher searcher = new IndexSearcher(directory);

    QueryParser parser = new QueryParser("contents",
                                         porterAnalyzer);
    parser.setPhraseSlop(1);

    Query query = parser.parse("\"over the lazy\"");

    Hits hits = searcher.search(query);
    assertEquals("hole accounted for", 1, hits.length());
}
```

The value of the phrase slop factor, in a simplified definition for this case, represents how many stop words could be present in the original text between indexed words. Introducing a slop factor greater than zero, however, allows even more inexact phrases to match. In this example, searching for "over lazy" also matches. With stop-word removal in analysis, doing *exact* phrase matches is, by definition, not possible: The words removed aren't there, so you can't know what they were.

The slop factor addresses the main problem with searching using stop-word removal that leaves holes; you can now see the benefit our analyzer provides, thanks to the stemming:

```
public void testStems() throws Exception {
    IndexSearcher searcher = new IndexSearcher(directory);
    Query query = QueryParser.parse("laziness",
                                    "contents",
                                    porterAnalyzer);
    Hits hits = searcher.search(query);
    assertEquals("lazi", 1, hits.length());

    query = QueryParser.parse("\"fox jumped\"",
                              "contents",
                              porterAnalyzer);
```

```
    hits = searcher.search(query);
    assertEquals("jump jumps jumped jumping", 1, hits.length());
}
```

Both *laziness* and the phrase "fox jumped" matched our indexed document, allowing users a bit of flexibility in the words used during searching.

4.8 Language analysis issues

Dealing with languages in Lucene is an interesting and multifaceted issue. How can text in various languages be indexed and subsequently retrieved? As a developer building I18N-friendly applications around Lucene, what issues do you need to consider?

You must contend with several issues when analyzing text in various languages. The first hurdle is ensuring that character-set encoding is done properly such that external data, such as files, are read into Java properly. During the analysis process, different languages have different sets of stop words and unique stemming algorithms. Perhaps accents should be removed from characters as well, which would be language dependent. Finally, you may require language detection if you aren't sure what language is being used. Each of these issues is ultimately up to the developer to address, with only basic building-block support provided by Lucene. However, a number of analyzers and additional building blocks such as `Tokenizers` and `TokenStreams` are available in the Sandbox (discussed in section 8.3) and elsewhere online.

This section discusses Lucene's built-in handling for non-English languages, but we begin first with a brief introduction to Unicode and character encodings.

4.8.1 Unicode and encodings

Internally, Lucene stores all characters in the standard UTF-8 encoding. Java frees us from many struggles by automatically handling Unicode within `Strings` and providing facilities for reading in external data in the many encodings. You, however, are responsible for getting external text into Java and Lucene. If you're indexing files on a file system, you need to know what encoding the files were saved as in order to read them properly. If you're reading HTML or XML from an HTTP server, encoding issues get a bit more complex. Encodings can be specified in an HTTP content-type header or specified within the document itself in the XML header or an HTML `<meta>` tag.

We won't elaborate on these encoding details, not because they aren't important, but because they're separate issues from Lucene. Please refer to appendix C for several sources of more detailed information on encoding topics. In particular, if you're new to I18N issues, read Joel Spolsky's excellent article "The Absolute Minimum Every Software Developer Absolutely, Positively Must Know About Unicode and Character Sets (No Excuses!)" (http://www.joelonsoftware.com/articles/Unicode.html) and the Java language Internationalization tutorial (http://java.sun.com/docs/books/tutorial/i18n/intro/). Additionally, the next version of the Java language (code-named Tiger) transitions towards Unicode 4.0 support for supplemental characters.

We'll proceed with the assumption that you have your text available as Unicode, and move on to the Lucene-specific language concerns.

4.8.2 *Analyzing non-English languages*

All the details of the analysis process apply when you're dealing with text in non-English languages. Extracting terms from text is the goal. With Western languages, where whitespace and punctuation are used to separate words, you must adjust stop-word lists and stemming algorithms to be specific to the language of the text being analyzed.

Beyond the built-in analyzers we've discussed, the core Lucene distribution provides two language-specific analyzers: `GermanAnalyzer` and `RussianAnalyzer`. Both of these employ language-specific stemming and stop-word removal. Also freely available is the `SnowballAnalyzer` family of stemmers, which supports many European languages. We discuss `SnowballAnalyzer` in section 8.3.1.

The `GermanAnalyzer` begins with a `StandardTokenizer` and `StandardFilter` (like the `StandardAnalyzer`) and then feeds the stream through a `StopFilter` and a `GermanStemFilter`. A built-in set of common German stop words is used by default; you can override it using the mechanism discussed in section 4.3.1. The `GermanStemFilter` stems words based on German-language rules and also provides a mechanism to provide an exclusion set of words that shouldn't be stemmed (which is empty by default).

The `RussianAnalyzer` begins with a `RussianLetterTokenizer`, which supports several character sets such as Unicode and CP1251, and then lowercases in a character set–specific manner using a `RussianLowerCaseFilter`. The `StopFilter` removes stop words using a default set of Russian words; it also lets you provide a custom set. Finally, the `RussianStemFilter` stems words using the Snowball algorithm (see section 8.3.1 for more details).

4.8.3 *Analyzing Asian languages*

Asian languages, such as Chinese, Japanese, and Korean (also denoted as CJK), generally use ideograms rather than an alphabet to represent words. These pictorial words may or may not be separated by whitespace and thus require a different type of analysis that recognizes when tokens should be split. The only built-in analyzer capable of doing anything useful with Asian text is the `Standard-Analyzer`, which recognizes some ranges of the Unicode space as CJK characters and tokenizes them individually.

However, two analyzers in the Lucene Sandbox are suitable for Asian language analysis (see section 8.1 for more details on the Sandbox). In our sample book data, the Chinese characters for the book *Tao Te Ching* were added to the title. Because our data originates in Java properties files, Unicode escape sequences are used:[8]

```
title=Tao Te Ching \u9053\u5FB7\u7D93
```

We used `StandardAnalyzer` for all tokenized fields in our index, which tokenizes each English word as expected (*tao*, *te*, and *ching*) as well as each of the Chinese characters as separate terms (*tao te ching*) even though there is no space between them. Our `ChineseTest` demonstrates that searching by the word *tao* using its Chinese representation works as desired:

```java
public class ChineseTest extends LiaTestCase {
  public void testChinese() throws Exception {
    IndexSearcher searcher = new IndexSearcher(directory);
    Hits hits = searcher.search(
        new TermQuery(new Term("contents", "道")));
    assertEquals("tao", 1, hits.length());
  }
}
```

Note that our ChineseTest.java file was saved in UTF-8 format and compiled using the UTF8 encoding switch for the javac compiler. We had to ensure that the representations of the Chinese characters are encoded and read properly, and use a CJK-aware analyzer.

Similar to the `AnalyzerDemo` in listing 4.2, we created a `ChineseDemo` (listing 4.9) program to illustrate how various analyzers work with Chinese text. This demo uses AWT `Label`s to properly display the characters regardless of your locale and console environment.

---

[8]   `java.util.Properties` loads properties files using the ISO-8859-1 encoding but allows characters to be encoded using standard Java Unicode `\u` syntax. Java includes a `native2ascii` program that can convert natively encoded files into the appropriate format.

Listing 4.9 `ChineseDemo`: illustrates what analyzers do with Chinese text

```
public class ChineseDemo {
  private static String[] strings = {"道德經"};      ←── Chinese text to
                                                           be analyzed
  private static Analyzer[] analyzers = {
    new SimpleAnalyzer(),
    new StandardAnalyzer(),
    new ChineseAnalyzer(),        │ Analyzers from
    new CJKAnalyzer()             │ Sandbox
  };

  public static void main(String args[]) throws Exception {

    for (int i = 0; i < strings.length; i++) {
      String string = strings[i];
      for (int j = 0; j < analyzers.length; j++) {
        Analyzer analyzer = analyzers[j];
        analyze(string, analyzer);
      }
    }

  }

  private static void analyze(String string, Analyzer analyzer)
          throws IOException {
    StringBuffer buffer = new StringBuffer();
    Token[] tokens =
          AnalyzerUtils.tokensFromAnalysis(analyzer, string);   ←──
    for (int i = 0; i < tokens.length; i++) {                     Retrieve tokens
      buffer.append("[");                                         from analysis using
      buffer.append(tokens[i].termText());                       AnalyzerUtils
      buffer.append("] ");
    }

    String output = buffer.toString();

    Frame f = new Frame();
    String name = analyzer.getClass().getName();
    f.setTitle(name.substring(name.lastIndexOf('.') + 1)
               + " : " + string);
    f.setResizable(false);

    Font font = new Font(null, Font.PLAIN, 36);
    int width = getWidth(f.getFontMetrics(font), output);

    f.setSize((width < 250) ? 250 : width + 50, 75);

    Label label = new Label(buffer.toString());    ←── AWT Label displays
    label.setSize(width, 75);                           analysis
    label.setAlignment(Label.CENTER);
    label.setFont(font);
    f.add(label);
```

```
      f.setVisible(true);
    }

    private static int getWidth(FontMetrics metrics, String s) {
      int size = 0;
      for (int i = 0; i < s.length(); i++) {
        size += metrics.charWidth(s.charAt(i));
      }

      return size;
    }
  }
```

CJKAnalyzer and ChineseAnalyzer are analyzers found in the Lucene Sandbox, they aren't included in the core Lucene distribution. ChineseDemo shows the output using an AWT Label component to avoid any confusion that might arise from console output encoding or limited fonts mangling things; you can see the output in figure 4.5.

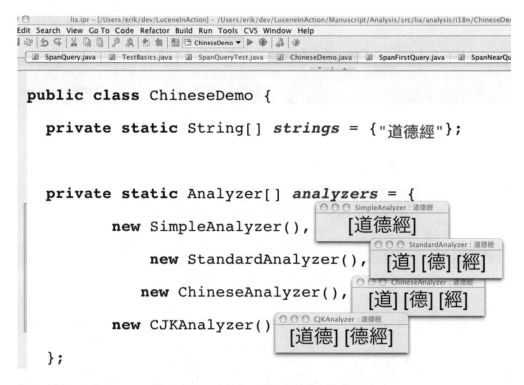

Figure 4.5 ChineseDemo illustrating analysis of the title *Tao Te Ching*

The `CJKAnalyzer` pairs characters in overlapping windows of two characters each. Many CJK words are two characters. By pairing characters in this manner, words are likely to be kept together (as well as disconnected characters, increasing the index size). The `ChineseAnalyzer` takes a simpler approach and, in our example, mirrors the results from the built-in `StandardAnalyzer` by tokenizing each Chinese character. Words that consist of multiple Chinese characters are split into terms for each component character.

4.8.4 Zaijian[9]

A major hurdle (unrelated to Lucene) remains when you're dealing with various languages: handling text encoding. The `StandardAnalyzer` it still the best built-in general-purpose analyzer, even accounting for CJK characters; however, the Sandbox `CJKAnalyzer` seems better suited for Asian language analysis.

When you're indexing documents in multiple languages into a single index, using a per-`Document` analyzer is appropriate. You may also want to add a field to documents indicating their language; this field can be used to filter search results or for display purposes during retrieval. In "Controlling date parsing locale" in section 3.5.5, we show how to retrieve the locale from a user's web browser; this could be automatically used in queries.

One final topic is language detection. This, like character encodings, is outside the scope of Lucene, but it may be important to your application. We don't cover language-detection techniques in this book, but it's an active area of research with several implementations to choose from (see appendix C).

4.9 *Nutch analysis*

We don't have the source code to Google, but we do have the open-source project Nutch, created by Lucene's creator Doug Cutting. Our Nutch case study in section 10.1 discusses the details of the Nutch architecture. There is another interesting facet to Nutch: how it analyzes text. Nutch does something very interesting with stop words, which it calls *common terms*. If all words are indexed, an enormous number of documents become associated with each common term, such as *the*. Querying for *the* is practically a nonsensical query, given that the majority of documents contain that term. When common terms are used in a query, but not within a phrase, such as *the quick brown* with no other adornments or quotes, common

---

[9] *Ziajian* means *good-bye* in Chinese.

terms are discarded. However, if a series of terms is surrounded by double-quotes, such as "the quick brown", a fancier trick is played, which we detail in this section.

Nutch combines an index-time analysis *bigram* (grouping two consecutive words as a single token) technique with a query-time optimization of phrases. This results in a far smaller document space considered during searching; for example, far fewer documents have *the quick* side by side than contain *the*. Using the internals of Nutch, we created a simple example to demonstrate the Nutch analysis trickery. Listing 4.10 first analyzes the phrase "The quick brown…" using the `NutchDocumentAnalyzer` and then parses a query of "the quick brown" to demonstrate the Lucene query created.

Listing 4.10 `NutchExample`: demonstrating the Nutch analysis and query-parsing techniques

```
public class NutchExample {
  public static void main(String[] args) throws IOException {    Custom analyzer
    NutchDocumentAnalyzer analyzer = new NutchDocumentAnalyzer();       ❶
    displayTokensWithDetails(analyzer, "The quick brown fox...");       ❷

                                                  displayTokensWithDetail method

                                                  Use fully qualified class names
    net.nutch.searcher.Query nutchQuery =
        net.nutch.searcher.Query.parse("\"the quick brown\"");         ❸
    Query query = QueryTranslator.translate(nutchQuery);      ❹
    System.out.println("query = " + query);      Translate Nutch Query
  }
}
```

❶ Nutch uses a custom analyzer, `NutchDocumentAnalyzer`.

❷ `displayTokensWithDetail` is similar to our previous `AnalyzerUtils` methods, except Nutch demands the field name `content`. So, we create a custom one-off version of this utility to inspect Nutch.

❸ Nutch clashes with some of Lucene's class names, so fully qualified class names are necessary. The `net.nutch.searcher.Query` class isn't related to Lucene's `Query` class.

❹ A Nutch `Query` is translated into a Lucene `Query` instance.

The analyzer output shows how "the quick" becomes a bigram, but the word *the* isn't discarded. The bigram resides in the same token position as *the*:

```
1: [the:<WORD>] [the-quick:gram]
2: [quick:<WORD>]
```

```
3: [brown:<WORD>]
4: [fox:<WORD>]
```

Because additional tokens are created during analysis, the index is larger, but the benefit of this trade-off is that searches for exact-phrase queries are much faster. And there's a bonus: No terms were discarded during indexing.

During querying, phrases are also analyzed and optimized. The query output (recall from section 3.5.1 that Query's toString() is handy) of the Lucene Query instance for the query expression "the quick brown" is

```
query = (+url:"the quick brown"^4.0)
⇒   (+anchor:"the quick brown"^2.0) (+content:"the-quick quick brown"
```

A Nutch query expands to search in the url and anchor fields as well, with higher boosts for those fields, using the exact phrase. The content field clause is optimized to only include the bigram of a position that contains an additional <WORD> type token.

This was a quick view of what Nutch does with indexing analysis and query construction. Nutch continues to evolve, optimize, and tweak the various techniques for indexing and querying. The bigrams aren't taken into consideration except in the content field; but as the document base grows, whether optimizations are needed on other fields will be reevaluated.

4.10 *Summary*

Analysis, while only a single facet of using Lucene, is the aspect that deserves the most attention and effort. The words that can be searched are those emitted during indexing analysis. Sure, using StandardAnalyzer may do the trick for your needs, and it suffices for many applications. However, it's important to understand the analysis process. Users who take analysis for granted often run into confusion later when they try to understand why searching for "to be or not to be" returns no results (perhaps due to stop-word removal).

It takes less than one line of code to incorporate an analyzer during indexing. Many sophisticated processes may occur under the covers, such as stop-word removal and stemming of words. Removing words decreases your index size but can have a negative impact on precision querying.

Because one size doesn't fit all when it comes to analysis, you may need to tune the analysis process for your application domain. Lucene's elegant analyzer architecture decouples each of the processes internal to textual analysis, letting you reuse fundamental building blocks to construct custom analyzers. When you're working with analyzers, be sure to use our `AnalyzerUtils`, or something similar, to see first-hand how your text is tokenized. If you're changing analyzers, you should rebuild your index using the new analyzer so that all documents are analyzed in the same manner.

*Advanced
search techniques*

149

Many applications that implement search with Lucene can do so using the API introduced in chapter 3. Some projects, though, need more than the basic searching mechanisms. In this chapter, we explore the more sophisticated searching capabilities built into Lucene.

A couple of odds and ends, PhrasePrefixQuery and MultiFieldQueryParser, round out our coverage of Lucene's additional built-in capabilities. If you've used Lucene for a while, you may not recognize some of these features. Sorting, span queries, and term vectors are all new in Lucene 1.4, dramatically increasing Lucene's power and flexibility.

5.1 *Sorting search results*

Until Lucene 1.4, search results were only returned in descending score order, with the most relevant documents appearing first. BookScene, our hypothetical bookstore, needs to display search results grouped into categories, and within the category results the books should be ordered by relevance to the query. Collecting all results and sorting them programmatically outside of Lucene is one way to accomplish this; however, doing so introduces a possible performance bottleneck if the number of results is enormous. Thankfully, expert developer Tim Jones contributed a highly efficient enhancement to Lucene, adding sophisticated sorting capabilities for search results. In this section, we explore the various ways to sort search results, including sorting by one or more field values in either ascending or descending order.

5.1.1 *Using a sort*

IndexSearcher contains several overloaded search methods. Thus far we've covered only the basic search(Query) method, which returns results ordered by decreasing relevance. The sorting version of this method has the signature search(Query, Sort). Listing 5.1 demonstrates the use of the sorting search method. The displayHits method uses the sorting search method and displays the Hits. The examples following will use the displayHits method to illustrate how various sorts work.

Listing 5.1 Sorting example

```
public class SortingExample {
  private Directory directory;

  public SortingExample(Directory directory) {
    this.directory = directory;
  }
```

```
public void displayHits(Query query, Sort sort)            ❶ Sort object encapsulates
    throws IOException {                                        sorting info
  IndexSearcher searcher = new IndexSearcher(directory);

  Hits hits = searcher.search(query, sort);           ❷ Overloaded search
                                                           method
  System.out.println("\nResults for: " +
      query.toString() + " sorted by " + sort);      ❸ toString output

  System.out.println(StringUtils.rightPad("Title", 30) +
      StringUtils.rightPad("pubmonth", 10) +
      StringUtils.center("id", 4) +
      StringUtils.center("score", 15));

  DecimalFormat scoreFormatter = new DecimalFormat("0.######");
  for (int i = 0; i < hits.length(); i++) {          StringUtils provides
    Document doc = hits.doc(i);                        columnar output
    System.out.println(
        StringUtils.rightPad                                            ❹
            StringUtils.abbreviate(doc.get("title"), 29), 30) +
        StringUtils.rightPad(doc.get("pubmonth"), 10) +
        StringUtils.center("" + hits.id(i), 4) +
        StringUtils.leftPad(
            scoreFormatter.format(hits.score(i)), 12));
    System.out.println("    " + doc.get("category"));
//      System.out.println(searcher.explain(query, hits.id(i)));  ❺
  }
                                                      Explanation commented
  searcher.close();                                         out for now
}}
```

❶ The Sort object encapsulates an ordered collection of field sorting information.

❷ We call the overloaded search method with the Sort object.

❸ The Sort class has informative toString() output.

❹ We use StringUtils from Jakarta Commons Lang for nice columnar output formatting.

❺ Later you'll see a reason to look at the explanation of score. For now, it's commented out.

Since our sample data set consists of only a handful of documents, the sorting examples use a query that returns all documents:

```
Term earliest = new Term("pubmonth", "190001");
Term latest = new Term("pubmonth", "201012");
RangeQuery allBooks = new RangeQuery(earliest, latest, true);
```

All books in our collection are in this publication month range. Next, the example runner is constructed based on the index path provided as a system property:

```
String indexDir = System.getProperty("index.dir");

FSDirectory directory =
    FSDirectory.getDirectory(indexDir, false);
SortingExample example = new SortingExample(directory);
```

Now that you've seen how to use sorting, let's explore various ways search results can be sorted.

5.1.2 Sorting by relevance

Lucene sorts by decreasing relevance, also called *score* by default. Sorting by score relevance works by either passing `null` as the `Sort` object or using the default `Sort` behavior. Each of the following variants returns results in the default score order. `Sort.RELEVANCE` is a shortcut to using new `Sort()`:

```
example.displayHits(allBooks, null);
example.displayHits(allBooks, Sort.RELEVANCE);
example.displayHits(allBooks, new Sort());
```

There is overhead involved in using a `Sort` object, though, so stick to using `search(Query)` or `search(Query, null)` if you want to sort by relevance. The output of using `Sort.RELEVANCE` is as follows (notice the decreasing score column):

```
Results for: pubmonth:[190001 TO 201012] sorted by <score>,<doc>
Title                      pubmonth   id      score
A Modern Art of Education  198106     0       0.086743
    /education/pedagogy
Imperial Secrets of Health... 199401  1       0.086743
    /health/alternative/chinese
Tao Te Ching 道德經          198810     2       0.086743
    /philosophy/eastern
Gödel, Escher, Bach: an Et... 197903  3       0.086743
    /technology/computers/ai
Mindstorms                 198001     4       0.086743
    /technology/computers/programming/education
Java Development with Ant  200208     5       0.086743
    /technology/computers/programming
JUnit in Action            200310     6       0.086743
    /technology/computers/programming
Lucene in Action           200406     7       0.086743
    /technology/computers/programming
Tapestry in Action         200403     9       0.086743
    /technology/computers/programming
Extreme Programming Explained 199910  8       0.062685
    /technology/computers/programming/methodology
The Pragmatic Programmer   199910     10      0.062685
    /technology/computers/programming
```

The output of `Sort`'s `toString()` shows `<score>,<doc>`. Score and index order are special types of sorting: The results are returned first in decreasing score order and, when the scores are identical, subsorted by increasing document ID order. Document ID order is the order in which the documents were indexed. In our case, index order isn't relevant, and order is unspecified (see section 8.4 on the Ant <index> task, which is how we indexed our sample data).

As an aside, you may wonder why the score of the last two books is different from the rest. Our query was on a publication date range. Both of these books have the same publication month. A RangeQuery expands, under the covers, into a BooleanQuery matching any of the terms in the range. The document frequency of the term *199910* in the pubmonth field is 2, which lowers the inverse document frequency (IDF) factor for those documents, thereby decreasing the score. We had the same curiosity when developing this example, and uncommenting the Explanation output in displayHits gave us the details to understand this effect. See section 3.3. for more information on the scoring factors.

5.1.3 *Sorting by index order*

If the order documents were indexed is relevant, you can use Sort.INDEXORDER. Note the increasing document ID column:

```
example.displayHits(allBooks, Sort.INDEXORDER);

Results for: pubmonth:[190001 TO 201012] sorted by <doc>
Title                       pubmonth   id     score
A Modern Art of Education   198106     0      0.086743
    /education/pedagogy
Imperial Secrets of Health... 199401   1      0.086743
    /health/alternative/chinese
Tao Te Ching 道德經          198810     2      0.086743
    /philosophy/eastern
Gödel, Escher, Bach: an Et... 197903   3      0.086743
    /technology/computers/ai
Mindstorms                  198001     4      0.086743
    /technology/computers/programming/education
Java Development with Ant   200208     5      0.086743
    /technology/computers/programming
JUnit in Action             200310     6      0.086743
    /technology/computers/programming
Lucene in Action            200406     7      0.086743
    /technology/computers/programming
Extreme Programming Explained 199910   8      0.062685
    /technology/computers/programming/methodology
Tapestry in Action          200403     9      0.086743
    /technology/computers/programming
The Pragmatic Programmer    199910     10     0.062685
    /technology/computers/programming
```

So far we've only sorted by score, which was already happening without using the sorting facility, and document order, which is probably only marginally useful at best. Sorting by one of our own fields is really what we're after.

5.1.4 Sorting by a field

Sorting by a field first requires that you follow the rules for indexing a sortable field, as detailed in section 2.6. Our `category` field was indexed as a single `Field.Keyword` per document, allowing it to be used for sorting. To sort by a field, you must create a new `Sort` object, providing the field name:

```
example.displayHits(allBooks, new Sort("category"));
```

```
Results for: pubmonth:[190001 TO 201012] sorted by "category",<doc>
Title                            pubmonth    id    score
A Modern Art of Education        198106      0     0.086743
    /education/pedagogy
Imperial Secrets of Health...    199401      1     0.086743
    /health/alternative/chinese
Tao Te Ching 道德經               198810      2     0.086743
    /philosophy/eastern
Gödel, Escher, Bach: an Et...    197903      3     0.086743
    /technology/computers/ai
Java Development with Ant        200208      5     0.086743
    /technology/computers/programming
JUnit in Action                  200310      6     0.086743
    /technology/computers/programming
Lucene in Action                 200406      7     0.086743
    /technology/computers/programming
Tapestry in Action               200403      9     0.086743
    /technology/computers/programming
The Pragmatic Programmer         199910      10    0.062685
    /technology/computers/programming
Mindstorms                       198001      4     0.086743
    /technology/computers/programming/education
Extreme Programming Explained    199910      8     0.062685
    /technology/computers/programming/methodology
```

The results now appear sorted by our `category` field in increasing alphabetical order. Notice the sorted-by output: The `Sort` class itself automatically adds document ID as the final sort field when a single field name is specified, so the secondary sort within category is by document ID.

5.1.5 Reversing sort order

The default sort direction for sort fields (including relevance and document ID) is natural ordering. Natural order is descending for relevance but increasing for all other fields. The natural order can be reversed per field. For example, here we list books with the newest publications first:

```
example.displayHits(allBooks, new Sort("pubmonth", true));

Results for: pubmonth:[190001 TO 201012] sorted by "pubmonth"!,<doc>
Title                           pubmonth   id     score
Lucene in Action                200406     7      0.086743
    /technology/computers/programming
Tapestry in Action              200403     9      0.086743
    /technology/computers/programming
JUnit in Action                 200310     6      0.086743
    /technology/computers/programming
Java Development with Ant        200208     5      0.086743
    /technology/computers/programming
Extreme Programming Explained   199910     8      0.062685
    /technology/computers/programming/methodology
The Pragmatic Programmer        199910     10     0.062685
    /technology/computers/programming
Imperial Secrets of Health...   199401     1      0.086743
    /health/alternative/chinese
Tao Te Ching 道德經               198810     2      0.086743
    /philosophy/eastern
A Modern Art of Education       198106     0      0.086743
    /education/pedagogy
Mindstorms                      198001     4      0.086743
    /technology/computers/programming/education
Gödel, Escher, Bach: an Et...   197903     3      0.086743
    /technology/computers/ai
```

The exclamation point in sorted by "pubmonth"!,<doc> indicates that the pubmonth field is being sorted in reverse natural order (descending publication months, newest first). Note that the two books with the same publication month are sorted in document id order.

5.1.6 *Sorting by multiple fields*

Implicitly we've been sorting by multiple fields, since the Sort object appends a sort by document ID in appropriate cases. You can control the sort fields explicitly using an array of SortFields. This example uses category as a primary alphabetic sort, with results within category sorted by score; finally, books with equal score within a category are sorted by decreasing publication month:

```
example.displayHits(allBooks,
    new Sort(new SortField[]{
      new SortField("category"),
      SortField.FIELD_SCORE,
      new SortField("pubmonth", SortField.INT, true)
    }));
```

```
Results for: pubmonth:[190001 TO 201012]
            sorted by "category",<score>,"pubmonth"!
Title                         pubmonth   id      score
A Modern Art of Education     198106     0       0.086743
    /education/pedagogy
Imperial Secrets of Health... 199401     1       0.086743
    /health/alternative/chinese
Tao Te Ching 道德經            198810     2       0.086743
    /philosophy/eastern
Gödel, Escher, Bach: an Et... 197903     3       0.086743
    /technology/computers/ai
Lucene in Action              200406     7       0.086743
    /technology/computers/programming
Tapestry in Action            200403     9       0.086743
    /technology/computers/programming
JUnit in Action               200310     6       0.086743
    /technology/computers/programming
Java Development with Ant     200208     5       0.086743
    /technology/computers/programming
The Pragmatic Programmer      199910     10      0.062685
    /technology/computers/programming
Mindstorms                    198001     4       0.086743
    /technology/computers/programming/education
Extreme Programming Explained 199910     8       0.062685
    /technology/computers/programming/methodology
```

The Sort instance internally keeps an array of SortFields, but only in this example have you seen it explicitly; the other examples used shortcuts to creating the SortField array. A SortField holds the field name, a field type, and the reverse order flag. SortField contains constants for several field types, including SCORE, DOC, AUTO, STRING, INT, and FLOAT. SCORE and DOC are special types for sorting on relevance and document ID. AUTO is the type used by each of our other examples, which sort by a field name.

The type of field is automatically detected as String, int, or float based on the value of the first term in the field. If you're using strings that may appear as numeric in some fields, be sure to specify the type explicitly as Sort-Field.STRING.

5.1.7 *Selecting a sorting field type*

By search time, the fields that can be sorted on and their corresponding types are already set. Indexing time is when the decision about sorting capabilities should be made; however, custom sorting implementations can do so at search time, as you'll see in section 6.1. Section 2.6 discusses index-time sorting design. By indexing an Integer.toString or Float.toString, sorting can be based on numeric values. In our example data, pubmonth was indexed as a String but is a valid, parsable `Integer`; thus it's treated as such for sorting purposes unless specified as `SortField.STRING` explicitly. Sorting by a numeric type consumes fewer memory resources than by `STRING`; section 5.1.9 discusses performance issues further.

It's important to understand that you index numeric values this way to facilitate sorting on those fields, not to constrain a search on a range of values. The numeric range query capability is covered in section 6.3.3; the padding technique will be necessary during indexing and searching in order to use numeric fields for searching. All terms in an index are `Strings`; the sorting feature uses the standard `Integer` and `Float` constructors to parse the string representations.

5.1.8 *Using a nondefault locale for sorting*

When you're sorting on a `SortField.STRING` type, order is determined under the covers using `String.compareTo` by default. However, if you need a different collation order, `SortField` lets you specify a locale. A `Collator` is determined for the provided locale using `Collator.getInstance(Locale)`, and the `Collator.compare` method determines the sort order. There are two overloaded `SortField` constructors for use when you need to specify locale:

```
public SortField (String field, Locale locale)
public SortField (String field, Locale locale, boolean reverse)
```

Both of these constructors imply the `SortField.STRING` type because locale applies only to string-type sorting, not to numerics.

5.1.9 *Performance effect of sorting*

Sorting comes at the expense of resources. More memory is needed to keep the fields used for sorting available. For numeric types, each field being sorted for each document in the index requires that four bytes be cached. For `String` types, each unique term is also cached for each document. Only the actual fields used for sorting are cached in this manner.

Plan your system resources accordingly if you want to use the sorting capabilities, knowing that sorting by a `String` is the most expensive type in terms of resources.

5.2 *Using PhrasePrefixQuery*

The built-in `PhrasePrefixQuery` is definitely a niche query, but it's potentially useful. The name is a bit confusing because this query isn't in any way related to `PrefixQuery`. It is, however, closely related to `PhraseQuery`.

PhrasePrefixQuery allows multiple terms per position, effectively the same as a BooleanQuery on multiple nonrequired PhraseQuery clauses. For example, suppose we want to find all documents about speedy foxes, with *quick* or *fast* followed by *fox*. One approach is to do a "quick fox" OR "fast fox" query. Another option is to use PhrasePrefixQuery. In our example, two documents are indexed with similar phrases. One document with uses "the quick brown fox jumped over the lazy dog", and the other uses "the fast fox hopped over the hound" as shown in our test setUp() method:

```
public class PhrasePrefixQueryTest extends TestCase {
  private IndexSearcher searcher;

  protected void setUp() throws Exception {
    RAMDirectory directory = new RAMDirectory();
    IndexWriter writer = new IndexWriter(directory,
        new WhitespaceAnalyzer(), true);
    Document doc1 = new Document();
    doc1.add(Field.Text("field",
            "the quick brown fox jumped over the lazy dog"));
    writer.addDocument(doc1);
    Document doc2 = new Document();
    doc2.add(Field.Text("field",
            "the fast fox hopped over the hound"));
    writer.addDocument(doc2);
    writer.close();

    searcher = new IndexSearcher(directory);
  }
}
```

Knowing that we want to find documents about speedy foxes, PhrasePrefix-Query lets us match phrases very much like PhraseQuery, but with a twist: Each term position of the query can have multiple terms. This has the same set of hits as a BooleanQuery consisting of multiple PhraseQuerys combined with an OR operator. The following test method demonstrates the mechanics of using the PhrasePrefixQuery API by adding one or more terms to a PhrasePrefixQuery instance in order:

```
public void testBasic() throws Exception {
  PhrasePrefixQuery query = new PhrasePrefixQuery();
  query.add(new Term[] {
    new Term("field", "quick"),          Any of these terms may be
    new Term("field", "fast")            in first position to match
  });
  query.add(new Term("field", "fox"));   Only one in
                                         second position
```

```
    Hits hits = searcher.search(query);
    assertEquals("fast fox match", 1, hits.length());

    query.setSlop(1);
    hits = searcher.search(query);
    assertEquals("both match", 2, hits.length());
}
```

Just as with `PhraseQuery`, the slop factor is supported. In `testBasic()`, the slop is used to match "quick brown fox" in the second search; with the default slop of zero, it doesn't match. For completeness, here is a test illustrating the described `BooleanQuery`, with a slop set for the phrase "quick fox":

```
public void testAgainstOR() throws Exception {
    PhraseQuery quickFox = new PhraseQuery();
    quickFox.setSlop(1);
    quickFox.add(new Term("field", "quick"));
    quickFox.add(new Term("field", "fox"));

    PhraseQuery fastFox = new PhraseQuery();
    fastFox.add(new Term("field", "fast"));
    fastFox.add(new Term("field", "fox"));

    BooleanQuery query = new BooleanQuery();
    query.add(quickFox, false, false);
    query.add(fastFox, false, false);
    Hits hits = searcher.search(query);
    assertEquals(2, hits.length());
}
```

One difference between `PhrasePrefixQuery` and the `BooleanQuery` of `Phrase-Query`'s approach is that the slop factor is applied globally with `PhrasePrefix-Query`—it's applied on a per-phrase basis with `PhraseQuery`.

Of course, hard-coding the terms wouldn't be realistic, generally speaking. One possible use of a `PhrasePrefixQuery` would be to inject synonyms dynamically into phrase positions, allowing for less precise matching. For example, you could tie in the WordNet-based code (see section 8.6 for more on WordNet and Lucene).

NOTE   Lucene's `QueryParser` doesn't currently support `PhrasePrefixQuery`.

5.3 *Querying on multiple fields at once*

In our book data, several fields were indexed. Users may want to query for terms regardless of which field they are in. One way to handle this is with `MultiField-`

QueryParser, which builds on QueryParser. Under the covers, it parses a query expression using QueryParser's static parse method for each field as the default field and combines them into a BooleanQuery. The default operator OR is used in the simplest parse method when adding the clauses to the BooleanQuery. For finer control, the operator can be specified for each field as required (REQUIRED_FIELD), prohibited (PROHIBITED_FIELD), or normal (NORMAL_FIELD), using the constants from MultiFieldQueryParser.

Listing 5.2 shows this heavier QueryParser variant in use. The testDefault-Operator() method first parses the query "development" using both the title and subjects fields. The test shows that documents match based on either of those fields. The second test, testSpecifiedOperator(), sets the parsing to mandate that documents must match the expression in all specified fields.

Listing 5.2 `MultiFieldQueryParser` in action

```
public class MultiFieldQueryParserTest extends LiaTestCase {
  public void testDefaultOperator() throws Exception {
    Query query = MultiFieldQueryParser.parse("development",
                              new String[] {"title", "subjects"},
                              new SimpleAnalyzer());

    IndexSearcher searcher = new IndexSearcher(directory);
    Hits hits = searcher.search(query);

    assertHitsIncludeTitle(hits, "Java Development with Ant");

    // has "development" in the subjects field
    assertHitsIncludeTitle(hits, "Extreme Programming Explained");
  }

  public void testSpecifiedOperator() throws Exception {
    Query query = MultiFieldQueryParser.parse("development",
                new String[] {"title", "subjects"},
                new int[] {MultiFieldQueryParser.REQUIRED_FIELD,
                           MultiFieldQueryParser.REQUIRED_FIELD},
                new SimpleAnalyzer());

    IndexSearcher searcher = new IndexSearcher(directory);
    Hits hits = searcher.search(query);

    assertHitsIncludeTitle(hits, "Java Development with Ant");
    assertEquals("one and only one", 1, hits.length());
  }
}
```

`MultiFieldQueryParser` has some limitations due to the way it uses `QueryParser`'s static `parse` method. You can't control any of the settings that `QueryParser` supports, and you're stuck with the defaults such as default locale date parsing and zero-slop default phrase queries.

> **NOTE** Generally speaking, querying on multiple fields isn't the best practice for user-entered queries. More commonly, all words you want searched are indexed into a `contents` or `keywords` field by combining various fields. A synthetic `contents` field in our test environment uses this scheme to put author and subjects together:
>
> ```
> doc.add(Field.UnStored("contents", author + " " + subjects));
> ```
>
> We used a space (`" "`) between author and subjects to separate words for the analyzer. Allowing users to enter text in the simplest manner possible without the need to qualify field names generally makes for a less confusing user experience.

If you choose to use `MultiFieldQueryParser`, be sure your queries are fabricated appropriately using the `QueryParser` and `Analyzer` diagnostic techniques shown in chapters 3 and 4. Plenty of odd interactions with analysis occur using `Query-Parser`, and these are compounded using `MultiFieldQueryParser`.

5.4 *Span queries: Lucene's new hidden gem*

Lucene 1.4 includes a new family of queries, all based on `SpanQuery`. A *span* in this context is a starting and ending position in a field. Recall from section 4.2.1 that tokens emitted during the analysis process include a position increment from the previous token. This position information, in conjunction with the new `SpanQuery` subclasses, allow for even more query discrimination and sophistication, such as all documents where `"quick fox"` is near `"lazy dog"`.

Using the query types we've discussed thus far, it isn't possible to formulate such a query. Phrase queries could get close with something like `"quick fox"` AND `"lazy dog"`, but these phrases may be too distant from one another to be relevant for our searching purposes. Happily, Doug Cutting graced us with his brilliance once again and added span queries to Lucene's core.

Span queries track more than the documents that match: The individual spans, perhaps more than one per field, are tracked. Contrasting with `TermQuery`, which simply matches documents, for example, `SpanTermQuery` keeps track of the positions of each of the terms that match.

There are five subclasses of the base `SpanQuery`, shown in table 5.1.

Table 5.1 SpanQuery family

SpanQuery type	Description
SpanTermQuery	Used in conjunction with the other span query types. On its own, it's functionally equivalent to `TermQuery`.
SpanFirstQuery	Matches spans that occur within the first part of a field.
SpanNearQuery	Matches spans that occur near one another.
SpanNotQuery	Matches spans that don't overlap one another.
SpanOrQuery	Aggregates matches of span queries.

We'll discuss each of these `SpanQuery` types within the context of a JUnit test case, `SpanQueryTest`. In order to demonstrate each of these types, a bit of setup is needed as well as some helper assert methods to make our later code clearer, as shown in listing 5.3. We index two similar phrases in a field f as separate documents and create `SpanTermQuerys` for several of the terms for later use in our test methods. In addition, we add three convenience assert methods to streamline our examples.

Listing 5.3 SpanQuery demonstration infrastructure

```
public class SpanQueryTest extends TestCase {
  private RAMDirectory directory;
  private IndexSearcher searcher;
  private IndexReader reader;

  private SpanTermQuery quick;
  private SpanTermQuery brown;
  private SpanTermQuery red;
  private SpanTermQuery fox;
  private SpanTermQuery lazy;
  private SpanTermQuery sleepy;
  private SpanTermQuery dog;
  private SpanTermQuery cat;
  private Analyzer analyzer;

  protected void setUp() throws Exception {
    directory = new RAMDirectory();

    analyzer = new WhitespaceAnalyzer();
    IndexWriter writer = new IndexWriter(directory,
        analyzer, true);
```

```
Document doc = new Document();
doc.add(Field.Text("f",
    "the quick brown fox jumps over the lazy dog"));
writer.addDocument(doc);

doc = new Document();
doc.add(Field.Text("f",
    "the quick red fox jumps over the sleepy cat"));
writer.addDocument(doc);

writer.close();

searcher = new IndexSearcher(directory);
reader = IndexReader.open(directory);

quick = new SpanTermQuery(new Term("f", "quick"));
brown = new SpanTermQuery(new Term("f", "brown"));
red = new SpanTermQuery(new Term("f", "red"));
fox = new SpanTermQuery(new Term("f", "fox"));
lazy = new SpanTermQuery(new Term("f", "lazy"));
sleepy = new SpanTermQuery(new Term("f", "sleepy"));
dog = new SpanTermQuery(new Term("f", "dog"));
cat = new SpanTermQuery(new Term("f", "cat"));
}

private void assertOnlyBrownFox(Query query)throws Exception {
  Hits hits = searcher.search(query);
  assertEquals(1, hits.length());
  assertEquals("wrong doc", 0, hits.id(0));
}

private void assertBothFoxes(Query query) throws Exception {
  Hits hits = searcher.search(query);
  assertEquals(2, hits.length());
}

private void assertNoMatches(Query query) throws Exception {
  Hits hits = searcher.search(query);
  assertEquals(0, hits.length());
}
}
```

With this necessary bit of setup out of the way, we can begin exploring span queries. First we'll ground ourselves with SpanTermQuery.

5.4.1 *Building block of spanning, SpanTermQuery*

Span queries need an initial leverage point, and SpanTermQuery is just that. Internally, a SpanQuery keeps track of its matches: a series of start/end positions for

Figure 5.1 `SpanTermQuery` for *brown*

each matching document. By itself, a `SpanTermQuery` matches documents just like `TermQuery` does, but it also keeps track of position of the same terms that appear within each document.

Figure 5.1 illustrates the `SpanTermQuery` matches for this code:

```
public void testSpanTermQuery() throws Exception {
  assertOnlyBrownFox(brown);
  dumpSpans(brown);
}
```

The *brown* `SpanTermQuery` was created in `setUp()` because it will be used in other tests that follow. We developed a method, `dumpSpans`, to visualize spans. The `dumpSpans` method uses some lower-level `SpanQuery` API to navigate the spans; this lower-level API probably isn't of much interest to you other than for diagnostic purposes, so we don't elaborate further on it. Each `SpanQuery` subclass sports a useful `toString()` for diagnostic purposes, which `dumpSpans` uses:

```
private void dumpSpans(SpanQuery query) throws IOException {
  Spans spans = query.getSpans(reader);
  System.out.println(query + ":");
  int numSpans = 0;

  Hits hits = searcher.search(query);
  float[] scores = new float[2];
  for (int i = 0; i < hits.length(); i++) {
    scores[hits.id(i)] = hits.score(i);
  }

  while (spans.next()) {
    numSpans++;

    int id = spans.doc();
    Document doc = reader.document(id);

    // for simplicity - assume tokens are in sequential,
    // positions, starting from 0
    Token[] tokens = AnalyzerUtils.tokensFromAnalysis(
        analyzer, doc.get("f"));
    StringBuffer buffer = new StringBuffer();
    buffer.append("   ");
    for (int i = 0; i < tokens.length; i++) {
```

```
        if (i == spans.start()) {
          buffer.append("<");
        }
        buffer.append(tokens[i].termText());
        if (i + 1 == spans.end()) {
          buffer.append(">");
        }
        buffer.append(" ");
      }
      buffer.append("(" + scores[id] + ") ");
      System.out.println(buffer);
//      System.out.println(searcher.explain(query, id));
    }

    if (numSpans == 0) {
      System.out.println("  No spans");
    }
    System.out.println();
  }
```

The output of `dumpSpans(brown)` is

```
f:brown:
    the quick <brown> fox jumps over the lazy dog (0.22097087)
```

More interesting is the `dumpSpans` output from a `SpanTermQuery` for *the*:

```
dumpSpans(new SpanTermQuery(new Term("f", "the")));

f:the:
    <the> quick brown fox jumps over the lazy dog (0.18579213)
    the quick brown fox jumps over <the> lazy dog (0.18579213)
    <the> quick red fox jumps over the sleepy cat (0.18579213)
    the quick red fox jumps over <the> sleepy cat (0.18579213)
```

Not only were both documents matched, but also each document had two span matches highlighted by the brackets. The basic `SpanTermQuery` is used as a building block of the other `SpanQuery` types.

5.4.2 *Finding spans at the beginning of a field*

To query for spans that occur within the first *n* positions of a field, use `Span-FirstQuery`. Figure 5.2 illustrates a `SpanFirstQuery`.

Figure 5.2 `SpanFirstQuery`

This test shows nonmatching and matching queries:

```
public void testSpanFirstQuery() throws Exception {
    SpanFirstQuery sfq = new SpanFirstQuery(brown, 2);
    assertNoMatches(sfq);

    sfq = new SpanFirstQuery(brown, 3);
    assertOnlyBrownFox(sfq);
}
```

No matches are found in the first query because the range of 2 is too short to find *brown*, but 3 is just long enough to cause a match in the second query (see figure 5.2). Any SpanQuery can be used within a SpanFirstQuery, with matches for spans that have an ending position in the first *n* (2 and 3 in this case) positions. The resulting span matches are the same as the original SpanQuery spans, in this case the same dumpSpans() output for *brown* as seen in section 5.4.1.

5.4.3 *Spans near one another*

A PhraseQuery (see section 3.4.5) matches documents that have terms near one another, with a slop factor to allow for intermediate or reversed terms. Span-NearQuery operates similarly to PhraseQuery, with some important differences. SpanNearQuery matches spans that are within a certain number of positions from one another, with a separate flag indicating whether the spans must be in the order specified or can be reversed. The resulting matching spans span from the start position of the first span sequentially to the ending position of the last span. An example of a SpanNearQuery given three SpanTermQuery objects is shown in figure 5.3.

Using SpanTermQuery objects as the SpanQuerys in a SpanNearQuery is much like a PhraseQuery. However, the SpanNearQuery slop factor is a bit less confusing than the PhraseQuery slop factor because it doesn't require at least two additional positions to account for a reversed span. To reverse a SpanNearQuery, set the inOrder flag (third argument to the constructor) to false. Listing 5.4 demonstrates a few variations of SpanNearQuery and shows it in relation to PhraseQuery.

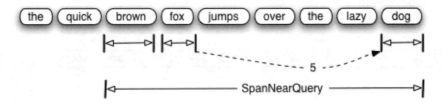

Figure 5.3 SpanNearQuery

Listing 5.4 SpanNearQuery

```
public void testSpanNearQuery() throws Exception {
  SpanQuery[] quick_brown_dog =
      new SpanQuery[]{quick, brown, dog};
  SpanNearQuery snq =
      new SpanNearQuery(quick_brown_dog, 0, true);      ❶ Query for three
  assertNoMatches(snq);                                      successive terms

  snq = new SpanNearQuery(quick_brown_dog, 4, true);    ❷ Same terms,
  assertNoMatches(snq);                                      slop of 4

  snq = new SpanNearQuery(quick_brown_dog, 5, true);    ❸ SpanNearQuery
  assertOnlyBrownFox(snq);                                   matches

  // interesting - even a sloppy phrase query would require
  // more slop to match
  snq = new SpanNearQuery(new SpanQuery[]{lazy, fox}, 3, false);   ❹
  assertOnlyBrownFox(snq);
                                                        Nested SpanTermQuery
                                                        objects in reverse order
  PhraseQuery pq = new PhraseQuery();
  pq.add(new Term("f", "lazy"));               ❺ Comparable
  pq.add(new Term("f", "fox"));                  PhraseQuery
  pq.setSlop(4);
  assertNoMatches(pq);

  pq.setSlop(5);                    ❻ PhraseQuery,
  assertOnlyBrownFox(pq);             slop of 5
}
```

❶ Querying for these three terms in successive positions doesn't match either document.

❷ Using the same terms with a slop of 4 positions still doesn't result in a match.

❸ With a slop of 5, the SpanNearQuery has a match.

❹ The nested SpanTermQuery objects are in reverse order, so the inOrder flag is set to false. A slop of only 3 is needed for a match.

❺ Here we use a comparable PhraseQuery, although a slop of 4 still doesn't match.

❻ A slop of 5 is needed for a PhraseQuery to match.

We've only shown SpanNearQuery with nested SpanTermQuerys, but SpanNearQuery allows for any SpanQuery type. A more sophisticated SpanNearQuery is demonstrated later in listing 5.5 in conjunction with SpanOrQuery.

5.4.4 *Excluding span overlap from matches*

The SpanNotQuery excludes matches where one SpanQuery overlaps another. The following code demonstrates:

```
public void testSpanNotQuery() throws Exception {
  SpanNearQuery quick_fox =
      new SpanNearQuery(new SpanQuery[]{quick, fox}, 1, true);
  assertBothFoxes(quick_fox);
  dumpSpans(quick_fox);

  SpanNotQuery quick_fox_dog = new SpanNotQuery(quick_fox, dog);
  assertBothFoxes(quick_fox_dog);
  dumpSpans(quick_fox_dog);

  SpanNotQuery no_quick_red_fox =
      new SpanNotQuery(quick_fox, red);
  assertOnlyBrownFox(no_quick_red_fox);
  dumpSpans(no_quick_red_fox);
}
```

The first argument to the SpanNotQuery constructor is a span to *include*, and the second argument is the span to *exclude*. We've strategically added dumpSpans to clarify what is going on. Here is the output with the Java query annotated above each:

```
SpanNearQuery quick_fox =
        new SpanNearQuery(new SpanQuery[]{quick, fox}, 1, true);
spanNear([f:quick, f:fox], 1, true):
   the <quick brown fox> jumps over the lazy dog (0.18579213)
   the <quick red fox> jumps over the sleepy cat (0.18579213)

SpanNotQuery quick_fox_dog = new SpanNotQuery(quick_fox, dog);
spanNot(spanNear([f:quick, f:fox], 1, true), f:dog):
   the <quick brown fox> jumps over the lazy dog (0.18579213)
   the <quick red fox> jumps over the sleepy cat (0.18579213)

SpanNotQuery no_quick_red_fox =
        new SpanNotQuery(quick_fox, red);
spanNot(spanNear([f:quick, f:fox], 1, true), f:red):
   the <quick brown fox> jumps over the lazy dog (0.18579213)
```

The SpanNear query matched both documents because both have *quick* and *fox* within one position of one another. The first SpanNotQuery, quick_fox_dog, continues to match both documents because there is no overlap with the quick_fox span and *dog*. The second SpanNotQuery, no_quick_red_fox, excludes the second document because *red* overlaps with the quick_fox span. Notice that the resulting span matches are the original included span. The excluded span is only used to determine if there is an overlap and doesn't factor into the resulting span matches.

5.4.5 Spanning the globe

Finally there is `SpanOrQuery`, which aggregates an array of `SpanQuerys`. Our example query, in English, is `all` `documents` `that` `have` `"quick fox"` near `"lazy dog"` or that have `"quick fox"` near `"sleepy cat"`. The first clause of this query is shown in figure 5.4. This single clause is `SpanNearQuery` nesting two `SpanNearQuerys`, which each consist of two `SpanTermQuerys`.

Our test case becomes a bit lengthier due to all the sub-`SpanQuerys` being built upon (see listing 5.5). Using `dumpSpans`, we analyze the code in more detail.

Listing 5.5 `SpanOrQuery`

```
public void testSpanOrQuery() throws Exception {
  SpanNearQuery quick_fox =
      new SpanNearQuery(new SpanQuery[]{quick, fox}, 1, true);
  SpanNearQuery lazy_dog =
      new SpanNearQuery(new SpanQuery[]{lazy, dog}, 0, true);

  SpanNearQuery sleepy_cat =
      new SpanNearQuery(new SpanQuery[]{sleepy, cat}, 0, true);

  SpanNearQuery qf_near_ld =
      new SpanNearQuery(
          new SpanQuery[]{quick_fox, lazy_dog}, 3, true);
  assertOnlyBrownFox(qf_near_ld);
  dumpSpans(qf_near_ld);

  SpanNearQuery qf_near_sc =
      new SpanNearQuery(
          new SpanQuery[]{quick_fox, sleepy_cat}, 3, true);
  dumpSpans(qf_near_sc);

  SpanOrQuery or = new SpanOrQuery(
      new SpanQuery[]{qf_near_ld, qf_near_sc});
  assertBothFoxes(or);
  dumpSpans(or);
}
```

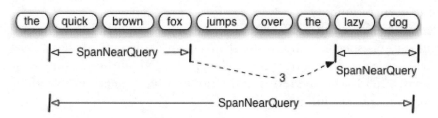

Figure 5.4 One clause of the `SpanOrQuery`

We've used our handy dumpSpans a few times to allow us to follow the progression as the final OR query is built. Here is the output, followed by our analysis of it:

```
SpanNearQuery qf_near_ld =
        new SpanNearQuery(
            new SpanQuery[]{quick_fox, lazy_dog}, 3, true);
spanNear([spanNear([f:quick, f:fox], 1, true),
        spanNear([f:lazy, f:dog], 0, true)], 3, true):
    the <quick brown fox jumps over the lazy dog> (0.3321948)


SpanNearQuery qf_near_sc =
        new SpanNearQuery(
            new SpanQuery[]{quick_fox, sleepy_cat}, 3, true);
spanNear([spanNear([f:quick, f:fox], 1, true),
        spanNear([f:sleepy, f:cat], 0, true)], 3, true):
    the <quick red fox jumps over the sleepy cat> (0.3321948)


SpanOrQuery or = new SpanOrQuery(
        new SpanQuery[]{qf_near_ld, qf_near_sc});
spanOr([spanNear([spanNear([f:quick, f:fox], 1, true),
                spanNear([f:lazy, f:dog], 0, true)], 3, true),
        spanNear([spanNear([f:quick, f:fox], 1, true),
                spanNear([f:sleepy, f:cat], 0, true)], 3, true)]):
    the <quick brown fox jumps over the lazy dog> (0.6643896)
    the <quick red fox jumps over the sleepy cat> (0.6643896)
```

Two SpanNearQuerys are created to match *quick fox* near *lazy dog* (qf_near_ld) and *quick fox* near *sleepy cat* (qf_near_sc) using nested SpanNearQuerys made up of SpanTermQuerys at the lowest level. Finally, these two SpanNearQuery instances are combined within a SpanOrQuery, which aggregates all matching spans. Whew!

5.4.6 *SpanQuery and QueryParser*

QueryParser doesn't currently support any of the SpanQuery types. Perhaps, though, support will eventually be added. At least one member of the Lucene community has created a query expression parser designed for span query expressions that may be part of the Lucene Sandbox by the time you read this. See the resources listed in appendix C for more details on how to tap into the Lucene user community.

Recall from section 3.4.5 that PhraseQuery is impartial to term order when enough slop is specified. Interestingly, you can easily extend QueryParser to use a SpanNearQuery with SpanTermQuery clauses instead, and force phrase queries to only match fields with the terms in the same order as specified. We demonstrate this technique in section 6.3.4.

5.5 *Filtering a search*

Filtering is a mechanism of narrowing the search space, allowing only a subset of the documents to be considered as possible hits. They can be used to implement search-within-search features to successively search within a previous set of hits or to constrain the document search space for security or external data reasons. A security filter is a powerful example, allowing users to only see search results of documents they own even if their query technically matches other documents that are off limits; we provide an example of a security filter in section 5.5.3.

You can filter any Lucene search, using the overloaded `search` methods that accept a `Filter` parameter. There are three built-in `Filter` implementations:

- `DateFilter` constrains the document space to only documents with a specified date field within a given range of dates.

- `QueryFilter` uses the results of query as the searchable document space for a new query.

- `CachingWrapperFilter` is a decorator over another filter caching its results to increase performance when used again.

Before you get concerned about mentions of caching results, rest assured that it's done with a tiny data structure (a `BitSet`) where each bit position represents a document.

Consider, also, the alternative to using a filter: aggregating required clauses in a `BooleanQuery`. In this section, we'll discuss each of the built-in filters as well as the `BooleanQuery` alternative.

5.5.1 *Using DateFilter*

The `date` field type is covered in section 2.4 along with its caveats. Having a `date` field, you filter as shown in `testDateFilter()` in listing 5.6. Our book data indexes the last modified date of each book data file as a `modified` field, indexed as a `Field.Keyword(String, Date)`. We test the date range filter by using an all-inclusive query, which by itself returns all documents.

Listing 5.6 Using `DateFilter`

```
public class FilterTest extends LiaTestCase {
  private Query allBooks;
  private IndexSearcher searcher;
  private int numAllBooks;
```

```
protected void setUp() throws Exception {        ❶  setUp() establishes
  super.setUp();                                      baseline book count

  allBooks = new RangeQuery(new Term("pubmonth","190001"),
                            new Term("pubmonth", "200512"),
                            true);
  searcher = new IndexSearcher(directory);
  Hits hits = searcher.search(allBooks);
  numAllBooks = hits.length();
}

public void testDateFilter() throws Exception {
  Date jan1 = parseDate("2004 Jan 01");
  Date jan31 = parseDate("2004 Jan 31");
  Date dec31 = parseDate("2004 Dec 31");

  DateFilter filter = new DateFilter("modified", jan1, dec31);

  Hits hits = searcher.search(allBooks, filter);
  assertEquals("all modified in 2004",
      numAllBooks, hits.length());

  filter = new DateFilter("modified", jan1, jan31);
  hits = searcher.search(allBooks, filter);
  assertEquals("none modified in January",
      0, hits.length());
}
}
```

❶ setUp() establishes a baseline count of all the books in our index, allowing for comparisons when we use an all inclusive date filter.

The first parameter to both of the DateFilter constructors is the name of a date field in the index. In our sample data this field name is modified; this field is the last modified date of the source data file. The two constructors differ only in the types of the second and third arguments: either java.util.Date (as in this example) or long, take your pick.

Open-ended date range filtering

DateFilter also supports open-ended date ranges. To filter on dates with one end of the range specified and the other end open, use one of the static factory methods on DateFilter:

```
filter = DateFilter.Before("modified", endDate);
filter = DateFilter.After("modified", startDate);
```

NOTE   `DateFilter` ranges are *inclusive* of the beginning and ending dates. The `Before` and `After` method names can be misleading given this fact. A `DateFilter.Before` range is really an "on or before" filter.

As with the `DateFilter` constructors, `Before` and `After` methods accept either a `java.util.Date` or a `long`.

You can leave both ends of the date range open, although doing so is effectively the same as using no filter—but with a performance hit for the comparisons. It's trickier to leave both ends unconstrained, because the only methods to get the special minimum and maximum dates return strings that must be converted to a date representation, as shown here:

```
Filter filter = new DateFilter("modified",
        DateField.stringToDate(DateField.MIN_DATE_STRING()),
        DateField.stringToDate(DateField.MAX_DATE_STRING()));
```

It wouldn't make much sense to hard-code such an open-ended `DateFilter`, but these constants would be useful as special cases when you're constructing a `Date-Filter` dynamically.

DateFilter and caching

Filters are ideally suited when they're reused for many searches, with the caveat that their work be cached initially. `DateFilter`, however, doesn't cache; and if you use it repeatedly, it will make the date-filtering decision each time with a noticeable performance degradation. When you reuse a `DateFilter` across multiple searches, wrap it with a `CachingWrappingFilter` to benefit from caching the document range that matches on the first search. See section 5.5.5 for details on caching a `DateFilter`.

5.5.2 Using QueryFilter

More generically useful than `DateFilter` is `QueryFilter`. `QueryFilter` uses the hits of one query to constrain available documents from a subsequent search. The result, a `BitSet` representing which documents were matched from the filtering query, is cached to maximize performance for future searches that use the same `QueryFilter` and `IndexSearcher` instances. Using a `QueryFilter`, we restrict the documents searched to a specific category:

```
public void testQueryFilter() throws Exception {
  TermQuery categoryQuery =
    new TermQuery(new Term("category", "/philosophy/eastern"));
```

```
Filter categoryFilter = new QueryFilter(categoryQuery);

Hits hits = searcher.search(allBooks, categoryFilter);
assertEquals("only tao te ching", 1, hits.length());
assertTrue(hits.score(0) < 1.0);
}
```

Here we're searching for all the books (see setUp() in listing 5.6) but constraining the search using a filter for a category which contains a single book. We explain the last assertion of testQueryFilter() shortly, in section 5.5.4.

QueryFilter can even replace DateFilter usage, although it requires a few more lines of code and isn't nearly as elegant looking. The following code demonstrates date filtering using a QueryFilter on a RangeQuery using the same date range and search as the first DateFilter example:

```
public void testQueryFilterWithRangeQuery() throws Exception {
    Date jan1 = parseDate("2004 Jan 01");        ◁──  Unshown method:
    Date dec31 = parseDate("2004 Dec 31");             returns Date as
                                                       expected
    Term start = new Term("modified",
        DateField.dateToString(jan1));
    Term end = new Term("modified",
        DateField.dateToString(dec31));

    Query rangeQuery = new RangeQuery(start, end, true);
    Filter filter = new QueryFilter(rangeQuery);

    Hits hits = searcher.search(allBooks, filter);
    assertEquals("all of 'em", numAllBooks, hits.length());
}
```

If you'll be hanging on to a filter instance for multiple searches, the caching of QueryFilter will result in more efficient searches than a similar DateFilter, which does no caching.

5.5.3 Security filters

Another example of document filtering constrains documents with security in mind. Our example assumes documents are associated with an owner, which is known at indexing time. We index two documents; both have the term *info* in their keywords field, but each document has a different owner:

```
public class SecurityFilterTest extends TestCase {
    private RAMDirectory directory;

    protected void setUp() throws Exception {
        IndexWriter writer = new IndexWriter(directory,
            new WhitespaceAnalyzer(), true);
```

```
    // Elwood
    Document document = new Document();
    document.add(Field.Keyword("owner", "elwood"));
    document.add(Field.Text("keywords", "elwoods sensitive info"));
    writer.addDocument(document);

    // Jake
    document = new Document();
    document.add(Field.Keyword("owner", "jake"));
    document.add(Field.Text("keywords", "jakes sensitive info"));
    writer.addDocument(document);

    writer.close();
  }
}
```

Using a `TermQuery` for *info* in the `keywords` field results in both documents found, naturally. Suppose, though, that Jake is using the search feature in our application, and only documents he owns should be searchable by him. Quite elegantly, we can easily use a `QueryFilter` to constrain the search space to only documents he is the owner of, as shown in listing 5.7.

Listing 5.7   Securing the search space with a filter

```
public void testSecurityFilter() throws Exception {
  directory = new RAMDirectory();
  setUp();

  TermQuery query = new TermQuery(new Term("keywords", "info"));    ❶
                                                          TermQuery for "info"
  IndexSearcher searcher = new IndexSearcher(directory);
  Hits hits = searcher.search(query);
  assertEquals("Both documents match", 2, hits.length());
                                                          ❷ Returns
                                                            documents
  QueryFilter jakeFilter = new QueryFilter(                 containing
      new TermQuery(new Term("owner", "jake")));            "info"
                                            ❸ Filter
  hits = searcher.search(query, jakeFilter);
  assertEquals(1, hits.length());                          ❹ Same
  assertEquals("elwood is safe",                             TermQuery,
      "jakes sensitive info", hits.doc(0).get("keywords"));  constrained
}                                                            results
```

❶ This is a general `TermQuery` for *info*.

❷ All documents containing *info* are returned.

❸ Here, the filter constrains document searches to only documents owned by "jake".

❹ Only Jake's document is returned, using the same *info* `TermQuery`.

If your security requirements are this straightforward, where documents can be associated with users or roles during indexing, using a QueryFilter will work nicely. However, this scenario is oversimplified for most needs; the ways that documents are associated with roles may be quite a bit more dynamic. QueryFilter is useful only when the filtering constraints are present as field information within the index itself. In section 6.4, we develop a more sophisticated filter implementation that leverages external information; this approach could be adapted to a more dynamic custom security filter.

5.5.4 A QueryFilter alternative

You can constrain a query to a subset of documents another way, by combining the constraining query to the original query as a *required* clause of a BooleanQuery. There are a couple of important differences, despite the fact that the same documents are returned from both. QueryFilter caches the set of documents allowed, probably speeding up successive searches using the same instance. In addition, normalized Hits scores are unlikely to be the same. The score difference makes sense when you're looking at the scoring formula (see section 3.3, page 78). The IDF factor may be dramatically different. When you're using BooleanQuery aggregation, all documents containing the terms are factored into the equation, whereas a filter reduces the documents under consideration and impacts the inverse document frequency factor.

This test case demonstrates how to "filter" using BooleanQuery aggregation and illustrates the scoring difference compared to testQueryFilter:

```
public void testFilterAlternative() throws Exception {
  TermQuery categoryQuery =
    new TermQuery(new Term("category", "/philosophy/eastern"));

  BooleanQuery constrainedQuery = new BooleanQuery();
  constrainedQuery.add(allBooks, true, false);
  constrainedQuery.add(categoryQuery, true, false);

  Hits hits = searcher.search(constrainedQuery);
  assertEquals("only tao te ching", 1, hits.length());
  assertTrue(hits.score(0) == 1.0);
}
```

The technique of aggregating a query in this manner works well with Query-Parser parsed queries, allowing users to enter free-form queries yet restricting the set of documents searched by an API-controlled query.

5.5.5 *Caching filter results*

The biggest benefit from filters comes when they cache and are reused. DateFilter doesn't cache, but QueryFilter does. Wrapping a noncaching filter with Caching-WrapperFilter takes care of caching automatically (internally using a WeakHash-Map, so that dereferenced entries get garbage collected). Filters cache by using the IndexReader as the key, which means searching should also be done with the same instance of IndexReader to benefit from the cache. If you aren't constructing IndexReader yourself, but rather are creating an IndexSearcher from a directory, you must use the same instance of IndexSearcher to benefit from the caching. When index changes need to be reflected in searches, discard IndexSearcher and IndexReader and reinstantiate.

Strictly speaking, CachingWrapperFilter is a third built-in filter within Lucene, although its purpose is to decouple filtering from caching and it doesn't filter. CachingWrapperFilter decorates an existing filter and caches the results in a similar manner to QueryFilter. To demonstrate its usage, we return to the date-range filtering example. We want to use DateFilter because the contortions of using a QueryFilter for dates are ugly, but we'd like to benefit from caching to improve performance:

```
public void testCachingWrapper() throws Exception {
  Date jan1 = parseDate("2004 Jan 01");
  Date dec31 = parseDate("2004 Dec 31");

  DateFilter dateFilter =
      new DateFilter("modified", jan1, dec31);

  cachingFilter =
      new CachingWrapperFilter(dateFilter);
  Hits hits = searcher.search(allBooks, cachingFilter);
  assertEquals("all of 'em", numAllBooks, hits.length());
}
```

Successive uses of the same CachingWrapperFilter instance with the same IndexSearcher instance will bypass using the wrapped filter, instead using the cached results.

5.5.6 *Beyond the built-in filters*

Lucene isn't restricted to using the built-in filters. An additional filter found in the Lucene Sandbox, ChainedFilter, allows for complex chaining of filters. We cover it in section 8.8, page 304.

Writing custom filters allows external data to factor into search constraints; however, a bit of detailed Lucene API know-how may be required to be highly efficient. We cover writing custom filters in section 6.4, page 209.

And if these filtering options aren't enough, Lucene 1.4 adds another interesting use of a filter. The `FilteredQuery` filters a query, like `IndexSearcher`'s `search(Query, Filter)` can, except it is itself a query: Thus it can be used as a single clause within a `BooleanQuery`. Using `FilteredQuery` seems to make sense only when using custom filters, so we cover it along with custom filters in section 6.4.

5.6 Searching across multiple Lucene indexes

If your architecture consists of multiple Lucene indexes, but you need to search across them using a single query with search results interleaving documents from different indexes, `MultiSearcher` is for you. In high-volume usage of Lucene, your architecture may partition sets of documents into different indexes.

5.6.1 Using MultiSearcher

With `MultiSearcher`, all indexes can be searched with the results merged in a specified (or descending-score) order. Using `MultiSearcher` is comparable to using `IndexSearcher`, except that you hand it an array of `IndexSearcher`s to search rather than a single directory (so it's effectively a decorator pattern and delegates most of the work to the subsearchers).

Listing 5.8 illustrates how to search two indexes that are split alphabetically by keyword. The index is made up of animal names beginning with each letter of the alphabet. Half the names are in one index, and half are in the other. A search is performed with a range that spans both indexes, demonstrating that results are merged together.

Listing 5.8 Securing the search space with a filter

```
public class MultiSearcherTest extends TestCase {
  private IndexSearcher[] searchers;

  public void setUp() throws Exception {
    String[] animals = { "aardvark", "beaver", "coati",
                         "dog", "elephant", "frog", "gila monster",
                         "horse", "iguana", "javelina", "kangaroo",
                         "lemur", "moose", "nematode", "orca",
                         "python", "quokka", "rat", "scorpion",
                         "tarantula", "uromastyx", "vicuna",
                         "walrus", "xiphias", "yak", "zebra"};
```

```
        Analyzer analyzer = new WhitespaceAnalyzer();

        Directory aTOmDirectory = new RAMDirectory();        ❶ Two
        Directory nTOzDirectory = new RAMDirectory();           indexes

        IndexWriter aTOmWriter = new IndexWriter(aTOmDirectory,
                                          analyzer, true);
        IndexWriter nTOzWriter = new IndexWriter(nTOzDirectory,
                                          analyzer, true);

        for (int i=0; i < animals.length; i++) {
          Document doc = new Document();
          String animal = animals[i];
          doc.add(Field.Keyword("animal", animal));
          if (animal.compareToIgnoreCase("n") < 0) {
            aTOmWriter.addDocument(doc);
          } else {                                    ❷ Indexing halves
            nTOzWriter.addDocument(doc);                 of the alphabet
          }
        }

        aTOmWriter.close();
        nTOzWriter.close();

        searchers = new IndexSearcher[2];
        searchers[0] = new IndexSearcher(aTOmDirectory);
        searchers[1] = new IndexSearcher(nTOzDirectory);
    }

    public void testMulti() throws Exception {

        MultiSearcher searcher = new MultiSearcher(searchers);

        Query query = new RangeQuery(new Term("animal", "h"),      ❸ Query
                          new Term("animal", "t"), true);            spans both
                                                                     indexes
        Hits hits = searcher.search(query);
        assertEquals("tarantula not included", 12, hits.length());
    }
}
```

❶ This code uses two indexes.

❷ The first half of the alphabet is indexed to one index, and the other half is indexed to the other index.

❸ This query spans documents in both indexes.

The inclusive RangeQuery matched animals that began with *h* through animals that began with *t*, with the matching documents coming from both indexes.

5.6.2 *Multithreaded searching using ParallelMultiSearcher*

A multithreaded version of `MultiSearcher` called `ParallelMultiSearcher` was added to Lucene 1.4. A search operation spins a thread for each `Searchable` and waits for them all to finish. The basic search and search with filter options are parallelized, but searching with a `HitCollector` has not yet been parallelized.

Whether you'll see performance gains using `ParallelMultiSearcher` greatly depends on your architecture. Supposedly, if the indexes reside on different physical disks and you're able to take advantage of multiple CPUs, there may be improved performance; but in our tests with a single CPU, single physical disk, and multiple indexes, performance with `MultiSearcher` was slightly better than `ParallelMultiSearcher`.

Using a `ParallelMultiSearcher` is identical to using `MultiSearcher`. An example, using `ParallelMultiSearcher` remotely, is shown in listing 5.9.

Searching multiple indexes remotely

Lucene includes remote index searching capability through Remote Method Invocation (RMI). There are numerous other alternatives to exposing search remotely, such as through web services. This section focuses solely on Lucene's built-in capabilities; other implementations are left to your innovation (you can also borrow ideas from projects like Nutch; see section 10.1).

An RMI server binds to an instance of `RemoteSearchable`, which is an implementation of the `Searchable` interface just like `IndexSearcher` and `MultiSearcher`. The server-side `RemoteSearchable` delegates to a concrete `Searchable`, such as a regular `IndexSearcher` instance.

Clients to the `RemoteSearchable` invoke search methods identically to searching through an `IndexSearcher` or `MultiSearcher`, as shown throughout this chapter. Figure 5.5 illustrates one possible remote-searching configuration.

Other configurations are possible, depending on your needs. The client could instantiate a `ParallelMultiSearcher` over multiple remote (and/or local) indexes, and each server could search only a single index.

In order to demonstrate `RemoteSearchable`, we put together a multi-index server configuration, similar to figure 5.5, using both `MultiSearcher` and `ParallelMultiSearcher` in order to compare performance. We split the WordNet index (a database of nearly 40,000 words and their synonyms) into 26 indexes representing *A* through *Z*, with each word in the index corresponding to its first letter. The server exposes two RMI client-accessible `RemoteSearchables`, allowing clients to access either the serial `MultiSearcher` or the `ParallelMultiSearcher`.

`SearchServer` is shown in listing 5.9.

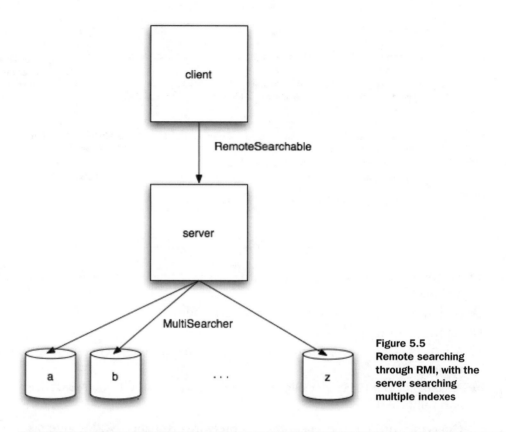

Figure 5.5
Remote searching through RMI, with the server searching multiple indexes

Listing 5.9 `SearchServer`: a remote search server using RMI

```
public class SearchServer {
  private static final String ALPHABET =
      "abcdefghijklmnopqrstuvwxyz";

  public static void main(String[] args) throws Exception {
    if (args.length != 1) {
      System.err.println("Usage: SearchServer <basedir>");
      System.exit(-1);
    }

    String basedir = args[0];              ❶ Indexes under basedir
    Searchable[] searchables = new Searchable[ALPHABET.length()];
    for (int i = 0; i < ALPHABET.length(); i++) {
      searchables[i] = new IndexSearcher(
          new File(basedir,
          "" + ALPHABET.charAt(i)).getAbsolutePath());    ❷ Open IndexSearcher
    }                                                         for each index
```

```
LocateRegistry.createRegistry(1099);         ❸ Create RMI registry

Searcher multiSearcher = new MultiSearcher(searchables);
RemoteSearchable multiImpl =                              ❹ MultiSearcher
    new RemoteSearchable(multiSearcher);                    over all
Naming.rebind("//localhost/LIA_Multi", multiImpl);         indexes

Searcher parallelSearcher =
    new ParallelMultiSearcher(searchables);     ParallelMultiSearcher  ❺
RemoteSearchable parallelImpl =                    over all indexes
    new RemoteSearchable(parallelSearcher);
Naming.rebind("//localhost/LIA_Parallel", parallelImpl);

System.out.println("Server started");
    }
}
```

❶ Twenty-six indexes reside under the basedir, each named for a letter of the
alphabet.

❷ A plain IndexSearcher is opened for each index.

❸ An RMI registry is created.

❹ A MultiSearcher over all indexes, named LIA_Multi, is created and published
through RMI.

❺ A ParallelMultiSearcher over the same indexes, named LIA_Parallel, is created
and published.

Querying through SearchServer remotely involves mostly RMI glue, as shown in
SearchClient in listing 5.10. Because our access to the server is through a Remote-
Searchable, which is a lower-level API than we want to work with, we wrap it inside
a MultiSearcher. Why MultiSearcher? Because it's a wrapper over Searchables,
making it as friendly to use as IndexSearcher.

Listing 5.10 SearchClient: accesses the RMI-exposed objects from
SearchServer

```
public class SearchClient {
  private static HashMap searcherCache = new HashMap();

  public static void main(String[] args) throws Exception {
    if (args.length != 1) {
      System.err.println("Usage: SearchClient <query>");
      System.exit(-1);
    }

    String word = args[0];
```

```
      for (int i=0; i < 5; i++) {              Multiple
        search("LIA_Multi", word);          ❶ identical
        search("LIA_Parallel", word);          searches
      }
  }

  private static void search(String name, String word)
      throws Exception {
    TermQuery query = new TermQuery(new Term("word", word));

    MultiSearcher searcher =
        (MultiSearcher) searcherCache.get(name);     ❷ Cache searchers

    if (searcher == null) {
      searcher =
        new MultiSearcher(new Searchable[]{lookupRemote(name)});  ❸
      searcherCache.put(name, searcher);
    }                                              Wrap Searchable in
                                                      MultiSearcher

    long begin = new Date().getTime();
    Hits hits = searcher.search(query);
    long end = new Date().getTime();          ❹ Time
                                                 searching
    System.out.print("Searched " + name +
        " for '" + word + "' (" + (end - begin) + " ms): ");

    if (hits.length() == 0) {
      System.out.print("<NONE FOUND>");
    }

    for (int i = 0; i < hits.length(); i++) {
      Document doc = hits.doc(i);
      String[] values = doc.getValues("syn");
      for (int j = 0; j < values.length; j++) {
        System.out.print(values[j] + " ");
      }
    }
    System.out.println();
    System.out.println();

    // DO NOT CLOSE searcher!   ❺ Don't close searcher
  }

  private static Searchable lookupRemote(String name)
      throws Exception {
    return (Searchable) Naming.lookup("//localhost/" + name);   ❻
  }                                                        RMI lookup
}
```

❶ We perform multiple identical searches to warm up the JVM and get a good sample of response time. The `MultiSearcher` and `ParallelMultiSearcher` are each searched.

❷ The searchers are cached, to be as efficient as possible.

❸ The remote `Searchable` is located and wrapped in a `MultiSearcher`.

❹ The searching process is timed.

❺ We don't close the searcher because it closes the remote searcher, thereby prohibiting future searches.

❻ Look up the remote interface.

> **WARNING** Don't `close()` the `RemoteSearchable` or its wrapping `MultiSearcher`. Doing so will prevent future searches from working because the server side will have closed its access to the index.

Let's see our remote searcher in action. For demonstration purposes, we ran it on a single machine in separate console windows. The server is started:

```
% java lia.advsearching.remote.SearchServer path/to/indexes/
Server started
```

The client connects, searches, outputs the results several times, and exits:

```
% java lia.advsearching.remote.SearchClient hello
Searched LIA_Multi for 'hello' (259 ms): hullo howdy hi

Searched LIA_Parallel for 'hello' (40 ms): hullo howdy hi

Searched LIA_Multi for 'hello' (17 ms): hullo howdy hi

Searched LIA_Parallel for 'hello' (83 ms): hullo howdy hi

Searched LIA_Multi for 'hello' (11 ms): hullo howdy hi

Searched LIA_Parallel for 'hello' (41 ms): hullo howdy hi

Searched LIA_Multi for 'hello' (30 ms): hullo howdy hi

Searched LIA_Parallel for 'hello' (50 ms): hullo howdy hi

Searched LIA_Multi for 'hello' (15 ms): hullo howdy hi

Searched LIA_Parallel for 'hello' (47 ms): hullo howdy hi
```

It's interesting to note the search times reported by each type of server-side searcher. The `ParallelMultiSearcher` is slower than the `MultiSearcher` in our environment (single CPU, single disk). Also, you can see the reason why we chose to run the search multiple times: The first search took much longer relative to the successive searches, which is probably due to JVM warmup. These results point out that performance testing is tricky business, but it's necessary in many environments. Because of the strong effect your environment has on performance, we urge you to perform your own tests with your own environment. Performance testing is covered in more detail in section 6.5, page 213.

If you choose to expose searching through RMI in this manner, you'll likely want to create a bit of infrastructure to coordinate and manage issues such as closing an index and how the server deals with index updates (remember, the searcher sees a snapshot of the index and must be reopened to see changes).

5.7 *Leveraging term vectors*

Term vectors are a new feature in Lucene 1.4, but they aren't new as an information retrieval concept. A *term vector* is a collection of term-frequency pairs. Most of us probably can't envision vectors in hyperdimensional space, so for visualization purposes, let's look at two documents that contain only the terms *cat* and *dog*. These words appear various times in each document. Plotting the term frequencies of each document in X, Y coordinates looks something like figure 5.6. What gets interesting with term vectors is the angle between them, as you'll see in more detail in section 5.7.2.

To enable term-vector storage, during indexing you enable the `store term vectors` attribute on the desired fields. `Field.Text` and `Field.Unstored` have additional overloaded methods with a boolean `storeTermVector` flag in the signature. Setting this value to `true` turns on the optional term vector support for the field, as we did for the `subject` field when indexing our book data (see figure 5.7).

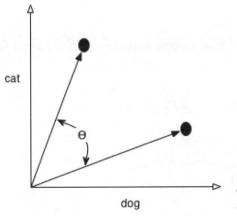

Figure 5.6
Term vectors for two documents containing the terms *cat* and *dog*

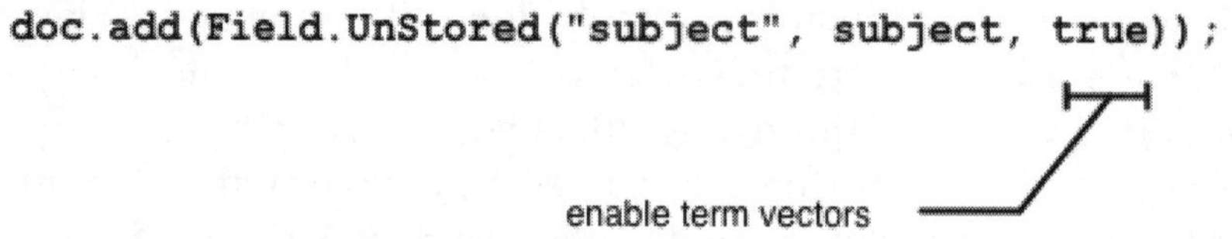

```
doc.add(Field.UnStored("subject", subject, true));
```

enable term vectors

Figure 5.7   Enabling term vectors during indexing

Retrieving term vectors for a field in a given document by ID requires a call to an `IndexReader` method:

```
TermFreqVector termFreqVector =
                    reader.getTermFreqVector(id, "subject");
```

A `TermFreqVector` instance has several methods for retrieving the vector information, primarily as matching arrays of `Strings` and `ints` (the term value and frequency in the field, respectively). You can use term vectors for some interesting effects, such as finding documents "like" a particular document, which is an example of latent semantic analysis. We built a `BooksLikeThis` feature as well as a proof-of-concept categorizer that can tell us the most appropriate category for a new book, as you'll see in the following sections.

5.7.1 *Books like this*

It would be nice to offer other choices to the customers of our bookstore when they're viewing a particular book. The alternatives should be related to the original book, but associating alternatives manually would be labor-intensive and would require ongoing effort to keep up to date. Instead, we use Lucene's boolean query capability and the information from one book to look up other books that are similar. Listing 5.11 demonstrates a basic approach for finding books like each one in our sample data.

Listing 5.11   Books like this

```
public class BooksLikeThis {

    public static void main(String[] args) throws IOException {
        String indexDir = System.getProperty("index.dir");

        FSDirectory directory =
            FSDirectory.getDirectory(indexDir, false);

        IndexReader reader = IndexReader.open(directory);
        int numDocs = reader.maxDoc();

        BooksLikeThis blt = new BooksLikeThis(reader);
```

```
    for (int i = 0; i < numDocs; i++) {
      System.out.println();
      Document doc = reader.document(i);
      System.out.println(doc.get("title"));

      Document[] docs = blt.docsLike(i, 10);
      if (docs.length == 0) {
        System.out.println("  None like this");
      }
      for (int j = 0; j < docs.length; j++) {
        Document likeThisDoc = docs[j];
        System.out.println("  -> " + likeThisDoc.get("title"));
      }
    }
  }

  private IndexReader reader;
  private IndexSearcher searcher;

  public BooksLikeThis(IndexReader reader) {
    this.reader = reader;
    searcher = new IndexSearcher(reader);
  }

  public Document[] docsLike(int id, int max) throws IOException {
    Document doc = reader.document(id);

    String[] authors = doc.getValues("author");
    BooleanQuery authorQuery = new BooleanQuery();
    for (int i = 0; i < authors.length; i++) {
      String author = authors[i];
      authorQuery.add(new TermQuery(new Term("author", author)),
          false, false);
    }
    authorQuery.setBoost(2.0f);

    TermFreqVector vector =
        reader.getTermFreqVector(id, "subject");

    BooleanQuery subjectQuery = new BooleanQuery();
    for (int j = 0; j < vector.size(); j++) {
      TermQuery tq = new TermQuery(
          new Term("subject", vector.getTerms()[j]));
      subjectQuery.add(tq, false, false);
    }

    BooleanQuery likeThisQuery = new BooleanQuery();
    likeThisQuery.add(authorQuery, false, false);
    likeThisQuery.add(subjectQuery, false, false);
```

2 Look up books like this

1 Iterate over every book

3 Boosts books by same author

4 Use terms from "subject" term vectors

5 Create final query

```
            // exclude myself                                    ⑥ Exclude
            likeThisQuery.add(new TermQuery(                        current book
                new Term("isbn", doc.get("isbn"))), false, true);

            //System.out.println("  Query: " +
            //    likeThisQuery.toString("contents"));
            Hits hits = searcher.search(likeThisQuery);
            int size = max;
            if (max > hits.length()) size = hits.length();

            Document[] docs = new Document[size];
            for (int i = 0; i < size; i++) {
              docs[i] = hits.doc(i);
            }

            return docs;
        }

    }
```

❶ As an example, we iterate over every book document in the index and find books like each one.

❷ Here we look up books that are like this one.

❸ Books by the same author are considered alike and are boosted so they will likely appear before books by other authors.

❹ Using the terms from the subject term vectors, we add each to a boolean query.

❺ We combine the author and subject queries into a final boolean query.

❻ We exclude the current book, which would surely be the best match given the other criteria, from consideration.

In ❸, we used a different way to get the value of the author field. It was indexed as multiple fields, in the manner (shown in more detail in section 8.4, page 284), where the original author string is a comma-separated list of author(s) of a book:

```
            String[] authors = author.split(",");
            for (int i = 0; i < authors.length; i++) {
              doc.add(Field.Keyword("author", authors[i]));
            }
```

The output is interesting, showing how our books are connected through author and subject:

```
A Modern Art of Education
   -> Mindstorms

Imperial Secrets of Health and Longevity
   None like this
```

```
Tao Te Ching 道德經
  None like this

Gödel, Escher, Bach: an Eternal Golden Braid
  None like this

Mindstorms
  -> A Modern Art of Education

Java Development with Ant
  -> Lucene in Action
  -> JUnit in Action
  -> Extreme Programming Explained

JUnit in Action
  -> Java Development with Ant

Lucene in Action
  -> Java Development with Ant

Extreme Programming Explained
  -> The Pragmatic Programmer
  -> Java Development with Ant

Tapestry in Action
  None like this

The Pragmatic Programmer
  -> Extreme Programming Explained
```

If you'd like to see the actual query used for each, uncomment the output lines toward the end of the docsLike.

The books-like-this example could have been done without term vectors, and we aren't really using them as vectors in this case. We've only used the convenience of getting the terms for a given field. Without term vectors, the subject field could have been reanalyzed or indexed such that individual subject terms were added separately in order to get the list of terms for that field (see section 8.4 for discussion of how the sample data was indexed). Our next example also uses the frequency component to a term vector in a much more sophisticated manner.

5.7.2 *What category?*

Each book in our index is given a single primary category: For example, this book is categorized as "/technology/computers/programming". The best category placement for a new book may be relatively obvious, or (more likely) several possible categories may seem reasonable. You can use term vectors to automate the decision. We've written a bit of code that builds a representative subject vector for each existing category. This representative, archetypical, vector is the sum of all vectors for each document's `subject` field vector.

With these representative vectors precomputed, our end goal is a calculation that can, given some subject keywords for a new book, tell us what category is the best fit. Our test case uses two example subject strings:

```
public void testCategorization() throws Exception {
  assertEquals("/technology/computers/programming/methodology",
               getCategory("extreme agile methodology"));
  assertEquals("/education/pedagogy",
               getCategory("montessori education philosophy"));

}
```

The first assertion says that, based on our sample data, if a new book has "extreme agile methodology" keywords in its subject, the best category fit is "/technology/computers/programming/methodology". The best category is determined by finding the closest category angle-wise in vector space to the new book's subject.

The test `setUp()` builds vectors for each category:

```
public class CategorizerTest extends LiaTestCase {
  Map categoryMap;

  protected void setUp() throws Exception {
    super.setUp();

    categoryMap = new TreeMap();

    buildCategoryVectors();
    //dumpCategoryVectors();
  }

  // . . .
}
```

Our code builds category vectors by walking every document in the index and aggregating book subject vectors into a single vector for the book's associated category. Category vectors are stored in a `Map`, keyed by category name. The value of each item in the category map is another map keyed by term, with the value an `Integer` for its frequency:

```
private void buildCategoryVectors() throws IOException {
  IndexReader reader = IndexReader.open(directory);

  int maxDoc = reader.maxDoc();

  for (int i = 0; i < maxDoc; i++) {
```

```
    if (!reader.isDeleted(i)) {
      Document doc = reader.document(i);
      String category = doc.get("category");

      Map vectorMap = (Map) categoryMap.get(category);
      if (vectorMap == null) {
        vectorMap = new TreeMap();
        categoryMap.put(category, vectorMap);
      }

      TermFreqVector termFreqVector =
          reader.getTermFreqVector(i, "subject");

      addTermFreqToMap(vectorMap, termFreqVector);
    }
  }
}
```

A book's term frequency vector is added to its category vector in `addTermFreq-ToMap`. The arrays returned by `getTerms()` and `getTermFrequencies()` align with one another such that the same position in each refers to the same term:

```
private void addTermFreqToMap(Map vectorMap,
                              TermFreqVector termFreqVector) {
  String[] terms = termFreqVector.getTerms();
  int[] freqs = termFreqVector.getTermFrequencies();

  for (int i = 0; i < terms.length; i++) {
    String term = terms[i];

    if (vectorMap.containsKey(term)) {
      Integer value = (Integer) vectorMap.get(term);
      vectorMap.put(term,
          new Integer(value.intValue() + freqs[i]));
    } else {
      vectorMap.put(term, new Integer(freqs[i]));
    }
  }
}
```

That was the easy part—building the category vector maps—because it only involved addition. Computing angles between vectors, however, is more involved mathematically. In the simplest two-dimensional case, as shown earlier in figure 5.6, two categories (A and B) have unique term vectors based on aggregation (as we've just done). The closest category, angle-wise, to a new book's subjects is the match we'll choose. Figure 5.8 shows the equation for computing an angle between two vectors.

$$\cos \theta = \frac{A \cdot B}{\| A \| \| B \|}$$

Figure 5.8
Formula for computing the
angle between two vectors

Our `getCategory` method loops through all categories, computing the angle between each category and the new book. The smallest angle is the closest match, and the category name is returned:

```
private String getCategory(String subject) {
   String[] words = subject.split(" ");

   Iterator categoryIterator = categoryMap.keySet().iterator();
   double bestAngle = Double.MAX_VALUE;
   String bestCategory = null;

   while (categoryIterator.hasNext()) {
     String category = (String) categoryIterator.next();

     double angle = computeAngle(words, category);
     if (angle < bestAngle) {
       bestAngle = angle;
       bestCategory = category;
     }
   }

   return bestCategory;
}
```

We assume that the subject string is in a whitespace-separated form and that each word occurs only once. The angle computation takes these assumptions into account to simplify a part of the computation. Finally, computing the angle between an array of words and a specific category is done in `computeAngle`, shown in listing 5.12.

Listing 5.12 Computing term vector angles for a new book against a given category

```
private double computeAngle(String[] words, String category) {
   Map vectorMap = (Map) categoryMap.get(category);

   int dotProduct = 0;
   int sumOfSquares = 0;
   for (int i = 0; i < words.length; i++) {
     String word = words[i];
     int categoryWordFreq = 0;

     if (vectorMap.containsKey(word)) {
       categoryWordFreq =
           ((Integer) vectorMap.get(word)).intValue();
     }
```

```
    dotProduct += categoryWordFreq;          ❶  Assume each word has frequency I
    sumOfSquares += categoryWordFreq * categoryWordFreq;
}


double denominator;                           ❷  Shortcut to prevent
if (sumOfSquares == words.length) {               precision issue
  denominator = sumOfSquares;
} else {
  denominator = Math.sqrt(sumOfSquares) *
                Math.sqrt(words.length);
}

double ratio = dotProduct / denominator;

return Math.acos(ratio);
}
```

❶ The calculation is optimized with the assumption that each word in the `words` array has a frequency of 1.

❷ We multiply the square root of N by the square root of N is N. This shortcut prevents a precision issue where the ratio could be greater than 1 (which is an illegal value for the inverse cosine function).

You should be aware that computing term vector angles between two documents or, in this case, between a document and an archetypical category, is computation-intensive. It requires square-root and inverse cosine calculations and may be prohibitive in high-volume indexes.

5.8 *Summary*

This chapter has covered some diverse ground, highlighting Lucene's additional built-in search features. Sorting is a dramatic new enhancement that gives you control over the ordering of search results. The new `SpanQuery` family leverages term-position information for greater searching precision. Filters constrain document search space, regardless of the query. Lucene includes support for multiple (including parallel) and remote index searching, giving developers a head start on distributed and scalable architectures. And finally, the new term vector feature enables interesting effects, such as "like this" term vector angle calculations.

Is this the end of the searching story? Not quite. Lucene also includes several ways to extend its searching behavior, such as custom sorting, filtering, and query expression parsing, which we cover in the following chapter.

Extending search

6

This chapter covers

- Creating a custom sort
- Using a HitCollector
- Customizing QueryParser
- Testing performance

Just when you thought we were done with searching, here we are again with even more on the topic! Chapter 3 discussed the basics of Lucene's built-in capabilities, and chapter 5 went well beyond the basics into Lucene's more advanced searching features. In those two chapters, we explored only the built-in features. Lucene also has several nifty extension points.

Our first custom extension demonstrates Lucene's custom sorting hooks, allowing us to implement a search that returns results in ascending geographic proximity order from a user's current location. Next, implementing your own `HitCollector` bypasses `Hits`; this is effectively an event listener when matches are detected during searches.

`QueryParser` is extensible in several useful ways, such as for controlling date parsing and numeric formatting, as well as for disabling potential performance degrading queries such as wildcard and fuzzy queries. Custom filters allow information from outside the index to factor into search constraints, such as factoring some information present only in a relational database into Lucene searches.

And finally, we explore Lucene performance testing using JUnitPerf. The performance-testing example we provide is a meaningful example of testing actually becoming a design tool rather than an after-the-fact assurance test.

6.1 *Using a custom sort method*

If sorting by score, ID, or field values is insufficient for your needs, Lucene lets you implement a custom sorting mechanism by providing your own implementation of the `SortComparatorSource` interface. Custom sorting implementations are most useful in situations when the sort criteria can't be determined during indexing.

An interesting idea for a custom sorting mechanism is to order search results based on geographic distance from a given location.[1] The given location is only known at search time. We've created a simplified demonstration of this concept using the important question, "What Mexican food restaurant is nearest to me?" Figure 6.1 shows a sample of restaurants and their fictitious grid coordinates on a sample 10x10 grid.[2]

The test data is indexed as shown in listing 6.1, with each place given a name, location in X and Y coordinates, and a type. The `type` field allows our data to

---

[1] Thanks to Tim Jones (the contributor of Lucene's sort capabilities) for the inspiration.
[2] These are real (tasty!) restaurants in Tucson, Arizona, a city Erik used to call home.

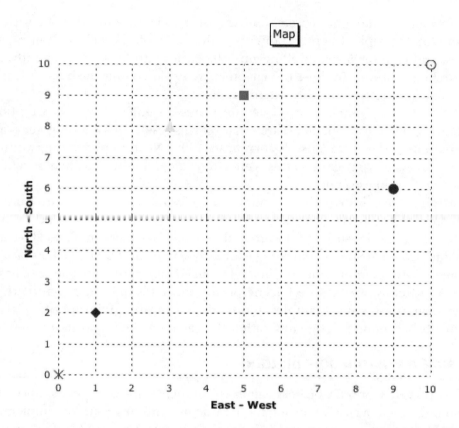

Figure 6.1 Which Mexican restaurant is closest to home (at 0,0) or work (at 10,10)?

accommodate other types of businesses and could allow us to filter search results to specific types of places.

Listing 6.1 Indexing geographic data

```
public class DistanceSortingTest extends TestCase {
  private RAMDirectory directory;
  private IndexSearcher searcher;
  private Query query;

  protected void setUp() throws Exception {
    directory = new RAMDirectory();
    IndexWriter writer =
      new IndexWriter(directory, new WhitespaceAnalyzer(), true);
    addPoint(writer, "El Charro", "restaurant", 1, 2);
    addPoint(writer, "Cafe Poca Cosa", "restaurant", 5, 9);
```

```
        addPoint(writer, "Los Betos", "restaurant", 9, 6);
        addPoint(writer, "Nico's Taco Shop", "restaurant", 3, 8);

        writer.close();

        searcher = new IndexSearcher(directory);

        query = new TermQuery(new Term("type","restaurant"));
    }

    private void addPoint(IndexWriter writer,
                          String name, String type, int x, int y)
        throws IOException {
        Document doc = new Document();
        doc.add(Field.Keyword("name", name));
        doc.add(Field.Keyword("type", type));
        doc.add(Field.Keyword("location", x+","+y));
        writer.addDocument(doc);
    }

}
```

The coordinates are indexed into a single location field as a string *x,y*. The location could be encoded in numerous ways, but we opted for the simplest approach for this example. Next we write a test that we use to assert that our sorting implementation works appropriately:

```
public void testNearestRestaurantToHome() throws Exception {
    Sort sort = new Sort(new SortField("location",
        new DistanceComparatorSource(0, 0)));

    Hits hits = searcher.search(query, sort);

    assertEquals("closest",
        "El Charro", hits.doc(0).get("name"));
    assertEquals("furthest",
        "Los Betos", hits.doc(3).get("name"));
}
```

Home is at coordinates (0,0). Our test has shown that the first and last documents in the Hits returned are the ones closest and furthest from home. *Muy bien!* Had we not used a sort, the documents would have been returned in insertion order, since the score of each hit is equivalent for the restaurant-type query. The distance computation, using the basic distance formula, is done under our custom DistanceComparatorSource, shown in listing 6.2.

Listing 6.2 `DistanceComparatorSource`

```
public class DistanceComparatorSource
    implements SortComparatorSource {        ❶ Implement SortComparatorSource
  private int x;
  private int y;

  public DistanceComparatorSource(int x, int y) {     ❷ Give constructor
    this.x = x;                                          base location
    this.y = y;
  }

  public ScoreDocComparator newComparator(    ❸ newComparator
      IndexReader reader, String fieldname) throws IOException {
    return new DistanceScoreDocLookupComparator(
        reader, fieldname, x, y);
  }

  private static class DistanceScoreDocLookupComparator    ❹
      implements ScoreDocComparator {                     ScoreDocComparator
    private float[] distances;       ❺ Array of
                                       distances
    public DistanceScoreDocLookupComparator(IndexReader reader,
              String fieldname, int x, int y) throws IOException {

      final TermEnum enumerator =
          reader.terms(new Term(fieldname, ""));
      distances = new float[reader.maxDoc()];
      if (distances.length > 0) {
        TermDocs termDocs = reader.termDocs();
        try {
          if (enumerator.term() == null) {
            throw new RuntimeException(
                "no terms in field " + fieldname);
          }
          do {                                            ❻ Iterate over
            Term term = enumerator.term();                  terms
            if (term.field() != fieldname) break;
            termDocs.seek(enumerator);
            while (termDocs.next()) {
              String[] xy = term.text().split(",");
              int deltax = Integer.parseInt(xy[0]) - x;
              int deltay = Integer.parseInt(xy[1]) - y;

              distances[termDocs.doc()] = (float) Math.sqrt(
                  deltax * deltax + deltay * deltay);      ❼
            }                                       ❽      Iterate over
          } while (enumerator.next());            Compute   documents
        } finally {                               and store containing
          termDocs.close();                       distance current term
        }
```

```
        }
      }

      public int compare(ScoreDoc i, ScoreDoc j) {
        if (distances[i.doc] < distances[j.doc]) return -1;         ❾  compare
        if (distances[i.doc] > distances[j.doc]) return 1;
        return 0;
      }

      public Comparable sortValue(ScoreDoc i) {
        return new Float(distances[i.doc]);
      }                                                        ❿  sortValue

      public int sortType() {
        return SortField.FLOAT;
      }
    }

    public String toString() {
      return "Distance from ("+x+","+y+")";
    }

  }
```

❶ First we implement SortComparatorSource.

❷ The constructor is handed the base location from which results are sorted by distance.

❸ This is SortComparatorSource's only method. Lucene itself handles the caching of ScoreDocComparators.

❹ This is our custom ScoreDocComparator implementation.

❺ Here we create an array of distances.

❻ We iterate over all the terms in the specified field.

❼ Next, we iterate over every document containing the current term.

❽ We compute and store the distance.

❾ The compare method is used by the high-level searching API when the actual distance isn't needed.

❿ The sortValue method is used by the lower-level searching API when the distance value is desired.

The sorting infrastructure within Lucene caches (based on a key combining the hashcode of the IndexReader, the field name, and the custom sort object) the result of newComparator. Our DistanceScoreDocLookupComparator implementation makes space to store a float for every document in the index and computes the distance from the base location to each document containing the specified sort field (location in our example). In a homogeneous index where all documents have the same fields, this would involve computing the distance for every document. Given these steps, it's imperative that you're aware of the resources utilized to sort; this topic is discussed in more detail in section 5.1.9 as well as in Lucene's Javadocs.

Sorting by runtime information such as a user's location is an incredibly powerful feature. At this point, though, we still have a missing piece: What is the distance from each of the restaurants to our current location? When using the Hits-returning search methods, we can't get to the distance computed. However, a lower-level API lets us access the values used for sorting.

6.1.1 Accessing values used in custom sorting

Beyond the IndexSearcher.search methods you've seen thus far, some lower-level methods are used internally to Lucene and aren't that useful to the outside. The exception enters with accessing custom sorting values, like the distance to each of the restaurants computed by our custom comparator source. The signature of the method we use, on IndexSearcher, is

```
public TopFieldDocs search(Query query, Filter filter,
                    final int nDocs, Sort sort)
```

TopFieldDocs contains the total number of Hits, the SortField array used for sorting, and an array of FieldDoc objects. A FieldDoc encapsulates the computed raw score, document ID, and an array of Comparables with the value used for each Sort-Field. TopFieldDocs and FieldDoc are specific to searching with a Sort, but a similar low-level API exists when sorting isn't being used: It returns TopDocs (parent class of TopFieldDocs) containing an array of ScoreDoc (parent class of FieldDoc) objects. Rather than concerning ourselves with the details of the API, which you can get from Lucene's Javadocs or the source code, let's see how to really use it.

Listing 6.3's test case demonstrates the use of TopFieldDocs and FieldDoc to retrieve the distance computed during sorting, this time sorting from Work at location (10,10).

Listing 6.3 Accessing custom sorting values for search results

```
public void testNeareastRestaurantToWork() throws Exception {
    Sort sort = new Sort(new SortField("location",        Specify maximum
        new DistanceComparatorSource(10, 10)));                hits returned

    TopFieldDocs docs = searcher.search(query, null, 3, sort);    ❶

    assertEquals(4, docs.totalHits);        ❷ Total number of hits
```

```
assertEquals(3, docs.scoreDocs.length);        ❸ Return total number
                                                   of documents
FieldDoc fieldDoc = (FieldDoc) docs.scoreDocs[0];      ❹ Get sorting
                                                          values
assertEquals("(10,10) -> (9,6) = sqrt(17)",
    new Float(Math.sqrt(17)),
    fieldDoc.fields[0]);     ❺ Give value of first
                                computation
Document document = searcher.doc(fieldDoc.doc);        ❻ Get Document
assertEquals("Los Betos", document.get("name"));
}
```

❶ This lower-level API requires that we specify the maximum number of hits returned.

❷ The total number of hits is still provided because all hits need to be determined to find the three best ones.

❸ The total number of documents (up to the maximum specified) are returned.

❹ `docs.scoreDocs(0)` returns a `ScoreDoc` and must be cast to `FieldDoc` to get sorting values.

❺ The value of the first (and only, in this example) `SortField` computation is available in the first `fields` slot.

❻ Getting the actual `Document` requires another call.

This lower-level API required that we specify how many search results we desired, which is different than `Hits`-returning methods. In this case, limiting our results to the three closest restaurants is more realistic anyway, because anything further away isn't what users want.

The lower-level `search` methods aren't useful to developers except in this particular case, so we don't discuss them elsewhere. However, this is currently the only way to get custom sort values. If you're sorting on any of the standard `Sort-Field` options, the values are available from `Hits` and the `Document` itself, so use this lower-level interface only in this custom sorting scenario.

6.2 *Developing a custom HitCollector*

In most applications with full-text search, users are looking for the most relevant documents from a query. The most common usage pattern is such that only the first few highest-scoring hits are visited. In some scenarios, though, users want to be shown all documents (by ID) that match a query without needing to access the contents of the document; search filters, discussed in section 5.5, may use `HitCollector`s efficiently in this manner. Another possible use, which we demonstrate in this section, is accessing every document's contents from a search in a direct fashion.

Using a Hits-returning search method will work to collect all documents if you traverse all the hits and process them manually, although you're incurring the effort of the caching mechanism within Hits. Using a custom HitCollector class avoids the Hits collection.

6.2.1 *About BookLinkCollector*

We've developed a custom HitCollector, called BookLinkCollector, which builds a map of all unique URLs and the corresponding book titles matching a query. The collect(int, float) method must be implemented from the HitCollector interface. BookLinkCollector is shown in listing 6.4.

Listing 6.4   Custom HitCollector: collects all book hyperlinks

```
public class BookLinkCollector extends HitCollector {
  private IndexSearcher searcher;
  private HashMap documents = new HashMap();

  public BookLinkCollector(IndexSearcher searcher) {
    this.searcher = searcher;
  }

  public void collect(int id, float score) {
    try {                                         Access documents
      Document doc = searcher.doc(id);         ◄─┘ by ID
      documents.put(doc.get("url"), doc.get("title"));
    } catch (IOException e) {
      // ignored
    }
  }

  public Map getLinks() {
    return Collections.unmodifiableMap(documents);
  }
}
```

Our collector collects all book titles (by URL) that match the query.

6.2.2 *Using BookLinkCollector*

Using a HitCollector requires the use of an use of IndexSearcher's search method variant as shown here:

```
public void testCollecting() throws Exception {
  TermQuery query = new TermQuery(new Term("contents", "junit"));
  IndexSearcher searcher = getSearcher();

  BookLinkCollector collector = new BookLinkCollector(searcher);
  searcher.search(query, collector);
  searcher.close();

  Map linkMap = collector.getLinks();
  assertEquals("Java Development with Ant",
               linkMap.get("http://www.manning.com/antbook"));;
}
```

Calling `IndexSearcher.doc(n)` or `IndexReader.document(n)` in the `collect` method can slow searches by an order of magnitude, so be sure your situation requires access to all the documents. In our example, we're sure we want the title and URL of each document matched. Stopping a `HitCollector` midstream is a bit of a hack, though, because there is no built-in mechanism to allow for this. To stop a `HitCollector`, you must throw a runtime exception and be prepared to catch it where you invoke `search`.

Filters (see section 5.5), such as `QueryFilter`, can use a `HitCollector` to set bits on a `BitSet` when documents are matched, and don't access the underlying documents directly; this is a highly efficient use of `HitCollector`.

The score passed to the `collect` method is the raw, denormalized, score. This can differ from `Hits.score(int)`, which will be normalized to be between 0 and 1 if the top-scoring document is greater than 1.0.

6.3 Extending QueryParser

In section 3.5, we introduced `QueryParser` and showed that it has a few settings to control its behavior, such as setting the locale for date parsing and controlling the default phrase slop. `QueryParser` is also extensible, allowing subclassing to override parts of the query-creation process. In this section, we demonstrate subclassing `QueryParser` to disallow inefficient wildcard and fuzzy queries, custom date-range handling, and morphing phrase queries into `SpanNearQuery`s instead of `PhraseQuery`s.

6.3.1 Customizing QueryParser's behavior

Although `QueryParser` has some quirks, such as the interactions with an analyzer, it does have extensibility points that allow for customization. Table 6.1 details the methods designed for overriding and why you may want to do so.

Table 6.1   `QueryParser`'s extensibility points

Method	Why override?
getFieldQuery(String field, Analyzer analyzer, String queryText) or getFieldQuery(String field, Analyzer analyzer, String queryText, int slop)	These methods are responsible for the construction of either a `TermQuery` or a `PhraseQuery`. If special analysis is needed, or a unique type of query is desired, override this method. For example, a `SpanNearQuery` can replace `PhraseQuery` to force ordered phrase matches.
getFuzzyQuery(String field, String termStr)	Fuzzy queries can adversely affect performance. Override and throw a `ParseException` to disallow fuzzy queries.
getPrefixQuery(String field, String termStr)	This method is used to construct a query when the term ends with an asterisk. The term string handed to this method doesn't include the trailing asterisk and isn't analyzed. Override this method to perform any desired analysis.
getRangeQuery(String field, Analyzer analyzer, String start, String end, boolean inclusive)	Default range-query behavior has several noted quirks (see section 3.5.5). Overriding could: ■ Lowercase the start and end terms ■ Use a different date format ■ Handle number ranges by padding to match how numbers were indexed
getWildcardQuery(String field, String termStr)	Wildcard queries can adversely affect performance, so overridden methods could throw a `ParseException` to disallow them. Alternatively, since the term string isn't analyzed, special handling may be desired.

All of the methods listed return a `Query`, making it possible to construct something other than the current subclass type used by the original implementations of these methods. Also, each of these methods may throw a `ParseException` allowing for error handling.

6.3.2   *Prohibiting fuzzy and wildcard queries*

The custom subclass in listing 6.5 demonstrates a custom query parser subclass that disables fuzzy and wildcard queries by taking advantage of the `Parse-Exception` option.

Listing 6.5   Disallowing wildcard and fuzzy queries

```
public class CustomQueryParser extends QueryParser {
  public CustomQueryParser(String field, Analyzer analyzer) {
```

```
        super(field, analyzer);
    }

    protected final Query getWildcardQuery(
            String field, String termStr) throws ParseException {
        throw new ParseException("Wildcard not allowed");
    }

    protected final Query getFuzzyQuery(
            String field, String termStr) throws ParseException {
        throw new ParseException("Fuzzy queries not allowed");
    }
}
```

To use this custom parser and prevent users from executing wildcard and fuzzy queries, construct an instance of CustomQueryParser and use it exactly as you would QueryParser, as shown in the following code. Be careful not to call the static parse method that uses the built-in QueryParser behavior:

```
public void testCustomQueryParser() {
    CustomQueryParser parser =
        new CustomQueryParser("field", analyzer);
    try {
        parser.parse("a?t");
        fail("Wildcard queries should not be allowed");
    } catch (ParseException expected) {
        // expected
        assertTrue(true);
    }

    try {
        parser.parse("xunit~");
        fail("Fuzzy queries should not be allowed");
    } catch (ParseException expected) {
        // expected
        assertTrue(true);
    }
}
```

With this implementation, both of these expensive query types are forbidden, giving you some peace of mind in terms of performance and errors that may arise from these queries expanding into too many terms.

6.3.3 *Handling numeric field-range queries*

Lucene is all about dealing with text. You've seen in several places how dates can be handled, which amounts to their being converted into a text representation that can be ordered alphabetically. Handling numbers is basically the same, except implementing a conversion to a text format is left up to you.

In this section, our example scenario indexes an integer id field so that range queries can be performed. If we indexed toString representations of the integers 1 through 10, the order in the index would be 1, 10, 2, 3, 4, 5, 6, 7, 8, 9— not the intended order at all. However, if we pad the numbers with leading zeros so that all numbers have the same width, the order is correct: 01, 02, 03, and so on. You'll have to decide on the maximum width your numbers need; we chose 10 digits and implemented the following pad(int) utility method:[3]

```
public class NumberUtils {
  private static final DecimalFormat formatter =
      new DecimalFormat("0000000000");

  public static String pad(int n) {
    return formatter.format(n);
  }
}
```

The numbers need to be padded during indexing. This is done in our test setUp() method on the id keyword field:

```
public class AdvancedQueryParserTest extends TestCase {
  private Analyzer analyzer;
  private RAMDirectory directory;

  protected void setUp() throws Exception {
    super.setUp();
    analyzer = new WhitespaceAnalyzer();

    directory = new RAMDirectory();
    IndexWriter writer = new IndexWriter(directory, analyzer,
      true);
    for (int i = 1; i <= 500; i++) {
      Document doc = new Document();
      doc.add(Field.Keyword("id", NumberUtils.pad(i)));
      writer.addDocument(doc);
    }
    writer.close();
  }
}
```

With this index-time padding, we're only halfway there. A query expression for IDs 37 through 346 phrased as id:[37 TO 346] won't work as expected with the

---

[3] Lucene stores term information with prefix compression so that no penalty is paid for large shared prefixes like this zero padding.

default RangeQuery created by QueryParser. The values are taken literally and aren't padded as they were when indexed. Fortunately we can fix this problem in our CustomQueryParser by overriding the getRangeQuery() method:

```
protected Query getRangeQuery(String field, Analyzer analyzer,
                              String part1, String part2,
                              boolean inclusive)
    throws ParseException {
  if ("id".equals(field)) {
    try {
      int num1 = Integer.parseInt(part1);
      int num2 = Integer.parseInt(part2);
      return new RangeQuery(
          new Term(field, NumberUtils.pad(num1)),
          new Term(field, NumberUtils.pad(num2)),
          inclusive);
    } catch (NumberFormatException e) {
      throw new ParseException(e.getMessage());
    }
  }

  return super.getRangeQuery(field, analyzer, part1, part2,
      inclusive);
}
```

This implementation is specific to our id field; you may want to generalize it for more fields. If the field isn't id, it delegates to the default behavior. The id field is treated specially, and the pad function is called just as with indexing. The following test case shows that the range query worked as expected, and you can see the results of the padding using Query's toString(String) method:

```
public void testIdRangeQuery() throws Exception {
  CustomQueryParser parser =
      new CustomQueryParser("field", analyzer);

  Query query = parser.parse("id:[37 TO 346]");

  assertEquals("padded", "id:[0000000037 TO 0000000346]",
                       query.toString("field"));

  IndexSearcher searcher = new IndexSearcher(directory);
  Hits hits = searcher.search(query);

  assertEquals(310, hits.length());
}
```

Our test shows that we've succeeded in allowing sensible-looking user-entered range queries to work as expected.

6.3.4 *Allowing ordered phrase queries*

When QueryParser parses a single term, or terms within double quotes, it delegates the construction of the Query to a getFieldQuery method. Parsing an unquoted term calls the getFieldQuery method without the slop signature (slop makes sense only on multiterm phrase query); parsing a quoted phrase calls the getFieldQuery signature with the slop factor, which internally delegates to the nonslop signature to build the query and then sets the slop appropriately. The Query returned is either a TermQuery or a PhraseQuery, by default, depending on whether one or more tokens are returned from the analyzer.[4] Given enough slop, PhraseQuery will match terms out of order in the original text. There is no way to force a PhraseQuery to match in order (except with slop of 0 or 1). However, SpanNearQuery does allow in-order matching. A straightforward override of get-FieldQuery allows us to replace a PhraseQuery with an ordered SpanNearQuery:

```
    protected Query getFieldQuery(
        String field, Analyzer analyzer, String queryText, int slop)
                                            throws ParseException {
      Query orig = super.getFieldQuery(field, analyzer, queryText);    ❶

      if (! (orig instanceof PhraseQuery)) {
        return orig;
      }

      PhraseQuery pq = (PhraseQuery) orig;
      Term[] terms = pq.getTerms();
      SpanTermQuery[] clauses = new SpanTermQuery[terms.length];
      for (int i = 0; i < terms.length; i++) {
        clauses[i] = new SpanTermQuery(terms[i]);
      }

      SpanNearQuery query = new SpanNearQuery(
          clauses, slop, true);

      return query;
    }
```

❶ **Delegate to QueryParser's implementation**

❷ **Only override PhraseQuery**

❸ **Pull all terms**

❹ **Create SpanNearQuery**

❶ We delegate to QueryParser's implementation for analysis and determination of query type.

❷ Here we override PhraseQuery and return anything else right away.

❸ We pull all terms from the original PhraseQuery.

❹ Finally, we create a SpanNearQuery with all the terms from the original PhraseQuery.

---

[4] A PhraseQuery could be created from a single term if the analyzer created more than one token for it.

Our test case shows that our custom `getFieldQuery` is effective in creating a `Span-NearQuery`:

```
public void testPhraseQuery() throws Exception {
  CustomQueryParser parser =
      new CustomQueryParser("field", analyzer);

  Query query = parser.parse("singleTerm");
  assertTrue("TermQuery", query instanceof TermQuery);

  query = parser.parse("\"a phrase\"");
  assertTrue("SpanNearQuery", query instanceof SpanNearQuery);
}
```

Another possible enhancement would add a toggle switch to the custom query parser, allowing the in-order flag to be controlled by the user of the API.

6.4 *Using a custom filter*

If all the information needed to perform filtering is in the index, there is no need to write your own filter because the `QueryFilter` can handle it. However, there are good reasons to factor external information into a custom filter. Using our book example data and pretending we're running an online bookstore, we want users to be able to search within our special hot deals of the day. One option is to store the specials flag in an index field. However, the specials change frequently. Rather than reindex documents when specials change, we opt to keep the specials flagged in our (hypothetical) relational database.

To do this right, we want it to be test-driven and demonstrate how our `Specials-Filter` can pull information from an external source without even having an external source! Using an interface, a mock object, and good ol' JUnit, here we go. First, here's the interface for retrieving specials:

```
public interface SpecialsAccessor {
  String[] isbns();
}
```

Since we won't have an enormous amount of specials at one time, returning all the ISBNs of the books on special will suffice.

Now that we have a retrieval interface, we can write our custom filter, `Specials-Filter`. Filters extend from the `org.jakarta.lucene.search.Filter` class and must implement the `bits(IndexReader reader)` method, returning a `BitSet`. Bit positions match the document numbers. Enabled bits mean the document for that position is available to be searched against the query, and unset bits mean the

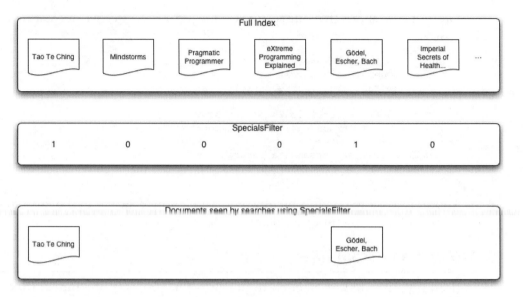

Figure 6.2 Filtering for books on special

document won't be considered in the search. Figure 6.2 illustrates an example `SpecialsFilter` that sets bits for books on special (see listing 6.6).

Listing 6.6 `SpecialsFilter`: a custom filter that retrieves information from an external source

```
public class SpecialsFilter extends Filter {
  private SpecialsAccessor accessor;

  public SpecialsFilter(SpecialsAccessor accessor) {
    this.accessor = accessor;
  }

  public BitSet bits(IndexReader reader) throws IOException {
    BitSet bits = new BitSet(reader.maxDoc());

    String[] isbns = accessor.isbns();          ❶ Fetch ISBNs

    int[] docs = new int[1];
    int[] freqs = new int[1];

    for (int i = 0; i < isbns.length; i++) {
      String isbn = isbns[i];
      if (isbn != null) {
        TermDocs termDocs =
            reader.termDocs(new Term("isbn", isbn));   ❷ Jump to term
```

```
            int count = termDocs.read(docs, freqs);
            if (count == 1) {
              bits.set(docs[0]);
            }
          }
        }

        return bits;
      }
    }
```

❸ Set corresponding bit

❶ Here, we fetch the ISBNs of the specials we want to enable for searching.

❷ isbn is indexed as a Keyword field and is unique, so we use IndexReader to jump directly to the term.

❸ With the matching document found, we set its corresponding bit.

Returning null from the bits() method is the same as lighting up all the bits. All documents will be considered, just as if the query had been done without the use of a filter.

To test that our filter is working, we created a simple MockSpecialsAccessor to return a specified set of ISBNs, giving our test case control over the set of specials:

```
public class MockSpecialsAccessor implements SpecialsAccessor {
  private String[] isbns;

  public MockSpecialsAccessor(String[] isbns) {
    this.isbns = isbns;
  }

  public String[] isbns() {
    return isbns;
  }
}
```

Here's how we test our SpecialsFilter, using the same setUp() that the other filter tests used:

```
public void testCustomFilter() throws Exception {
  String[] isbns = new String[] {"0060812451"};

  SpecialsAccessor accessor = new MockSpecialsAccessor(isbns);
  Filter filter = new SpecialsFilter(accessor);
  Hits hits = searcher.search(allBooks, filter);
  assertEquals("the specials", isbns.length, hits.length());
}
```

We use a generic query that is broad enough to retrieve all the books, making assertions easier to craft; but because our filter trimmed the search space, only the specials are returned. With this infrastructure in place, implementing a `Specials-Accessor` to retrieve a list of ISBNs from a database should be easy; doing so is left as an exercise for the savvy reader.

Note that we made an important implementation decision *not* to cache the `Bit Set` in `SpecialsFilter`. Decorating `SpecialsFilter` with a `CachingWrapperFilter` frees us from that aspect.

6.4.1 *Using a filtered query*

To add to the *filter* terminology overload, one final option is new in Lucene 1.4: `FilteredQuery`.[5] `FilteredQuery` inverts the situation that searching with a `Filter` presents. Using a `Filter` an `IndexSearcher`'s search method applies a single filter prior to querying. Using the new `FilteredQuery`, though, you can apply a `Filter` to a particular query clause of a `BooleanQuery`.

Let's take the `SpecialsFilter` as an example again. This time, we want a more sophisticated query: books in an education category on special, or books on Logo.[6] We couldn't accomplish this with a direct query using the techniques shown thus far, but `FilteredQuery` makes this possible. Had our search been only for books in the education category on special, we could have used the technique shown in the previous code snippet, instead.

Our test case, in listing 6.7, demonstrates the described query using a `Boolean-Query` with a nested `TermQuery` and `FilteredQuery`.

Listing 6.7 Using a `FilteredQuery`

```
public void testFilteredQuery() throws Exception {
    String[] isbns = new String[] {"0854402624"};        ❶ Rudolf Steiner's book

    SpecialsAccessor accessor = new MockSpecialsAccessor(isbns);
    Filter filter = new SpecialsFilter(accessor);

    WildcardQuery educationBooks =
        new WildcardQuery(new Term("category", "*education*"));
    FilteredQuery edBooksOnSpecial =                       All education  ❷
        new FilteredQuery(educationBooks, filter);          books on
                                                             special
```

---

[5] We're sorry! We know that `Filter`, `QueryFilter`, `FilteredQuery`, and the completely unrelated `Token-Filter` names can be confusing.

[6] Erik began his programming adventures with Logo on an Apple][e. Times haven't changed much; now he tinkers with StarLogo on a PowerBook.

```
TermQuery logoBooks =
    new TermQuery(new Term("subject", "logo"));

BooleanQuery logoOrEdBooks = new BooleanQuery();
logoOrEdBooks.add(logoBooks, false, false);
logoOrEdBooks.add(edBooksOnSpecial, false, false);

Hits hits = searcher.search(logoOrEdBooks);
System.out.println(logoOrEdBooks.toString());
assertEquals("Papert and Steiner", 2, hits.length());
}
```

❸ All books with "logo" in subject

❹ Combine queries

❶ This is the ISBN number for Rudolf Steiner's *A Modern Art of Education*.

❷ We construct a query for education books on special, which only includes Steiner's book in this example.

❸ We construct a query for all books with *logo* in the subject, which only includes *Mindstorms* in our sample data.

❹ The two queries are combined in an OR fashion.

The `bits()` method of the nested `Filter` is called each time a `FilteredQuery` is used in a search, so we recommend that you use a caching filter if the query is to be used repeatedly and the results of a filter don't change.

6.5 *Performance testing*

Lucene is fast and scalable. But how fast is it? Is it fast enough? Can you guarantee that searches are returned within a reasonable amount of time? How does Lucene respond under load?

If your project has high performance demands, you've done the right thing by choosing Lucene, but don't let performance numbers be a mystery. There are several ways Lucene's performance can be negatively impacted by how you use it—like using fuzzy or wildcard queries or a range query, as you'll see in this section.

We've been highlighting unit testing throughout the book using the basics of JUnit. In this section, we utilize another unit-testing gem, JUnitPerf. JUnitPerf, a JUnit decorator, allows JUnit tests to be measured for load and speed.

6.5.1 *Testing the speed of a search*

We've discussed how `FuzzyQuery` and `WildcardQuery` have the potential to get out of control. In a similar fashion, `RangeQuery` can, too: As it enumerates all the terms in the range, it forms a `BooleanQuery` that can potentially be large.

The infamous Mike "addicted to the green bar" Clark has graciously donated some Lucene performance tests to us.[7] Let's examine a concrete example in which we determine that a searching performance issue is caused by how we index, and find out how we can easily fix this issue. We rely on JUnitPerf to identify the issue and ensure that it's fixed and stays fixed.

We're indexing documents that have a last-modified timestamp. For example purposes, we index a sample of 1,000 fabricated documents with timestamps increasing in 1-second increments, starting yesterday:

```
Calendar timestamp = GregorianCalendar.getInstance();
timestamp.set(Calendar.DATE,
    timestamp.get(Calendar.DATE) - 1);          ❶ Yesterday

for (int i = 0; i < size; i++) {
  timestamp.set(Calendar.SECOND,
      timestamp.get(Calendar.SECOND) + 1);      ❷ Increase I second
  Date now = timestamp.getTime();
  Document document = new Document();
  document.add(Field.Keyword("last-modified", now));   ❸ As Date
  writer.addDocument(document);
}
```

Being the test-infected coders we are, we even ensure that our search is returning the expected results by searching over a timestamp range that encompasses all documents indexed:

```
public void testSearchByTimestamp() throws Exception {
  Search s = new Search();
  Hits hits = s.searchByTimestamp(janOneTimestamp,
                                  todayTimestamp);
  assertEquals(1000, hits.length());
}
```

searchByTimestamp performs a RangeQuery:[8]

```
public Hits searchByTimestamp(Date begin, Date end)
    throws Exception {
  Term beginTerm = new Term("last-modified",
      DateField.dateToString(begin));
  Term endTerm = new Term("last-modified",
      DateField.dateToString(end));
```

---

[7] Mike is the coauthor of *Bitter EJB* (Manning) and the author of *Pragmatic Automation* (Pragmatic Bookshelf); http://www.clarkware.com.

[8] We're intentionally skipping bits of Mike's test infrastructure to keep our discussion focused on the performance-testing aspect rather than get bogged down following his nicely decoupled code. See the "about this book" section at the beginning of the book for details on obtaining the full source code.

```
    Query query = new RangeQuery(beginTerm, endTerm, true);

    return newSearcher(
        index.byTimestampIndexDirName()).search(query);
}
```

At this point, all is well. We've indexed 1,000 documents and found them all using an encompassing date RangeQuery. Ship it! Whoa...not so fast...what if we had indexed 2,000 documents? Here's what happens when we run the test-SearchByTimestamp() test method:

org.apache.lucene.search.BooleanQuery$TooManyClauses
```
        at org.apache.lucene.search.BooleanQuery.add(BooleanQuery.java:109)
        at org.apache.lucene.search.BooleanQuery.add(BooleanQuery.java:101)
        at org.apache.lucene.search.RangeQuery.rewrite(RangeQuery.java:137)
        at
    org.apache.lucene.search.IndexSearcher.rewrite(IndexSearcher.java:227)
        at org.apache.lucene.search.Query.weight(Query.java:84)
        at
    org.apache.lucene.search.IndexSearcher.search(IndexSearcher.java:129)
        at org.apache.lucene.search.Hits.getMoreDocs(Hits.java:102)
        at org.apache.lucene.search.Hits.<init>(Hits.java:81)
        at org.apache.lucene.search.Searcher.search(Searcher.java:71)
        at org.apache.lucene.search.Searcher.search(Searcher.java:65)
        at lia.advsearching.perf.Search.searchByTimestamp(Search.java:40)
        at
    lia.advsearching.perf.SearchTest.testSearchByTimestamp(SearchTest.java:24)
```

Our dataset is only 2,000 documents, which is no problem for Lucene to handle. But a RangeQuery internally rewrites itself to a BooleanQuery with a nonrequired clause for every term in the range. That is, with 2,000 documents being indexed, the searchByTimestamp() method will cause 2,000 OR'd TermQuerys nested in a BooleanQuery. This exceeds the default limit of 1,024 clauses to a BooleanQuery, which prevents queries from getting carried away.

Modifying the index

For searching purposes, though, the goal is to be able to search by date range. It's unlikely we'll need to search for documents in a range of seconds, so using this fine-grained timestamp isn't necessary. In fact, it's problematic. Indexing 1,000 or 2,000 documents in successive second timestamp increments gives each document a completely unique term, all within the span of less than an hour's worth of timestamps.

Since searching by day, not second, is the real goal, let's index the documents by day instead:

```
String today = Search.today();

for (int i = 0; i < size; i++) {
  Document document = new Document();
  document.add(Field.Keyword("last-modified", today));
  writer.addDocument(document);
}
```

Here, `today` is set to YYYYMMDD format. Remember, terms are sorted alphabetically, so numbers need to take this into account (see section 6.3.3 for a number-padding example):

```
public static String today() {
  SimpleDateFormat dateFormat =
      (SimpleDateFormat) SimpleDateFormat.getDateInstance();
  dateFormat.applyPattern("yyyyMMdd");
  return dateFormat.format(todayTimestamp());
}
```

Notice that we're using a `String` value for `today` (such as 20040715) rather than using the `DateField.dateToString()` method. Regardless of whether you index by timestamp or by YYYYMMDD format, the documents all have the same year, month, and day; so in our second try at indexing a last-modified field, there is only a single term in the index, not thousands. This is a dramatic improvement that's easily spotted in JUnitPerf tests. You can certainly keep a timestamp field in the document, too—it just shouldn't be a field used in range queries.

Testing the timestamp-based index

Listing 6.8 is a JUnitPerf `TimedTest`, testing that our original 1,000 documents are found in 100 milliseconds or less.

Listing 6.8   JUnitPerf-decorated timed test

```
public class SearchTimedTest {

  public static Test suite() {
    int maxTimeInMillis = 100;

    Test test = new SearchTest("testSearchByTimestamp");
    TestSuite suite = new TestSuite();

    suite.addTest(test);              ❶ Warmup test
    suite.addTest(new TimedTest(test, maxTimeInMillis));   ❷ Wrap test in
                                                              TimedTest
    return suite;
  }
}
```

❶ We first run one test to warm up the JVM prior to timing.

❷ Then, we wrap the simple test inside a `TimedTest`, asserting that it runs in 100 milliseconds or less.

This test fails because it exceeds the 100-millisecond constraint:

```
[junit] Testcase: testSearchByTimestamp(lia.advsearching.perf.SearchTest):
  FAILED
    [junit] Maximum elapsed time exceeded! Expected 100ms, but was 138ms.
    [junit] junit.framework.AssertionFailedError: Maximum elapsed time
  exceeded! Expected 100ms, but was 138ms.
    [junit]        at
  com.clarkware.junitperf.TimedTest.runUntilTestCompletion(Unknown Source)
    [junit]        at com.clarkware.junitperf.TimedTest.run(Unknown Source)
```

The test failed, but not by much. Of course, when 2,000 documents are attempted it fails horribly with a `TooManyClauses` exception.

Testing the date-based index

Now let's write a unit test that uses the YYYYMMDD range:

```
public void testSearchByDay() throws Exception {
  Search s = new Search();
  Hits hits = s.searchByDay("20040101", today);
  assertEquals(1000, hits.length());
}
```

The value of `today` in `testSearchByDay()` is the current date in YYYYMMDD format. Now we replace one line in `SearchTimedTest` with a `testSearchByDay()`:

```
Test test = new SearchTest("testSearchByDay");
```

Our `SearchTimedTest` now passes with flying colors (see figure 6.3 for timings of `SearchTest` under load).

6.5.2 Load testing

Not only can JUnitPerf decorate a test and assert that it executes in a tolerated amount of time, it can also perform load tests by simulating a number of concurrent users. The same decorator pattern is used as with a `TimedTest`. Decorating a `TimedTest` with a `LoadTest` is the general usage, as shown in listing 6.9.

> **Listing 6.9 Load test**

```
public class SearchLoadTest {

  public static Test suite() {

    int maxTimeInMillis = 100;
```

```
        int concurrentUsers = 10;

        Test test = new SearchTest("testSearchByDay");

        TestSuite suite = new TestSuite();
        suite.addTest(test);
        Test timedTest = new TimedTest(test, maxTimeInMillis);
        LoadTest loadTest = new LoadTest(timedTest, concurrentUsers);
        suite.addTest(loadTest);

        return suite;
    }
}
```

**Wrap basic test
with TimedTest** ❶

❷

**Wrap TimedTest
in LoadTest**

❶ We wrap the basic test (ensuring that 1,000 hits are found) with a `TimedTest`.

❷ Then we wrap the `TimedTest` in a `LoadTest`, which executes the `TimedTest` 10 times concurrently.

`SearchLoadTest` executes `testSearchByDay()` 10 times concurrently, with each thread required to execute in under 100 milliseconds. It should be no surprise that switching the `SearchLoadTest` to run `SearchTest.testSearchByTimestamp()` causes a failure, since it fails even the `SearchTimedTest`. The timings of each `SearchTest`, run as 10 concurrent tests, are shown in figure 6.3.

The results indicate that each test performed well under the 100-millisecond requirement, even running under concurrent load.

6.5.3 *QueryParser again!*

`QueryParser` rears its ugly head again with our changed date format. The built-in date-range handling parses `DateFormat.SHORT` formats into the `DateField` text conversions. It would be nice to let users enter a typical date format like 1/1/04 and have it converted to our revised date format of YYYYMMDD. This can be

Test	Time elapsed
Total:	**0.154 s**
testSearchByDay	0.016 s
testSearchByDay	0.009 s
testSearchByDay	0.006 s
testSearchByDay	0.005 s
testSearchByDay	0.006 s
testSearchByDay	0.007 s
testSearchByDay	0.069 s
testSearchByDay	0.005 s
testSearchByDay	0.009 s
testSearchByDay	0.022 s

**Figure 6.3
Performance test results for 10 concurrent
`SearchTests`, each required to complete
in 100 milliseconds or less**

done in a similar fashion to what we did in section 6.3.3 to pad integers for range queries. The desired effect is shown in the following test:

```
public void testQueryParsing() throws Exception {
   SmartDayQueryParser parser =
      new SmartDayQueryParser("contents",
         new StandardAnalyzer());

   Query query =
      parser.parse("last-modified:[1/1/04 TO 2/29/04]");

   assertEquals("last-modified:[20040101 TO 20040229]",
      query.toString("contents"));
}
```

Now that we have our desired effect coded as a test case, let's make it pass by coding SmartDayQueryParser.

Understanding *SmartDayQueryParser*

The SmartDayQueryParser is a simple adaptation of the built-in QueryParser's getRangeQuery method:

```
public class SmartDayQueryParser extends QueryParser {
   public static final DateFormat formatter =
      new SimpleDateFormat("yyyyMMdd");

   public SmartDayQueryParser(String field, Analyzer analyzer) {
      super(field, analyzer);
   }

   protected Query getRangeQuery(String field, Analyzer analyzer,
                                 String part1, String part2,
                                 boolean inclusive)
      throws ParseException {

      try {
         DateFormat df =
            DateFormat.getDateInstance(DateFormat.SHORT,
               getLocale());
         df.setLenient(true);
         Date d1 = df.parse(part1);
         Date d2 = df.parse(part2);
         part1 = formatter.format(d1);
         part2 = formatter.format(d2);
      } catch (Exception ignored) {
      }

      return new RangeQuery(new Term(field, part1),
         new Term(field, part2),
```

```
                inclusive);
        }
    }
```

The only difference between our overridden `getRangeQuery` and the original implementation is the use of YYYYMMDD formatting.

6.5.4 *Morals of performance testing*

In addition to testing whether Lucene can perform acceptably with your environment and data, unit performance testing assists (as does basic JUnit testing) in the design of your code. In this case, you've seen how our original method of indexing dates was less than desirable even though our first unit test succeeded with the right number of results. Only when we tested with more data or with time and load constraints did an issue present itself. We could have swept the data failure under the rug temporarily by setting `BooleanQuery`'s `setMaxClause-Count(int)` to `Integer.MAX_VALUE`. However, we wouldn't be able to hide a performance test failure.

We strongly encourage you to adopt unit testing in your projects and to continue to evolve the testing codebase into performance unit testing. As you can tell from the code examples in this book, we are highly test-centric, and we also use tests for learning purposes by exploring APIs. Lucene itself is built around a strong set of unit tests, and it improves on a regular basis.

> **NOTE** We would be remiss not to recommend further reading on unit testing. *Pragmatic Unit Testing* by Dave Thomas and Andy Hunt is a concise and elegant introduction to unit testing. Manning's *JUnit in Action* is fantastic; it goes beyond the basics and delves into topics like performance testing and mock unit testing, both of which we have incorporated into the books' source code.

6.6 *Summary*

Lucene offers developers extreme flexibility in searching capabilities. Custom sorting and filters, `QueryParser` subclassing, and a `HitCollector` implementation all received attention in this chapter. Equipped with the searching features from this chapter and chapters 3 and 5, you have more than enough power and flexibility to integrate Lucene searching into your applications.

Part 2

Applied Lucene

Lucene itself is just a JAR, with the real fun and power coming from what you build around it. This section explores various ways to leverage Lucene. Projects commonly demand full-text searching of Microsoft Word, PDF, HTML, XML, and other document formats. "Parsing common document formats" illuminates the various ways to index these document types into Lucene, ultimately providing a reusable generic document-handling framework. Many "Tools and extensions" have been developed to augment and extend Lucene, with the finest ones being covered here. Although Java is the primary language used with Lucene, the index format is language neutral. The "Lucene ports" chapter details Lucene usage from languages such as C++, C#, and Python. Last, but certainly not least, several superb "Case studies" have been graciously contributed, giving you a deep look into projects that have achieved great success with Lucene's power.

7

Parsing common document formats

So far in this book, we have covered various aspects of Lucene usage. In all cases, however, we have dealt exclusively with plain-text data. In the real world, documents in plain-text format are diminishing, and in their place we increasingly find information presented in rich media documents. For example:

- Corporate environments most frequently work with PDF, Microsoft Word, or Excel documents.
- The World-Wide Web typically contains data in HTML.
- Software applications are increasingly using XML to exchange data.

Can you use Lucene to search rich-text documents like these? Yes, you can!

Although Lucene doesn't include tools to automatically index documents that aren't plain text, there are a number of free and commercial tools that you can use to extract the textual data from rich media.[1] Once extracted, you can index the data with Lucene as discussed in chapter 2.

In this chapter, we'll start by presenting a simple `DocumentHandler` interface as an abstraction to nest within a rich framework for parsing and indexing documents of any type.

Next, we'll walk through examples to show you how to parse and index various document types such as plain text, PDF, Microsoft Word, HTML, XML, and RTF with Lucene. Each example uses a third-party tool to extract the text. In addition, each example implements a specialized version of the `DocumentHandler` interface.

Finally, we'll develop a small framework capable of indexing multiple file formats. We'll use this framework to write a full-blown file-system indexer sample application.

7.1 *Handling rich-text documents*

In addition to showing you how to parse and index individual document formats, our goal in this chapter is to create a small framework that you can use to index documents commonly found in the office environment as well as on the Internet. Such a framework is useful when your goal is to index and enable users to search for files that reside in multiple directories and are of different formats, or if you need to fetch and index web pages of different content types. In both cases, using a framework that handles multiple file types automates the process of extracting the text from each file format so that you don't need to concern yourself with how

---

[1] Lucene developers purposely keep the Lucene core small and focused. Since a number of tools exist that extract text from rich media, there is no need to include duplicate functionality in Lucene.

exactly it's accomplished. We start by defining a generic `DocumentHandler` interface that defines a contract for individual document parsers.

7.1.1 *Creating a common DocumentHandler interface*

The simple interface shown in listing 7.1 consists of a single method, `get-Document(InputStream)`, which returns an instance of the Lucene `Document`. Each of the document parsers that we'll create in this chapter must implement this single method.

We use `InputStream` as the input type because all tools that we use in this chapter allow text extraction from `InputStream`. Using `InputStream` is also handy when you're indexing files in a file system, because you can turn each `File` class instance into a `FileInputStream` by using the `java.io.FileInputStream(File)` constructor.

Listing 7.1 `DocumentHandler` interface that all document format parsers will implement

```
public interface DocumentHandler {

  /**
   * Creates a Lucene Document from an InputStream.
   * This method can return <code>null</code>.
   *
   * @param is the InputStream to convert to a Document
   * @return a ready-to-index instance of Document
   */
  Document getDocument(InputStream is)
    throws DocumentHandlerException;
}
```

All implementations of this handler return an instance of the Lucene `Document` class with one or more `Field`s. Because different types of documents store different meta-data, the returned `Document` instances contain different `Field`s. For example, HTML documents typically have titles, whereas XML documents don't. Thus, the HTML `DocumentHandler` may return a `Document` with a title `Field`, but the XML `DocumentHandler` may not.

If any kind of error occurs, all classes implementing the `DocumentHandler` interface throw a `DocumentHandlerException`. This is a checked exception, a simple subclass of Java's `Exception` class, so we'll omit its listing.

In general, all the parsers in this chapter follow the steps outlined in table 7.1.

Table 7.1 Common DocumentHandler implementation steps

Step	Description
1. Process InputStream.	Take InputStream input. Read and parse the InputStream. Extract text from the InputStream.
2. Create Lucene Document.	Create an instance of Lucene Document. Create Lucene Fields with textual values extracted from the InputStream. Add Fields to the Lucene Document. Return the Lucene Document, ready to be indexed by the caller.

Finally, each implementation of DocumentHandler that we present in this chapter includes a main method, allowing you to invoke it from the command line. All main methods expect a single command-line parameter that represents a path to a file. To keep the code listings as short and simple as possible, we don't check for valid input, so make sure you always provide valid input.

The parsers you will learn about focus exclusively on input parsing and creation of Lucene Document instances, not on the actual indexing. After all, once these parsers convert their input to ready-to-index Lucene Documents, the indexing step is identical for all document types; we don't want to duplicate it in every parser implementation. Furthermore, having the wrapping framework handle the indexing decouples the architecture nicely and allows the framework to add common fields for all documents if desired (such as last modified date, file system path, URL, and so on).

Now that you have a high-level understanding of how rich-text document parsers work and how the pieces will fit together in the end, let's start with the parser implementation. XML is a common document format these days—even office applications such as OpenOffice use it as their main on-disk document format—so we'll begin with an XML parser.

7.2 *Indexing XML*

In this section, we'll convert a snippet of an XML document into a Lucene Document. First we'll use the SAX API, and then we'll use the Jakarta Commons Digest. Then we'll index the snippet with Lucene.

Listing 7.2 is an XML snippet that represents a single entry from an imaginary address book. Our ultimate goal is to make this address book searchable so we can find matching entries in it using a simple search syntax, such as name:Zane or city:"New York" (see section 3.1.2 for more details on QueryParser syntax).

```
<?xml version='1.0' encoding='utf-8'?>
<address-book>
    <contact type="individual">
        <name>Zane Pasolini</name>
        <address>999 W. Prince St.</address>
        <city>New York</city>
        <province>NY</province>
        <postalcode>10013</postalcode>
        <country>USA</country>
        <telephone>+1 212 345 6789</telephone>
    </contact>
</address-book>
```

Although it would be possible to create a powerful and flexible application that can handle XML for any Document Type Definition (DTD), the two XML `Document-Handler` implementations in this section assume the address book XML format shown in listing 7.2, in order to keep things simple.

Our XML `DocumentHandler` implementations index each subelement of the `<contact>` element. Note that the `<contact>` element has an attribute `type`. In both the SAX and Digester implementations of our `DocumentHandler`, we'll treat this attribute as just another field.

7.2.1 *Parsing and indexing using SAX*

Simple API for XML (SAX) defines an event-driven interface in which the parser invokes one of several methods supplied by the caller when a parsing event occurs. Events include beginnings and endings of documents and their elements, parsing errors, and so on.

To provide an example of extracting textual data from XML documents, we use Xerces2 Java Parser. Xerces2 Java Parser is developed under the Apache XML project and can be found at http://xml.apache.org/xerces2-j/index.html. It implements version 2.0.1 of the SAX API. This isn't the fastest XML parser currently available, but it's one of the most widely used Java XML parsers, and it has been around for many years.

Listing 7.3 shows our solution for parsing the XML address book and converting it to a Lucene `Document`.

```
public class SAXXMLHandler
  extends DefaultHandler implements DocumentHandler {
```

```
/** A buffer for each XML element */
private StringBuffer elementBuffer = new StringBuffer();
private HashMap attributeMap;

private Document doc;

public Document getDocument(InputStream is)                ❶ Implement DocumentHandler
  throws DocumentHandlerException {                          interface; start parser

  SAXParserFactory spf = SAXParserFactory.newInstance();
  try {
    SAXParser parser = spf.newSAXParser();
    parser.parse(is, this);
  }
  catch (IOException e) {
    throw new DocumentHandlerException(
      "Cannot parse XML document", e);
  }
  catch (ParserConfigurationException e) {
    throw new DocumentHandlerException(
      "Cannot parse XML document", e);
  }
  catch (SAXException e) {
    throw new DocumentHandlerException(
      "Cannot parse XML document", e);
  }

  return doc;
}

public void startDocument() {            ❷ Called when
  doc = new Document();                     parsing begins
}

public void startElement(String uri, String localName,    ❸ Beginning of new
  String qName, Attributes atts) throws SAXException {        XML element

  elementBuffer.setLength(0);
  attributeMap.clear();
  if (atts.getLength() > 0) {
    attributeMap = new HashMap();
    for (int i = 0; i < atts.getLength(); i++) {
      attributeMap.put(atts.getQName(i), atts.getValue(i));
    }
  }
}

// called when cdata is found
public void characters(char[] text, int start, int length) {   ❹
  elementBuffer.append(text, start, length);
}                                         Append element contents
                                             to elementBuffer
```

```
      // called at element end
      public void endElement(String uri, String localName, String qName)    ❺
        throws SAXException {
        if (qName.equals("address-book")) {
          return;
        }
        else if (qName.equals("contact")) {
          Iterator iter = attributeMap.keySet().iterator();
          while (iter.hasNext()) {
            String attName = (String) iter.next();
            String attValue = (String) attributeMap.get(attName);
            doc.add(Field.Keyword(attName, attValue));
          }
        }
        else {
          doc.add(Field.Keyword(qName, elementBuffer.toString()));
        }
      }

      public static void main(String args[]) throws Exception {
        SAXXMLHandler handler = new SAXXMLHandler();
        Document doc = handler.getDocument(
          new FileInputStream(new File(args[0])));
        System.out.println(doc);
      }
    }
```

Called when closing XML elements are processed

The five key methods in this listing are getDocument, startDocument, startElement, characters, and endElement. Also note the elementBuffer StringBuffer and the attributeMap HashMap. The former is used to store the textual representation of the CDATA enclosed by the current document element. Some elements may contain attributes, such as the <contact> element containing attribute type, in our address book entry. The attributeMap is used for storing names and the value of the current element's attributes.

❶ The getDocument method doesn't do much work: It creates a new SAX parser and passes it a reference to the InputStream of the XML document. From there, the parser implementation calls the other four key methods in this class, which together create a Lucene Document that is eventually returned by the getDocument method.

❷ In startDocument, which is called when XML document parsing starts, we only create a new instance of Lucene Document. This is the Document that we'll eventually populate with Fields.

❸ The startElement method is called whenever the beginning of a new XML element is found. We first erase the elementBuffer StringBuffer by setting its length to zero, and clear the attributeMap to remove data associated with the previous element. If the current element has attributes, we iterate through them and save their names and values in the `attributeMap`. In the case of the XML document in listing 7.2, this happens only when `startElement` method is called for the `<contact>` element, because only that element has an attribute.

4 The `characters` method may be called multiple times during the processing of a single XML element. In it we append to our `elementBuffer` the element contents passed into the method.

5 The last method of interest is `endElement`, where you can finally see more of Lucene in action. This method is called when the parser processes the closing tag of the current element. Therefore, this is the method where we have all the information about the XML element that was just processed. We aren't interested in indexing the top level element, `<address book>`, so we immediately return from the method in that case. Similarly, we aren't interested in indexing the `<contact>` element. However, we are interested in indexing that `<contact>`'s attributes, so we use `attributeMap` to get attribute names and values, and add them to the Lucene `Document`. All other elements of our address book entry are treated equally, and we blindly index them as keyword `Field.Keyword`. Attribute values as well element data are indexed.

If you look back to table 7.1, you'll see that the XML parser in listing 7.3 follows all the steps we outlined. As a result, we get a ready-to-index Lucene `Document` populated with `Field`s whose names are derived from XML elements' names and whose values correspond to the textual content of those elements. Although this code alone will let you index XML documents, let's look at another handy tool for parsing XML: Digester.

7.2.2 *Parsing and indexing using Digester*

Digester, located at http://jakarta.apache.org/commons/digester, is a subproject of the Jakarta Commons project. It offers a simple, high-level interface for mapping XML documents to Java objects; some developers find it easier to use than DOM or SAX XML parsers. When Digester finds developer-defined patterns in an XML document, it takes developer-specified actions.

The `DigesterXMLHandler` class in listing 7.4 parses XML documents, such as our address book entry (shown in listing 7.2), and returns a Lucene `Document` with XML elements represented as `Field`s.

Listing 7.4 `DocumentHandler` using Jakarta Commons Digester to parse XML

```
public class DigesterXMLHandler implements DocumentHandler {

    private Digester dig;
```

```
private static Document doc;

public DigesterXMLHandler() {

    // instantiate Digester and disable XML validation
    dig = new Digester();
    dig.setValidating(false);
```

**Rule 1: Create instance of
DigesterXMLHandler**

```
    // instantiate DigesterXMLHandler class
    dig.addObjectCreate("address-book", DigesterXMLHandler.class);    ❶
    // instantiate Contact class
    dig.addObjectCreate("address-book/contact", Contact.class);       ❷
```

Rule 2: Create instance of Contact

```
    // set type property of Contact instance when 'type'
    // attribute is found
    dig.addSetProperties("address-book/contact", "type", "type");     ❸
```

Rule 3: Set Contact's type attribute

```
    // set different properties of Contact instance using
    // specified methods
    dig.addCallMethod("address-book/contact/name",           ❹  Rule 4: Set Contact's
        "setName", 0);                                               name property
    dig.addCallMethod("address-book/contact/address",
        "setAddress", 0);
    dig.addCallMethod("address-book/contact/city",
        "setCity", 0);
    dig.addCallMethod("address-book/contact/province",
        "setProvince", 0);
    dig.addCallMethod("address-book/contact/postalcode",
        "setPostalcode", 0);
    dig.addCallMethod("address-book/contact/country",
        "setCountry", 0);
    dig.addCallMethod("address-book/contact/telephone",
        "setTelephone", 0);

    // call 'populateDocument' method when the next
    // 'address-book/contact' pattern is seen
    dig.addSetNext("address-book/contact", "populateDocument");       ❺
}
```

Rule 5: Call populateDocument

```
public synchronized Document getDocument(InputStream is)          ❻
    throws DocumentHandlerException {
```

**Implement
DocumentHandler interface**

```
    try {
        dig.parse(is);          ❼  Start parsing XML
    }                               InputStream
    catch (IOException e) {
        throw new DocumentHandlerException(
            "Cannot parse XML document", e);
    }
    catch (SAXException e) {
        throw new DocumentHandlerException(
```

```
            "Cannot parse XML document", e);
    }

    return doc;
}

public void populateDocument(Contact contact) {
```
                                                    **⑧ Populate Lucene
                                                    Document with Fields**
```
    // create a blank Lucene Document
    doc = new Document();

    doc.add(Field.Keyword("type", contact.getType()));
    doc.add(Field.Keyword("name", contact.getName()));
    doc.add(Field.Keyword("address", contact.getAddress()));
    doc.add(Field.Keyword("city", contact.getCity()));
    doc.add(Field.Keyword("province", contact.getProvince()));
    doc.add(Field.Keyword("postalcode", contact.getPostalcode()));
    doc.add(Field.Keyword("country", contact.getCountry()));
    doc.add(Field.Keyword("telephone", contact.getTelephone()));
}

/**
 * JavaBean class that holds properties of each Contact
 * entry.  It is important that this class be public and
 * static, in order for Digester to be able to instantiate
 * it.
 */
public static class Contact {
    private String type;
    private String name;
    private String address;
    private String city;
    private String province;
    private String postalcode;
    private String country;
    private String telephone;

    public void setType(String newType) {
        type = newType;
    }
    public String getType() {
        return type;
    }

    public void setName(String newName) {
        name = newName;
    }
    public String getName() {
        return name;
    }
```

```java
    public void setAddress(String newAddress) {
      address = newAddress;
    }
    public String getAddress() {
      return address;
    }

    public void setCity(String newCity) {
      city = newCity;
    }
    public String getCity() {
      return city;
    }

    public void setProvince(String newProvince) {
      province = newProvince;
    }
    public String getProvince() {
      return province;
    }

    public void setPostalcode(String newPostalcode) {
      postalcode = newPostalcode;
    }
    public String getPostalcode() {
      return postalcode;
    }

    public void setCountry(String newCountry) {
      country = newCountry;
    }
    public String getCountry() {
      return country;
    }

    public void setTelephone(String newTelephone) {
      telephone = newTelephone;
    }
    public String getTelephone() {
      return telephone;
    }
  }

  public static void main(String[] args) throws Exception {
    DigesterXMLHandler handler = new DigesterXMLHandler();
    Document doc =
      handler.getDocument(new FileInputStream(new File(args[0])));
    System.out.println(doc);
  }
}
```

This is a lengthy piece of code, and it deserves a few explanations. In the `Digester-XMLHandler` constructor we create an instance of Digester and configure it by specifying several rules. Each rule specifies an action and a pattern that will trigger the action when encountered.

❶ The first rule tells Digester to create an instance of the `DigesterXMLHandler` class when the pattern `"address-book"` is found. It does that by using Digester's `addObjectCreate` method. Because `<address-book>` is the opening element in our XML document, this rule is triggered first.

❷ The next rule instructs Digester to create an instance of class `Contact` when it finds the `<contact>` child element under the `<address-book>` parent, specified with the `"address-book/contact"` pattern.

❸ To handle the `<contact>` element's attribute, we set the `type` property of the `Contact` instance when Digester finds the `type` attribute of the `<contact>` element. To accomplish that, we use Digester's `addSetProperties` method. The `Contact` class is written as an inner class and contains only setter and getter methods.

❹ Our `DigesterXMLHandler` class contains several similar-looking rules, all of which call Digester's `addCallMethod` method. They're used to set various `Contact` properties. For instance, a call such as `dig.addCallMethod("address-book/contact/name", "setName", 0)` calls the `setName` method of our `Contact` instance. It does this when Digester starts processing the `<name>` element, found under the parent `<address-book>` and `<contact>` elements. The value of the `setName` method parameter is the value enclosed by `<name>` and `</name>` tags. If you consider our sample address book from listing 7.2, this would call `setName("Zane Pasolini")`.

❺ We use Digester's `addSetNext` method to specify that the `populateDocument(Contact)` method should be called when the closing `</contact>` element is processed.

❻ The `DocumentHandler`'s `getDocument` method takes an `InputStream` to the XML document to parse.

❼ Here we begin parsing the XML `InputStream`.

❽ Finally, we populates a Lucene `Document` with `Fields` containing data collected by the `Contact` class during parsing.

It's important that you consider the order in which the rules are passed to Digester. Although we could change the order of various `addSetProperties()` rules in our class and still have properly functioning code, switching the order of `addObjectCreate()` and `addSetNext()` would result in an error.

As you can see, Digester provides a high-level interface for parsing XML documents. Because we have specified our XML parsing rules programmatically, our `DigesterXMLHandler` can parse only our address book XML format. Luckily, Digester lets you specify these same rules declaratively using the XML schema described in the digester-rules DTD, which is included in the Digester distribution. By using such a declarative approach, you can design a Digester-based XML parser that can be configured at runtime, allowing for greater flexibility. If you're curious, an example of digester-rules appears in section 10.7.

Under the covers, Digester uses Java's reflection features to create instances of classes, so you have to pay attention to access modifiers to avoid stifling Digester. For instance, the inner `Contact` class is instantiated dynamically, so it must be public. Similarly, our `populateDocument(Contact)` method needs to be public because it, too, will be called dynamically. Digester also required that our `Document` instance be declared as static; in order to make `DigesterXMLHandler` thread-safe, we have to synchronize access to the `getDocument(InputStream)` method.

By now you've gotten a feel for how our `DocumentHandler` implementations work, and you know how to use both the SAX API and Digester. Let's move onto the next popular format: PDF.

7.3 *Indexing a PDF document*

Portable Document Format (PDF) is a document format invented by Adobe Systems over a decade ago. This format goes beyond simple textual data by allowing document authors to embed pictures, hyperlinks, colors, and more. Today, PDF is widespread, and in some domains it's the dominant format. For instance, official forms such as travel visa application forms, health insurance forms, U.S. tax declaration forms, product manuals, and so on most often come as PDF documents. Even this book is available as PDF; Manning Publications sells chapters of most of its books electronically, allowing customers to buy individual chapters and immediately download them.

If you've ever opened PDF documents, you most likely used an application called Adobe Reader. Although this application has a built-in search, that feature isn't very powerful, allowing the user only two search options: matching whole or partial words, and running a case-sensitive or insensitive search. Your PDF search needs may go beyond this. Moreover, what do you do if you need to search a whole collection of PDF documents? You use Lucene, of course!

In this section, you'll learn how to use PDFBox, a third-party Java library, to parse PDF documents, while sticking with our `DocumentHandler` interface. In addition to our own integration of Lucene and PDFBox, we'll show you how to use PDFBox's built-in Lucene integration classes.

7.3.1 *Extracting text and indexing using PDFBox*

PDFBox is a free, open-source library written by Ben Litchfield; you can find it at http://www.pdfbox.org/. There are several free tools capable of extracting text from PDF files; we chose PDFBox for its popularity, the author's dedicated support on the Lucene mailing lists, and the fact that this library includes classes that work with Lucene particularly well.

Listing 7.5 shows how to extract textual content from a PDF document, as well as document meta-data, and create a Lucene Document suitable for indexing.

> **Listing 7.5** DocumentHandler using the PDFBox library to extract text from PDF files

```
public class PDFBoxPDFHandler implements DocumentHandler {

  public static String password = "-password";

  public PDFBoxPDFHandler() {
  }

  public Document getDocument(InputStream is)        ❶  getDocument method
    throws DocumentHandlerException {

    COSDocument cosDoc = null;
    try {
      cosDoc = parseDocument(is);       ❷  Load InputStream into memory
    }
    catch (IOException e) {
      closeCOSDocument(cosDoc);
      throw new DocumentHandlerException(
        "Cannot parse PDF document", e);
    }

    // decrypt the PDF document, if it is encrypted
    try {
      if (cosDoc.isEncrypted()) {       ❸  Decrypt document
        DecryptDocument decryptor = new DecryptDocument(cosDoc);
        decryptor.decryptDocument(password);
      }
    }
    catch (CryptographyException e) {
      closeCOSDocument(cosDoc);
      throw new DocumentHandlerException(
        "Cannot decrypt PDF document", e);
    }
    catch (InvalidPasswordException e) {
      closeCOSDocument(cosDoc);
      throw new DocumentHandlerException(
```

```
      "Cannot decrypt PDF document", e);
}
catch (IOException e) {
  closeCOSDocument(cosDoc);
  throw new DocumentHandlerException(
    "Cannot decrypt PDF document", e);
}

// extract PDF document's textual content
String docText = null;
try {
  PDFTextStripper stripper = new PDFTextStripper();
  docText = stripper.getText(new PDDocument(cosDoc));
}
catch (IOException e) {
  closeCOSDocument(cosDoc);
  throw new DocumentHandlerException(
    "Cannot parse PDF document", e);
}

Document doc = new Document();
if (docText != null) {
  doc.add(Field.UnStored("body", docText));
}

// extract PDF document's meta-data
PDDocument pdDoc = null;
try {
  PDDocumentInformation docInfo =
    pdDoc.getDocumentInformation();
  String author   = docInfo.getAuthor();
  String title    = docInfo.getTitle();
  String keywords = docInfo.getKeywords();
  String summary  = docInfo.getSubject();
  if ((author != null) && !author.equals("")) {
    doc.add(Field.Text("author", author));
  }
  if ((title != null) && !title.equals("")) {
    doc.add(Field.Text("title", title));
  }
  if ((keywords != null) && !keywords.equals("")) {
    doc.add(Field.Text("keywords", keywords));
  }
  if ((summary != null) && !summary.equals("")) {
    doc.add(Field.Text("summary", summary));
  }
}
catch (Exception e) {
  closeCOSDocument(cosDoc);
  closePDDocument(pdDoc);
  System.err.println("Cannot get PDF document meta-data: "
```

❹ Extract textual content

❺ Save UnStored Field in Lucene Document

❻ Extract document meta-data

```
                       + e.getMessage());
             }

      return doc;
   }

   private static COSDocument parseDocument(InputStream is)
      throws IOException {
      PDFParser parser = new PDFParser(is);
      parser.parse();
      return parser.getDocument();
   }

   private void closeCOSDocument(COSDocument cosDoc) {
      if (cosDoc != null) {
         try {
            cosDoc.close();
         }
         catch (IOException e) {
            // eat it, what else can we do?
         }
      }
   }

   private void closePDDocument(PDDocument pdDoc) {
      if (pdDoc != null) {
         try {
            pdDoc.close();
         }
         catch (IOException e) {
            // eat it, what else can we do?
         }
      }
   }

   public static void main(String[] args) throws Exception {
      PDFBoxPDFHandler handler = new PDFBoxPDFHandler();
      Document doc = handler.getDocument(
         new FileInputStream(new File(args[0])));
      System.out.println(doc);
   }
}
```

❶ The DocumentHandler's getDocument method takes a reference to the PDF document's InputStream.

❷ Here we load the InputStream into memory; it's represented as an instance of a COSDocument object.

❸ PDF documents can be password-protected, and PDFBox allows you to decrypt them prior to parsing them. Our `PDFBoxPDFHandler` exposes the password to be used for decryption as a public static variable, which should be explicitly set by the caller, before parsing encrypted documents.

❹ Now we extract the textual content from the document, ignoring formatting and other PDF structures.

❺ We save the `UnStored Field` in a Lucene `Document` and use the extracted text as its value.

❻ As you can see in this code listing, PDFBox makes use of the PDF document's structure and extracts the document meta-data, such as author, keywords, summary, and title, in addition to pulling out the textual content from the document body. This allows us to add richer `Documents` to the index and provide better search results in the end.

We store the meta-data in the following `Fields`: `author`, `keywords`, `summary`, and `title`. We have to be careful not to store null values, because null `Fields` are invalid. We also don't want to store blank `Fields`, so we perform appropriate checks before adding meta-data to an instance of Lucene `Document`.

Since document meta-data isn't crucial to have, if PDFBox throws an `IOException` while extracting meta-data we choose only to print out a warning instead of throwing a `DocumentHandlerException`.

7.3.2 *Built-in Lucene support*

Listing 7.5 demonstrates the low-level way of extracting data from a PDF document. The PDFBox distribution also comes with two classes that Lucene users may want to consider using if you don't need fine control over Lucene `Document` creation. If you just need a quick way to index a directory of PDF files or a single PDF file, of if you only want to test PDFBox, you can use the Lucene support built into PDFBox. This approach can be quick, as you're about to see, but it also limits what is extracted from the PDF file, what Lucene `Document Fields` are created, and how they're analyzed and indexed.

PDFBox's `org.pdfbox.searchengine.lucene` package contains two classes: `IndexFiles` and `LucenePDFDocument`. We discuss them next.

Using the IndexFiles class

`IndexFiles` is a simple class that exposes a single method for indexing a single file system directory. Here's how you can use it:

```
public class PDFBoxIndexFiles {
  public static void main(String[] args) throws Exception {
```

```
    IndexFiles indexFiles = new IndexFiles();
    indexFiles.index(new File(args[0]), true, args[1]);
  }
}
```

This code calls the `index` method in `IndexFiles` class passing it arguments from the command line. The output of this program is as follows (of course, you have to ensure that your classpath includes the PDFBox and Lucene JARs, as well as the JAR that comes with this book):

```
$ java lia.handlingtypes.pdf.PDFBoxIndexFiles
           /home/otis/PDFs /tmp/pdfindex

Indexing PDF document: /home/otis/PDFs/Concurrency-j-jtp07233.pdf
Indexing PDF document: /home/otis/PDFs/CoreJSTLAppendixA.pdf
Indexing PDF document: /home/otis/PDFs/CoreJSTLChapter2.pdf
Indexing PDF document: /home/otis/PDFs/CoreJSTLChapter5.pdf
Indexing PDF document: /home/otis/PDFs/Google-Arch.pdf
Indexing PDF document: /home/otis/PDFs/JavaCookbook-Chapter22-RMI.pdf
Indexing PDF document: /home/otis/PDFs/JavaSockets.pdf
Indexing PDF document: /home/otis/PDFs/LinuxBackup.pdf
Indexing PDF document: /home/otis/PDFs/SEDA.pdf
Indexing PDF document: /home/otis/PDFs/ViTutorialWithCheatSheet.pdf
Indexing PDF document: /home/otis/PDFs/design-patterns.pdf
Indexing PDF document: /home/otis/PDFs/jndi.pdf
Indexing PDF document: /home/otis/PDFs/pagerank.pdf
Indexing PDF document: /home/otis/PDFs/servlet-2_3-fcs-spec.pdf
Indexing PDF document: /home/otis/PDFs/tilesAdvancedFeatures.pdf
Optimizing index...
42971 total milliseconds
```

The `IndexFiles` class did everything for us: It found all the PDFs in a given directory, it parsed them, and it indexed them with Lucene. This may be a bit too much for those who like to keep some control in their own hands. Thus, PDFBox comes with a `LucenePDFDocument` class that's even simpler: It parses a given PDF file and returns a populated Lucene `Document` instance. Let's see how it works.

Using the LucenePDFDocument class

The `LucenePDFDocument` class is somewhat similar to our `DocumentHandler`'s `getDocument(InputStream)` method. It offers two static methods that return a Lucene `Document` when passed an instance of `File` or an instance of a `URL` object. The following code demonstrates the use of the method that takes a `File` object as a parameter:

```
public class PDFBoxLucenePDFDocument {
  public static void main(String[] args) throws Exception {
    Document doc = LucenePDFDocument.getDocument(new File(args[0]));
```

```
        System.out.println(doc);
    }
}
```

This class is a simple wrapper around PDFBox's `LucenePDFDocument` class. After adding all the needed JARs to the classpath, we pass the name of the file specified on the command line to this class and then print out the resulting Lucene `Document`. As shown here, this class creates a Lucene `Document` with `Fields` named `summary`, `producer`, `contents`, `modified`, `url`, and `path`:

```
$ java lia.handlingtypes.pdf.PDFBoxLucenePDFDocument
⇒  /home/otis/PDFs/Google-Arch.pdf
Document<Unindexed<summary:22
Few Web services require as much
computation per request as search engines.
On average, a single query on Google reads
hundreds of megabytes of data and consumes
tens of billions of CPU cycles. Supporting a
peak request stream of thousands of queries
per second requires an infrastructure compa-
rable in size to that of the largest supercom-
puter installations. Combining more than
15,000 commodity-class PCs with fault-tol-
erant software creates a solution that is more
cost-effective than a c>
Text<Producer:Acrobat Distiller 4.05 for Macintosh>
Text<CreationDate:0demeknhc>
Text<contents:java.io.InputStreamReader@1193779>
org.apache.lucene.document.Field@8916a2
Keyword<modified:0dhb25ujs>
Unindexed<url:/home/otis/PDFs/Google-Arch.pdf>
Unindexed<path:/home/otis/PDFs/Google-Arch.pdf>>
```

PDFBox and Lucene make a good couple. More important, they make it easy for us to make collections of PDF documents searchable.

7.4 Indexing an HTML document

HTML is everywhere. Most web documents are in HTML format. The Web is currently the largest repository of information on the planet. Add two and two together, and it's clear that we need to be able to index and search volumes of existing HTML documents. That is the bread and butter of web search engines, and many companies have built businesses based on this need. Parsing HTML is nontrivial, though, because many sites still don't conform to the latest W3C standards for XHTML (HTML as an XML dialect). Specialized parsers have been developed that can leniently interpret various bastardizations of HTML.

7.4.1 Getting the HTML source data

Listing 7.6 contains the HTML document that we'll be parsing using the HTML parsers featured in this section. A large percentage of HTML documents available on the Web aren't well formed, and not all parsers deal with that situation equally well. In this section, we use the JTidy and NekoHTML parsers, both of which are solid HTML parsers capable of dealing with broken HTML.

Listing 7.6   The HTML document that we'll parse, index, and ultimately search

```
<html>
  <head>
    <title>
      Letter press supplies are available in First Class only
    </title>
  </head>
  <body>
    <h1>Code, Write, Fly</h1>
    This chapter is being written 11,000 meters above New Foundland.
  </body>
</html>
```

Now that we have some HTML to work with, let's see how we can process it with JTidy.

7.4.2 Using JTidy

With a decade behind it, Tidy is an old-timer among HTML parsers. The original Tidy was implemented in C by Dave Raggett, but the project's development stopped in 2000. A group of enthusiastic developers recently took over the project and gave it a second life. Tidy is now actively developed at http://tidy.sourceforge.net/.

JTidy is a Java port of Tidy, written by Andy Quick; its home is at http://jtidy.sourceforge.net/. After four years without a release, the JTidy project recently got a new project administrator and developer, Fabrizio Giustina; he started working on JTidy at the beginning of 2004 and began preparing it for new releases.

The code in listing 7.7 represents a JTidy-based implementation of our `DocumentHandler` interface. JTidy is invoked by its `parseDOM` method, to which we pass an HTML document's `InputStream`. From there on we use standard DOM API methods to get textual values for two HTML elements that we want to index: the document's `title` and `body`.

Listing 7.7 `DocumentHandler` using JTidy to extract text from HTML documents

```
public class JTidyHTMLHandler implements DocumentHandler {

  public org.apache.lucene.document.Document
    getDocument(InputStream is) throws DocumentHandlerException {    ❶

                                                            getDocument method
    Tidy tidy = new Tidy();
    tidy.setQuiet(true);
    tidy.setShowWarnings(false);                                ❷  Parse HTML
    org.w3c.dom.Document root = tidy.parseDOM(is, null);           InputStream
    Element rawDoc = root.getDocumentElement();

    org.apache.lucene.document.Document doc =
      new org.apache.lucene.document.Document();

    String title = getTitle(rawDoc);     ❸  Get title
    String body = getBody(rawDoc);                ❹  Get text in all elements
    if ((title != null) && (!title.equals(""))) {    between <body> and
      doc.add(Field.Text("title", title));           </body>
    }
    if ((body != null) && (!body.equals(""))) {
      doc.add(Field.Text("body", body));
    }

    return doc;
  }

  /**
   * Gets the title text of the HTML document.
   *
   * @rawDoc the DOM Element to extract title Node from
   * @return the title text
   */
  protected String getTitle(Element rawDoc) {
    if (rawDoc == null) {
      return null;
    }

    String title = "";
                                                            Get text of
                                                            first <title>
    NodeList children = rawDoc.getElementsByTagName("title");
    if (children.getLength() > 0) {                            ❺
      Element titleElement = ((Element) children.item(0));
      Text text = (Text) titleElement.getFirstChild();
      if (text != null) {
        title = text.getData();
      }
    }
    return title;
  }
```

```
/**
 * Gets the body text of the HTML document.
 *
 * @rawDoc the DOM Element to extract body Node from
 * @return the body text
 */
protected String getBody(Element rawDoc) {
  if (rawDoc == null) {
    return null;
  }
  String body = "";
  NodeList children = rawDoc.getElementsByTagName("body");
  if (children.getLength() > 0) {
    body = getText(children.item(0));
  }
  return body;
}

/**
 * Extracts text from the DOM node.
 *
 * @param node a DOM node
 * @return the text value of the node
 */
protected String getText(Node node) {
  NodeList children = node.getChildNodes();
  StringBuffer sb = new StringBuffer();
  for (int i = 0; i < children.getLength(); i++) {
    Node child = children.item(i);
    switch (child.getNodeType()) {
      case Node.ELEMENT_NODE:
        sb.append(getText(child));
        sb.append(" ");
        break;
      case Node.TEXT_NODE:
        sb.append(((Text) child).getData());
        break;
    }
  }
  return sb.toString();
}

public static void main(String args[]) throws Exception {
  JTidyHTMLHandler handler = new JTidyHTMLHandler();
  org.apache.lucene.document.Document doc = handler.getDocument(
    new FileInputStream(new File(args[0])));
  System.out.println(doc);
}
}
```

⑥ Get references to **<body>**

⑦ **Extract all text between**
ⵜbodyⵜ and ⵜ/bodyⵜ

⑧ **Extract all text in all elements**
under specified Node

❶ DocumentHandler's getDocument method, to which we pass HTML document's InputStream, calls JTidy's DOM parser and then creates a Lucene Document.

❷ The call to JTidy's parseDOM method parses the given HTML InputStream and forms a DOM tree, suitable for traversal.

❸ The call to getTitle gets the textual value of the HTML document title. This text is then used to populate the Lucene Document instance.

❹ The call to getBody gets the full text of the HTML document. This text is then used to populate the Lucene Document instance.

❺ The getTitle method traverses the DOM tree and returns the textual value of the first <title> element it finds.

❻ We use the standard DOM API call to get a list of references to all <body> elements. Normally there is just one <body> container element present in an HTML document.

❼ The getBody method calls the generic getText method to pull out all the text from the HTML document. All text found between <body> and </body> elements is returned.

❽ The getText method is a generic method for extracting all text found in all elements under the specified DOM Node.

As was the case elsewhere in this chapter, Fields can be null or empty, so we perform the necessary checks before adding title and body to the index. Because the DOM API contains a class called Document (org.w3c.dom.Document), we avoid namespace clashes with Lucene's Document by using fully qualified class names for both Document classes.

Next, let's look at JTidy's younger cousin, NekoHTML.

7.4.3 *Using NekoHTML*

NekoHTML is a relative newcomer to the work of HTML parsers, but its author Andy Clark is not. His is a known name in the world of parsers, and a lot of his work can be found in the Xerces-J XML parser. As such, it's no surprise that NekoHTML is written using the Xerces Native Interface (XNI), which is the foundation of the Xerces2 implementation.

NekoHTML is a simple HTML scanner and tag balancer that enables application programmers to parse HTML documents and access them using standard XML interfaces. The parser can scan HTML files and fix up a number of common mistakes that human and computer authors make in writing HTML documents. NekoHTML adds missing parent elements, automatically closes elements with optional end tags, and can handle mismatched inline element tags.

NekoHTML is part of Andy Clark's set of CyberNeko Tools for XNI; you can
find it at http://www.apache.org/~andyc/neko/doc/index.html. Listing 7.8 shows
our `DocumentHandler` implementation based on NekoHTML. It uses the DOM
API, just like the JTidy example. However, here we go a step further and provide
a bit more general implementation in the two `getText` methods.

**Listing 7.8 `DocumentHandler` using the NekoHTML to extract text from HTML
documents**

```
public class NekoHTMLHandler implements DocumentHandler {
  private DOMFragmentParser parser = new DOMFragmentParser();   ❶
                                              Neko's DOM parser for HTML
  public Document getDocument(InputStream is)       ❷  getDocument method
    throws DocumentHandlerException {

    DocumentFragment node =
      new HTMLDocumentImpl().createDocumentFragment();   ❸  Create
    try {                                                     DocumentFragment
      parser.parse(new InputSource(is), node);   ❹  Parse InputStream
    }
    catch (IOException e) {
      throw new DocumentHandlerException(
        "Cannot parse HTML document: ", e);
    }
    catch (SAXException e) {
      throw new DocumentHandlerException(
        "Cannot parse HTML document: ", e);
    }

    org.apache.lucene.document.Document doc =
      new org.apache.lucene.document.Document();

    StringBuffer sb = new StringBuffer();     ❺  Extract/
    getText(sb, node, "title");                   store text
    String title = sb.toString();                 of <title>

    sb.setLength(0);     ❻  Clear StringBuffer
    getText(sb, node);
    String text = sb.toString();        ❼  Extract all text
                                            from DOM Node
    if ((title != null) && (!title.equals(""))) {
      doc.add(Field.Text("title", title));
    }
    if ((text != null) && (!text.equals(""))) {
      doc.add(Field.Text("body", text));
    }

    return doc;
  }
```

```
    private void getText(StringBuffer sb, Node node) {
      if (node.getNodeType() == Node.TEXT_NODE) {
        sb.append(node.getNodeValue());
      }
      NodeList children = node.getChildNodes();
      if (children != null) {
        int len = children.getLength();
        for (int i = 0; i < len; i++) {
          getText(sb, children.item(i));
        }
      }
    }

    private boolean getText(StringBuffer sb, Node node,
      String element) {
      if (node.getNodeType() == Node.ELEMENT_NODE) {
        if (element.equalsIgnoreCase(node.getNodeName())) {
          getText(sb, node);
          return true;
        }
      }
      NodeList children = node.getChildNodes();
      if (children != null) {
        int len = children.getLength();
        for (int i = 0; i < len; i++) {
          if (getText(sb, children.item(i), element)) {
            return true;
          }
        }
      }
      return false;
    }

    public static void main(String args[]) throws Exception {
      NekoHTMLHandler handler = new NekoHTMLHandler();
      org.apache.lucene.document.Document doc = handler.getDocument(
        new FileInputStream(new File(args[0])));
      System.out.println(doc);
    }
  }
```

8 Extract all text from DOM Node that represents specified element

9 Extract text from Nodes that represent specified element

1 NekoHTML offers several HTML parsers. In this implementation we use NekoHTML's `DOMFragmentParser`, which is capable of processing even incomplete HTML documents.

2 The implementation of `DocumentHandler`'s `getDocument` method takes the HTML document as `InputStream`, uses NekoHTML's API to parse it into a DOM tree, and then pulls the needed textual values from the tree.

❸ We create a blank instance of Xerces' `DocumentFragment` class that we'll later populate with DOM data.

❹ The call to NekoHTML's parser processes the given `InputStream` and stores its DOM representation in the blank `DocumentFragment` instance that we created earlier.

❺ We extract the text of the `<title>` element in the given DOM `Node` by calling one version of the generic `getText` method. The textual value is stored in the specified `StringBuffer`.

❻ Recycling the `StringBuffer` isn't necessary, but we do it anyway, just to be nice.

❼ Using the other variant of the generic `getText` method, we extract all of the HTML document's text.

❽ The generic and recursive `getText` method is used to extract textual values from all DOM `Nodes` that contain text. The `getText(StringBuffer, Node)` method pulls all textual data it finds in the HTML document. It does so by calling itself recursively as it traverses the DOM tree and collecting text from all DOM text `Nodes` on the way. Because we use this version of the `getText` method to get the body of our sample HTML document, we end up collecting all textual data from the document, not just that found between the `<body>` and `</body>` elements.

❾ This is another variant of the generic and recursive `getText` method. This one, however, limits itself to DOM `Nodes` with the given name. We used this method to extract the text between `<title>` and `</title>` elements.

> **NOTE** Although we showed you how to use its DOM parser, you should be aware that NekoHTML also provides a SAX HTML parser.

You now know how to parse HTML, the most popular file format on the Web. Although HTML is the dominant web file format, Microsoft Word documents still rule in corporate environments. Let's look how to parse them.

7.5 *Indexing a Microsoft Word document*

Like it or not, virtually every business on Earth uses Microsoft Word.[2] If you were to print all the MS Word documents in existence and stack them on top of each other, you could probably reach far-away planets in our solar system. How do you drill through such a big pile of killed trees to find something you're looking for? Instead of printing anything, you read the following section and learn how to parse MS Word documents and make them searchable with Lucene.

---

[2] Painfully, even this book was written in Microsoft Word.

Unlike all other document formats covered in this chapter, the format of MS Word documents is proprietary. In other words, Microsoft Corporation keeps the exact format a secret, making it difficult for others to write applications to read and write documents in MS Word format. Luckily, several open-source projects made it their goal to overcome this obstacle. In this section, you'll see how to use tools created by two such projects: Jakarta POI and TextMining.org text extractors.

7.5.1 *Using POI*

POI is a Jakarta project; you can find it at http://jakarta.apache.org/poi. It's a highly active project whose goal is to provide a Java API for manipulation of various file formats based on Microsoft's OLE 2 Compound Document format. Thus, POI lets you extract textual data from Microsoft Word documents, as well as Excel and other documents, using the OLE 2 Compound Document format.

In the example presented in listing 7.9, we use a single POI class, `WordDocument`, to extract text from a sample Microsoft Word document; we then use the text to populate a Lucene `Document` instance. In addition to the document contents, Microsoft Word documents also hold some meta-data, such as the document summary and the name of the author; although our example doesn't extract this meta-data, you can certainly use POI for that, if you need to index document meta-data, too.

Listing 7.9 POI `DocumentHandler` for parsing Microsoft Word documents

```
public class POIWordDocHandler implements DocumentHandler {

  public Document getDocument(InputStream is)        ❶ getDocument method
    throws DocumentHandlerException {

    String bodyText = null;

    try {
      WordDocument wd = new WordDocument(is);
      StringWriter docTextWriter = new StringWriter();      ❷ Extract textual
      wd.writeAllText(new PrintWriter(docTextWriter));         data from MS
      docTextWriter.close();                                   Word document
      bodyText = docTextWriter.toString();
    }
    catch (Exception e) {
      throw new DocumentHandlerException(
        "Cannot extract text from a Word document", e);
    }

    if ((bodyText != null) && (bodyText.trim().length() > 0)) {
      Document doc = new Document();
```

```
        doc.add(Field.UnStored("body", bodyText));
        return doc;
    }
    return null;
}

public static void main(String[] args) throws Exception {
    POIWordDocHandler handler = new POIWordDocHandler();
    Document doc = handler.getDocument(
        new FileInputStream(new File(args[0])));
    System.out.println(doc);
}
}
```

❶ This is the `DocumentHandler`'s `getDocument` method, to which we pass the MS Word document's `InputStream`.

❷ POI makes text extraction simple. Its `WordDocument` class readily takes a reference to the `InputStream` of a Microsoft Word document and allows us to extract the text by writing it to a `Writer` class. Since we need the text in a `String` variable, we use the combination of `StringWriter` and `PrintWriter` to get the document's textual value. Any structure is discarded. Like the other examples in this chapter, we save this data in a `body` `Field`.

Simple, isn't it? Believe it or not, TextMining.org text extractors, described next, make this task even simpler.

7.5.2 *Using TextMining.org's API*

The TextMining.org API provides an alternative interface to the Jakarta POI API, making text extraction from Microsoft Word documents a breeze. It's interesting to note that Ryan Ackley, the author of the TextMining.org text extractors, is also one of the developers of the Jakarta POI project. Besides the simpler API, you ought to be aware of the following advantages that the TextMining.org API has over POI:

- This library is optimized for extracting text. POI is not.

- The TextMining.org library supports extracting text from Word 6/95, whereas POI does not.

- The TextMining.org library doesn't extract deleted text that is still present in the document for the purposes of revision marking. On the other hand, POI doesn't handle this.

Listing 7.10 shows you how easy it is to use the TextMining.org toolkit: It takes only one line!

Listing 7.10 TextMining.org `DocumentHandler` for Microsoft Word documents

```
public class TextMiningWordDocHandler implements DocumentHandler {

  public Document getDocument(InputStream is)            ❶ getDocument method
    throws DocumentHandlerException {

    String bodyText = null;
    try {
      bodyText = new WordExtractor().extractText(is);    ❷ Extract raw text
    }                                                       from InputStream
    catch (Exception e) {
      throw new DocumentHandlerException(
        "Cannot extract text from a Word document", e);
    }

    if ((bodyText != null) && (bodyText.trim().length() > 0)) {
      Document doc = new Document();
      doc.add(Field.UnStored("body", bodyText));
      return doc;
    }
    return null;
  }

  public static void main(String[] args) throws Exception {
    TextMiningWordDocHandler handler =
      new TextMiningWordDocHandler();
    Document doc = handler.getDocument(
      new FileInputStream(new File(args[0])));
    System.out.println(doc);
  }
}
```

❶ This is the `DocumentHandler`'s `getDocument` method to which we pass the MS Word document `InputStream`.

❷ TextMining.org's simple API requires that we deal with only a single class, `WordExtractor`, and a single method of that class, `extractText(InputStream)`, which pulls all of the Microsoft Word document's text into a string. Once we have a reference to the document's text, we add it to an instance of a Lucene `Document` the same way we have been doing in other examples in this chapter.

Next, you'll learn how to parse RTF documents. Although such documents aren't nearly as popular as Microsoft Word documents, the RTF format is attractive because it offers platform and application portability.

7.6 *Indexing an RTF document*

Although we needed third-party libraries to extract text from all rich media documents covered in this chapter, for documents in Rich Text Format (RTF) we can use classes that are part of Java's standard distribution. They hide in the `javax.swing.text` and `javax.swing.text.rtf` packages but deliver the promised functionality when used, as shown in listing 7.11.

Listing 7.11 `DocumentHandler` using Java's built-in RTF text extractor

```
public class JavaBuiltInRTFHandler implements DocumentHandler {

  public Document getDocument(InputStream is)                     ❶ getDocument method
      throws DocumentHandlerException {
                                                          Instance of javax.swing.text.Document
    String bodyText = null;
    DefaultStyledDocument styledDoc = new DefaultStyledDocument();     ❷
    try {
      new RTFEditorKit().read(is, styledDoc, 0);            ❸ Load InputStream
      bodyText = styledDoc.getText(0, styledDoc.getLength());     ❹
    }                                                          Extract text
    catch (IOException e) {
      throw new DocumentHandlerException(
        "Cannot extract text from a RTF document", e);
    }
    catch (BadLocationException e) {
      throw new DocumentHandlerException(
        "Cannot extract text from a RTF document", e);
    }

    if (bodyText != null) {
      Document doc = new Document();
      doc.add(Field.UnStored("body", bodyText));
      return doc;
    }
    return null;
  }

  public static void main(String[] args) throws Exception {
    JavaBuiltInRTFHandler handler = new JavaBuiltInRTFHandler();
    Document doc = handler.getDocument(
      new FileInputStream(new File(args[0])));
    System.out.println(doc);
  }
}
```

❶ This is the DocumentHandler's getDocument method, to which we pass the RTF document's InputStream.

❷ We instantiate the specific implementation of the javax.swing.text.Document interface and later use it to read in the RTF document contents.

❸ To extract text from a RTF document, we use Java's built-in RTFEditorKit class. With its read method, we read our RTF document into an instance of Default-StyledDocument.

❹ To get all text from the RTF document we read it in full from the DefaultStyled-Document. This class implements a javax.swing.text.Document interface, which allows us to get any range of document characters. We are, of course, interested in all textual data, so we specify the range from the very first to the very last character. By specifying different offset and length we could have extracted only a portion of the whole text.

After all the text has been pulled out of the RTF document, we see the familiar block of code that adds the extracted text to a Lucene Document as Field.UnStored. Our last DocumentHandler will handle plain-text files. Let's take a look.

7.7 *Indexing a plain-text document*

Finally, let's implement a DocumentHandler for plain-text documents, shown in listing 7.12. This is the simplest class in this chapter, and it requires very little explanation because it uses only the familiar, core Java classes—it has no third-party dependencies.

Listing 7.12 Plain-text DocumentHandler using only core Java classes

```
public class PlainTextHandler implements DocumentHandler {

  public Document getDocument(InputStream is)        ❶ getDocument method
    throws DocumentHandlerException {

    String bodyText = "";

    try {
      BufferedReader br =
        new BufferedReader(new InputStreamReader(is));
      String line = null;
      while ((line = br.readLine()) != null) {
        bodyText += line;                            ❷ Read InputStream
      }                                                  a line at a time
      br.close();
    }
    catch(IOException e) {
```

```
        throw new DocumentHandlerException(
          "Cannot read the text document", e);
      }

      if (!bodyText.equals("")) {
        Document doc = new Document();
        doc.add(Field.UnStored("body", bodyText));
        return doc;
      }

      return null;
    }

    public static void main(String[] args) throws Exception {
      PlainTextHandler handler = new PlainTextHandler();
      Document doc = handler.getDocument(
        new FileInputStream(new File(args[0])));
      System.out.println(doc);
    }
  }
```

❶ This is the DocumentHandler's getDocument method, to which we pass the plain-text document's InputStream.

❷ This DocumentHandler implementation reads the plain-text document a line at a time and appends each line to a String, which ends up containing the full content of the original document. This text is then indexed as a Field.UnStored called body.

As we stated in the introduction to this chapter, our goal is to create a small framework for parsing and indexing document of various formats. All the Document-Handler implementations presented so far are the first step in that direction. We now move on to our next step, where things get interesting: We'll begin gluing things together, and the framework will start to take shape.

7.8 *Creating a document-handling framework*

So far in this chapter, we've presented standalone solutions: individual Document-Handler implementations for parsing several common document formats. Because all the classes we've presented implement our generic DocumentHandler interface, defined at the beginning of this chapter, it's easy to create a minimal framework for handling and indexing documents of various types without worrying about individual files' formats.

To our existing infrastructure, consisting of the `DocumentHandler` interface and accompanying `DocumentHandlerException`, we now add a new `FileHandler` interface and `FileHandlerException`. Furthermore, we implement the `FileHandler` interface with a class called `ExtensionFileHandler`. Table 7.2 summarizes the framework components.

Table 7.2 Java classes that compose a file-indexing framework

Java class	Purpose
DocumentHandler	Defines the `getDocument(InputStream)` method implemented by all document parsers
DocumentHandlerException	Checked exception thrown by all parsers in case of error
FileHandler	Defines the `getDocument(File)` method implemented by `ExtensionFileHandler`
FileHandlerException	Checked exception thrown by concrete `FileHandler` implementations
ExtensionFileHandler	Implementation of `FileHandler` that acts as a façade for individual `DocumentHandler` implementations, by invoking the appropriate parser based on the extension of the file passed to it via the `getDocument(File)` method

Finally, we create a `FileIndexer` command-line application that uses all of the components listed in figure 7.1 as well as all the parsers presented in this chapter. This ready-to-use application can recursively traverse file-system directories, along the way indexing files in all the formats we've covered. Figure 7.1 shows the framework after everything has been put together.

With this high-level picture in mind, let's take a more detailed look at the individual components that make up the system.

7.8.1 *FileHandler interface*

By now you should be familiar with the `DocumentHandler` and a number of its implementations. `FileHandler`, presented in listing 7.13, is a simple interface, very similar to that of a `DocumentHandler`. However, unlike `DocumentHandler`, which exposes the generic `InputStream` as the acceptable input type, the `FileHandler` interface defines `File` as its input type, thus making it easier to work with for higher-level classes that deal with `File` objects.

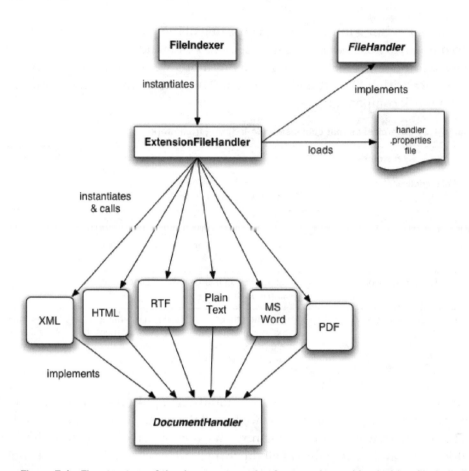

Figure 7.1 The structure of the document-parsing framework, combined with a file-indexing application that uses it

Listing 7.13 `FileHandler` interface for creating Lucene `Documents` from files

```
public interface FileHandler {

  /**
   * Creates a Lucene Document from a File.
   * This method can return <code>null</code>.
   *
   * @param file the File to convert to a Document
   * @return a ready-to-index instance of Document
   */
  Document getDocument(File file)          Convert File object to
    throws FileHandlerException;          Lucene Document
}
```

Given an instance of a `File` class, an implementation of the `FileHandler` interface returns a populated instance of a Lucene `Document` to its caller. Every `FileHandler` implementation wraps any exceptions it encounters and rethrows them wrapped in a `FileHandlerException`, a class as boring as most other exception classes. Instead of listing that exception class here, let's look at `ExtensionFileHandler`.

7.8.2 *ExtensionFileHandler*

`ExtensionFileHandler`, shown in listing 7.14, is our only implementation of the `FileHandler` interface. Its implementation of the `getDocument(File)` method uses the extension of the given file to deduce the type of the file and call the appropriate parser implementation. Because all our parsers implement the common `DocumentHandler` interface, the `ExtensionFileHandler` can blindly pass them the `File` object wrapped in a `FileInputStream`, which parsers know how to handle.

Listing 7.14 `ExtensionFileHandler`: a `FileHandler` based on file extensions

```
/**
 * A FileHandler implementation that delegates responsibility to
 * appropriate DocumentHandler implementation, based on a file
 * extension.
 */
public class ExtensionFileHandler implements FileHandler {
  private Properties handlerProps;

  public ExtensionFileHandler(Properties props) throws IOException {
    handlerProps = props;          ❶ Map file extension
  }

  public Document getDocument(File file)
    throws FileHandlerException {

    Document doc = null;
    String name = file.getName();
    int dotIndex = name.indexOf(".");                    ❷ Extract
    if ((dotIndex > 0) && (dotIndex < name.length())) {     filename
      String ext = name.substring(dotIndex + 1, name.length());  extension
      String handlerClassName = handlerProps.getProperty(ext);

                                      Look up parser ❸
      try {                              class name
        Class handlerClass = Class.forName(handlerClassName);
        DocumentHandler handler =
          (DocumentHandler) handlerClass.newInstance();
        return handler.getDocument(new FileInputStream(file));  ❹
      }
                            Pass File to parser implementation
      catch (ClassNotFoundException e) {
        throw new FileHandlerException(
```

```
                 "Cannot create instance of : "
                 + handlerClassName, e);
            }
            catch (InstantiationException e) {
              throw new FileHandlerException(
                "Cannot create instance of : "
                + handlerClassName, e);
            }
            catch (IllegalAccessException e) {
              throw new FileHandlerException(
                "Cannot create instance of : "
                + handlerClassName, e);
            }
            catch (FileNotFoundException e) {
              throw new FileHandlerException(
                "File not found: "
                + file.getAbsolutePath(), e);
            }
            catch (DocumentHandlerException e) {
              throw new FileHandlerException(
                "Document cannot be handler: "
                + file.getAbsolutePath(), e);
            }
          }
        }
        return null;
      }

      public static void main(String[] args) throws Exception {
        if (args.length < 2) {
          usage();
          System.exit(0);
        }

        Properties props = new Properties();
        props.load(new FileInputStream(args[0]));

        ExtensionFileHandler fileHandler =
          new ExtensionFileHandler(props);
        Document doc = fileHandler.getDocument(new File(args[1]));
      }

      private static void usage() {
        System.err.println("USAGE: java "
          + ExtensionFileHandler.class.getName()
          + " /path/to/properties /path/to/document");
      }
    }
```

❺ Load properties file

❶ The `Properties` instance maps file extensions to the `DocumentHandler` classes capable of parsing files with those extensions.

② To extract the filename extension, we look for the last dot in the filename and grab everything from that offset to the end of the filename.

③ We use the extracted filename extension and the `Properties` instance to instantiate the appropriate `DocumentHandler`.

④ After we dynamically instantiate our `DocumentHandler`, we pass it the `File` wrapped by `FileInputStream` for parsing.

⑤ The properties file specified on the command line is loaded into the `Properties` instance.

There are several important parts in this implementation worth noting. The first thing to observe is that the only constructor is the one that takes an instance of a `Properties` class. This is important because this `FileHandler` needs a configuration that maps different file extensions to different `DocumentHandler` classes. Here is an example properties file. We've mapped several common file extensions to various `DocumentHandler` implementations presented earlier in the chapter:

```
txt  = lia.handlingtypes.text.PlainTextHandler
html = lia.handlingtypes.html.JTidyHTMLHandler
rtf  = lia.handlingtypes.rtf.JavaBuiltInRTFHandler
doc  = lia.handlingtypes.msdoc.TextMiningWordDocHandler
pdf  = lia.handlingtypes.pdf.PDFBoxPDFHandler
xml  = lia.handlingtypes.xml.DigesterXMLHandler
```

Looking beyond the constructor and into the `getDocument(File)` method, you can see that the code extracts the filename extension and uses it to create the appropriate `DocumentHandler`, after consulting the `Properties` instance set in the constructor. The matching `DocumentHandler` is dynamically instantiated, which is possible because all `DocumentHandler` implementations contain a public default constructor. Finally, the input file is converted to a `FileInputStream`, a subclass of `InputStream`, and passed to the `getDocument(InputStream)` method defined in the `DocumentHandler` interface. A number of exceptions that we're catching are related to instantiation of `DocumentHandler` implementations using Java reflection.

You may choose to call `ExtensionFileHandler` from another Java class, but we included the `main` method, which allows you to run this class from the command line as well. Two command-line arguments must be specified: the path to the properties file that maps file extensions to `DocumentHandler`s, and a path to the file that needs to be processed.

The `main` method is only a convenience method. The real power of `Extension-FileHandler` is apparent when it's called programmatically—and that is exactly what we do from the `FileIndexer` application, described in the next section.

7.8.3 *FileIndexer application*

Listing 7.15 shows a class called `FileIndexer`, the final product of this chapter. It ties together all the components described in this chapter in a command-line application capable of recursively traversing file-system directories and indexing all files found along the way, as long as we have a parser capable of handling their file format. `FileIndexer` may remind you of the `Indexer` application from section 1.4. Both of them recursively traverse file-system directories. However, whereas `Indexer` is limited to indexing plain-text files, `FileIndexer` can parse and index all the document formats covered in this chapter.

Listing 7.15 `FileIndexer`: a recursive file-system indexer

```
/**
 * A File Indexer capable of recursively indexing a directory tree.
 */
public class FileIndexer
{
  protected FileHandler fileHandler;

  public FileIndexer(Properties props) throws IOException {
    fileHandler = new ExtensionFileHandler(props);      ❶ ExtensionFileHandler
  }

  public void index(IndexWriter writer, File file)      ❷ index method
    throws FileHandlerException {

    if (file.canRead()) {
      if (file.isDirectory()) {
        String[] files = file.list();                   ❸ Traverse readable
        if (files != null) {                               directories
          for (int i = 0; i < files.length; i++) {         recursively
            index(writer, new File(file, files[i]));
          }
        }
      }
      else {
        System.out.println("Indexing " + file);
        try {
        Document doc = fileHandler.getDocument(file);   ❹ Hand off files to
          if (doc != null) {                               ExtensionFileHandler
            writer.addDocument(doc);                    ❺ Add returned
          }                                                Lucene Document
          else {                                           to index
            System.err.println("Cannot handle"
              + file.getAbsolutePath() + "; skipping");
          }
        }
        catch (IOException e) {
```

```
            System.err.println("Cannot index "
                + file.getAbsolutePath() + "; skipping ("
                + e.getMessage() + ")");
          }
        }
      }
    }

    public static void main(String[] args) throws Exception {
      if (args.length < 3) {
        usage();
        System.exit(0);
      }

      Properties props = new Properties();
      props.load(new FileInputStream(args[0]));
      Directory dir = FSDirectory.getDirectory(args[2], true);
      Analyzer analyzer = new SimpleAnalyzer();
      IndexWriter writer = new IndexWriter(dir, analyzer, true);

      FileIndexer indexer = new FileIndexer(props);

      long start = new Date().getTime();
      indexer.index(writer, new File(args[1]));
      writer.optimize();
      writer.close();
      long end = new Date().getTime();
      System.out.println();
      IndexReader reader = IndexReader.open(dir);
      System.out.println("Documents indexed: " + reader.numDocs());
      System.out.println("Total time: " + (end - start) + " ms");
      reader.close();
    }

    private static void usage() {
      System.err.println("USAGE: java "
        + FileIndexer.class.getName()
        + " /path/to/properties /path/to/file/or/directory"
        + " /path/to/index");
    }
  }
```

6 Load properties specified on command line

Open index

7

8 Create FileIndexer instance

9 First call to index method

10 Optimize index; close index writer

User-friendly summary **11**

1 FileIndexer has a private default constructor and a public constructor that takes an instance of Properties class as a parameter for the same reasons that ExtensionFileHandler required a Properties instance. Moreover, looking at File-Indexer's public constructor reveals that the specified Properties are passed to the ExtensionFileHandler constructor.

② The meat of `FileIndexer` is in the `index(IndexWriter, File)` method. This is where we implement file indexing.

③ If the specified instance of `File` class represents a file system directory, the `index(IndexWriter, File)` method calls itself recursively.

④ Eventually, though, `index(IndexWriter, File)` calls itself with a `File` instance that represents a real file. At that point the `ExtensionFileHandler` comes into play, because the execution control is passed to it with a call to its `getDocument(File)` method.

⑤ The call to `getDocument(File)` returns a populated Lucene `Document`, if one of the `DocumentHandler` implementations was able to parse the specified file. If no `DocumentHandler` was capable of processing the file, a null Lucene `Document` is returned. Thus, we check the returned object for null, and add it to the Lucene index only if the `Document` isn't null.

⑥ The properties file specified on the command line is loaded into an instance of `Properties`.

⑦ The index to which all `Files` converted to Lucene `Documents` are added to is opened for writing with Lucene's `IndexWriter` class.

⑧ The instance of `FileIndexer` to perform directory traversal and file indexing is created with the `Properties` that will eventually be passed to `ExtensionFileHandler`.

⑨ The first call to `FileIndexer`'s `index` method starts directory and file processing. We pass it the `IndexWriter` we previously opened, and the starting point—the name of the file or directory specified on the command line.

⑩ Once it has traversed the whole directory tree, the recursive `index` method returns the execution control to its caller. It's then the responsibility of the caller to handle the `IndexWriter` properly by closing it, optionally optimizing it first.

⑪ Our user-friendly summary informs the user about the number of files indexed and the time taken.

7.8.4 Using FileIndexer

The `FileIndexer` class includes a `main` method that can be used to invoke the class from the command line and recursively index files in a given directory tree. To run `FileIndexer` from the command line, pass it a path to the properties file as the first argument, similar to the one shown in the following example; as a second argument, pass it a path to a directory tree or a single file that you want to index:

```
$ java lia.handlingtypes.framework.FileIndexer
⇒  ~/handler.properties ~/data ~/index
Indexing /home/otis/data/FileWithoutExtension
Cannot handle /home/otis/data/FileWithoutExtension; skipping
```

```
Indexing /home/otis/data/HTML.html
Indexing /home/otis/data/MSWord.doc
Indexing /home/otis/data/PlainText.txt
Indexing /home/otis/data/PowerPoint.ppt
Cannot handle /home/otis/data/PowerPoint.ppt; skipping
Indexing /home/otis/data/RTF.rtf
Indexing /home/otis/data/addressbook-entry.xml

Documents indexed: 6
Total time: 3046 ms
```

As it works through a directory tree, `FileIndexer` prints out information about its progress. You can see here that it indexes only files with extensions we have mapped to specific `DocumentHandlers`; all other files are skipped.

7.8.5 *FileIndexer drawbacks, and how to extend the framework*

This framework has one obvious, although minor, flaw: It assumes that the file extensions don't lie, and it requires that all files have them. For example, it assumes that a plain-text file always has a .txt file extension, and no other; that the .doc extension is reserved for Microsoft Word documents; and so on.

The framework that we developed in this chapter includes parsers that can handle the following types of input:

- XML
- PDF
- HTML
- Microsoft Word
- RTF
- Plain text

So, what do you do if you need to index and make searchable files of a type that our framework doesn't handle? You extend the framework, of course! More precisely, you follow these steps:

1 Write a parser for the desired file type and implement the `DocumentHandler` interface.

2 Add your parser class to the `handler.properties` file, mapping it to the appropriate file extension.

3 Keep using `FileIndexer` as shown.

This leads us into the next section, where you can find a list of document-parsing tools you can use in addition to the ones presented in this chapter.

7.9 *Other text-extraction tools*

In this chapter, we've presented text extraction from, and indexing of, the most common document formats. We chose tools that are the most popular among developers, tools that are still being developed (or at least maintained), and tools that are easy to use. All libraries that we've presented are freely available. There are, of course, a number of other free and commercial tools that you could use; several that we know of are listed in table 7.3.

Table 7.3 Tools for parsing different document formats, which can be used with Lucene to make documents in these formats searchable

Document format	Tool	Where to download
PDF	Xpdf	http://www.foolabs.com/xpdf/
	JPedal	http://www.jpedal.org/
	Etymon PJ	http://www.etymon.com/
	PDF Text Stream	http://snowtide.com/home/PDFTextStream
	Multivalent	http://multivalent.sourceforge.net/
XML	JDOM	http://www.jdom.org/
	Piccolo	http://piccolo.sourceforge.net/
HTML	HTMLParser	http://htmlparser.sourceforge.net/
	Multivalent	http://multivalent.sourceforge.net/
Microsoft Word	Antiword	http://www.winfield.demon.nl/
	OpenOffice SDK	http://www.openoffice.org/
Microsoft Excel	POI	http://jakarta.apache.org/poi

7.9.1 *Document-management systems and services*

In addition to individual libraries that you can use to implement document parsing and indexing the way we did in this chapter, a few free software packages and services already do that—and, interestingly enough, rely on Lucene to handle document indexing:

- DocSearcher (http://www.brownsite.net/docsearch.htm) is described by its author as follows: "DocSearcher uses the Open Source Lucene and POI Apache APIs as well as the Open Source PDF Box API to provide searching capabilities for HTML, MS Word, MS Excel, RTF, PDF, Open Office (and Star Office) documents, and text documents."

- Docco (http://tockit.sourceforge.net/docco/index.html) is a small, personal document management system built on top of Lucene. It provides indexing and searching with Lucene; the latter is enhanced by using Formal Concept Analysis's visualization techniques. According to the documentation on its home page, Docco can handle a number of document formats: plain text, XML, HTML, PDF, Microsoft Word and Excel, OpenOffice, and StarOffice 6.0, as well as UNIX man pages. Note that the list doesn't include RTF documents.

- SearchBlox (http://www.searchblox.com/) is a J2EE search component that is deployed as a web application. It's controlled and customized via a web browser interface, and it can index and search HTML, PDF, Word, Excel, and PowerPoint documents. You can read a SearchBlox case study in section 10.3.

- Simpy (http://www.simpy.com/) is a free online service created by one of the authors of this book. It lets you save links to your online documents, be they HTML web pages; PDF, Microsoft Word, or RTF documents; or any other format. Besides the meta-data that you can enter for each document, Simpy will crawl and index the full text of your documents, allowing you to search them from any computer. Your documents can be kept private or can be shared, allowing you to form online collaboration circles. Of course, all the indexing and searching is powered by Lucene, and some portions of the back end use Nutch (see the case study in section 10.1).

New Lucene document-management systems and services will undoubtedly emerge after this book goes into print. A good place to look for Lucene-powered solutions is the Lucene Wiki, as well as SourceForge.

7.10 Summary

In this code-rich chapter, you learned how to handle several common document formats, from the omnipresent but proprietary Microsoft Word format to the omnipresent and open HTML. As you can see, any type of data that can be converted to text can be indexed and made searchable with Lucene. If you can extract textual data from sound or graphics files, you can index those, too. As a matter of fact, section 10.6 describes one interesting approach to indexing JPEG images.

We used a number of freely available parsers to parse different document formats: Xerces and Digester for XML, JTidy and NekoHTML for HTML, PDFBox for PDF, and POI and TextMining.org extractors for Microsoft Word documents. To parse RTF and plain-text documents, we relied on core Java classes.

Early in the chapter, we defined a `DocumentHandler` interface that helped us define the standard invocation mechanism for all our document parsers. This, in turn, made it simple for us to bundle all the parsers in a small turnkey framework capable of recursively parsing and indexing a file system.

What you've learned in this chapter isn't limited to indexing files stored in your local file system. You can use the same framework to index web pages, files stored on remote FTP servers, files stored on remote servers on your LAN or WAN, incoming and outgoing email or instant messenger messages, or anything else you can turn into text. Your imagination is the limit.

8

Tools and extensions

You've built an index, but can you browse or query it without writing code? Absolutely! In this chapter, we'll discuss three tools to do this. Do you need analysis beyond what the built-in analyzers provide? Several specialized analyzers for many languages are available in Lucene's Sandbox. How about providing Google-like term highlighting in search results? We've got that, too!

This chapter examines third-party (non-Jakarta) software as well as several Sandbox projects. Jakarta hosts a separate CVS repository where add-ons to Lucene are kept. Deliberate care was taken with the design of Lucene to keep the core source code cohesive yet extensible. We're taking the same care in this book by keeping an intentional separation between what is in the core of Lucene and the tools and extensions that have been developed to augment it.

8.1 Playing in Lucene's Sandbox

In an effort to accommodate the increasing contributions to the Lucene project that are above and beyond the core codebase, a Sandbox CVS repository was created to house them. The Sandbox is continually evolving, making it tough to write about concretely. We'll cover the stable pieces and allude to the other interesting bits. We encourage you, when you need additional Lucene pieces, to consult the Sandbox repository and familiarize yourself with what is there—you may find that one missing piece you need. And in the same vein, if you've developed Lucene pieces and want to share the maintenance efforts, contributions are more than welcome.

Table 8.1 lists the current major contents of the Sandbox with pointers to where each is covered in this book.

Table 8.1   Major Sandbox component cross reference

Sandbox area	Description	Coverage
analyzers	Analyzers for various languages	Section 8.3
ant	An Ant `<index>` task	Section 8.4
db	Berkeley DB Directory implementation	Section 8.9
highlighter	Search result snippet highlighting	Section 8.7
javascript	Query builder and validator for web browsers	Section 8.5
lucli	Command-line interface to interact with an index	Section 8.2.1
miscellaneous	A few odds and ends, including the `ChainedFilter`	Section 8.8

continued on next page

Table 8.1   Major Sandbox component cross reference *(continued)*

Sandbox area	Description	Coverage
snowball	Sophisticated family of stemmers and wrapping analyzer	Section 8.3.1
WordNet	Utility to build a Lucene index from WordNet database	Section 8.6

There are a few more Sandbox components than those we cover in this chapter. Refer to the Sandbox directly to dig around and to see any new goodies since this was printed.

8.2   *Interacting with an index*

You've created a great index. Now what? Wouldn't it be nice to browse the index and perform ad hoc queries? You will, of course, write Java code to integrate Lucene into your applications, and you could fairly easily write utility code as a JUnit test case, a command-line utility, or a web application to interact with the index. Thankfully, though, some nice utilities have already been created to let you interact with Lucene file system indexes. We'll explore three such utilities, each unique and having a different type of interface into an index:

- *lucli (Lucene Command-Line Interface)*—A CLI that allows ad-hoc querying and index inspection
- *Luke (Lucene Index Toolbox)*—A desktop application with nice usability
- *LIMO (Lucene Index Monitor)*—A web interface that allows remote index browsing

8.2.1   *lucli: a command-line interface*

Rather than write code to interact with an index, it can be easier to do a little command-line tap dancing for ad-hoc searches or to get a quick explanation of a score. The Sandbox contains the Lucene Command-Line Interface (lucli) contribution from Dror Matalon. Lucli provides an optional readline capability (on supporting operating systems), which lets you scroll through a history of commands and reexecute a previously entered command to enhance its usability.

Using the WordNet index we'll build in section 8.6 as an example, listing 8.1 demonstrates an interactive session.

Listing 8.1   lucli in action

```
% java lucli.Lucli

Lucene CLI. Using directory:index          ⟵  Open existing
lucli> index ../WordNet/index                  index by path
Lucene CLI. Using directory:../WordNet/index
Index has 39718 documents
All Fields:[syn, word]
Indexed Fields:[word]               Perform
lucli> search jump              ⟵   search
Searching for: syn:jump word:jump    ⟵
1 total matching documents                Query on all
------------------------------------     terms
--------------- 0 score:1.0---------------------
syn:startle
syn:start
syn:spring
syn:skip
syn:rise
syn:parachuting
syn:leap
syn:jumpstart
syn:jumping
syn:derail
syn:bound
syn:alternate
word:jump
##################################################    lucli explanations
lucli> help                               ⟵        of commands
        count: Return the number of hits for a search.
              Example: count foo
        explain: Explanation that describes how the document
                 scored against query. Example: explain foo
        help: Display help about commands.
        index: Choose a different lucene index.
              Example index my_index
        info: Display info about the current Lucene Index.
              Example:info
        optimize: Optimize the current index
        quit: Quit/exit the program
        search: Search the current index. Example: search foo
        terms: Show the first 100 terms in this index.
              Supply a field name to
              only show terms in a specific field. Example: terms
        tokens: Does a search and shows the top 10 tokens for each
              document.
                 Verbose! Example: tokens foo
lucli> explain dog                    ⟵
Searching for: syn:dog word:dog            Search, and
1 total matching documents                 explain results
```

```
Searching for: word:dog
-------------------------------------
--------------- 0 score:1.0---------------------
syn:trail
syn:track
syn:tail
syn:tag
syn:pawl
syn:hound
syn:heel
syn:frump
syn:firedog
syn:dogtooth
syn:dogiron
syn:detent
syn:click
syn:chase
syn:cad
syn:bounder
syn:blackguard
syn:andiron
word:dog
Explanation:10.896413 = fieldWeight(word:dog in 262), product of:
   1.0 = tf(termFreq(word:dog)=1)
   10.896413 = idf(docFreq=1)
   1.0 = fieldNorm(field=word, doc=262)

#################################################
```

Lucli is relatively new to the scene, and as such it still has room to evolve in features and presentation. It has a couple of limitations to note, but generally they don't detract from its usefulness: The current version of lucli uses the `MultiFieldQuery-Parser` for search expressions and is hard-coded to use `StandardAnalyzer` with the parser.

8.2.2 *Luke: the Lucene Index Toolbox*

Andrzej Bialecki created Luke (found at http://www.getopt.org/luke/), an elegant Lucene index browser. This gem provides an intimate view inside a file system–based index from an attractive desktop Java application (see figure 8.1). We highly recommend having Luke handy when you're developing with Lucene because it allows for ad-hoc querying and provides insight into the terms and structure in an index.

Luke has become a regular part of our Lucene development toolkit. Its interconnected user interface allows for rapid browsing and experimentation. Luke

Figure 8.1
Luke's About page

can force an index to be unlocked when opening, optimize an index, and also delete and undelete documents, so it's really only for developers or, perhaps, system administrators. But what a wonderful tool it is!

You can launch Luke via Java WebStart from the Luke web site or install it locally. It's a single JAR file that can be launched directly (by double-clicking from a file-system browser, if your system supports that) or running `java -jar luke.jar` from the command line. The latest version at the time of this writing is 0.5; it embeds a prefinal release of Lucene 1.4. A separate JAR is available without Lucene embedded; you can use it if you wish to use a different version of Lucene.[1] Of course, the first thing Luke needs is a path to the index file, as shown in the file-selection dialog in figure 8.2.

Luke's interface is nicely interconnected so that you can jump from one view to another in the same context. The interface is divided into five tabs: Overview, Documents, Search, Files, and Plugins. The Tools menu provides options to optimize the current index, undelete any documents flagged for deletion, and switch the index between compound and standard format.

Overview: seeing the big picture

Luke's Overview tab shows the major pieces of a Lucene index, including the number of fields, documents, and terms (figure 8.3). The top terms in one or more selected fields are shown in the "Top ranking terms" pane. Double-clicking a term opens the Documents tab for the selected term, where you can browse all documents containing that term. Right-clicking a term brings up a menu with two options: "Show all term docs" opens the Search tab for that term so all

---

[1] The usual issues of Lucene version and index compatibility apply.

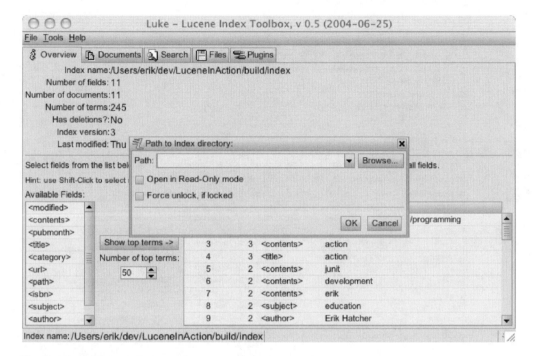

Figure 8.2 Luke: opening an index

documents appear in a list, and "Browse term docs" opens the Documents tab for the selected term.

Document browsing

The Documents tab is Luke's most sophisticated screen, where you can browse documents by document number and by term (see figure 8.4). Browsing by document number is straightforward; you can use the arrows to navigate through the documents sequentially. The table at the bottom of the screen shows all stored fields for the currently selected document.

Browsing by term is trickier; you can go about it several ways. Clicking First Term navigates the term selection to the first term in the index. You can scroll through terms by clicking the Next Term button. The number of documents containing a given term is shown as the "Doc freq of this term" value. To select a specific term, type all but the last character in the text box, click Next Term, and navigate forward until you find the desired term.

Just below the term browser is the term document browser, which lets you navigate through the documents containing the term you selected. The First Doc

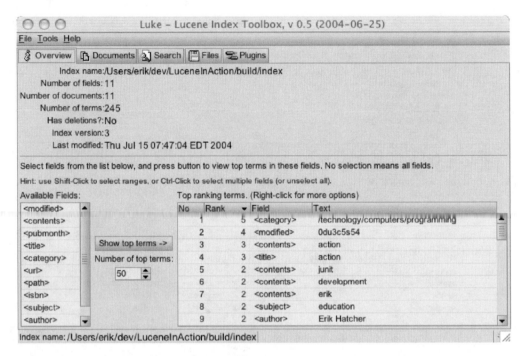

Figure 8.3 Luke: index overview, allowing you to browse fields and terms

button selects the first document that contains the selected term; and, as when you're browsing terms, Next Doc navigates forward.

The selected document, or all documents containing the selected term, can also be deleted from this screen (use caution if this is a production index, of course!).

Another feature of the Documents tab is the "Copy text to Clipboard" feature. All fields shown, or the selected field, may be copied to the clipboard. For example, copying the entire document to the clipboard places the following text there:

```
Keyword<modified:0du3cd068>
Keyword<pubmonth:200310>
Text<title:JUnit in Action>
Keyword<category:/technology/computers/programming>
Unindexed<url:http://www.manning.com/massol>
Keyword<path:C:\dev\LuceneInAction\Manuscript\data\technology\
        computers\programming\jia.properties>
Keyword<isbn:1930110995>
Keyword<author:Vincent Massol>
Keyword<author:Ted Husted>
```

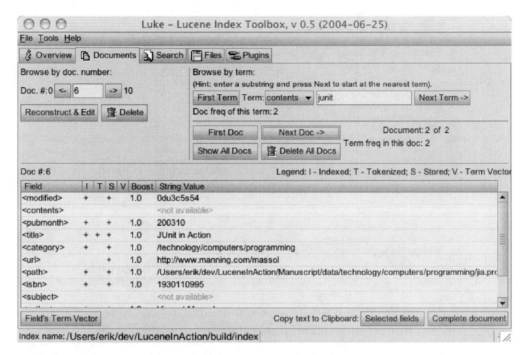

Figure 8.4   Luke's Documents tab: feel the power!

NOTE   It's important to note that Luke can only work within the constraints of a Lucene index, and unstored fields don't have the text available in its original form. The terms of those fields, of course, are navigable with Luke, but those fields aren't available in the document viewer or for copying to the clipboard (for example, our `contents` field in this case).

Clicking the Show All Docs button shifts the view to the Search tab with a search on the selected term, such that all documents containing this term are displayed. If a field's term vectors have been stored, the Field's Term Vector button displays a window showing terms and frequencies.

One final feature of the Documents tab is the "Reconstruct & Edit" button. Clicking this button opens a document editor allowing you to edit (delete and re-add) the document in the index or add a new document. Figure 8.5 shows a document being edited.

Luke reconstructs fields that were tokenized but not stored, by aggregating in position order all the terms that were indexed. Reconstructing a field is a potentially lossy operation, and Luke warns of this when you view a reconstructed field

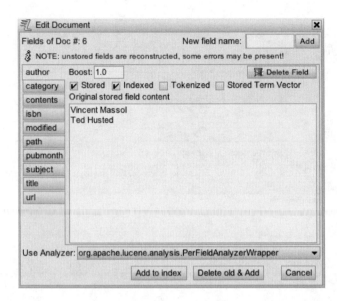

**Figure 8.5
Document editor**

(for example, if stop words were removed or tokens were stemmed during the analysis process then the original value isn't available).

Still searching over here, boss

We've already shown two ways to automatically arrive at the Search tab: choosing "Show all term docs" from the right-click menu of the "Top ranking terms" section of the Overview tab, and clicking Show All Docs from the term browser on the Documents tab.

You can also use the Search tab manually, entering `QueryParser` expression syntax along with your choice of `Analyzer` and default field. Click Search when the expression and other fields are as desired. The bottom table shows all the documents from the search hits, as shown in figure 8.6.

Double-clicking a document shifts back to the Documents tab with the appropriate document preselected. It's useful to interactively experiment with search expressions and see how `QueryParser` reacts to them (but be sure to commit your assumptions to test cases, too!). Luke shows all analyzers it finds in the classpath, but only analyzers with no-arg constructors may be used with Luke. Luke also provides insight document scoring with the explanation feature.

To view score explanation, select a result and click the Explanation button; an example is shown in figure 8.7.

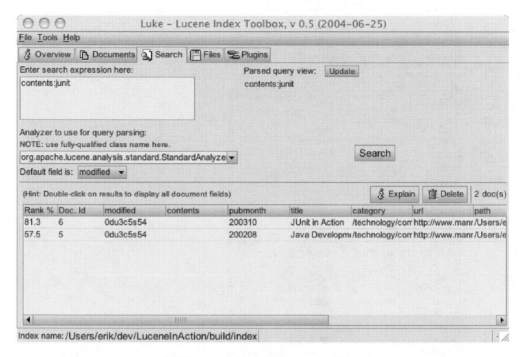

Figure 8.6   Searching: an easy way to experiment with `QueryParser`

Files view

The final view in Luke displays the files (and their sizes) that make up the internals of a Lucene index directory. The total index size is also shown, as you can see in figure 8.8.

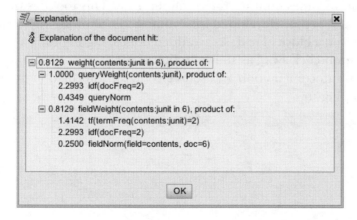

**Figure 8.7
Lucene's scoring explanation**

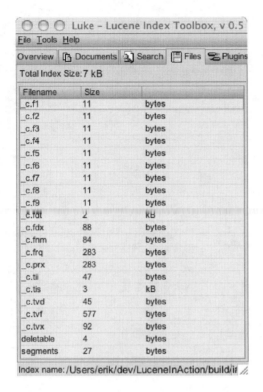

Filename	Size	
_c.f1	11	bytes
_c.f2	11	bytes
_c.f3	11	bytes
_c.f4	11	bytes
_c.f5	11	bytes
_c.f6	11	bytes
_c.f7	11	bytes
_c.f8	11	bytes
_c.f9	11	bytes
_c.fdt	2	kB
_c.fdx	88	bytes
_c.fnm	84	bytes
_c.frq	283	bytes
_c.prx	283	bytes
_c.tii	47	bytes
_c.tis	3	kB
_c.tvd	45	bytes
_c.tvf	577	bytes
_c.tvx	92	bytes
deletable	4	bytes
segments	27	bytes

Index name:/Users/erik/dev/LuceneInAction/build/in

Figure 8.8
Luke's Files view shows how big an index is.

Plugins view

As if the features already described about Luke weren't enough, Andrzej has gone the extra kilometer and added a plug-in framework so that others can add tools to Luke. One plug-in comes built in: the Analyzer Tool. This tool has the same purpose as the `AnalyzerDemo` developed in section 4.2.3, showing the results of the analysis process on a block of text. As an added bonus, highlighting a selected token is a mere button-click away, as shown in figure 8.9.

Consult the Luke documentation and source code for information on how to develop your own plug-in.

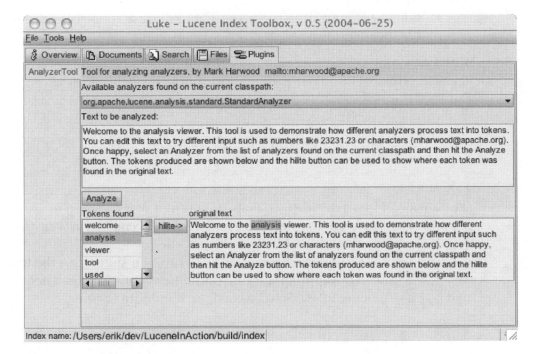

Figure 8.9 Analyzer Tool plug-in

8.2.3 *LIMO: Lucene Index Monitor*

Julien Nioche is the creator of Lucene Index Monitor (LIMO).[2] It's available online at http://limo.sourceforge.net/. LIMO provides a web browser interface to Lucene indexes, giving you a quick look at index status information such as whether an index is locked, the last modification date, the number of documents, and a field summary. In addition, a rudimentary document browser lets you scroll through documents sequentially.

Figure 8.10 shows the initial page, where you can select one or more preconfigured indexes.

To install LIMO, follow these steps:

1 Download the LIMO distribution, which is a WAR file.

2 Expand the WAR file in the Tomcat webapps/limo webapps directory.

---

[2] LIMO v0.3 is the most recent version at the time of this writing.

3   Edit the limo/WEB-INF/web.xml file, adding a couple of references to Lucene index directories.

LIMO uses context parameters in the web.xml file for controlling which indexes are made visible. One of our entries appears in web.xml like this:

```
<context-param>
  <param-name>LIA</param-name>
  <param-value>
    /Users/erik/dev/LuceneInAction/build/index
  </param-value>
  <description>Lucene In Action sample index</description>
</context-param>
```

The version of LIMO that we used embeds Lucene 1.3; if you need to use a newer version of Lucene than LIMO embeds, replace the Lucene JAR in WEB-INF/lib by removing the existing file and adding a newer one.

After you follow the installation and configuration steps, start the web container. Navigate to the appropriate URL (http://localhost:8080/limo/ in our case), and take a seat in the LIMO. Select a configured index to browse.

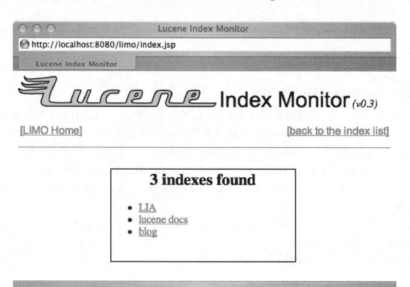

Figure 8.10   LIMO: selecting an index

Browsing an index

LIMO's only other screen is the index summary and document browser view. Figure 8.11 shows a sample.

Click the Prev and Next links to navigate through the documents. All the stored fields are shown on the right, indicating whether they are stored and/or indexed.

Using LIMO

LIMO's user interface isn't fancy, but it does the job. You may want to have LIMO installed on a secured Tomcat instance on a production server. Being able to get a quick view of how many documents are in an index, whether it's locked, and when it was last updated can be helpful for monitoring purposes. Also, using the LIMO JSP pages as a basis for building your own custom monitoring view could be a time saver. Because LIMO functions as a web application and doesn't allow any destructive operations on an index, it provides a handy way to peek into a remote index.

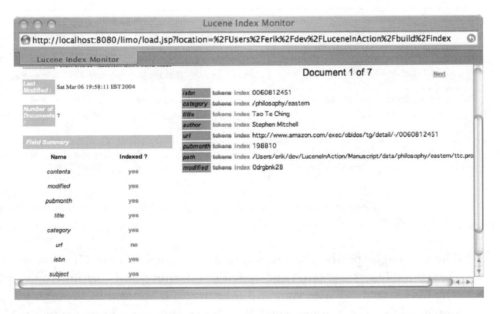

Figure 8.11   Cruising in the LIMO

8.3 *Analyzers, tokenizers, and TokenFilters, oh my*

The more analyzers, the merrier, we always say. And the Sandbox doesn't disappoint in this area: It houses several language-specific analyzers, a few related filters and tokenizers, and the slick Snowball algorithm analyzers. The analyzers are listed in table 8.2.

Table 8.2   Sandbox analyzers

Analyzer[a]	TokenStream flow
`org.apache.lucene.analysis.` `br.BrazilianAnalyzer`	`StandardTokenizer` ➜ `StandardFilter` ➜ `StopFilter` (custom stop table) ➜ `BrazilianStemFilter` ➜ `LowerCaseFilter`
`org.apache.lucene.analysis.` `cjk.CJKAnalyzer`	`CJKTokenizer` ➜ `StopFilter` (custom English stop words ironically)
`org.apache.lucene.analysis.` `cn.ChineseAnalyzer`	`ChineseTokenizer` ➜ `ChineseFilter`
`org.apache.lucene.analysis.` `cz.CzechAnalyzer`	`StandardTokenizer` ➜ `StandardFilter` ➜ `LowerCaseFilter` ➜ `StopFilter` (custom stop list)
`org.apache.lucene.analyzer.` `nl.DutchAnalyzer`	`StandardTokenizer` ➜ `StandardFilter` ➜ `StopFilter` (custom stop table)➜ `DutchStemFilter`
`org.apache.lucene.analyzer.` `fr.FrenchAnalyzer`	`StandardTokenizer` ➜ `StandardFilter` ➜ `StopFilter` (custom stop table)➜ `FrenchStemFilter` ➜ `LowerCaseFilter`
`org.apache.lucene.analysis.` `snowball.SnowballAnalyzer`	`StandardTokenizer` ➜ `StandardFilter` ➜ `LowerCaseFilter` [➜ `StopFilter`] ➜ `SnowballFilter`

[a] *Note the different package name for the* `SnowballAnalyzer`*—it is housed in a different sandbox directory than the others.*

The language-specific analyzers vary in how they tokenize. The Brazilian and French analyzers use language-specific stemming and custom stop-word lists. The Czech analyzer uses standard tokenization, but also incorporates a custom stop word list. The Chinese and CJK (Chinese-Japanese-Korean) analyzers tokenize double-byte characters as a single token to keep a logical character intact. We demonstrate analysis of Chinese characters in section 4.8.3, illustrating how these two analyzers work.

Each of these analyzers, including the `SnowballAnalyzer` discussed in the next section, lets you customize the stop-word list just as the `StopAnalyzer` does (see section 4.3.1). Most of these analyzers do quite a bit in the filtering process. If the stemming or tokenization is all you need, borrow the relevant pieces, and construct your own custom analyzer from the parts here. Section 4.6 covers creating custom analyzers.

8.3.1 *SnowballAnalyzer*

The `SnowballAnalyzer` deserves special mention because it serves as a driver of an entire family of stemmers for different languages. Stemming was first introduced in section 4.7. Dr. Martin Porter, who also developed the Porter stemming algorithm, created the Snowball algorithm.[3] The Porter algorithm was designed for English only; in addition, many "purported" implementations don't adhere to the definition faithfully.[4] To address these issues, Dr. Porter rigorously defined the Snowball system of stemming algorithms. Through these algorithmic definitions, accurate implementations can be generated. In fact, the snowball project in Lucene's Sandbox has a build process that can pull the definitions from Dr. Porter's site and generate the Java implementation.

One of the test cases demonstrates the result of the English stemmer stripping off the trailing *ming* from *stemming* and the *s* from *algorithms*:

```
public void testEnglish() throws Exception {
  Analyzer analyzer = new SnowballAnalyzer("English");

  assertAnalyzesTo(analyzer,
      "stemming algorithms", new String[] {"stem", "algorithm"});
}
```

`SnowballAnalyzer` has two constructors; both accept the stemmer name only, and one specifies a `String[]` stop-word list to use. Many unique stemmers exist for various languages. The non-English stemmers include Danish, Dutch, Finnish, French, German, German2, Italian, Kp (Kraaij-Pohlmann algorithm for Dutch), Norwegian, Portuguese, Russian, Spanish, and Swedish. There are a few English-specific stemmers named English, Lovins, and Porter. These exact names are the valid argument values to the `SnowballAnalyzer` constructors. Here is an example using the Spanish stemming algorithm:

---

[3] The name *Snowball* is a tribute to the string-manipulation language SNOBOL.

[4] From http://snowball.tartarus.org/texts/introduction.html

```
public void testSpanish() throws Exception {
   Analyzer analyzer = new SnowballAnalyzer("Spanish");

   assertAnalyzesTo(analyzer,
       "algoritmos", new String[] {"algoritm"});
}
```

If your project demands stemming, we recommend that you give the Snowball analyzer your attention first since an expert in the stemming field developed it. And, as already mentioned but worth repeating, you may want to use the clever piece of this analyzer (the `SnowballFilter`) wrapped in your own custom analyzer implementation. Several sections in chapter 4 discuss writing custom analyzers in great detail.

8.3.2 Obtaining the Sandbox analyzers

Depending on your needs, you may want JAR binary distributions of these analyzers or raw source code from which to borrow ideas. Section 8.10 provides details on how to access the Sandbox CVS repository and how to build binary distributions. Within the repository, the Snowball analyzer resides in contributions/snowball; the other analyzers discussed here are in contributions/analyzers. There are no external dependencies for these analyzers other than Lucene itself, so they are easy to incorporate. A test program called `TestApp` is included for the Snowball project. It's run in this manner:

```
> java -cp dist/snowball.jar net.sf.snowball.TestApp
Usage: TestApp <stemmer name> <input file> [-o <output file>]

> java -cp dist/snowball.jar
⇒  net.sf.snowball.TestApp Lovins spoonful.txt
... output of stemmer applied to specified file
```

The Snowball `TestApp` bypasses `SnowballAnalyzer`. Only the Snowball stemmer itself is used with rudimentary text splitting at whitespace.

8.4 Java Development with Ant and Lucene

A natural integration point with Lucene incorporates document indexing into a build process. As part of *Java Development with Ant* (Hatcher and Loughran, Manning Publications, 2002), Erik created an Ant task to index a directory of file-based documents. This code has since been enhanced and is maintained in the Sandbox.

Why index documents during a build process? Imagine a project that is providing an embedded help system with search capability. The documents are probably static for a particular version of the system, and having a read-only index created at build-time fits perfectly. For example, what if the Ant, Lucene, and other projects had a domain-specific search on their respective web sites? It makes sense for the searchable documentation to be the latest release version; it doesn't need to be dynamically updated.

8.4.1 Using the <index> task

Listing 8.2 shows a simplistic Ant 1.6.x–compatible build file that indexes a directory of text and HTML files.

Listing 8.2 Using the Ant `<index>` task

```xml
<?xml version="1.0"?>
<project name="ant-example" default="index">

  <description>
    Lucene Ant index example
  </description>

  <property name="index.base.dir" location="build"/>      Parent of index directory
  <property name="files.dir" location="."/>               Root directory of documents to index

  <target name="index">
    <mkdir dir="${index.base.dir}"/>

    <index index="${index.base.dir}/index"
           xmlns="antlib:org.apache.lucene.ant">
      <fileset dir="${files.dir}"/>
    </index>
  </target>

</project>
```

The Ant integration is Ant 1.6 Antlib compatible, as seen with the xmlns specification. The legacy `<taskdef>` method can still be used, too. Listing 8.2 shows the most basic usage of the `<index>` task, minimally requiring specification of the index directory and a fileset of files to consider for indexing. The default file-handling mechanism indexes only files that end with .txt or .html.[5] Table 8.3 lists the fields created by the index task and the default document handler. Only `path` and `modified` are fixed fields; the others come from the document handler.

---

[5] JTidy is currently used to extract HTML content for indexing. See section 7.4 for more on indexing HTML.

Table 8.3 `<index>` task default fields

Field name	Field type	Comments
path	Keyword	Absolute path to a file
modified	`Keyword` (as `Date`)	Last-modified date of a file
title	Text	`<title>` in HTML files; and filename for .txt files.
Contents	Text	Complete contents of .txt files; parsed `<body>` of HTML files
rawcontents	UnIndexed	Raw contents of the file

It's very likely that the default document handler is insufficient for your needs. Fortunately, a custom document handler extension point exists.

8.4.2 *Creating a custom document handler*

A swappable document-handler facility is built into the `<index>` task, allowing custom implementations to handle different document types and control the Lucene fields created.[6] Not only can the document handler be specified, configuration parameters can be passed to the custom document handler. We used the Ant `<index>` task, as shown in listing 8.3, to build the index used in the majority of the code for this book.

Listing 8.3 Use of the `<index>` task to build the sample index for this book

```
<target name="build-index" depends="compile">
  <typedef resource="org/apache/lucene/ant/antlib.xml">
    <classpath>
      <path refid="compile.classpath"/>
      <pathelement location="${build.dir}/classes"/>
    </classpath>
  </typedef>

  <index index="${build.dir}/index"
         documenthandler="lia.common.TestDataDocumentHandler">
    <fileset dir="${data.dir}"/>
    <config basedir="${data.dir}"/>
  </index>
</target>
```

❶ `<typedef>`

Use custom document handler ❷

❸ **basedir configuration property**

---

[6] The `<index>` task document handler facility was developed long before the framework Otis built in chapter 7. At this point, the two document-handling frameworks are independent of one another, although they're similar and can be easily merged.

① We use `<typdef>` because we need an additional dependency added to the class-path for our document handler. If we didn't need a custom document handler, the `<typedef>` would be unnecessary.

② We use a custom document handler to process files differently.

③ Here we hand our document handler a configuration property, `basedir`. This allows relative paths to be extracted cleanly.

The directory, referred to as ${data.dir}, contains a hierarchy of folders and .properties files. Each .properties file contains information about a single book, as in this example:

```
title=Tao Te Ching \u9053\u5FB7\u7D93
isbn=0060812451
author=Stephen Mitchell
subject=taoism
pubmonth=198810
url=http://www.amazon.com/exec/obidos/tg/detail/-/0060812451
```

The folder hierarchy serves as meta-data also, specifying the book categories. Figure 8.12 shows the sample data directory. For example, the .properties example just shown is the ttc.properties file that resides in the data/philosophy/eastern directory. The base directory points to data and is stripped off in the document handler as shown in listing 8.4.

To write a custom document handler, pick one of the two interfaces to implement. If you don't need any additional meta-data from the Ant build file, implement `DocumentHandler`, which has the following single method returning a Lucene `Document` instance:

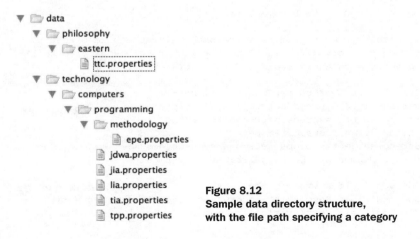

Figure 8.12
Sample data directory structure,
with the file path specifying a category

```
public interface DocumentHandler {
   Document getDocument(File file)
            throws DocumentHandlerException;
}
```

Implementing `ConfigurableDocumentHandler` allows the `<index>` task to pass additional information as a `java.util.Properties` object:

```
public interface ConfigurableDocumentHandler
                     extends DocumentHandler {
   void configure(Properties props);
}
```

Configuration options are passed using a single `<config>` subelement with arbitrarily named attributes. The `<config>` attribute names become the keys to the properties. Our complete `TestDataDocumentHandler` class is shown in listing 8.4.

Listing 8.4   `TestDataDocumentHandler`: how we built our sample index

```
public class TestDataDocumentHandler
              implements ConfigurableDocumentHandler {
   private String basedir;

   public Document getDocument(File file)
            throws DocumentHandlerException {
     Properties props = new Properties();
     try {
       props.load(new FileInputStream(file));
     } catch (IOException e) {
       throw new DocumentHandlerException(e);
     }

     Document doc = new Document();

     // category comes from relative path below the base directory
     String category = file.getParent().substring(basedir.length());
     category = category.replace(File.separatorChar,'/');
                                                          Get category ❶

     String isbn = props.getProperty("isbn");
     String title = props.getProperty("title");
     String author = props.getProperty("author");       ❷ Pull fields
     String url = props.getProperty("url");
     String subject = props.getProperty("subject");
     String pubmonth = props.getProperty("pubmonth");

     doc.add(Field.Keyword("isbn", isbn));             Add fields to ❸
     doc.add(Field.Keyword("category", category)); Document instance
     doc.add(Field.Text("title", title));
```

```
// split multiple authors into unique field instances
String[] authors = author.split(",");
for (int i = 0; i < authors.length; i++) {
  doc.add(Field.Keyword("author", authors[i]));
}

doc.add(Field.UnIndexed("url", url));
doc.add(Field.UnStored("subject", subject, true));

doc.add(Field.Keyword("pubmonth", pubmonth));

doc.add(Field.UnStored("contents",
    aggregate(new String[] { title, subject, author})));

return doc;
}

private String aggregate(String[] strings) {
  StringBuffer buffer = new StringBuffer();

  for (int i = 0; i < strings.length; i++) {
    buffer.append(strings[i]);
    buffer.append(" ");
  }

  return buffer.toString();
}

public void configure(Properties props) {
  this.basedir = props.getProperty("basedir");
}
}
```

Add fields to ❸ **Document instance**

❹ **Flag subject field**

Add contents field ❺

❶ We base the category on the relative path from the base data directory, ensuring that forward slashes are used as separators.

❷ Here we pull each field from the values in the .properties file.

❸ We add each field to the Document instance; note the different types of fields used.

❹ The subject field is flagged for term vector storage.

❺ The contents field is an aggregate field: We can search a single field containing both the author and subject.

When you use a custom document handler, in addition to the fields the handler creates, the <index> task automatically adds path and modified fields. These two fields are used for incremental indexing, allowing only newly modified files to be processed.

The build file can also control the analyzer and merge factor. The merge factor defaults to 20, but you can set it to another value by specifying `mergeFactor="..."` as an attribute to the `<index>` task. The analyzer is specified in one of two ways. The built-in analyzers are available using `analyzer="..."`, where the value is `simple`, `standard`, `stop`, `whitespace`, `german`, or `russian`. If you need to use any other analyzer, specify `analyzerClass="..."` instead, with the fully qualified class name. Currently, only analyzers that have a no-argument constructor can be used with `<index>`; this rules out using the `SnowballAnalyzer` directly, for example.

There are several interesting possibilities, thanks to the flexibility of the `<index>` task, such as indexing documentation in multiple languages. You may have documents separated by directory structure (docs/en, docs/fr, docs/nl, and so on), by filename (index.html.en, index.html.fr, and so on), or by some other scheme. You could use the `<index>` task multiple times in a build process to build a separate index for each language, or you could write them all to the same index and use a different analyzer for each language.

8.4.3 *Installation*

The `<index>` task requires three libraries and at least Ant 1.5.4 (although Ant 1.6 or higher is recommended to take advantage of the Antlib feature). The Lucene JAR, JTidy's JAR, and the JAR of the `<index>` task itself are required. Obtain these JARs, place them in a single directory together, and use the `-lib` Ant 1.6 command-line switch to point to this directory (or use `<taskdef>` with the proper classpath). See section 8.10 for elaboration on how to obtain JARs from the Sandbox component, and refer to Ant's documentation and Manning's *Java Development with Ant* for specifics on working with Ant.

8.5 *JavaScript browser utilities*

Integrating Lucene into an application often requires placing a search interface in a web application. `QueryParser` is handy, and it's easy to expose a simple text box allowing the user to enter a query; but it can be friendlier for users to see query options separated into fields, such as a date-range selection in conjunction with a text box for free-text searching. The JavaScript utilities in the Sandbox assist with browser-side usability in constructing and validating sophisticated expressions suitable for `QueryParser`.

8.5.1 *JavaScript query construction and validation*

As we've explored in several previous chapters, exposing `QueryParser` directly to end users can lead to confusion. If you're providing a web interface to search a Lucene index, you may want to consider using the nicely done JavaScript query constructor and validator in the Sandbox, originally written by fellow Lucene developer Kelvin Tan. The javascript Sandbox project includes a sample HTML file that mimics Google's advanced searching options, as shown in figure 8.13.

The query constructor supports all HTML fields including text and hidden fields, radio buttons, and single and multiple selects. Each HTML field must have a corresponding HTML field named with the suffix *Modifier*, controlling how the terms are added to the query. The modifier field can be a hidden field to prevent a user from controlling it, as in the case of the text fields in figure 8.12. The constructed query is placed in an HTML field (typically a hidden one), which is handed to `QueryParser` on the server side.

The query validator uses regular expressions to do its best approximation of what is acceptable to `QueryParser`. Both JavaScript files allow customization with features like debug mode to alert you to what is happening, modifier field suffixes, specifying whether to submit the form upon construction, and more. The JavaScript files are well documented and easy to drop into your own environment.

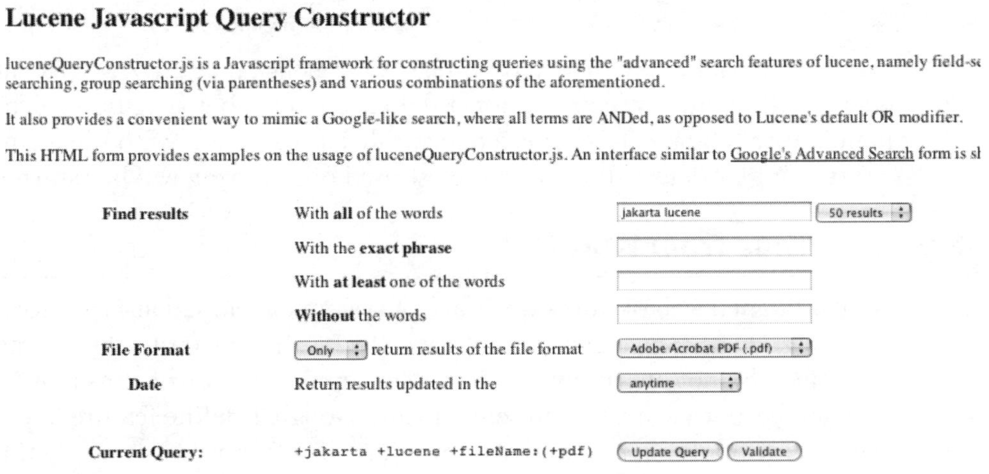

Figure 8.13   JavaScript example

At the time of this writing, the javascript Sandbox was being enhanced. Rather than show potentially out-of-date HTML, we refer you to the examples in the Sandbox when you need this capability.

8.5.2 *Escaping special characters*

QueryParser uses many special characters for operators and grouping. The characters must be escaped if they're used in a field name or as part of a term (see section 3.5 for more details on QueryParser escape characters). Using the luceneQueryEscaper.js support from the Sandbox, you can escape a query string.

You should use the query escaper only on fields or strings that should not contain any Lucene special characters already. For example, it would be incorrect to escape a query built with the query constructor, since any parentheses and operators it added would be subsequently escaped.

8.5.3 *Using JavaScript support*

Adding JavaScript support to your HTML file only requires grabbing (see section 8.10) the JavaScript files and referring to them in the <head> section in this manner:

```
<script type="text/javascript"
        src="luceneQueryConstructor.js"></script>
<script type="text/javascript"
        src="luceneQueryValidator.js"></script>
<script type="text/javascript" src="luceneQueryEscaper.js"></script>
```

Call doMakeQuery to construct a query and doCheckLuceneQuery to validate a query. Both methods require a form field argument that specifies which field to populate or validate. To escape a query, call doEscapeQuery with the form field or a text string (it detects the type); the escaped query string will be returned.

8.6 *Synonyms from WordNet*

What a tangled web of words we weave. A system developed at Princeton University's Cognitive Science Laboratory, driven by Psychology Professor George Miller, illustrates the net of synonyms.[7] WordNet represents word forms that are interchangeable, both lexically and semantically. Google's define feature (type **define: word** as a Google search, and see for yourself) often refers users to the online

---

[7] Interestingly, this is the same George Miller who reported on the phenomenon of seven plus or minus two chunks in immediate memory.

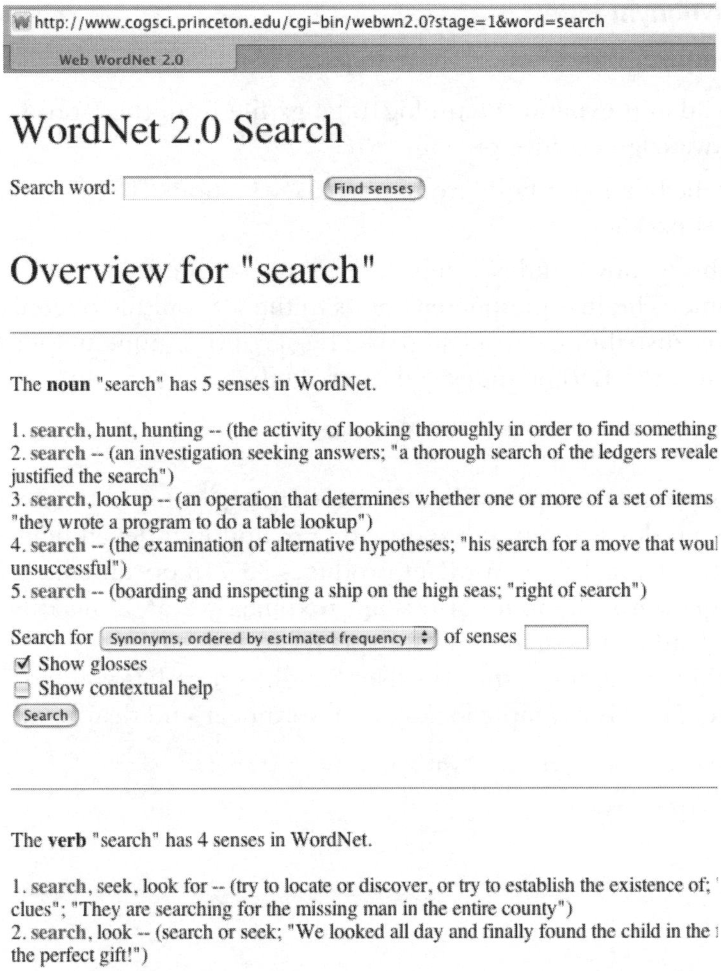

```
http://www.cogsci.princeton.edu/cgi-bin/webwn2.0?stage=1&word=search
Web WordNet 2.0
```

WordNet 2.0 Search

Search word: [_____] (Find senses)

Overview for "search"

The **noun** "search" has 5 senses in WordNet.

1. search, hunt, hunting -- (the activity of looking thoroughly in order to find something
2. search -- (an investigation seeking answers; "a thorough search of the ledgers reveale
justified the search")
3. search, lookup -- (an operation that determines whether one or more of a set of items
"they wrote a program to do a table lookup")
4. search -- (the examination of alternative hypotheses; "his search for a move that woul
unsuccessful")
5. search -- (boarding and inspecting a ship on the high seas; "right of search")

Search for [Synonyms, ordered by estimated frequency ‡] of senses [_____]
☑ Show glosses
☐ Show contextual help
(Search)

The **verb** "search" has 4 senses in WordNet.

1. search, seek, look for -- (try to locate or discover, or try to establish the existence of;
clues"; "They are searching for the missing man in the entire county")
2. search, look -- (search or seek; "We looked all day and finally found the child in the
the perfect gift!")

**Figure 8.14
Caught in the WordNet:
word interconnections
for *search***

WordNet system, allowing you to navigate word interconnections. Figure 8.14 shows the results of searching for *search* at the WordNet site.

What does all this mean to developers using Lucene? With Dave Spencer's contribution to Lucene's Sandbox, the WordNet synonym database can be churned into a Lucene index. This allows for rapid synonym lookup—for example, for synonym injection during indexing or querying (see section 8.6.2 for such an implementation).

8.6.1 *Building the synonym index*

To build the synonym index, follow these steps:

1   Download and expand the prolog16.tar.gz file from the WordNet site at http://www.cogsci.princeton.edu/~wn.

2   Obtain the binary (or build from source; see section 8.10) of the Sandbox WordNet package.

3   Build the synonym index using the Syns2Index program from the command line. The first parameter points to the wn_s.pl file obtained in the WordNet distribution from step 1. The second argument specifies the path where the Lucene index will be created:

```
java org.apache.lucene.wordnet.Syns2Index
⇒   prologwn/wn_s.pl wordnetindex
```

The Syns2Index program converts the WordNet Prolog synonym database into a standard Lucene index with an indexed field word and unindexed fields syn for each document. Version 1.6 of WordNet produces 39,718 documents, each representing a single word; the index size is approximately 2.5MB, making it compact enough to load as a RAMDirectory for speedy access.

A second utility program in the WordNet Sandbox area lets you look up synonyms of a word. Here is a sample lookup of a word near and dear to our hearts:

```
java org.apache.lucene.wordnet.SynLookup wordnetindex search

Synonyms found for "search":
seek
searching
research
lookup
look
hunting
hunt
explore
```

Figure 8.15 shows these same synonyms graphically using Luke.

To use the synonym index in your applications, borrow the relevant pieces from SynLookup, as shown in listing 8.5.

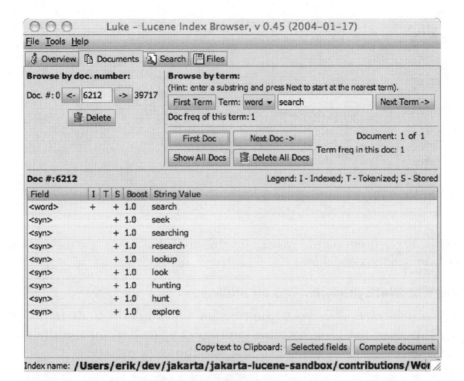

Figure 8.15   Cool app Luke: inspecting WordNet synonyms

Listing 8.5   Looking up synonyms from a WordNet-based index

```java
public class SynLookup {

  public static void main(String[] args) throws IOException {
    if (args.length != 2) {
      System.out.println(
    "java org.apache.lucene.wordnet.SynLookup <index path> <word>");
    }

    FSDirectory directory = FSDirectory.getDirectory(args[0], false);
    IndexSearcher searcher = new IndexSearcher(directory);

    String word = args[1];
    Hits hits = searcher.search(
      new TermQuery(new Term("word", word)));

    if (hits.length() == 0) {
      System.out.println("No synonyms found for " + word);
    } else {
      System.out.println("Synonyms found for \"" + word + "\":");
    }
```

```
    for (int i = 0; i < hits.length(); i++) {
      Document doc = hits.doc(i);

      String[] values = doc.getValues("syn");        Enumerate
                                                      synonyms
      for (int j = 0; j < values.length; j++) {      for word
        System.out.println(values[j]);
      }
    }

    searcher.close();
    directory.close();
  }
}
```

The SynLookup program was written for this book, but it has been added into the
WordNet Sandbox codebase.

8.6.2 *Tying WordNet synonyms into an analyzer*

The custom SynonymAnalyzer from section 4.6 can easily hook into WordNet
synonyms using the SynonymEngine interface. Listing 8.6 contains the WordNet-
SynonymEngine, which is suitable for use with the SynonymAnalyzer.

Listing 8.6 WordNetSynonymEngine

```
public class WordNetSynonymEngine implements SynonymEngine {
  RAMDirectory directory;
  IndexSearcher searcher;

  public WordNetSynonymEngine(File index) throws IOException {
    directory = new RAMDirectory(
                      FSDirectory.getDirectory(index, false));   ◄─┐
    searcher = new IndexSearcher(directory);          Load synonym
  }                                                   index into RAM
                                                      for rapid access
  public String[] getSynonyms(String word) throws IOException {

    ArrayList synList = new ArrayList();

    Hits hits = searcher.search(
                  new TermQuery(new Term("word", word)));

    for (int i = 0; i < hits.length(); i++) {
      Document doc = hits.doc(i);

      String[] values = doc.getValues("syn");
```

```
      for (int j = 0; j < values.length; j++) {
        synList.add(values[j]);
      }
    }

    return (String[]) synList.toArray(new String[0]);
  }
}
```

Adjusting the `SynonymAnalyzerViewer` from section 4.6 to use the `WordNetSynonym-Engine`, our sample output is as follows:

```
1: [quick] [agile] [fast] [flying] [immediate] [nimble] [prompt]
   [promptly] [quickly] [ready] [speedy] [spry] [straightaway]
   [warm]
2: [brown] [brownish] [brownness]
3: [fox] 8 [bedevil] [befuddle] [confound] [confuse]
   [discombobulate] [dodger] [fob] [fuddle] [slyboots] [throw]
   [trick]
4: [jumps]
5: [over] [across] [o]
6: [lazy] [slothful] [otiose] [indolent] [faineant]
7: [dogs]
```

Interestingly, WordNet synonyms do exist for *jump* and *dog* (see the lucli output in listing 8.1), but only in singular form. Perhaps stemming should be added to our `SynonymAnalyzer` prior to the `SynonymFilter`, or maybe the `WordNetSynonym-Engine` should be responsible for stemming words before looking them up in the WordNet index. These are issues that need to be addressed based on your environment. This emphasizes again the importance of the analysis process and the fact that it deserves your attention.

The Lucene WordNet code requires an older version (1.6) of the WordNet database. If you want to hook into the more recent 2.x versions of WordNet, you'll need to either manually adjust the Lucene Sandbox code or tie into JWordNet, a Java API into WordNet housed at http://jwn.sourceforge.net/.

8.6.3 *Calling on Lucene*

With the increasing pervasiveness of mobile devices and their shrinking size, we need clever text-input methods. The T9 interface present on most phones is far

---

[8] We've apparently befuddled or outfoxed the WordNet synonym database because the synonyms injected for *fox* don't relate to the animal noun we intended.

Figure 8.16
Cell-phone-like Swing interface

more efficient than requiring exact character input.[9] As a prototype of something potentially useful, we put Lucene and WordNet under a cell-phone-like Swing interface, as shown in figure 8.16.[10]

The buttons 2–9 are mapped to three or four letters of the alphabet each, identical to an actual phone. Each click of these numbers appends the selected digit to an internal buffer; a Lucene search is performed to match words for those digits. The buttons that aren't mapped to letters are used for additional capabilities: 1 scrolls the view through the list of matching words (the status bar shows how many words match the digits entered); the asterisk (*) backspaces one digit, undoing the last number entered; 0 enables debugging diagnostic output to the console; and pound (#) clears all digits entered, allowing you to start a new entry.

Constructing the T9 index

We wrote a utility class to preprocess the original WordNet index into a specialized T9 index. Each word is converted into a t9 keyword field. Each word, its T9 equivalent, and the text length of the word are indexed, as shown here:

```
Document newDoc = new Document();
newDoc.add(Field.Keyword("word", word));
newDoc.add(Field.Keyword("t9", t9(word)));
newDoc.add(new Field("length",
    Integer.toString(word.length()), false, true, false));
```

---

[9] T9 is an input method that maps each numeric button to multiple letters of the alphabet. A series of numbers logically corresponds to a subset of sensible words. For example, 732724 spells *search*.

[10] Many thanks to Dave Engler for building the base Swing application framework.

The t9 method is not shown, but it can be obtained from the book's source code distribution (see the "About this book" section). The word length is indexed as its Integer.toString() value to allow for sorting by length using the sort feature discussed in section 5.1.

Searching for words with T9

To have a little fun with Lucene, we query for a sequence of digits using a Boolean-Query with a slight look-ahead so a user doesn't have to enter all the digits. For example, if the digits 73272 are entered, *search* is the first word shown, but two others also match (*secpar*[11] and *peasant*). The query uses a boosted TermQuery on the exact digits (to ensure that exact matches come first) and a wildcard query matching words with one or two more characters more. Here's the BooleanQuery code:

```
BooleanQuery query = new BooleanQuery();
Term term = new Term("t9", number);
TermQuery termQuery = new TermQuery(term);
termQuery.setBoost(2.0f);
WildcardQuery plus2 = new WildcardQuery(
                          new Term("t9", number + "??"));
query.add(termQuery, false, false);
query.add(plus2, false, false);
```

The search results are sorted first by score, then by length, and finally alphabetically within words of the same length:

```
Hits hits = searcher.search(query,
    new Sort(new SortField[] {SortField.FIELD_SCORE,
                        new SortField("length",
                            SortField.INT),
                        new SortField("word")}));
```

Search results are timed and cached. The status bar displays the time the search took (often under 30ms). The cache allows the user to scroll through words.

Just a prototype

This desktop cell-phone prototype is a compellingly fast and accurate T9 lookup implementation. However, the Lucene index used is over 2MB in size and is unsuitable given current mobile-phone memory constraints. With a smaller set of words and some indexing optimizations (using an unstored t9 field instead of a keyword), the index could be dramatically reduced in size. With persistent, fast, and cheap server connectivity from mobile devices, some word lookups could

---

[11] "A unit of astronomical length based on the distance from Earth at which stellar parallax is 1 second of arc; equivalent to 3.262 light years" (according to a Google **define: secpar** result from WordNet).

perhaps be performed on the server rather than the client. Searching Google is already a common mobile device activity!

8.7 *Highlighting query terms*

Giving users of your search engine some context around hits from their searches is friendly and, more important, useful. A prime example is Google search results. Each hit, as shown in figure 1.1, includes up to three lines of the matching document highlighting the terms of the query. Often a brief glimpse of the surrounding context of the search terms is enough to know if that result is worth investigating further.

Thanks to Mark Harwood's contribution, the Sandbox includes infrastructure to highlight text based on a Lucene query. Figure 8.17 is an example of using Highlighter on a sample of text based on a term query for *ipsum*.

The Highlighter code has recently evolved substantially into a sophisticated and flexible utility. The Highlighter includes three main pieces: Fragmenter, Scorer, and Formatter. These correspond to Java interfaces by the same names, and each has a built-in implementation for ease of use. The simplest example of Highlighter returns the best fragment, surrounding each matching term with HTML <B> tags:

```
String text = "The quick brown fox jumps over the lazy dog";

TermQuery query = new TermQuery(new Term("field", "fox"));
Scorer scorer = new QueryScorer(query);
Highlighter highlighter = new Highlighter(scorer);

TokenStream tokenStream =
    new SimpleAnalyzer().tokenStream("field",
        new StringReader(text));

System.out.println(highlighter.getBestFragment(tokenStream, text));
```

Contrary to popular belief, Lorem Ipsum..., from a Lorem Ipsum passage, and going through..., discovered the undoubtable source. Lorem Ipsum comes... the Renaissance. The first line of Lorem Ipsum, "Lorem ipsum dolor sit amet..", comes from a line

Figure 8.17
Highlighting query terms

The previous code produces this output:

```
The quick brown <B>fox</B> jumps over the lazy dog
```

Highlighter requires that you provide not only a scorer and the text to highlight, but also a `TokenStream`. Analyzers produce `TokenStreams` (see chapter 4). To successfully highlight terms, the terms in the `Query` need to match `Tokens` emitted from the `TokenStream`. The same text should be used to generate the `TokenStream` as is used for the original text to highlight. Each `Token` emitted from a `TokenStream` contains positional information, indicating where in the original text to begin and end highlighting.

The Highlighter breaks the original text into fragments, using a Fragmenter. The built-in `SimpleFragmenter` splits the original text into same-size fragments with the default size of 100 characters. The size of fragments is controllable, as you'll see in listing 8.6.

`QueryScorer` is the built-in Scorer. The Scorer's job is primarily to rank fragments. `QueryScorer` uses the terms from the query; it extracts them from primitive term, phrase, and Boolean queries and weights them based on their corresponding boost factor. A query must be rewritten in its most primitive form for `QueryScorer` to be happy. For example, wildcard, fuzzy, prefix, and range queries rewrite themselves to a `BooleanQuery` of all the matching terms. Call `Query.rewrite(IndexReader)` to rewrite a query prior to passing the `Query` to `QueryScorer` (unless, as in this example, you're sure the query is a primitive one).

Finally, the Formatter decorates term text. The built-in `SimpleHTMLFormatter`, unless specified otherwise, uses begin and end HTML bold tags to surround the highlighted term text. Highlighter uses both the `SimpleHTMLFormatter` and `SimpleFragmenter` by default. For each term it's highlighting, the Formatter is handed a token score. This score is, when using `QueryScorer`, is the boost factor of the query clause of that term. This token score could be used to affect the decoration based on the importance of the term. A custom Formatter would need to be implemented to take advantage of this feature, but this is beyond the scope of this section.

8.7.1 *Highlighting with CSS*

Using `<B>` tags to surround text that will be rendered by browsers is a reasonable default. Fancier styling should be done with cascading style sheets (CSS) instead. Our next example uses custom begin and end tags to wrap highlighted terms with a `<span>` using the custom CSS class `highlight`. Using CSS attributes, the color and formatting of highlighted terms is decoupled from highlighting, allowing much more control for the web designers who are tasked with beautifying our search results page.

Listing 8.7 demonstrates the use of custom a custom Fragmenter, setting the fragment size to 50, and a custom Formatter to style highlights with CSS. In our first example, only the best fragment was returned, but Highlighter shines in returning multiple fragments. `HighlightIt`, in listing 8.7, uses the Highlighter method to concatenate the best fragments with an ellipsis (...) separator; however you could also have a `String[]` returned by not passing in a separator, so that your code could deal with each fragment individually.

Listing 8.7   Highlighting terms using cascading style sheets

```
public class HighlightIt {
  private static final String text =
      "Contrary to popular belief, Lorem Ipsum is" +
      " not simply random text. It has roots in a piece of" +
      " classical Latin literature from 45 BC, making it over" +
      " 2000 years old. Richard McClintock, a Latin professor" +
      " at Hampden-Sydney College in Virginia, looked up one" +
      " of the more obscure Latin words, consectetur, from" +
      " a Lorem Ipsum passage, and going through the cites" +
      " of the word in classical literature, discovered the" +
      " undoubtable source. Lorem Ipsum comes from sections" +
      " 1.10.32 and 1.10.33 of \"de Finibus Bonorum et" +
      " Malorum\" (The Extremes of Good and Evil) by Cicero," +
      " written in 45 BC. This book is a treatise on the" +
      " theory of ethics, very popular during the" +
      " Renaissance. The first line of Lorem Ipsum, \"Lorem" +
      " ipsum dolor sit amet..\", comes from a line in" +
      " section 1.10.32.";  // from http://www.lipsum.com/

  public static void main(String[] args) throws IOException {
    String filename = args[0];

    if (filename == null) {
      System.err.println("Usage: HighlightIt <filename>");
      System.exit(-1);
    }

    TermQuery query = new TermQuery(new Term("f", "ipsum"));
    QueryScorer scorer = new QueryScorer(query);           Customize   ❶
    SimpleHTMLFormatter formatter =                     surrounding tags
        new SimpleHTMLFormatter("<span class=\"highlight\">",
            "</span>");
    Highlighter highlighter = new Highlighter(formatter, scorer);
    Fragmenter fragmenter = new SimpleFragmenter(50);      ❷ Reduce default
    highlighter.setTextFragmenter(fragmenter);                fragment size
```

```
TokenStream tokenStream = new StandardAnalyzer()
    .tokenStream("f", new StringReader(text));

String result =
    highlighter.getBestFragments(tokenStream, text, 5, "...");

FileWriter writer = new FileWriter(filename);
writer.write("<html>");
writer.write("<style>\n" +
    ".highlight {\n" +
    " background: yellow;\n" +
    "}\n" +
    "</style>");
writer.write("<body>");
writer.write(result);
writer.write("</body></html>");
writer.close();
    }
}
```

③ Tokenize text

**Highlight best 5 ④
fragments**

**⑤ Write
highlighted
HTML**

❶ We customize the surrounding tags for each highlighted term.

❷ This code reduces the default fragment size from 100 to 50 characters.

❸ Here we tokenize the original text, using `StandardAnalyzer`.

❹ We highlight the best five fragments, separating them with an ellipsis (…).

❺ Finally we write the highlighted HTML to a file, as shown in figure 8.15.

In neither of our examples did we perform a search and highlight actual hits. The text to highlight was hard-coded. This brings up an important issue when dealing with the Highlighter: where to get the text to highlight. This is addressed in the next section.

8.7.2 *Highlighting Hits*

Whether to store the original field text in the index is up to you (see section 2.2 for field indexing options). If the original text isn't stored in the index (generally for size considerations), it will be up to you to retrieve the text to be highlighted from its original source. If the original text is stored with the field, it can be retrieved directly from the `Document` obtained from `Hits`, as shown in the following piece of code:

```
IndexSearcher searcher = new IndexSearcher(directory);

TermQuery query = new TermQuery(new Term("title", "action"));
Hits hits = searcher.search(query);
```

```
QueryScorer scorer = new QueryScorer(query);
Highlighter highlighter = new Highlighter(scorer);

for (int i = 0; i < hits.length(); i++) {
  String title = hits.doc(i).get("title");

  TokenStream stream =
      new SimpleAnalyzer().tokenStream("title",
          new StringReader(title));
  String fragment =
      highlighter.getBestFragment(stream, title);

  System.out.println(fragment);
}
```

With our sample book index, the output is

```
JUnit in <B>Action</B>
Lucene in <B>Action</B>
Tapestry in <B>Action</B>
```

Notice that it was still our responsibility to tokenize the text. This is duplicated effort, since the original text was tokenized during indexing. However, during indexing, the positional information is discarded (that is, the character position of each term in the original text, but the term position offsets are stored in the index). Because of the computational needs of highlighting, it should only be used for the hits displayed to the user.

8.8 *Chaining filters*

Using a search filter, as we've discussed in section 5.5, is a powerful mechanism for selectively narrowing the document space to be searched by a query. The Sandbox contains an interesting meta-filter in the misc project, contributed by Kelvin Tan, which chains other filters together and performs AND, OR, XOR, and ANDNOT bit operations between them. ChainedFilter, like the built-in CachingWrapperFilter, isn't a concrete filter; it combines a list of filters and performs a desired bit-wise operation for each successive filter, allowing for sophisticated combinations.

It's slightly involved to demonstrate ChainedFilter because it requires a diverse enough dataset to showcase how the various scenarios work. We've set up an index with 500 documents including a key field with values 1 through 500; a date field with successive days starting from January 1, 2003; and an owner field with the first half of the documents owned by bob and the second half owned by sue:

```
public class ChainedFilterTest extends TestCase {
  public static final int MAX = 500;
```

```
private RAMDirectory directory;
private IndexSearcher searcher;
private Query query;
private DateFilter dateFilter;
private QueryFilter bobFilter;
private QueryFilter sueFilter;

public void setUp() throws Exception {
  directory = new RAMDirectory();
  IndexWriter writer =
    new IndexWriter(directory, new WhitespaceAnalyzer(), true);

  Calendar cal = Calendar.getInstance();
  cal.setTimeInMillis(1041397200000L); // 2003 January 01

  for (int i = 0; i < MAX; i++) {
    Document doc = new Document();
    doc.add(Field.Keyword("key", "" + (i + 1)));
    doc.add(
        Field.Keyword("owner", (i < MAX / 2) ? "bob" : "sue"));
    doc.add(Field.Keyword("date", cal.getTime()));
    writer.addDocument(doc);

    cal.add(Calendar.DATE, 1);
  }

  writer.close();

  searcher = new IndexSearcher(directory);

  // query for everything to make life easier
  BooleanQuery bq = new BooleanQuery();
  bq.add(new TermQuery(new Term("owner", "bob")), false, false);
  bq.add(new TermQuery(new Term("owner", "sue")),false, false);
  query = bq;

  // date filter matches everything too
  Date pastTheEnd = parseDate("2099 Jan 1");
  dateFilter = DateFilter.Before("date", pastTheEnd);

  bobFilter = new QueryFilter(
      new TermQuery(new Term("owner", "bob")));
  sueFilter = new QueryFilter(
      new TermQuery(new Term("owner", "sue")));
}

// ...
}
```

In addition to the test index, setUp defines an all-encompassing query and some
filters for our examples. The query searches for documents owned by either bob
or sue; used without a filter, it will match all 500 documents. An all-encompassing

DateFilter is constructed, as well as two QueryFilters, one to filter on owner bob and the other for sue.

Using a single filter nested in a ChainedFilter has no effect beyond using the filter without ChainedFilter, as shown here with two of the filters:

```
public void testSingleFilter() throws Exception {
  ChainedFilter chain = new ChainedFilter(
      new Filter[] {dateFilter});
  Hits hits = searcher.search(query, chain);
  assertEquals(MAX, hits.length());

  chain = new ChainedFilter(new Filter[] {bobFilter});
  hits = searcher.search(query, chain);
  assertEquals(MAX / 2, hits.length());
}
```

The real power of ChainedFilter comes when we chain multiple filters together. The default operation is OR, combining the filtered space as shown when filtering on bob or sue:

```
public void testOR() throws Exception {
  ChainedFilter chain = new ChainedFilter(
    new Filter[] {sueFilter, bobFilter});

  Hits hits = searcher.search(query, chain);
  assertEquals("OR matches all", MAX, hits.length());
}
```

Rather than increase the document space, AND can be used to narrow the space:

```
public void testAND() throws Exception {
  ChainedFilter chain = new ChainedFilter(
    new Filter[] {dateFilter, bobFilter}, ChainedFilter.AND);

  Hits hits = searcher.search(query, chain);
  assertEquals("AND matches just bob", MAX / 2, hits.length());
  assertEquals("bob", hits.doc(0).get("owner"));
}
```

The testAND test case shows that the dateFilter is AND'd with the bobFilter, effectively restricting the search space to documents owned by bob since the dateFilter is all encompassing. In other words, the intersection of the provided filters is the document search space for the query.

```
Filter bit sets can be XOR'd (exclusively OR'd, meaning one or the other,
  but not both):
public void testXOR() throws Exception {
  ChainedFilter chain = new ChainedFilter(
    new Filter[]{dateFilter, bobFilter}, ChainedFilter.XOR);
```

```
    Hits hits = searcher.search(query, chain);
    assertEquals("XOR matches sue", MAX / 2, hits.length());
    assertEquals("sue", hits.doc(0).get("owner"));
}
```

The `dateFilter` XOR'd with `bobFilter` effectively filters for owner sue in our test data. And finally, the ANDNOT operation allows only documents that match the first filter but not the second filter to pass through:

```
public void testANDNOT() throws Exception {
   ChainedFilter chain = new ChainedFilter(
     new Filter[]{dateFilter, sueFilter},
       new int[] {ChainedFilter.AND, ChainedFilter.ANDNOT});

   Hits hits = searcher.search(query, chain);
   assertEquals("ANDNOT matches just bob",
       MAX / 2, hits.length());
   assertEquals("bob", hits.doc(0).get("owner"));
}
```

In `testANDNOT`, given our test data, all documents in the date range except those owned by sue are available for searching, which narrows it down to only documents owned by bob.

Depending on your needs, the same effect can be obtained by combining query clauses into a `BooleanQuery` or using the new `FilteredQuery` (see section 6.4.1, page 212). Keep in mind the performance caveats to using filters; and, if you're reusing filters without changing the index, be sure you're using a caching filter. `Chained-Filter` doesn't cache, but wrapping it in a `CachingWrappingFilter` will take care of that aspect.

8.9 *Storing an index in Berkeley DB*

The low-key Chandler project (http://www.osafoundation.org) is an ongoing effort to build an open-source Personal Information Manager. Chandler aims to manage diverse types of information such as email, instant messages, appointments, contacts, tasks, notes, web pages, blogs, bookmarks, photos, and much more. It's an extensible platform, not just an application. As you suspected, search is a crucial component to the Chandler infrastructure.

Chandler's underlying repository uses Sleepycat's Berkeley DB in a vastly different way than a traditional relational database, inspired by RDF and associative databases. The Chandler codebase uses Python primarily, with hooks to native code where necessary. We're going to jump right to how the Chandler developers use Lucene; refer to the Chandler site for more details on this fascinating project.

Lucene is compiled to the native platform using GCJ and is accessed from Python through SWIG. Lupy (the Python port of Lucene) was considered, but for speed a more native approach was deemed more appropriate.

Andi Vajda, one of Chandler's key developers, created a Lucene directory implementation that uses Berkeley DB as the underlying storage mechanism. An interesting side-effect of having a Lucene index in a database is the transactional support it provides. Andi donated his implementation to the Lucene project, and it's maintained in the Db contributions area of the Sandbox. The Chandler project has also open-sourced its PyLucene code, which is discussed in section 9.6.

8.9.1 *Coding to DbDirectory*

DbDirectory is more involved to use than the built in RAMDirectory and FSDirectory. It requires constructing and managing two Berkeley DB Java API objects, DbEnv and Db. Listing 8.8 shows DbDirectory being used for indexing.

Listing 8.8 Indexing with DbDirectory

```
public class BerkeleyDbIndexer {
  public static void main(String[] args)
                      throws IOException, DbException {
    if (args.length != 1) {
      System.err.println("Usage: BerkeleyDbIndexer <index dir>");
      System.exit(-1);
    }
    String indexDir = args[0];

    DbEnv env = new DbEnv(0);
    Db index = new Db(env, 0);
    Db blocks = new Db(env, 0);
    File dbHome = new File(indexDir);
    int flags = Db.DB_CREATE;

    if (dbHome.exists()) {
      File[] files = dbHome.listFiles();

      for (int i = 0; i < files.length; i++)
        if (files[i].getName().startsWith("__"))
          files[i].delete();
      dbHome.delete();
    }

    dbHome.mkdir();

    env.open(indexDir, Db.DB_INIT_MPOOL | flags, 0);
    index.open(null, "__index__", null, Db.DB_BTREE, flags, 0);
    blocks.open(null, "__blocks__", null, Db.DB_BTREE, flags, 0);
```

```
    DbDirectory directory = new DbDirectory(null, index, blocks, 0);
    IndexWriter writer = new IndexWriter(directory,
        new StandardAnalyzer(),
        true);

    Document doc = new Document();
    doc.add(Field.Text("contents", "The quick brown fox..."));
    writer.addDocument(doc);

    writer.optimize();
    writer.close();

    index.close(0);
    blocks.close(0);
    env.close(0);

    System.out.println("Indexing Complete");
  }
}
```

Once you have an instance of DbDirectory, using it with Lucene is no different than using the built-in Directory implementations. Searching with DbDirectory uses the same mechanism, but you use the flags value of 0 to access an already-created index.

8.9.2 *Installing DbDirectory*

Erik had a hard time getting DbDirectory working, primarily because of issues with building and installing Berkeley DB 4.2.52 on Mac OS X. After many emails back and forth with Andi, the problems were resolved, and the index (and unshown searching) example worked.

Follow the instructions for obtaining and installing Berkeley DB. Be sure to configure the Berkeley DB build with Java support enabled (./configure --enable-java). You need Berkeley DB's db.jar as well as the DbDirectory (and friends) code from the Sandbox in your classpath. At least on Mac OS X, setting the environment variable DYLD_LIBRARY_PATH to /usr/local/BerkeleyDB.4.2/lib was also required.

8.10 *Building the Sandbox*

The Sandbox repository has historically been a "batteries not included" area. Work is in progress to improve the visibility and ease of using the Sandbox components, and this area may change from the time of this writing until you read this book. Initially, each contribution to the Sandbox had its own Ant build file and wasn't integrated into a common build, but this situation has improved; now, most of the Sandbox pieces are incorporated into a common build infrastructure.

Unless more current documentation online says otherwise, we recommend that you obtain the Sandbox components directly from Jakarta's anonymous CVS access and either build the JAR files and incorporate the binaries into your project or copy the desired source code into your project and build it directly into your own binaries.

8.10.1 Check it out

Using a CVS client, follow the instructions provided at the Jakarta site: http://jakarta.apache.org/site/cvsindex.html. Specifically, this involves executing the following commands from the command line:

```
% cvs -d :pserver:anoncvs@cvs.apache.org:/home/cvspublic login
password: anoncvs

% cvs -d :pserver:anoncvs@cvs.apache.org:/home/cvspublic checkout
  jakarta-lucene-sandbox
```

The password is *anoncvs*. This is read-only access to the repository. In your current directory, you'll now have a subdirectory named jakarta-lucene-sandbox. Under that directory is a contributions directory where all the goodies discussed here, and more, reside.

8.10.2 Ant in the Sandbox

Next, let's build the components. You'll need Ant 1.6.x in order to run the Sandbox build files. At the root of the contributions directory is a build.xml file. From the command line, with the current directory jakarta-lucene-sandbox/contributions, execute ant. Most of the components will build, test, and create a distributable JAR file in the dist subdirectory.

Some components, such as javascript, aren't currently integrated into this build process, so you need to copy the necessary files into your project. Some outdated contributions are still there as well (these are the ones we didn't mention in this chapter), and additional contributions will probably arrive after we've written this.

Each contribution subdirectory, such as analyzers and ant, has its own build.xml file. To build a single component, set your current working directory to the desired component's directory and execute ant. This is still a fairly crude way of getting your hands on these add-ons to Lucene, but it's useful to have direct access to the source. You may want to use the Sandbox for ideas and inspiration, not necessarily for the exact code.

8.11 Summary

Don't reinvent the wheel. Someone has probably encountered the same situation you're struggling with—you need language-specific analysis, or you want to build an index during an Ant build process, or you want query terms highlighted in search results. The Sandbox and the other resources listed on the Lucene web site should be your first stops.

If you end up rolling up your sleeves and creating something new and generally useful, please consider donating it to the Sandbox or making it available to the Lucene community. We're all more than grateful for Doug Cutting's generosity for open-sourcing Lucene itself. By also contributing, you benefit from a large number of skilled developers who can help review, debug, and maintain it; and, most important, you can rest easy knowing you have made the world a better place!

Lucene ports

9

This chapter covers

- Using Lucene ports to other programming languages
- Comparing ports' APIs, features, and performance

Over the past few years, Lucene's popularity has grown dramatically. Today, Lucene is the de facto standard open-source Java IR library. Although surveys have shown that Java is currently the most widespread programming language, not everyone uses Java. Luckily, a number of Lucene ports are available in different languages for those whose language of choice is not Java.

In this chapter, we'll give you an overview of all the Lucene ports currently available. We'll provide brief examples of the ports' use, but keep in mind that each port is an independent project with its own mailing lists, documentation, tutorials, user, and developer community that will be able to provide more detailed information.

9.1 Ports' relation to Lucene

Table 9.1 shows a summary of the most important aspects of each port. As you can see, the ports lag behind Lucene. Don't be discouraged by that, though; all the Lucene port projects are actively developed.

Table 9.1 The summary of all existing Lucene ports

	CLucene	dotLucene	Plucene	Lupy	PyLucene
Port language	C++	C#	Perl	Python	GCJ + SWIG
Current version	0.8.11	1.4	1.19	0.2.1	0.9.2
Java version	1.2	1.4-final	1.3	1.2 (partial)	1.4 (partial)
Compatible index	Yes (1.2)	Yes (1.4)	Yes (1.3)	Yes (1.2)	Yes

Each of the featured ports is currently an independent project. This means that each port has its own web site, mailing lists, and everything else that typically goes along with open-source projects. Each port also has its own group of founders and developers.

Although each port tries to remain in sync with the latest Lucene version, they all lag behind it a bit. Furthermore, most of the ports are relatively young, and from what we could gather, there are no developer community overlaps. Each port takes some and omits some of the concepts from Lucene, but because Lucene was well designed, they all mimic its architecture. There is also little communication between the ports' developers and Lucene's developers, although we're all aware of each project's existence. This may change with time, especially since the authors of this book would like to see all ports gathered around Lucene in order to ensure parallel development, a stronger community, minimal API changes, a compatible index format, and so on. With this said, let's look at each port, starting with CLucene.

9.2 *CLucene*

CLucene is Ben van Klinken's open-source port of Apache Jakarta Lucene to C++. It's released under the LGPL license and hosted at http://sourceforge.net/ projects/clucene/. Ben is an Australian pursuing a Masters Degree in International Relations and Asian Politics. Although his studies aren't in a technology-related field, he has strong interest in Information Retrieval. Ben was kind enough to provide this overview of CLucene.

The current version of CLucene is 0.8.11; it's based on Lucene version 1.2. Due to Unicode problems (outlined later), there are some compatibility issues on Linux between non-Unicode indexes and Unicode indexes. Linux-based CLucene will read Unicode indexes but may produce strange results. The version compiled for the Microsoft Windows platform has no problems with Unicode support.

The distribution package of CLucene includes many of the same components as Lucene, such as tests and demo examples. It also contains wrappers that allow CLucene to be used with other programming languages. Currently there are wrappers for PHP, .NET (read-only), and a Dynamic Link Library (DLL) that can be shared between different programs, and separately developed wrappers for Python and Perl.

9.2.1 *Supported platforms*

CLucene was initially developed in Microsoft Visual Studio, but now it also compiles in GCC, MinGW32, and (reportedly) the Borland C++ compiler (although no build scripts are currently being distributed). In addition to the MS Windows platform, CLucene has also been successfully built on Red Hat 9, Mac OS X, and Debian. The CLucene team is making use of SourceForge's multiplatform compile farm to ensure that CLucene compiles and runs on as many platforms as possible. The activity on the CLucene developers' mailing lists indicates that support for AMD64 architecture and FreeBSD is being added.

9.2.2 *API compatibility*

The CLucene API is similar to Lucene's. This means that code written in Java can be converted to C++ fairly easily. The drawback is that CLucene doesn't follow the generally accepted C++ coding standards. However, due to the number of classes that would have to redesigned, CLucene continues to follow a "Javaesque" coding standard. This approach also allows much of the code to be converted using macros and scripts. The CLucene wrappers for other languages, which are included in the distribution, all have different APIs.

Listing 9.1 shows a command-line program that illustrates the indexing and searching API and its use. This program first indexes several documents with a single `contents` field. Following that, it runs a few searches against the generated index and prints out the search results for each query.

Listing 9.1 Using CLucene's `IndexWriter` and `IndexSearcher` API

```
int main( int argc, char** argv){

try {
  SimpleAnalyzer* analyzer = new SimpleAnalyzer();
  IndexWriter writer( _T("testIndex"), *analyzer, true);

 wchar_t* docs[] = {
  _T("a b c d e"),
  _T("a b c d e a b c d e"),
  _T("a b c d e f g h i j"),
  _T("a c e"),
  _T("e c a"),
  _T("a c e a c e"),
  _T("a c e a b c")
 };

 for (int j = 0; j < 7; j++) {
  Document* d = new Document();
  Field& f = Field::Text(_T("contents"), docs[j]);
  d->add(f);

  writer.addDocument(*d);
  // no need to delete fields - document takes ownership
  delete d;
 }
 writer.close();

 IndexSearcher searcher(_T("testIndex"));
 wchar_t* queries[] = {
  _T("a b"),
  _T("\"a b\""),
  _T("\"a b c\""),
  _T("a c"),
  _T("\"a c\""),
  _T("\"a c e\""),
 };
```

```
Hits* hits = NULL;
QueryParser parser(_T("contents"), *analyzer);

parser.PhraseSlop = 4;
for (int j = 0; j < 6; j++) {

  Query* query = &parser.Parse(queries[j]);
  const wchar_t* qryInfo = query->toString(_T("contents"));
  _cout << _T("Query: ") << qryInfo << endl;
  delete qryInfo;

  Hits* hits = &searcher.search(*query);
  _cout << hits->Length() << _T(" total results") << endl;

  for (int i=0; i<hits->Length() && i<10; i++) {
    Document* d = &hits->doc(i);
    cout << i << _T(" ") << hits->score(i) <<
    _T(" ") << d->get(_T("contents")) << endl;
  }
  delete hits;
  delete query;
}

searcher.close();
if ( analyzer )
  delete analyzer;
} catch (THROW_TYPE e) {
 _cout << _T(" caught a exception: ") <<
  e.what() << _T("\n");
} catch (...){
 _cout << _T(" caught an unknown exception\n");
}
```

Many applications have to deal with characters outside the ASCII range. Let's
look at some Unicode-related issues we mentioned earlier.

9.2.3 *Unicode support*

CLucene was originally written to be as fast and lightweight as possible. In the
interest of speed, the decision was made not to incorporate any external libraries
for string handling and reference counting. However, there are some drawbacks
to this. Linux suffers from a lack of good Unicode support, and since CLucene
doesn't use external libraries, Linux builds had to be built without Unicode. This
led to CLucene using the _UNICODE pre-processor directive: When it's specified,
the Unicode characters are used; otherwise, non-Unicode (narrow) characters are
used. However, support for Unicode is included in CLucene and can be enabled

at compile-time. Future version may also solve this problem by optionally including a Unicode library.

9.2.4 Performance

According to a couple of reports captured in the archives of the Lucene Developers mailing list, CLucene indexes documents faster than Lucene. We haven't done any benchmarks ourselves because doing so would require going back to version 1.2 of Lucene (not something a new Lucene user would do).

9.2.5 Users

Although the CLucene port has been around for a while and has an active user mailing list, we haven't been able to locate many actual CLucene users to list here. This could be due to the fact that the CLucene development team is small and has a hard time keeping up with features being added to Lucene. We did find out about Awasu, a personal knowledge–management tool that uses CLucene under the covers (http://www.awasu.com/).

9.3 dotLucene

When we first wrote this chapter, we discussed a .NET port of Lucene called Lucene.Net. Unfortunately, the people behind Lucene.Net decided to withdraw their port and its source code from the SourgeForge site, where the project was hosted. However, Lucene.Net was released under the Apache Software License (ASL), which made it possible for a new group of developers to take over the project. This new incarnation of the .NET port is dotLucene, and you can find it at http://www.sourceforge.net/projects/dotlucene/. The distribution package of dotLucene consists of the same components as the distribution package of Lucene. It includes the source code, tests, and a few demo examples.

In addition to dotLucene, there is another port of Lucene to the .NET platform: NLucene, which is hosted at http://www.sourceforge.net/projects/nlucene/. However, this port appears hopelessly out of date—the last version was released in the summer of 2002—and so doesn't merit full coverage.

9.3.1 API compatibility

Although it's written in C#, dotLucene exposes an API that is nearly identical to that of Lucene. Consequently, code written for Lucene can be ported to C# with minimal effort. This compatibility also allows .NET developers to use documentation for the Java version, such as this book.

The difference is limited to the Java and C# naming styles. Whereas Java's method names begin with lowercase letters, the .NET version uses the C# naming style in which method names typically begin with uppercase letters.

9.3.2 Index compatibility

dotLucene is compatible with Lucene at the index level. That is to say, an index created by Lucene can be read by dotLucene and vice versa. Of course, as Lucene evolves, indexes between versions of Lucene itself may not be portable, so this compatibility is currently limited to Lucene version 1.4.

9.3.3 Performance

The developers of dotLucene don't have any performance numbers at this time, and they're focused on adding features to their port to ensure it stays as close to Lucene as possible. However, it would be safe to assume that dotLucene's performance is similar to that of its precursor; according to Lucene.Net's author, its performance was comparable to that of Lucene.

9.3.4 Users

In the course of our research of Lucene.Net, we found several interesting users of that Lucene port. The most notable user of Lucene.Net is Lookout Software (http://www.lookoutsoft.com/Lookout/), which was recently acquired by Microsoft Corporation. It's the creator of Lookout, a popular Microsoft Outlook add-on that provides search functionality superior to that of Outlook's built-in search feature.

Another interesting user of Lucene.Net is Beagle (http://www.gnome.org/projects/beagle/), a GNOME component for indexing and searching of all kinds of files, including pictures. Beagle is still in the very early phases of development.

Because the dotLucene project is so new, we didn't look for users of this new port. However, since the last version of Lucene.Net was used to start the dotLucene project, both Lookout Software and Beagle are effectively using dotLucene. Furthermore, we're certain that with time, all users of the Lucene.Net port will migrate to dotLucene.

9.4 Plucene

Plucene is a Perl port of Lucene; you can find it on CPAN (http://search.cpan.org/dist/Plucene/). Version 1.19 of Plucene was released in July 2004, and it's a straight port of version 1.3 of Lucene. Most of the work was done by Simon Cozens, and although his involvement with Plucene development has lessened, he remains involved and active on the Plucene mailing list.

9.4.1 API compatibility

Being a direct port of Lucene, Plucene preserves the API to a large extent. The only obvious difference is in the code-naming style, which follows the standards for the naming and structure of Perl modules, classes, method, and such. In listing 9.2, you can see an example of IndexWriter and IndexSearcher usage in Plucene.

Listing 9.2 Using Plucene's IndexWriter and IndexSearcher API

```
my $writer = Plucene::Index::Writer->new("/tmp/index",
Plucene::Plugin::Analyzer::PorterAnalyzer->new(), 1);
$writer->set_mergefactor(100);
while (($key, $value) = each (%hash)) {
  $doc = Plucene::Document->new;
  $doc->add(Plucene::Document::Field->Keyword(id => $key));
  $doc->add(Plucene::Document::Field->UnStored('text' => $value));
  $writer->add_document($doc);
};
$writer->optimize;
undef $writer;
my $parser = Plucene::QueryParser->new({
  analyzer => Plucene::Plugin::Analyzer::PorterAnalyzer->new(),
  default  => "text"
});
my $queryStr = "+mango +ginger";
my $query = $parser->parse($queryStr);
my $searcher = Plucene::Search::IndexSearcher->new("/tmp/index");
my $hc = Plucene::Search::HitCollector->new(collect => sub {
  my ($self, $doc, $score)= @_;
  push @docs, $searcher->doc($doc);
});
$searcher->search_hc($query, $hc);
```

As you can tell from the listing, if you're familiar with Perl, you'll be able to translate between the Java and Perl versions with ease.

Although the Plucene API resembles that of Lucene, there are some internal implementation differences between the two codebases. One difference is that Lucene uses method overloading, whereas Plucene uses different method names in most cases. The other difference, according to Plucene's developers, is that Java uses 64-bit long integers, but most Perl versions use 32 bits.

9.4.2 *Index compatibility*

According to Plucene's author, indexes created by Lucene 1.3 and Plucene 1.19 are compatible. A Java application that uses Lucene 1.3 will be able to read and digest an index created by Plucene 1.19 and vice versa. As is the case for other ports with compatible indexes, indexes between versions of Lucene itself may not be portable as Lucene evolves, so this compatibility is restricted to Lucene version 1.3.

9.4.3 *Performance*

Version 1.19 of Plucene is significantly slower than the Java version. One Plucene developer attributed this to differences in advantages and weaknesses between the implementation languages. Because Plucene is a fairly direct port, many of Java strengths hit Perl's weak spots. However, according to the same source, fixes for performance problems are in the works. Some recent activity on Plucene's mailing lists also suggests that developers are addressing performance issues.

9.4.4 *Users*

According to Plucene consultants, Plucene is used by Gizmodo (http://www.gizmodo.com/), a site that reviews cutting-edge consumer electronic devices. It's also used by Twingle (http://www.twingle.com), a web-mail site run by Kasei, the company that sponsored the development of Plucene. Plucene has also been integrated into Movable Type, a popular blogging software.

9.5 *Lupy*

Lupy is a pure Python port of Lucene 1.2. The main developers of Lupy are Amir Bakhtiar and Allen Short. Some core Lucene functionality is missing from Lupy, such as `QueryParser`, some of the analyzers, index merging, locking, and a few other small items. Although Lupy is a port of a rather old Lucene version, its developers are busy adding features that should bring it closer to Lucene 1.4. The current version of Lupy is 0.2.1; you can find it at http://www.divmod.org/Home/Projects/Lupy/.

9.5.1 *API compatibility*

Python syntax aside, Lupy's API resembles that of Lucene. In listing 9.3, which shows how to index a `Document` with Lupy, you see familiar classes and methods. However, note that we can create `IndexWriter` without specifying the analyzer—that is something we can't do in Lucene.

Listing 9.3   Indexing a file with Lupy, and demonstrating Lupy's indexing API

```
from lupy.index.indexwriter import IndexWriter
from lupy import document

# open index for writing
indexer = IndexWriter('/tmp/index', True)

# create document
d = document.Document()

# add fields to document
f = document.Keyword('filename', fname)
d.add(f)
f = document.Text('title', title)
d.add(f)

# Pass False as the 3rd arg to ensure that
# the actual text of s is not stored in the index
f = document.Text('text', s, False)
d.add(f)

# add document to index, optimize and close index
indexer.addDocument(d)
indexer.optimize()
indexer.close
```

Listing 9.4 shows how we can use Lupy to search the index we created with the code from listing 9.3. After opening the index with `IndexSearcher`, we create a `Term` and then a `TermQuery` in the same fashion we would with Lucene. After executing the query, we loop through all hits and print out the results.

Listing 9.4   Searching an index with Lupy, and demonstrating Lupy's searching API

```
from lupy.index.term import Term
from lupy.search.indexsearcher import IndexSearcher
from lupy.search.term import TermQuery

# open index for searching
searcher = IndexSearcher('/tmp/index')

# look for the word 'mango' in the 'text' field
t = Term('text', 'mango')
q = TermQuery(t)

# execute query and get hits
hits = searcher.search(q)
```

```
# loop through hits and print them
for hit in hits:
    print 'Found in document %s (%s)' % (hit.get('filename'),
        hit.get('title'))
```

As you can see, the Lupy API feels only a little different from that of Lucene. That is to be expected—Lupy's developers are big Python fans. Regardless, the API is simple and resembles Lucene's API closely.

9.5.2 *Index compatibility*

As is the case with dotLucene and Plucene, an index created with Lupy is compatible with that of Lucene. Again, that compatibility is limited to a particular version. In Lupy's case, indexes are compatible with Lucene 1.2's indexes.

9.5.3 *Performance*

Like Plucene, Lupy is a direct port of the original Lucene, which affects its performance. There are no Python-specific tricks in Lupy to ensure optimal performance of the Python port. However, we spoke to Lupy's developers, and in addition to adding newer Lucene features to Lupy, they will also be addressing performance issues in upcoming releases.

9.5.4 *Users*

The primary user of Lupy is Divmod (http://www.divmod.com/). As you can tell from the URL, this site is related to the site that hosts Lupy project.

9.6 *PyLucene*

PyLucene is the most recent Lucene port; it's released under the MIT license and led by Andi Vajda, who also contributed Berkeley DbDirectory (see section 8.9) to the Lucene codebase. It began as an indexing and searching component of Chandler (described briefly in section 8.9), an extensible open-source PIM, but it was split into a separate project in June 2004. You can find PyLucene at http://pylucene.osafoundation.org/.

Technically speaking, PyLucene isn't a true port. Instead, it uses GNU Java Compiler (GCJ) and SWIG to export the Lucene API and make it available to a Python interpreter. GCJ is distributed as part of the GCC toolbox, which can be used to compile Java code into a native shared library. Such a shared library exposes Java classes as C++ classes, which makes integration with Python simple.

SWIG (http://www.swig.org) is a software development tool that connects programs written in C and C++ with a variety of high-level programming languages such as Python, Perl, Ruby, and so on. PyLucene is essentially a combination of the output of GCJ applied to Lucene's source code and "SWIG gymnastics," as Andi Vajda put it.

9.6.1 *API compatibility*

Because PyLucene was originally a component of Chandler, its authors exposed only those Lucene classes and methods that they needed. Consequently, not all Lucene functionality is available in PyLucene. However, since PyLucene has become a separate project, users have begun requesting more from it, so Andi and his team are slowly exposing more of the Lucene API via SWIG. In time, they intend to expose all functionality. Because adding Lucene's latest features to PyLucene is simple and quick, the PyLucene team believes PyLucene will always be able to remain in sync with Lucene; this was one of the reasons its developers embarked on it instead of trying to use Lupy.

As far as its structure is concerned, the API is virtually the same, which makes it easy for users of Lucene to learn how to use PyLucene. Another convenient side effect is that all existing Lucene documentation can be used for programming with PyLucene.

9.6.2 *Index compatibility*

Because of the nature of PyLucene ("compiler and SWIG gymnastics"), its indexes are compatible with those of Lucene.

9.6.3 *Performance*

The aim of the PyLucene project isn't to be the fastest Lucene port but to be the closest port. Because of the GCJ and SWIG approach, this shouldn't be difficult to achieve, because it requires less effort than manually writing a port to another programming language. Despite the fact that high performance isn't the primary goal, PyLucene outperforms Lucene, although it doesn't match the performance of CLucene.

9.6.4 *Users*

Being a very recent Lucene port, PyLucene doesn't have many public users yet. So far, the only serious project we know of that uses PyLucene is Chandler (http://www.osafoundation.org/).

9.7 Summary

In this chapter, we discussed all currently existing Lucene ports known to us: CLucene, dotLucene, Plucene, Lupy, and PyLucene. We looked at their APIs, supported features, Lucene compatibility, and performance as compared to Lucene, as well as some of the users of each port. The future may bring additional Lucene ports; the Lucene developers keep a list on the Lucene Wiki at http://wiki.apache.org/jakarta-lucene/.

By covering the Lucene ports, we have stepped outside the boundaries of core Lucene. In the next chapter we'll go even further by examining several interesting Lucene case studies.

Case studies

This chapter covers

- Using Lucene in the real world
- Undertaking architectural design
- Addressing language concerns
- Handling configuration and threading concerns

A picture is worth a thousand words. Examples of Lucene truly "in action" are invaluable. Lucene is the driving force behind many applications. There are countless proprietary or top-secret uses of Lucene that we may never know about, but there are also numerous applications that we can see in action online. Lucene's Wiki has a section titled PoweredBy, at http://wiki.apache.org/jakarta-lucene/PoweredBy, which lists many sites and products that use Lucene.

Lucene's API is straightforward, almost trivial, to use. The magic happens when Lucene is used cleverly. The case studies that follow are prime examples of very intelligent uses of Lucene. Read between the lines of the implementation details of each of them, and borrow the gems within. For example, Nutch delivers an open-source, highly scalable, full-Internet search solution that should help keep Google honest and on its toes. jGuru is focused on a single domain—Java—and has tuned its search engine specifically for Java syntax. SearchBlox delivers a product (limited free version available) based on Lucene, providing intranet search solutions. LingPipe's case study is intensely academic and mind-bogglingly powerful for domain-focused linguistic analysis. Showing off the cleverness factor, Michaels.com uses Lucene to index and search for *colors*. And finally, TheServer-Side intelligently wraps Lucene with easily configurable infrastructure, enabling you to easily find articles, reviews, and discussions about Java topics.

If you're new to Lucene, read these case studies at a high level and gloss over any technical details or code listings; get a general feel for how Lucene is being used in a diverse set of applications. If you're an experienced Lucene developer or you've digested the previous chapters in this book, you'll enjoy the technical details; perhaps some are worth borrowing directly for your applications.

We're enormously indebted to the contributors of these case studies who took time out of their busy schedules to write what you see in the remainder of this chapter.

10.1 Nutch: "The NPR of search engines"

Contributed by Michael Cafarella

Nutch is an open-source search engine that uses Lucene for searching the entire web's worth of documents, or in a customized form for an intranet or subset of the Web. We want to build a search engine that is as good as anything else available: Nutch needs to process at least as many documents, search them at least as fast, and be at least as reliable, as any search engine you've ever used.

There is a lot of code in Nutch (the HTTP fetcher, the URL database, and so on), but text searching is clearly at the center of any search engine. Much of the code and effort put into Nutch exist for just two reasons: to help build a Lucene index, and to help query that index.

In fact, Nutch uses lots of Lucene indexes. The system is designed to scale to process Web-scale document sets (somewhere between 1 and 10 billion documents). The set is so big that both indexing and querying must take place across lots of machines simultaneously. Further, the system at query time needs to process searches quickly, and it needs to survive if some machines crash or are destroyed.

The Nutch query architecture is fairly simple, and the protocol can be described in just a few steps:

1   An HTTP server receives the user's request. There is some Nutch code running there as a servlet, called the Query Handler. The Query Handler is responsible for returning the result page HTML in response to the user's request.

2   The Query Handler does some light processing of the query and forwards the search terms to a large set of Index Searcher machines. The Nutch query system might seem much simpler than Lucene's, but that's largely because search engine users have a strong idea of what kind of queries they like to perform. Lucene's system is very flexible and allows for many different kinds of queries. The simple-looking Nutch query is converted into a very specific Lucene one. This is discussed further later. Each Index Searcher works in parallel and returns a ranked list of document IDs.

3   There are now many streams of search results that come back to the Query Handler. The Query Handler collates the results, finding the best ranking across all of them. If any Index Searcher fails to return results after a second or two, it is ignored, and the result list is composed from the successful repliers.

10.1.1 *More in depth*

The Query Handler does some very light processing of the query, such as throwing away stop words such as *the* and *of*. It then performs a few operations so that Nutch can work well at large scale. It contacts many Index Searchers simultaneously because the document set is too large to be searched by any single one. In fact, for system-wide robustness, a single segment of the document set will be copied to several different machines. For each segment in the set, the Query Handler randomly contacts one of the Index Searchers that can search it. If an

Index Searcher cannot be contacted, the Query Handler marks it as unavailable for future searches. (The Query Handler will check back every once in a while, in case the machine comes available again.)

One common search engine design question is whether to divide the overall text index by document or by search term. Should a single Index Searcher be responsible for, say, all occurrences of *parrot*? Or should it handle all possible queries that hit the URL http://nutch.org?

Nutch has decided on the latter, which definitely has some disadvantages. Document-based segmentation means every search has to hit every segment; with term-based segmentation, the Query Handler could simply forward to a single Index Searcher and skip the integration step.[1]

The biggest advantage of segmenting by document is when considering machine failures. What if a single term-segment becomes unavailable? Engine users suddenly cannot get any results for a nontrivial number of terms. With the document-based technique, a dead machine simply means some percentage of the indexed documents will be ignored during search. That's not great, but it's not catastrophic. Document-based segmentation allows the system to keep chugging in the face of failure.

10.1.2 *Other Nutch features*

- The Query Handler asks each Index Searcher for only a small number of documents (usually 10). Since results are integrated from many Index Searchers, there's no need for a lot of documents from any one source, especially when users rarely move beyond the first page of results.

- Each user query is actually expanded to quite a complicated Lucene query before it is processed.[2] Each indexed document contains three fields: the content of the web page itself, the page's URL text, and a synthetic document that consists of all the anchor text found in hyperlinks leading to the web page. Each field has a different weight. The Nutch Query Handler generates a Lucene boolean query that contains the search engine user's text in each of the three fields.

- Nutch also specially indexes combinations of words that occur extremely frequently on the Web. (Many of these are HTTP-related phrases.) These sequences of words occur so often that it's needless overhead to search for

[1] Except in the case of multiword queries, which would require a limited amount of integration.

[2] Authors' note: See more on this query expansion in section 4.9.

each component of the sequence independently and then find the intersection. Rather than search for these terms as separate word pairs, we can search for them as a single unit Nutch must detect at index-time. Also, before contacting the Index Searcher, the Query Handler looks for any of these combinations in the user's query string. If such a sequence does occur, its component words are agglomerated into a single special search term.

- The Nutch fetcher/indexer prepares HTML documents before indexing them with Lucene. It uses the NekoHTML parser to strip out most HTML content and indexes just the nonmarkup text. NekoHTML is also useful to extract the title from an HTML document.

- Nutch does not use stemming or term aliasing of any kind. Search engines have not historically done much stemming, but it is a question that comes up regularly.

- The Nutch interprocess communication network layer (IPC) maintains a long-lasting TCP/IP connection between each Query Handler and each Index Searcher. There are many concurrent threads on the Query Handler side, any of which can submit a call to the remote server at a given address. The server receives each request and tries to find a registered service under the given string (which runs on its own thread). The client's requesting thread blocks until notified by the IPC code that the server response has arrived. If the response takes longer than the IPC timeout, the IPC code will declare the server dead and throw an exception.

10.2 *Using Lucene at jGuru*

Contributed by Terence Parr

jGuru.com is a community-driven site for Java developers. Programmers can find answers among our 6,500 FAQ entries and ask questions in our forums. Each topic is managed by a guru (a topic expert selected by jGuru management) who mines the forum questions and responses looking for interesting threads that he or she can groom into a good FAQ entry. For example, the authors of this book, Erik Hatcher and Otis Gospodneti, are gurus of the Ant and Lucene topics, respectively, at jGuru. Launched in December 1999, jGuru now has more than 300,000 unique visitors per month, nearly 300,000 registered users, and over 2,000,000 page views per month.

Although the site appears fairly simple on the outside, the server is a 110k line pure-Java behemoth containing all sorts of interesting goodies such as its

`StringTemplate` engine (http://www.antlr.org/stringtemplate/index.tml) for generating multiskin dynamic web pages. Despite its size and complexity, jGuru barely exercises a Linux-based dual-headed 800Mhz Pentium server with 1Gb RAM running JDK 1.3. I will limit my discussion here, however, to jGuru's use of Lucene and other text-processing mechanisms.

Before Lucene became available, we used a commercially available search engine that essentially required your server to spider its own site rather than directly fill the search database from the main server database. Spidering took many days to finish even when our site had few FAQ entries and users. By building search indexes with Lucene directly from our database instead of spidering, the time dropped to about 30 minutes. Further, the previous search engine had to be separately installed and had its own bizarre XML-based programming language (See my article "Humans should not have to grok XML" [http://www-106.ibm.com/developerworks/xml/library/x-sbxml.html] for my opinions on this), making the system more complicated and unreliable. Lucene, in contrast, is just another JAR file deployed with our server.

This description is a nuts-and-bolts description of how jGuru uses Lucene and other text-processing facilities to provide a good user experience.

10.2.1 *Topic lexicons and document categorization*

One of the design goals of jGuru is to make it likely you will receive an answer to your question. To do that, we try to increase the signal-to-noise ratio in our forums, spider articles from other sites, and allow users to filter content according to topic preferences. All of this relies on knowing something about topic terminology employed by the users.

For example, consider our noise-reduction procedure for forum postings. There is nothing worse than an already-answered question, a database question in the Swing forum, or a thread where people say "You're an idiot." "No, *you*'re an idiot." We have rather successfully solved this problem by the following procedure:

1   If there are no Java-related keywords in the post, ask the user to rephrase.

2   If the post uses terminology most likely from a different topic, suggest the other likely topic(s) and let them click to move the post to the appropriate forum.

3   Use Lucene to search existing FAQ entries to see if the question has already been answered. If the user does not see the right answer, he or she must manually click Continue to actually submit something to the forum.

How do we know what the lexicon (that is, the vocabulary or terminology) for a particular topic is? Fortunately, jGuru is a domain-specific site. We know that Java is the main topic and that there are subtopics such as JSP. First, I spidered the New York Times and other web sites, collecting a pool of generic English words. Then I collected words from our FAQ system, figuring that it was English+Java. Doing a fuzzy set difference, (Java+English)-English, should result in a set of Java-specific words. Using something like TFIDF (term frequency, inverse document frequency), I reasoned that the more frequently a word was in our FAQs and the less frequently it was used in the plain English text, the more likely it was to be a Java keyword (and vice versa). A similar method gets you the Java subtopic lexicons. As time progresses, existing topic lexicons drift with each new FAQ entry. The corresponding lexicon is updated automatically with any new words and their frequencies of occurrence; the server operator does not have to do anything in order to track changes in programmer word usage.

jGuru snoops other Java-related sites for articles, tutorials, forums, and so on that may be of interest to jGuru users. Not only are these items indexed by Lucene, but we use our topic vocabularies to compute the mostly likely topic(s). Users can filter for only, say, snooped JDBC content.

10.2.2 *Search database structure*

On to Lucene. jGuru has 4 main Lucene search databases stored in directories:

- /var/data/search/faq—Content from jGuru FAQs
- /var/data/search/forum—Content from jGuru forums
- /var/data/search/foreign—Content spidered from non-jGuru sources
- /var/data/search/guru—Content related to jGuru users

Within the server software, each database has a search resource name similar to a URL:

- jGuru:forum
- jGuru:faq
- foreign
- jGuru:guru

The reason we have separate search databases is that we can rebuild and search them separately (even on a different machine), a corruption in one database does not affect the others, and highly specific searches are often faster due to partitioning (searching only FAQs, for example).

The jGuru software also has groups of resources such as `universe` that means every search resource. Search resources may also have topics. For example, `jGuru:` `faq/Lucene` indicates only the Lucene FAQ entries stored in the `jGuru` database.

Within the foreign resource are sites such as

- foreign:devworks
- foreign:javaworld

The search boxes are context-sensitive so that when viewing a JDBC forum page, you'll see the following in the HTML form for the search box:

```
<INPUT type=hidden NAME=resource VALUE="jGuru:faq/JDBC">
<INPUT type=hidden NAME=resource VALUE="jGuru:forum/JDBC">
```

This indicates jGuru should search only the FAQ/forum associated with JDBC. If you are on the FAQ or Forum zone home page, you'll see

```
<INPUT type=hidden NAME=resource VALUE="jGuru:faq">
<INPUT type=hidden NAME=resource VALUE="jGuru:forum">
```

From the home page, you'll see:

```
<INPUT type=hidden NAME=resource VALUE="universe">
```

Further, related topics are grouped so that requesting a search in, say, Servlets also searches JSP and Tomcat topics. The search manager has predefined definitions such as

```
new SearchResourceGroup("jGuru:faq/Servlets",
        "Servlets and Related FAQs",
        new String[] {"jGuru:faq/Servlets",
                "jGuru:faq/JSP",
                "jGuru:faq/Tomcat"}
            )
```

jGuru will launch most multiple resource searches in parallel to take advantage of our dual-headed server unless the results must be merged into a single result.

Finally, it is worth noting that search resources are not limited to Lucene databases. jGuru has a number of snoopers that scrape results on demand from search engines on other sites. The jGuru querying and search result display software does not care where a list of search results comes from.

10.2.3 *Index fields*

All jGuru Lucene databases have the same form for consistency, although some fields are unused depending on the indexed entity type. For example, the foreign search database stores a site ID, but it is unused in the regular jGuru Lucene database. Some fields are used for display, and some are used for searching. The complete list of fields is shown in table 10.1.

Table 10.1 jGuru Lucene index fields

Field name	Description
EID	Keyword used as unique identifier
site	Keyword used by foreign db only
date	Keyword (format `DateField.dateToString(...)`)
type	Keyword (one word) in set {`forum, article, course, book, doc, code, faq, people`}
title	Text (such as FAQ question, Forum subject, article title)
link	`UnIndexed` in jGuru; keyword in foreign db (link to entity)
description	`UnIndexed` (for display)
topic	Text (one or more topics separated by spaces)
contents	`UnStored` (the main search field)

When an entry is returned as part of a search, the title, link, date, type, and description fields are displayed.

All the FAQ entries, forums, foreign articles, guru bios, and so on use the `contents` field to store indexed text. For example, a FAQ entry provides the question, answer, and any related comments as `contents` (that is, the indexed text). The title is set to the FAQ question, the link is set to /faq/view.jsp?EID=*n* for ID *n*, and so on. The search display software does not need to know the type of an entity—it can simply print out the title, link, and description.

10.2.4 *Indexing and content preparation*

There are two things you need to know to create a Lucene search database: how you are going to get information to spider, and what processing you are going to do on the text to increase the likelihood of a successful query.

You should never build a search database by crawling your own site. Using the HTTP port to obtain information and then removing HTML cruft when you have direct access to the database is insanity. Not only is direct transfer of information much faster, you have more control over what part of the content is indexed.

jGuru indexes new content as it is added so you can post a question and then immediately search and find it or register and then immediately find your name.

After a search database is built, it is dynamically kept up to date. There is never a need to spider unless the database does not exist. A useful automation is to have your server sense missing search databases and build them during startup.

jGuru highly processes content before letting Lucene index it. The same processing occurs for index and query operations; otherwise, queries probably will not find good results. jGuru converts everything to lowercase, strips plurals, strips punctuation, strips HTML tags (except for code snippets in `<pre>` tags), and strips English stop words (discussed later).

Because jGuru knows the Java lexicon, I experimented with removing non-Java words during indexing/querying. As it turns out, users want to be able to find non-Java keywords such as *broken* as well as Java keywords, so this feature was removed.

Stripping plurals definitely improved accuracy of queries. You do not want *window* and *windows* to be considered different words, and it also screws up the frequency information Lucene computes during indexing. I gradually built up the following routine using experience and some simple human and computer analysis applied to our corpus of FAQ entries:

```
/** A useful, but not particularly efficient plural stripper */
public static String stripEnglishPlural(String word) {
    // too small?
    if ( word.length()<STRIP_PLURAL_MIN_WORD_SIZE ) {
        return word;
    }
    // special cases
    if ( word.equals("has") ||
        word.equals("was") ||
        word.equals("does") ||
        word.equals("goes") ||
        word.equals("dies") ||
        word.equals("yes") ||
        word.equals("gets") ||  // means too much in java/JSP
        word.equals("its") )
        {
            return word;
        }
    String newWord=word;
    if ( word.endsWith("sses") ||
        word.endsWith("xes") ||
        word.endsWith("hes") ) {
        // remove 'es'
        newWord = word.substring(0,word.length()-2);
    }
    else if ( word.endsWith("ies") ) {
        // remove 'ies', replace with 'y'
        newWord = word.substring(0,word.length()-3)+'y';
    }
```

```
        else if ( word.endsWith("s") &&
                !word.endsWith("ss") &&
                !word.endsWith("is") &&
                !word.endsWith("us") &&
                !word.endsWith("pos") &&
                !word.endsWith("ses") ) {
        // remove 's'
        newWord = word.substring(0,word.length()-1);
    }
    return newWord;
}
```

After looking at the histogram from about 500,000 English words I grabbed from various web sites, I found the following list to be effective in reducing indexing noise:

```
public static final String[] EnglishStopWords = {
    "I", "about", "also", "an", "and", "any", "are", "aren", "arent",
    "around", "as", "at", "be", "because", "been", "before", "being",
    "between", "both", "but", "by", "can", "cannot", "cant", "come",
    "could", "day", "did", "do", "doe", "does", "doesn", "doesnt",
    "dont","either", "even", "every", "for", "from", "get",
    "great", "had", "has", "hasn", "hasnt", "have", "havn",
    "havnt", "he", "help", "her", "here", "him", "his", "how",
    "in", "info", "into", "is", "it", "its", "just", "let", "life",
    "live", "many", "may", "me", "most", "much", "must", "my",
    "need", "not", "of", "on", "one", "only", "or", "other", "our",
    "please", "question", "re", "really", "regard", "said", "say",
    "see", "she", "should", "since", "so", "some", "still", "story",
    "such", "take", "than", "thank", "that", "the", "their", "them",
    "then", "there", "these", "they", "thing", "those", "thought",
    "through", "thru", "thus", "to", "told", "too", "use", "used",
    "uses", "using", "ve", "very", "want", "was", "way", "we",
    "well", "were", "what", "when", "where", "which", "who", "why",
    "will", "with", "without", "won", "wont", "would", "you", "your"
};
```

Words like *hasn* are the result of *hasn't* being stripped of punctuation.

10.2.5 *Queries*

jGuru works hard to provide good, consistent search results. From carefully prepared indexes, jGuru grooms search words and translates them to Lucene-specific queries. This section summarizes how results are displayed, outlines how queries are generated, provides an English plural stripper, and finally characterizes jGuru search words from the year 2002.

Search results display and search types

Regardless of the source or type of entity, all results are normalized to show title, link, date, and description. jGuru can provide results merged from multiple databases and can provide results per source such as entries in the FAQs, entries in the Forums, and so on. This is often useful because some content is edited and some is not. You may want to ignore unedited content like forums occasionally. Queries can also be limited to specific databases, topics, or sites by specifying a resource name such as `jGuru:faq/Lucene`.

Handling multiple pages of search results is an interesting problem. You do not want to have to save and manage search results in a session variable so that page 2 can be displayed when a user clicks the next page link. Fortunately, this problem is easily solved: it turns out that Lucene is fast enough to just requery on every results page and then ask for nth page of results.

> **NOTE** We'd like to emphasize Terrence's last sentence here: *"...Lucene is fast enough to just requery on every results page...."* We mentioned this previously in section 3.2.2.

Computing Lucene queries from search words

jGuru first processes queries in the same manner it uses for preparing text to index. Then, because Lucene assumes an OR-like default logic and users expect AND logic, jGuru inserts AND in between the words of the query after normal text processing such as stop-word removal. A search string of "close the database" should find only those documents containing both *close* and *database*. If, however, the number of words is bigger than a threshold, the query is left as is. As the number of words increases, the probability of an AND-condition matching anything at all approaches zero.

To further improve search accuracy, queries sent to Lucene contain terms for both title and content. The more of a field that a query matches, the more likely you have a good match. So if you search for "class not found" and there is a FAQ entry title "Why do I get class not found," this entry should get a good score. If you only searched the indexed content, the FAQ entry would incorrectly get a much lower score.

jGuru uses one final trick to improve search results. Keywords found in a query such as methods and class names from the Java API are boosted to indicate their importance. Getting the list of keywords from the API was a simple matter of using javap on the .class files and parsing the results with ANTLR (http://www.antlr.org).

Query characteristics

jGuru logs all search queries because it will eventually use this feedback to automatically improve search results (for example, by watching which FAQ entries users visit after a search—those entries could then be boosted for similar queries in the future). In this section, I have collected some statistics the reader may find interesting.

In the last full year of statistics, 2002, there were 1,381,842 total searches, 554,403 of which were unique (vis-à-vis `equals()`). There were 820,800 multi-word and 561,042 single-word searches (about 40%). 829,825 queries referenced jGuru databases specifically (versus foreign ones like developerWorks), with 597,402 searches in a particular topic.

Most popular Java search strings

Table 10.2 shows the top 35 terms of a search histogram (frequency count out of 1,381,842 searches). It provides a measure of the most popular terms in 2002.

Table 10.2 Top 35 most popular Java search terms

Frequency	Full query string	Frequency	Full query string	Frequency	Full query string
4527	struts	1796	print	1442	log4j
3897	tomcat	1786	date	1414	jar
3641	JTable	1756	upload	1403	mod_jk
3371	jtable	1720	classpath	1369	mod_webapp
2950	session	1683	image	1330	blob
2702	jboss	1650	JTree	1323	apache
2233	jsp	1627	applet	1320	weblogic
2116	jdbc	1559	javascript	1267	ant
2112	xml	1536	servlet	1246	ejb
1989	jtree	1526	ftp	1229	connection pool
1884	javamail	1525	thread	1217	file upload
1827	web.xml	1476	cookie		

Considering only the multiword queries, table 10.3 shows the 35 most popular searches.

Table 10.3   35 most popular multi-word queries

Frequency	Full query string	Frequency	Full query string	Frequency	Full query string
1229	connection pool	376	properties file	276	back button
1217	file upload	362	jsp include	270	memory leak
741	entry stream	360	web services	266	property file
618	session timeout	360	copy file	264	garbage collection
603	tomcat apache	355	nt service	253	inner class
553	connection pooling	342	file download	243	primary key
502	upload file	336	virtual host	242	jsp session
500	read file	329	tomcat 4	242	class not found
494	apache tomcat	327	out of memory	239	jdk 1.4
428	stored procedure	322	error page	239	applet servlet
422	java mail	301	http post	233	jsp forward
384	drag and drop	281	date format		

As for topics (see table 10.4), the logs reveal the following histogram (truncated to 35 entries) of 597,402 total FAQ or Forum topic-specific searches. Naturally, topics introduced partway through 2002 are artificially less popular in this list.

Table 10.4   Top 35 topics

Frequency	Specific FAQ or Forum topic	Frequency	Specific FAQ or Forum topic	Frequency	Specific FAQ or Forum topic
191013	Tomcat	22118	AWT	9120	Collections
129035	JSP	21940	Applets	8242	Threads
96480	Servlets	21288	Networking	8183	IntellijIDEA
84893	Struts	18100	VAJ	7764	Tools
72015	Swing	17663	AppServer	7446	JMS
51871	JDBC	17321	XML	7428	I18N
47092	JavaMail	14603	JNI	7269	J2ME

continued on next page

Table 10.4   Top 35 topics *(continued)*

Frequency	Specific FAQ or Forum topic	Frequency	Specific FAQ or Forum topic	Frequency	Specific FAQ or Forum topic
46471	JavaScript	14373	JBuilder	6828	Linux
38083	EJB	13584	Security	5884	Media
33765	JavaLanguage	10560	ANTLR	4886	CORBA
33546	Ant	10090	RMI	4876	Serialization
24075	IO	9395	JNDI		

10.2.6 *JGuruMultiSearcher*

Lucene does not have a standard object for searching multiple indexes with different queries. Because jGuru needs to search the foreign database versus its internal search databases with slightly different query terms, I made a subclass of Lucene's `MultiSearcher`, `JGuruMultiSearcher` (shown in listing 10.1), to correct the situation.

> **NOTE**   `JGuruMultiSearcher` uses a bit of low-level internal Lucene API that is not covered in this book. Please refer to Lucene's Javadocs for more details on `TopDocs` and `ScoreDoc` as well as the `Searcher` interface.

Listing 10.1   Searching multiple indexes with different queries

```
/** Since lucene's multisearcher was final,3 I had to wholesale
 *   copy it to fix a limitation that you cannot
 *   have multiple queries, hence, no heterogeneous lucene
 *   search db's.
 */
public class JGuruMultiSearcher extends MultiSearcher {
  Query[] queries = null;

  /** Creates a searcher which searches <i>searchers</i>. */
  public JGuruMultiSearcher(Searcher[] searchers,
                            Query[] queries) throws IOException {
    super(searchers);
    this.queries = queries;
  }
```

---

[3] This is no longer the case (as of Lucene 1.4). `MultiSearcher` has been opened up, and a `Parallel-MultiSearcher` subclass has been added to the core. However, nothing is currently built in that performs a different query on each index and merges the results like this `JGuruMultiSearcher`.

```
protected TopDocs search(Query query /* ignored */,
                         Filter filter, int nDocs)
    throws IOException {
    HitQueue hq = new HitQueue(nDocs);
    float minScore = 0.0f;
    int totalHits = 0;

    // search each searcher
    for (int i = 0; i < searchers.length; i++) {
        if ( queries[i]==null || searchers[i]==null ) {
            continue;
        }
        TopDocs docs =
            searchers[i].search(queries[i], filter, nDocs);
        totalHits += docs.totalHits;    // update totalHits
        ScoreDoc[] scoreDocs = docs.scoreDocs;
        for (int j = 0; j < scoreDocs.length; j++) {
            // merge scoreDocs into hq
            ScoreDoc scoreDoc = scoreDocs[j];
            if (scoreDoc.score >= minScore) {
                scoreDoc.doc += starts[i];// convert doc
                hq.put(scoreDoc);       // update hit queue
                if (hq.size() > nDocs) {    // if hit queue overfull
                    hq.pop();       // remove lowest in hit queue
                    // reset minScore
                    minScore = ((ScoreDoc)hq.top()).score;
                }
            } else {
                break;              // no more scores > minScore
            }
        }
    }

    ScoreDoc[] scoreDocs = new ScoreDoc[hq.size()];
    for (int i = hq.size()-1; i >= 0; i--) {  // put docs in array
        scoreDocs[i] = (ScoreDoc)hq.pop();
    }

    return new TopDocs(totalHits, scoreDocs);
    }
}
```

10.2.7 *Miscellaneous*

Lucene makes a lot of files before you can perform an optimize() sometimes. We had to up our Linux max file descriptions to 4,000 with ulimit -n 4000 to prevent the search system from going insane.[4]

I used to run a cron job in the server to optimize the various Lucene databases (being careful to synchronize with database insertions). Before I discovered the file descriptor issue mentioned earlier, I moved optimization to the insertion point; that is, I optimized upon every insert. This is no longer necessary and makes insertions artificially slow.

The Lucene query string parser isn't exactly robust. For example, querying "the AND drag" screws up with *the* first because it is a stop word. The bug report status was changed to "won't fix" on the web site, oddly enough.[5] Eventually I built my own mechanism.

10.3 *Using Lucene in SearchBlox*

Contributed by Robert Selvaraj, SearchBlox Software Inc.

When we started to design SearchBlox, we had one goal—to develop a 100% Java search tool that is simple to deploy and easy to manage. There are numerous search tools available in the market but few have been designed with the manageability of the tool in mind. With searching for information becoming an increasing part of our daily lives, it is our view that manageability is the key to the widespread adoption of search tools, especially in companies where the complexity of the existing tools is the major stumbling block in implementing search applications, not to mention the cost. Companies must be able to deploy search functionality in the matter of minutes, not months.

10.3.1 *Why choose Lucene?*

While selecting an indexing and searching engine for SearchBlox, we were faced with two choices: either use one of the several open-source toolkits that are available or build our own search toolkit. After looking at several promising toolkits, we decided to use Lucene. The reasons behind this decision were

- *Performance*—Lucene offers incredible search performance. Typical search times are in milliseconds, even for large collections. This is despite the fact that it is 100% Java, which is slow compared to languages like C++. In the search tools industry, it is extremely important to have fast and relevant search results.

- *Scalability*—Even though SearchBlox is optimized for small to medium-sized document collections (<250,000 documents), scalability was also a

---

[4] Lucene 1.3 added the compound index format, making the file handle situation much less of an issue.

[5] There are still open issues regarding stop words and `QueryParser`.

critical criteria in choosing Lucene. We wanted to keep open the option of supporting larger collections in SearchBlox at a later date. Lucene is certainly up to the task in terms of scalability. We are aware of a particular project where Lucene is being used for 4 million document index with <100 millisecond search times.

■ *Extensive adoption*—Usage of Lucene has grown tremendously over the last couple of years. It has become highly popular with Information Retrieval (IR) experts who have used Lucene as the search toolkit for their projects. This has resulted in a great deal of Lucene add-on open-source code being available to accomplish various specialized IR tasks. This can be a great bonus when you wish to offer your users/customers new features on very short development cycles.

10.3.2 *SearchBlox architecture*

Figure 10.1 shows the overall architecture of SearchBlox. Compared to Lucene, which is a text indexing and search API, SearchBlox is a complete search tool. It features integrated crawlers, support for different document types, provision for

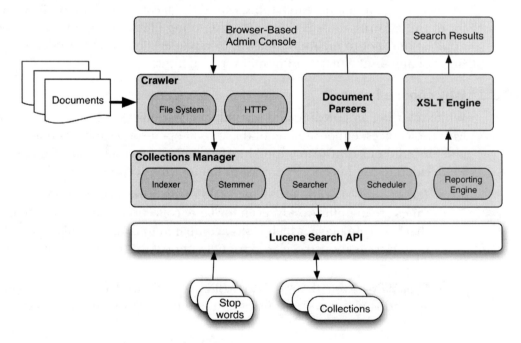

Figure 10.1 SearchBlox system architecture

several languages, and customizable search results; all controlled from a browser-based Admin Console. As a pure Java solution, SearchBlox can be deployed to any Servlet/JSP container, giving the customer complete flexibility in choosing the hardware, operating system and application server.

10.3.3 *Search results*

SearchBlox provides the user with the option to see search results sorted by relevance, sorted by date, or sorted alphabetically on the title. Search results in SearchBlox are completely customizable using XSL style sheets. The search results can also be delivered as XML to be consumed by an external application. This is achieved by generating an XML document for each search result page. In the results page, each search result is represented as shown here:

```
<result no="1">
   <score>27</score>
   <url>http://www.searchblox.com/faqs/question.php?qstId=22</url>
   <lastmodified>24 Nov 2003 07:40:15 EST</lastmodified>
   <indexdate>24 Nov 2003 07:40:15 EST</indexdate>
   <size>7408</size>
<title>SearchBlox<highlight>FAQs</highlight></title>
   <keywords />
   <contenttype>HTML</contenttype>
    <description><highlight>FAQs</highlight>
  Home / Browse Categories / Collections /
  Why is there a limit on the number of collections?
  Why is there a limit on the number of collections?
  There is a limit on the number of collections due to
  performance reasons. User Comments Why is t...
</description>
   <language>en</language>
   </result>
```

This XML segment is generated from the Lucene `Hits` object. The data for the `title` and `description` fields is then passed through a `Highlighter` class to highlight the query terms. The highlighted terms are marked using the `<highlight>` tag.

This mechanism gives the developer complete flexibility in customizing the search results, choosing only the XML elements that are of significance to the end user.

10.3.4 *Language support*

SearchBlox currently supports 17 languages including Japanese, Chinese (Simplified and Traditional), and Korean. There are two main challenges in creating a search tool that supports searching across multiple collections in several languages

- *Indexing documents with different encodings*—The solution to this problem is to normalize the document encoding. In the case of SearchBlox, all content is converted to UTF-8 before indexing. SearchBlox uses several mechanisms to detect the encoding of the document that is to be indexed.

- *Detecting the language of the content*—The language of the content is required for two purposes when indexing: to choose the correct analyzer and to use the correct stop-words list. SearchBlox uses the language setting specified at the time of collection creation as the language of the content.

10.3.5 Reporting Engine

A key element of SearchBlox is the Reporting Engine. It is crucial to know what end users are searching for. Most commercial search tools provide a reporting tool, which is either a log analyzer or a database-based tool. In SearchBlox, the Reporting Engine is based on Lucene. Details of every search query are indexed as a Lucene document. Precanned searches are executed on this Lucene index to retrieve the various reporting statistics. This Lucene-based reporting engine offers all the advantages of a database-based reporting system without the overhead of using a database.

10.3.6 Summary

SearchBlox leverages the Lucene API to deliver a pure Java search tool. Using Lucene has allowed SearchBlox to focus on the designing the usability of the search tool rather than developing a new search API from scratch. With Java having become a widespread enterprise standard and the increasing requirement for search, SearchBlox will provide a truly usable search tool incorporating Lucene.

10.4 Competitive intelligence with Lucene in XtraMind's XM-InformationMinder™

Contributed by Karsten Konrad, Ralf Steinbach, and Holger Stenzhorn

Detailed knowledge about competitors, markets, costumers, and products is a vital strategic advantage for any enterprise. But in the ever-growing flood of information available today, the truly relevant information cannot be looked up with common search methodologies anymore, even in a particular, narrow domain. In this regard, aggregating information has become by far more time consuming than its focused evaluation. Systematically and efficiently searching and identifying all important correlations, current trends, and developments in the amount of data coming in every day has become more and more difficult, if not impossible. Yet the paramount task of intelligence groups in companies is exactly this: to keep track of all potentially important current news and to subsequently inform marketing, sales, or the strategic planning groups of any developments that might change the company's business environment or direction.

Hence, there is some real need for specialized sophisticated tools that provide help in collecting and evaluating information for the knowledge workers in the intelligence departments. XtraMind Technologies—a technology and solution provider for natural-language and artificial intelligence–oriented systems such as those used for automated text classification, document clustering, topic detection, and so forth—developed the XM-InformationMinder to target exactly those needs in a web-based client/server application. One of the staple technologies we use in this application is Lucene.

XM-InformationMinder was initially developed as a custom solution for a large German generic drug manufacturer. They wanted a simple tool that could on one hand supervise news about themselves, their competitors, and their products on the Internet and on the other hand gather information on chemical compounds and formulations used for the company's drugs regarding pending patents and counterindications, for example. The final product has become a multipurpose application targeted at competitive and product intelligence in any business area.

XM-InformationMinder can basically be split into two subapplications: first, a web-based information access portal that allows the user to perform searches for particular documents or topics, the management of found documents via categories, the generation of reports for executives and so on; and second, an agent that scours around the Internet and gathers the information to be prepared and presented. Lucene is especially important to us in the information access portal.

Some of the key points of the information access portal are

- *Full text and similarity* search—XM-InformationMinder supports concept-based, fuzzy, and similarity search and sorts the results by relevance. At this, the search is able to tolerate misspellings. For interactive search by the user, all retrieved information and relevant pages are then made accessible through concept-based navigation methods.

- *Reporting*—The reporting function is used to transform relevant information into qualified statements and strategies. The application provides a report editor where the user can insert and comment search results. The

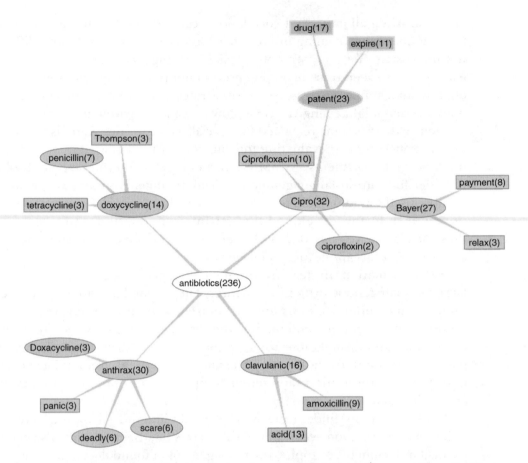

Figure 10.2   Visualization indicating relations between antibiotics, anthrax, and the anti-anthrax drug Cipro, manufactured by Bayer

resulting report documents can be made available by email or via the search portal itself.

- *Visualization and navigation*—Search strings and relevant related terms are computed dynamically and are visualized through a graphical user interface (see figure 10.2). Users can extend and control the search interactively and intuitively navigate through the information space. This aids users who may not be aware of some existent relevant cross-links, relations, or important new topics within the given domain and enables the user to detect and explore them. Their visualization through a user interface shows directly the connections between documents within their contexts. Starting with one search string, users see documents related to their query in the form of a graphical network. The visual navigation tool induces the search and automatically extends the query. The relevant relations to other terms are always computed at run-time relative to the original search term and the available information in the document base, thus assuring precision and topicality.

The second subapplication is the agent, an information gatherer that is based on a technology of intelligent software agents that are capable of distinguishing essential from nonessential information. Through methods of machine learning and language technology, the system achieves high levels of accuracy.

To train the system, users provide relevant sample texts, which XM-Information-Minder analyses for common properties within their content. XM-Information-Minder then uses this acquired knowledge (the so-called *relevance model*) for its search and the evaluation of new information. As a second set of clues, users indicate to XM-InformationMinder where relevant information is likely to be found or which sources (web pages, competitors' sites, portals, newsgroups, newsletters, and so on) should be monitored systematically. In this process, the agent removes redundant information automatically through the mentioned machine learning and language technologies.

10.4.1 *The system architecture*

XM-InformationMinder has been designed and developed as a pure Java, J2EE-based enterprise application that can be run on any standard application server platform.

The functional partition introduced earlier is directly reflected in the system's design: there exists first a software agent that collects information and second a search portal that provides this information and helps in preparing reports on certain developments and trends. The two parts are loosely linked via Java Messaging Service, and so this makes it possible to distribute the two parts and their tasks on more than one machine—that is, the agent part runs on one machine, and the portal part on another.

The software agent is an intelligent agent that uses a machine learning text classifier for distinguishing between relevant and irrelevant information. It basically works as a flexible web crawler that is able to stop crawling whenever it finds the currently visited web page not "interesting" or suitable. The decisions of the agent are based on a predefined relevance model (as mentioned earlier) that has been trained from both examples and terminology from the particular area of interest, in this case the generics pharmaceutical drug industry. The starting

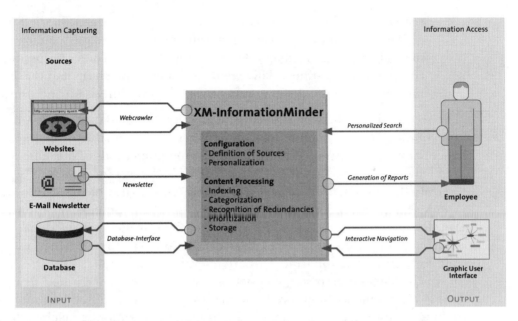

Figure 10.3 Depiction of the overall design and workflow of the system

points for the agent's searches are mostly newsletters from several online news-wire agencies that it receives via subscribed email services. It also reacts to changes on (user-defined) important web pages such as competitors' web sites. Furthermore, there also exist several newsgroups together with the usual articles on the industry (found, for instance, in Yahoo's directory) that can be scanned for suitable input for the agent. See figure 10.3.

The actual core of both system parts is based upon the functionalities provided by Lucene, with each employing its own index that it works on directly. Additionally, each part employs a database to hold basic infrastructure information, such as user and configuration management. The database also redundantly keeps some of the information that can be found in the Lucene index for two specific reasons:

- *Failure recovery*—If the index somehow becomes corrupted (for example, through disk failure), it can easily and quickly be rebuilt from the data stored in the database without any information loss. This is further leveraged by the fact that the database can reside on a different machine.

- *Access speed*—Each document is marked with a unique identifier. So, in the case that the application needs to access a certain document by a given identifier, the database can return it more efficiently than Lucene could. (the identifier is the primary key of a document in the database). If we would employ Lucene here, it would have to search its whole index for the document with the identifier stored in one of the document's fields.

The interaction of the agent and the information access portal subapplications is presented in the following brief workflow overview:

1   The agent first reads newsletter emails sent to it and inspects them as well as all the given other sources for new links that it should process.

2   The agent performs the crawling process and fetches all relevant web pages, PDF, Word, Rich Text, and other documents that can be converted to plain text. (This usually happens during nighttime because of the reduced Internet traffic.) During this procedure, all crawled data is first converted on the fly from the original format into plain text and subsequently stored into a database for further processing.

3   The agent process continues by feeding the Lucene indexer with the stored content data and putting the results into its proper index.

4   After the indexing, the agent sends a message to the portal application. This in turn starts to merge the agent index into its own, inserts the data (including all metadata—, such as the crawling time of a document) from the agent database into the portal database, and transfers the stored web pages and documents to a place for the portal to access.

One additional point to note is that transaction handling is supported: If the system (either the agent or the information access portal) or a user adds a new document into the index, then the agent first tries to write the data into the database and then into the index. If one of the two steps fails, the whole transaction is rolled back; by doing so, data integrity is ensured. The same applies for the deletion of documents from the application.

For our application, we modified the Lucene engine in such a way that it can support advanced search methods like visual explorative topic maps and search for similar documents. Because the information gathered by the software agent often contains redundant information, we also had to extended Lucene's indexing by automated redundancy filtering. Although Lucene certainly becomes more powerful and flexible with our own algorithms and extensions, the excellent basic data structures and persistence of Lucene are used without any modification. We found Lucene an ideal platform for our technologies and still apply Lucene's basic full-text search functionality in our application.

10.4.2 *How Lucene has helped us*

There can be no discussion on this matter: Lucene is a heaven-sent tool for any Java developer who needs an open-source, extensible full-text search engine. It outperforms expensive commercially available systems, yet it comes with a clean and easy-to-understand design that is open to extensions. XtraMind's business is—in a way—to provide services and solutions around advanced natural-language processing, and Lucene represents a very efficient information retrieval platform in that context.

Of course, we made some improvements to Lucene to suit our needs. First, we found the fuzzy expansion (`FuzzyEnum`) of Lucene to be too inefficient on very large collections of text; therefore, we replaced the original with one of our own methods that reduces the number of words expanded. Second, we extended the result collection mechanism with a priority queue that restricts the result sets to a few best dozen hits for certain time-consuming searches. There have been almost no changes to the core of Lucene, because all changes we had to make for language preprocessing could be done by inheriting and modifying class variants, mainly for the `Similarity` class and the `HitCollector`. For instance, we extended the `Similarity` class by a method that collects the actual terms of a query such that we could do highlighting and text extraction more easily.

We developed a wrapper for the core engine of Lucene into an additional comfort layer that performs additional functions like automated spelling correction and advanced query processing; this helps us integrate cross-lingual information retrieval capabilities into the existing framework.

Having said this, we do not have a particularly long list of wishes for Lucene. But one of the problems where we could not find any good solution was the fast generation of extracts for a given search result hit. We currently index the document content and then retokenize the content when we generate short text extracts. The problem is that this method is not really efficient when indexing long documents: the index becomes very large, and the extract generation takes up way too much time. Therefore we would like to see some method introduced that can quickly compute a window of words around a given search term for any document without having to access its content.

10.5 Alias-i: orthographic variation with Lucene

Contributed by Bob Carpenter of Alias-i, Inc.

Users seeking information in a large document collection are typically interested in individuals, not tokens. This goal is subverted by two facts of human language: name overloading and name variation. *Name overloading* involves using the same name to refer to different people. *Name variation* involves using different names to refer to the same person.

The focus of this discussion is name variation and how Lucene can be used to improve searches for something with many aliases. Specifically, we model a term as a bag of character subsequences and store each such bag of sequences as a Lucene document. Queries are similarly parsed into bags of character subsequences from which boolean query clauses are formed. The hits resulting from a query term will be the documents representing the terms in order of their fuzzy string similarity to the query term. Jumping ahead a bit, we tokenize a term such as *Al Jazeerah* as subsequences of length 2 to 4:

```
"Al", "l ", " J", ..., "ah",
...,
"Al Ja", "l Ja", " Jaz", ..., "erah"
```

Used as a query, `"Al Jazeerah"` returns the responses above the threshold shown in table 10.5.

Table 10.5 Orthographic variation used in a query for "Al Jazeerah"

Score	Result
999	Al Jazeerah
787	Al Jazeera
406	Jazeera
331	Al-Jazeera
304	al-Jazeera
259	Jazeera al-Jazirah
253	al-Jazeera TV
252	Al Jazirah

continued on next page

Table 10.5   Orthographic variation used in a query for "Al Jazeerah" *(continued)*

Score	Result
222	Arab channel al-Jazeera
213	Al-jazeera

10.5.1 *Alias-i application architecture*

At Alias-i, we have concentrated on building tools and interfaces to be used by professional information analysts, concentrating on two application domains: government intelligence analysts tracking the world's news, and biomedical researchers tracking the genomics and proteomics research literature. Specializing in particular subdomains is often necessary in order to import the necessary knowledge to solve the problems introduced by name overloading and variation.

The high-level information flow and data-storage architecture of the Alias-i Tracker system is illustrated in figure 10.4.

From the highest level, the standard three-tier web architecture is organized form left-to-right in figure 10.4. The tiers consist of an external interface, an internal model (the so-called *business logic*), and an encapsulated data store. Document processing within the model follows a queue-based pipeline. This arrangement was chosen primarily for its scalability properties. Even within a single JVM, I/O load balancing can be performed with very good responsiveness using the lock-split queues of Doug Lea's `util.concurrent` package. The queue-based architecture easily scales to multiple machines with transactional robustness by implementing the queues as a Java 2 Enterprise Edition (J2EE) Java Message Service (JMS) provider.

Document feeds gather documents from external sources and push them onto the first queue in the pipeline. Current implementations include a subscriber in a Publish/Subscribe pattern, a web-page downloader based on searches through the Google API, and a disk-based directory walker. Documents are transformed by their feed handler, based on their provenance, into our standardized XML format for news documents and placed in the incoming document queue. HTML is normalized with Andy Clark's NekoHTML and processed with SAX.

The first two steps in the pipeline store the documents and index them. Indexing is carried out with the Apache Lucene search engine. The Lucene indexer itself buffers documents in a `RAMDirectory`, using a separate thread to merge them periodically with an on-disk index.

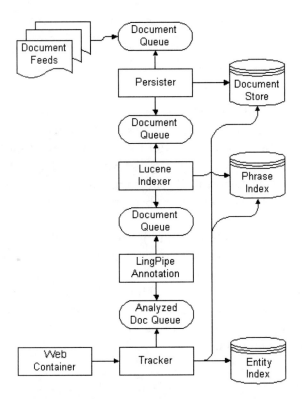

Figure 10.4 Alias-i Tracker architecture

The next two stages of processing are linguistic in nature. LingPipe, Alias-i's open-source linguistic annotation package, is used to annotate sentence boundaries, extract names of relevant individuals for a particular application, and determine when two names in the same document refer to the same individual.

Finally, a linguistically annotated document is processed by the tracker module to cluster names that refer to the same individual across documents and store the entities in a database.

For instance, typical output would look like this:

```
<DOCUMENT>
  <P>
    <sent>
      <ENAMEX id="393" type="PERSON">John Smith</ENAMEX>
      lives in <ENAMEX id="394" type="LOCATION">Washington</ENAMEX>.
    </sent>
    <sent>
      Mr. <ENAMEX id="393" type="PERSON">Smith</ENAMEX> works for
```

```
    <ENAMEX id="395" type="ORGANIZATION">
      American Airlines
    </ENAMEX>.
  </sent>
 </P>
</DOCUMENT>
```

We have applied LingPipe to applications in several domains and languages, including Hindi, Spanish, Dutch and English news, and English genomics/proteomics. LingPipe is distributed with a model for English news that labels people, places, and organizations. It is also distributed with a model for English genomics that labels proteins, DNA, and RNA, subcategorizing them based on whether they are a family, structure, molecule, substructure, or binding site, as well as labeling cells and organisms.

The user-interface architecture follows the ubiquitous model-view-control pattern. The tracker plays the role of model, accepting control in the form of document addition from the back-end document-processing queue. It also accepts control from the user's end application. The model acts as a façade to the databases, providing views of the data to the front-end interface. The controller handling the application control flow is implemented as part of the application and run within the web container.

10.5.2 *Orthographic variation*

There is a range of causes for name variation:

- *Misspellings*—A query term such as *Smith* may be spelled accidentally as *Smth* or *Smiht*. Search engines such as Google now normally provide alternative suggestions for terms that appear very unlikely compared to high-likelihood variants.

- *Alternative spellings*—Some terms simply have more than one conventionally acceptable spelling, either within or across dialects. Consider *colour* and *color* in British and American English or, on the same topic, the colors *grey* and *gray*. Even proper names may vary, such as MacDonald and McDonald or O'Leary and Oleary.

- *Reduced character sets*—Often terms from languages with character sets that are richer than English, such as German, are reduced to different forms in English, such as *Schütze* being rendered as *Schuetze* or *Schutze*, or the English word *naïve* alternating with the simpler character set version *naive*.

- *Alternative punctuation and tokenization*—Some terms vary with respect to how they are tokenized. This is particularly common with biological terminology, where the same protein may be referred to as *SLP-76* or *SLP76*. Person names suffer the same problem, with variations such as *Jun'ichi* versus *Junichi*. Company names suffer the same problem, with users potentially writing *FooBar Corp* as *Foo Bar Corp*, or common names such as *cybercafe* versus *cyber cafe*. Even simple prefixes and suffixes are sometimes hyphenated and sometimes not, as in *coordinate* vs. *co-ordinate*, or in acronyms, with *IBM* alternating with *I.B.M.*.

- *Transliteration*—Alternate transliteration of foreign names leads to variations such as translations into English from Russian such as *Tschaikowsky*, *Tchaikovsky*, and *Chaikovsky*, or from Chinese such as *Looi*, *Lui*, and *Loui*. These may affect tokenization as well, as in the variation between *Abd al* and *Abdul* or among *Sa ad*, *Sa'ad*, and *Saad*, transliterated from Arabic.

- *Name specificity variation*—There are various levels of specificity for names, such as the generic protein *p53* versus its bacterial and insect varieties *p53b* and *p53i*.

- *Abbreviated forms*—Biological terminology is full of semi-standardized abbreviations for terms, such as *linDNA* for *linearized DNA*.

- *Morphological variation*—There is also a wide range of morphological variation, from simple suffixes like plural *gene* versus *genes* to prefixes such as *binding*, *cobinding*, and *co-binding*.

A final problem we have in the biomedical domain is that many common stop words are also acronyms or names of genes, and are even written lowercase, as in genes *not*, *if*, and *for*.

The tokenization and variant problems are partly ameliorated by standard tokenization, stemming, and stop lists. For instance, *p53* will match *p53b* if the latter is tokenized as *p*, *53*, and *b*. Standard stemmers handle some of the problems with morphological variation, while at the same time introducing problems for search precision by equating two terms that should be kept separate and removing relevant terms such as the gene names *not*, *if*, and *for*. Stop lists can deal with some of the problems with mismatched punctuation if punctuation is removed from search.

10.5.3 *The noisy channel model of spelling correction*

The standard spelling correction model is based on Claude Shannon's *noisy-channel model* (Manning and Schütze 2003). The noisy channel model assumes that messages are being chosen according to a probabilistic distribution, P(message), and rendered as a signal that is received by a listener, P(signal|message).

The recipient's job is to decode the intended message from the retrieved signal. Shannon showed that this process is optimized in the case where the message decoded from a given signal is the message that maximizes the joint probability `P(message,signal) = P(message) * P(signal|message)`.

For spelling correction, suppose we are able to estimate the probability `P(spelling|word)` of a spelling given a word. For instance, `P("Jones"|"Jones")` will be very high, but the transposition typo case `P("Jnoes"|"Jones")` and the deletion typo case `P("Jone"|"Jones")` will be higher than a fully reversed spelling `P("senoJ"|"Jones")` or completely unrelated outcome `P("Smith"|"Jones")`. Similarly `P("confusible"|"confusable")` will be high in a good model because reduced *i* and *a* sound the same and are often confused in spelling. Probabilistic models of this kind are typically implemented through a notion of edit distance (Gusfield 1997).

There will also be a probability for the underlying words in question. For instance, *IBM* might have a much higher probability (say, 1/1000) than *BM* (say, 1/10,000,000) in text. Then when a term like *BM* is seen, we measure `P("BM") * P("BM"|"BM")` versus `P("IBM") * P("BM"|"IBM")`. In essence, we ask whether the probability of a *BM* times the probability of spelling the word *BM* as *BM* is greater or less than the probability of *IBM* times the probability of mistyping *IBM* as *BM*. In addition to the first-best hypothesis, the top *N* hypotheses are also easy to decode. This is how Microsoft Office is able to convert *hte* into *the* and to provide more suggestions in cases where it's not 100% confident in its alternate choice. It is also how Google is able to provide alternate spelling suggestions.

10.5.4 *The vector comparison model of spelling variation*

A popular statistical (although not probabilistic) model for comparing two words for similarity of spelling involves comparing their character subsequences (Anglell et al 1983). A sequence of *n* characters is typically called a *character n-gram*. The character n-grams for *John* are the 0-gram ""; the unigrams "J", "o", "h", "n"; the bigrams "Jo", "oh", "hn"; the trigrams "Joh" and "ohn"; and the 4-gram "John". The term *Jon* has n-grams "", "J", "o", "n", "Jo", "on", and "Jon".

In fact, it's been demonstrated for text search that replacing a text with all of its 4-grams, and analyzing queries with TF/IDF-weighted cosine term vectors, provides precision and recall results for search very similar to using whole word search (Cavnar 1994). The analyzer and query parser we present next could be used to implement a full information retrieval system based on n-grams.

10.5.5 *A subword Lucene analyzer*

It is simple to extract the n-grams from a word with Lucene by using a specialized analyzer. The token stream class shown in listing 10.2 does the job.

Listing 10.2 n-gramming `TokenStream`

```
private static int MIN_NGRAM = 2;
private static int MAX_NGRAM = 4;

public static class NGramTokenStream extends TokenStream {
    private int mLength = MIN_NGRAM;
    private int mStart = 0;
    private final String mToken;
    public NGramTokenStream(String token) {
        mToken = token;
    }
    public Token next() {
        int mEnd = mStart + mLength;
        if (mLength > MAX_NGRAM || mEnd > mToken.length())
            return null;
        String s = mToken.substring(mStart,mEnd);
        Token result = new Token(s,mStart,mEnd);
        if (mEnd == mToken.length()) {
            ++mLength;
            mStart = 0;
        } else {
            ++mStart;
        }
        return result;
    }
}
```

Assuming we have a method `String readerToString(Reader)` that reads the contents of a reader into a string without throwing exceptions, we can convert the token stream into an analyzer class directly:[6]

```
public static class SubWordAnalyzer extends Analyzer {
    public TokenStream tokenStream(String fieldName, Reader reader) {
        String content = readerToString(reader);
        return new NGramTokenStream(content);
    }
}
```

---

[6] Authors' note: The `KeywordAnalyzer` in section 4.4 converts a `Reader` to a `String` and could be adapted for use here.

With the analyzer and the set of terms we are interested in, it is straightforward to construct documents corresponding to terms with the following method:

```
public static Directory index(String[] terms) {
    Directory indexDirectory = new RAMDirectory();
    IndexWriter indexWriter
        = new IndexWriter(indexDirectory,new SubWordAnalyzer(),true);
    for (int i = 0; i < lines.length; ++i) {
        Document doc = new Document();
        doc.add(new Field(NGRAM_FIELD,lines[i],false,true,true));
        doc.add(
            new Field(FULL_NAME_FIELD,lines[i],true,false,false));
        indexWriter.addDocument(doc);
    }
    indexWriter.optimize();
    indexWriter.close();
    return indexDirectory;
}
```

Note that it stores the full name in its own field to display retrieval results. We employ the same n-gram extractor, converting the n-gram tokens into term query clauses:

```
public static class NGramQuery extends BooleanQuery {
    public NGramQuery(String queryTerm) throws IOException {
        TokenStream tokens = new NGramTokenStream(queryTerm);
        Token token;
        while ((token = tokens.next()) != null) {
            Term t = new Term(NGRAM_FIELD,token.termText());
            add(new TermQuery(t),false,false);
        }
    }
}
```

Note that they are added to the boolean query as optional terms that are neither required nor prohibited so that they will contribute to the TF/IDF matching supplied by Lucene. We simply extend the IndexSearcher to build in the n-gram query parser:

```
public static class NGramSearcher extends IndexSearcher {
    public NGramSearcher(Directory directory) {
        super(IndexReader.open(indexDirectory));
    }
    public Hits search(String term) {
        Hits = search(new NGramQuery(term));
    }
}
```

The nice part about this implementation is that Lucene does all the heavy lifting behind the scenes. Among the services provided are TF/IDF weighting of the n-gram vectors, indexing of terms by n-grams, and cosine computation and result ordering.

Here's an example of some of the queries run over 1,307 newswire documents selected from a range of American and Middle Eastern sources. Among these documents, there were 14,411 unique people, organizations, and locations extracted by LingPipe's named entity detector. These entity names were then indexed using 2-grams, 3-grams, and 4-grams. Then each of the names was used as a query. Total processing time was under two minutes on a modest personal computer, including the time to read the strings from a file, index them in memory, optimize the index, and then parse and execute each name as a query and write out the results. In addition to the one in the introduction, consider the following result. The number of hits indicates the total number of names that shared at least one n-gram, and only hits scoring 200 or above are returned:

```
Query=Mohammed Saeed al-Sahaf
Number of hits=7733
1000      Mohammed Saeed al-Sahaf
819       Muhammed Saeed al-Sahaf
769       Mohammed Saeed al-Sahhaf
503       Mohammed Saeed
493       Mohammed al-Sahaf
490       Saeed al-Sahaf
448       Mohammed Said el-Sahaf
442       Muhammad Saeed al-Sahhaf
426       Mohammed Sa'id al-Sahhaf
416       Mohammed Sahaf
368       Mohamed Said al-Sahhaf
341       Mohammad Said al-Sahaf
287       Mohammad Saeed
270       Mohammad Said al-Sahhaf
267       Muhammad Saeed al-Tantawi
254       Mohammed Sadr
254       Mohammed Said
252       Mohammed Bakr al-Sadr
238       Muhammad Said al-Sahaf
227       Mohammed Sadeq al-Mallak
219       Amer Mohammed al- Rasheed
```

In each of these cases, transliteration from Arabic presents spelling variation that goes well beyond the ability of a stemmer to handle. Also note that not every answer is a correct variation. On the other hand, the work of a stemmer is handled neatly, as exemplified by

```
Query=Sweden
Number of hits=2216
1000      Sweden
736       Swede
277       Swedish
```

In particular, the larger the substring overlap, the larger the errors. For instance, "Defense Ministry", in addition to matching the correct variation "Ministry of Defence" at 354, matches "Defense Analyst" at 278 and "Welfare Ministry" and "Agriculture Ministry", both at 265. At Alias-i, we blend character-level models with token-level models for increased accuracy.

10.5.6 *Accuracy, efficiency, and other applications*

Accuracy can be tuned with precision/recall trade-offs in various ways. For a start, terms can be lowercased. Alternatively, both lowercase and uppercase variants of n-grams with uppercase in them can be supplied. Furthermore, n-grams can be weighted based on their length, which is easily supported by Lucene. With longer n-grams being upweighted, the returned distributions will be sharpened, but the long-token overlap problem becomes more pronounced.

The previous implementations are intended for expository purposes, not a scalable application. For efficiency, the construction of Token objects could be bypassed in the query constructor. A priority-queue-based HitCollector, or simply one that applied a threshold, should significantly reduce object allocation during queries. Finally, a file-system directory could be applied to store more data on disk.

10.5.7 *Mixing in context*

In addition to orthographic term variation, we also consider the context in which a term occurs before deciding if two terms refer to the same individual. If the words in a window around the term in question are taken into account, it is quite possible to sort the three dozen different John Smiths appearing in two years of *New York Times* articles based on the similarity of their contexts (Bagga and Baldwin 1998). This performs at roughly 80% precision and recall as measured over the relations between pairs of individuals that are the same; thus a true-positive is a pair of mentions that are related, a false positive involves relating two mentions that should not be linked, and a false negative involves failing to relate two mentions that should be linked. Together, the string variation and the context variation are merged into an overall similarity score, to which clustering may be applied to extract the entities (Jain and Dubes 1988).

10.5.8 References

- Alias-i. 2003. LingPipe 1.0. http://www.aliasi.com/lingpipe.

- Anglell, R., B. Freund, and P. Willett. 1983. Automatic spelling correction using a trigram similarity measure. Information Processing & Management 19(4):305–316.

- Bagga, Amit, and Breck Baldwin. 1998. Entity-Based Cross-Document Coreferencing Using the Vector Space Model. Proceedings of the 36th Meeting of the Association for Computational Linguistics. 79–85.

- Cavnar, William B. 1994. Using an n-gram-based document representation with a vector processing retrieval model. In Proceedings of the Third Text Retrieval Conference. 269–277.

- Clark, Andy. 2003. CyberNeko HTML Parser 0.9.3. http://www.apache.org/~andyc/neko/doc/html/.

- Gusfield, Dan. 1997. Algorithms on Strings, Trees and Sequences: *Computer Science and Computational Biology*. Cambridge University Press.

- Jain, Anil K., and Richard C. Dubes. 1988. *Algorithms for Clustering Data*. Prentice Hall.

- Lea, Doug. 2003. Overview of package util.concurrent Release 1.3.4. http://gee.cs.oswego.edu/dl/classes/EDU/oswego/cs/dl/util/concurrent/intro.html.

- Manning, Christopher D., and Hinrich Schütze. 2003. *Foundations of Statistical Natural Language Processing*. MIT Press.

- Sun Microsystems. 2003. J2EE Java Message Service (JMS). http://java.sun.com/products/jms/.

10.6 *Artful searching at Michaels.com*

Contributed by Craig Walls

Michaels.com is the online presence for Michaels Stores, Inc., an arts and crafts retailer with more than 800 stores in the United States and Canada. Using this web site, Michaels targets crafting enthusiasts with articles, project ideas, and product information designed to promote the crafting pastime and the Michaels brand. In addition, Michaels.com also offers a selection of over 20,000 art prints for purchase online.

With such a vast offering of ideas and products, Michaels.com requires quick and robust search facility to help their customers locate the information they need to enjoy their craft.

When first launched, Michaels.com employed a naïve approach to searching. With all of the site's content stored in a relational database, they used basic SQL queries involving LIKE clauses. Because the content tables were very large and contained lengthy columns, searching in this manner was very slow. Furthermore, complex searches involving multiple criteria were not possible.

Realizing the limitations of searching by SQL, Michaels.com turned to a commercial search solution. Although this tool offered an improved search facility over SQL searching, it was still not ideal. Search results were often inconsistent, omitting items that should have matched the search criteria. Rebuilding the search index involved taking the search facility offline. And, to make matters worse, documentation and technical support for the product came up lacking.

After much frustration with the commercial product, Michaels.com began seeking a replacement. The following criteria were set for finding a suitable replacement:

- *Performance*—Any search, no matter how complicated, must return results quickly. Although *quickly* never was quantified, it was understood that web surfers are impatient and that any search that took longer than a few seconds would outlast the customer's patience.

- *Scalability*—The tool must scale well both in terms of the amount of data indexed as well as with the site's load during peak traffic.

- *Robustness*—The index must be frequently rebuilt without taking the search facility offline.

Following a brief evaluation period, Michaels.com chose Lucene to fulfill their search requirements. What follows is a description of how Lucene drives Michaels.com's search facility.

10.6.1 *Indexing content*

Michaels.com has four types of searchable content: art prints, articles, in-store products information, and projects.

All searchable types are indexed in Lucene with a document containing at least two fields: an ID field and a keywords field. Although Lucene is used for searching on Michaels.com, a relational database contains the actual content. Therefore, the ID field in each Lucene document contains the value of the primary key of the

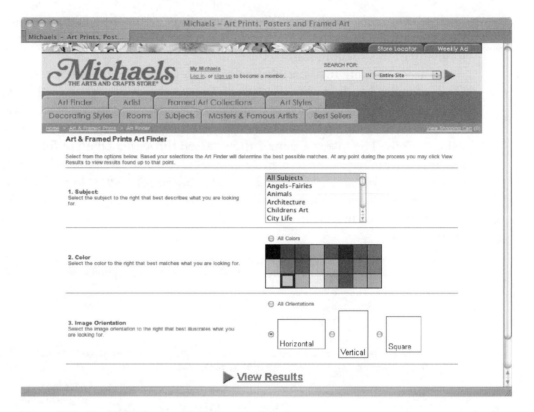

Figure 10.5   The Michaels.com Art Finder search tool

content in the database. The `keywords` field contains one or more words that may be searched upon.

Art prints have special search requirements beyond simple keyword searching. Michaels.com offers an Art Finder tool (figure 10.5) that enables an art print customer to locate a suitable print based upon one or more of a print's orientation (landscape, portrait, or square), subject, and dominant colors. As such, an art print is indexed in Lucene with a document containing orientation, subject, and color fields in addition to the ID and keywords fields.

Analyzing keyword text

One of the requirements placed upon Michaels.com's search facility was the ability to match search terms against synonyms and common misspellings. For example, the Xyron line of crafting products is very popular among scrapbookers and other paper-crafting enthusiasts. Unfortunately, many visitors to

Michaels.com mistakenly spell *Xyron* as it sounds: *Zyron*. To enable those users to find the information that they are looking for, Michaels.com's search must be forgiving of this spelling mistake.

To accommodate this, the Michaels.com development team created a custom Lucene analyzer called `AliasAnalyzer`. An `AliasAnalyzer` starts with an `Alpha-numericTokenizer` (a subclass of `org.apache.lucene.analysis.LetterTokenizer` that also accepts numeric digits in a token) to break the keyword string into individual tokens. The token stream is then passed through a chain of filters, including `org.apache.lucene.analysis.LowerCaseFilter`, `org.apache.lucene.analysis.StopFilter`, and `org.apache.lucene.analysis.PorterStemFilter`. The last filter applied to the token stream is a custom `AliasFilter` (listing 10.3) that looks up a token's aliases from a property file and introduces the aliases (if any) into the token stream.

Listing 10.3 `AliasFilter` introduces synonym tokens into the token stream

```
class AliasFilter extends TokenFilter {
  private final static MultiMap ALIAS_MAP = new MultiHashMap();
  private Stack currentTokenAliases = new Stack();

  static {
    ResourceBundle aliasBundle = ResourceBundle.getBundle("alias");
    Enumeration keys = aliasBundle.getKeys();

    while (keys.hasMoreElements()) {            Load alias list from
      String key = (String)keys.nextElement();    properties file
      loadAlias(key, aliasBundle.getString(key));
    }
  }

  private static void loadAlias(String word, String aliases) {

    StringTokenizer tokenizer = new StringTokenizer(aliases);
      while(tokenizer.hasMoreTokens()) {
      String token = tokenizer.nextToken();
      ALIAS_MAP.put(word, token);
      ALIAS_MAP.put(token, word);      Allow for bidirectional aliasing
    }
  }

  AliasFilter(TokenStream stream) {
    super(stream);
  }

  public Token next() throws IOException {
    if (currentTokenAliases.size() > 0) {
      return (Token)currentTokenAliases.pop();    Return next alias
    }                                               as next token
```

```
        Token nextToken = input.next();

        if (nextToken == null) return null;

        Collection aliases =                                  Look up aliases
            (Collection) ALIAS_MAP.get(nextToken.termText());  for next token

        pushAliases(aliases);      ◁─┐  Push aliases
                                        onto stack
        return nextToken;          ◁─  Return
    }                                   next token

    private void pushAliases(Collection aliases) {

        if (aliases == null) return;                          Load alias list from
                                                              properties file
        for (Iterator i = aliases.iterator(); i.hasNext();) {
          String token = (String) i.next();
          currentTokenAliases.push(new Token(token, 0, token.length()));
        }
    }
}
```

For example, if the keyword text is "The Zyron machine" and the following properties file is used, the resulting token stream would contain the following tokens: *zyron*, *xyron*, *device*, and *machine*:

```
zyron=xyron
machine=device
```

Analyzing art print colors

Initially, each print's dominant color was to be chosen manually by the production staff. However, this plan was flawed in that analysis of colors by a human is subjective and slow. Therefore, the Michaels.com team developed an analysis tool to determine a print's dominant colors automatically.

To begin, a finite palette of colors was chosen to match each print against. The palette size was kept small to avoid ambiguity of similar colors but was still large enough to accommodate most decorators' expectations. Ultimately a palette of 21 colors and 3 shades of grey were chosen (see table 10.6).

Table 10.6   The Michaels.com color palette for finding art prints

#000000	#CCCCCC	#FFFFFF
#663300	#CC6600	#FFCC99

continued on next page

Table 10.6 The Michaels.com color palette for finding art prints (continued)

#006633	#666600	#CCCC66
#CCCC00	#FFCC33	#FFFFCC
#006699	#99CCFF	#99CCCC
#330066	#663399	#6633CC
#993333	#CC6666	#FF9999
#FF3333	#FF6600	#FF99CC

The analysis tool processes JPEG images of each print. Each pixel in the image is compared to each color in the color palette in an attempt to find the palette color that most closely matches the pixel color. Each color in the palette has an associated score that reflects the number of pixels in the image that matched to that color.

When matching a pixel's color to the palette colors, a color distance formula is applied. Consider the RGB (red/green/blue) components of a color being mapped in Euclidean space. Finding the distance between two colors is simply a matter of determining the distance between two points in Euclidean space using the formula shown in figure 10.6.[7]

After every pixel is evaluated against the color palette, the three colors with the highest score are considered the dominant colors for the art print. Furthermore, if any of the colors accounts for less than 25% of the pixels in the print, then that color is considered insignificant and is thrown out.

Once the dominant colors have been chosen, their hexadecimal triples (such as FFCC99) are stored in the relational database along with the print's other

$$distance = \sqrt{(r_1 - r_2)^2 + (g_1 - g_2)^2 + (b_1 - b_2)^2}$$

Figure 10.6   Color distance formula

---

[7] Actually, the formula employed by Michaels.com is slightly more complicated than this. The human eye is more sensitive to variations of some colors than others. Changes in the green component are more noticeable than changes in the red component, which are more noticeable than changes in the blue component. Therefore, the formula must be adjusted to account for the human factor of color. The actual formula used by Michaels.com is a derivative of the formula explained at http://www.compuphase.com/cmetric.htm.

information. The color analysis routine is a one-time routine applied when a print is first added to the site and is not performed every time that a print is indexed in Lucene.

Running the indexers

The search index is rebuilt from scratch once per hour. A background thread awakens, creates a new empty index, and then proceeds to add content data to the index. This is simply a matter of drawing a content item's data from the relational database, constructing a Lucene document to contain that data, and then adding it to the index.

So that the search facility remains available during indexing, there are two indexes: an active index and a working index. The active index is available for searching by Michaels.com customers, whereas the working index is where indexing occurs. Once the indexer is complete, the working and active directories are swapped so that the new index becomes the active index and the old index waits to be rebuilt an hour later.

To avoid multiple index files, Michaels.com recently began using the new compound index format available in Lucene 1.3.

10.6.2 *Searching content*

Several HTML forms drive the search for Michaels.com. In the case of a simple keywords search, the form contains a `keywords` field. In the case of an Art Finder search, the form contains an HTML `<select>` named `subject`, a hidden field (populated through JavaScript) named `color`, and a set of radio buttons named `orientation`.

When the search is submitted, each of these fields is placed into a `java.util.Map` (where the parameter name is the key and the parameter value is the value) and passed into the Lucene query constructor method shown in listing 10.4.

```
private static final String[] IGNORE_WORDS =
    new String[] { "and", "or" };

public static String constructLuceneQuery(Map fields) {
  StringBuffer queryBuffer = new StringBuffer();

  for(Iterator keys=fields.keySet().iterator(); keys.hasNext();) {      ◁──┐  Cycle over each
    String key = (String) keys.next();                                          field in Map
    String field = (String) fields.get(key);

    if(key.equals("keywords")) {                        Strip nonalphanumeric
      String keywords =                             characters from keywords  ◁
          removeNonAlphaNumericCharacters(field).toLowerCase();
```

Listing 10.4   Constructing a Lucene query from a map of fields

```
    StringTokenizer tokenizer = new StringTokenizer(keywords);

    while(tokenizer.hasMoreTokens()) {                        Separate keywords
      String nextToken = tokenizer.nextToken();               on space delimiter
      if (Arrays.binarySearch(IGNORE_WORDS, nextToken) > 0) {
        continue;                                              If reserved
      }                                                        word, ignore
      if(!StringUtils.isEmpty(keywords)) {
        queryBuffer.append("+").append(nextToken).append(" ");
      }                                                        Add keyword
    }                                                          to query
  }
  else {
    queryBuffer.append("+").append(key).append(":").
      append(field).append(" ");                              Add nonkeyword field
  }                                                            and value to query
}

return queryBuffer.toString();
}
```

When dealing with keywords, care must be taken to ensure that no characters with special meaning to Lucene are passed into the query. A call to the removeNonAlphaNumericCharacters() utility method strips out all characters that aren't A-Z, 0-9, or spaces. The keywords field is also normalized to lowercase and stripped of any words with special meaning to Lucene (in this case, *and* and *or*).

At this point, the keywords string is clean and ready to be added to the search query. If we wanted the query to be an inclusive query (including all documents matching any of the keywords), we could just append the keywords string to the query and be done. Instead, each word in the string is prepended with a plus sign (+) indicating that matching documents must contain the word.[8]

For example, given a search phrase of "Mother and child", the resulting Lucene query would be "+mother +child".

In the case of the nonkeywords search fields, we simply append the name and value of the field into the query, separated by a colon (:). For example, had the customer used Art Finder to locate a horizontal art print in any subject with dark

---

[8] Authors' note: There are enough odd interactions between analyzers and QueryParser for us to add a warning here. Building a query expression in code to be parsed by QueryParser may be quirky. An alternative is to build a BooleanQuery with nested TermQuerys directly.

brown as its dominant color, the query would be `"orientation:horizontal color:663300"`.

With the query constructed, we are now ready to perform the search.

Submitting the query

The `findDocuments()` method (listing 10.5) is responsible for querying a given Lucene index and returning a list of documents that match that query.

Listing 10.5   The `findDocuments()` method returns a list of matching documents

```
private List findDocuments(String queryString,
    String indexDirectory) {

  IndexSearcher searcher = null;
  try {
    searcher = new IndexSearcher(indexDirectory);      ◁──┘  Open IndexSearcher
                                                             on specified directory

    Query query = QueryParser.parse(
        queryString, "keywords", new SearchAnalyzer());      Parse query

    Hits hits = searcher.search(query);      ◁─┐  Do search

    List documentList = new ArrayList();

    for (int i = 0; i < hits.length()⁹; i++) {
      documentList.add(
          new BaseDocument(hits.doc(i), hits.score(i)));
    }
    return documentList;
  }
  catch(Exception e) {
    throw new SystemException("An search error occured");
  }
  finally {
    LuceneUtils.close(searcher);
  }
}
```

---

[9] Authors' note: Be aware of the potential number of hits, the size of your documents, and the scalability needs of your application when you choose to iterate over all hits, especially if you collect them using `hits.doc(i)` like this. As noted in this case study, the performance in this scenario has been more than acceptable, but much larger indexes and arbitrary queries change the landscape dramatically.

The BaseDocument class (listing 10.6) is simply a means to tie a Lucene Document to its relevancy score. As eluded to by the getId() method, the only thing we care about within a returned document is its ID. We'll use this value to look up the complete piece of data from the relational database.

Listing 10.6 BaseDocument **associates a** Document **and its score**

```
public class BaseDocument {
  protected final Document document;
  protected final float score;

  BaseDocument(Document document, float score) {
    this.document = document;
    this.score = score;
  }

  public int getId() {
    return Integer.parseInt(document.get("id"));
  }

  String getFieldValue(String fieldName) {
    return document.get(fieldName);
  }
}
```

With the list of BaseDocuments returned from findDocuments(), we're ready to pare down the results into a page's worth of data:

```
List documentList = findDocuments(query, indexPath);
List subList = documentList.subList(start,
    Math.min(start + count, documentList.size()));
```

The start variable indicates the first document for the current page, whereas the count variable indicates how many items are on the current page.

Using the ID of each document in subList as a primary key, the last step is to retrieve additional data about each document from the relational database.

10.6.3 *Search statistics*

At the time this was written (March 2004), Michaels.com boasted 23,090 art prints, 3,327 projects, 385 in-store product promotions, and 191 crafting articles—all searchable through Lucene.

During the 2003 holiday shopping period, typically a time of peak traffic for Michaels.com, the search facility was engaged approximately 60,000 times per day. Without fail, Lucene returned results in subsecond time for each request.

10.6.4 Summary

Michaels.com has had tremendous success in employing Lucene to drive its search facility, enabling customers to find the art and craft information and products that they are looking for. Using its simple and intuitive API, we were able to integrate Lucene into our site's codebase quickly. Unlike its predecessors, Lucene has proven to be stable, robust, and very quick. Furthermore, it runs virtually hands-free, not requiring any developer intervention in well over a year and a half.

10.7 I love Lucene: TheServerSide

Contributed by Dion Almaer

"TheServerSide.com is an online community for enterprise Java architects and developers, providing daily news, tech talk interviews with key industry figures, design patterns, discussion forums, satire, tutorials, and more."

—http://www.theserverside.com

TheServerSide historically had a poor search engine. Thanks to Jakarta Lucene, we could fix the problem with a high quality open source solution. This case study discusses how TheServerSide implemented Lucene as its underlying search technology.

10.7.1 Building better search capability

There are a lot of areas on TheServerSide that we would like to change. Trust us. Ever since I joined TheServerSide I have cringed at our search engine implementation. It didn't do a good job, and that meant that our users couldn't get to information that they wanted. User interface analysis has shown that search functionality is *very* important on the web (see http://www.useit.com/alertbox/20010513.html), so we really had to clean up our act here. This case study discusses how TheServerSide built an infrastructure that allows us to index and search our different content using Lucene. We will chat about our high-level infrastructure, how we index and search, as well as how we are easily able to tweak the configuration.

So, we wanted a good search engine, but what are the choices? We were using ht://Dig and having it crawl our site, building the index as it went along.[10] This

---

[10] For more on ht://Dig, visit http://www.htdig.org/.

process wasn't picking up all of the content and didn't give us a nice clean API for us to tune the search results. It did do *one* thing well, and that was searching through our news. This was a side effect of having news on the home page, which helps the rankings (the more clicks ht://Dig needed to navigate from the home page, the lower the rankings).

Although ht://Dig wasn't going a great job, we could have tried to help it on its way. For example, we could have created a special HTML file that linked to various areas of the site and used that as the root page for it to crawl. Maybe we could have put a servlet filter that checked for the ht://Dig user agent and returned back content in a different manner (cleaning up the HTML and such).

We looked into using Google to manage our searching for us. I mean, they are pretty good at searching, aren't they?! Although I am sure we could have had a good search using them, we ran into a couple of issues:

- It wasn't that easy for us (a small company) to get much information from them.
- For the type of search that we needed, it was looking very expensive.
- We still have the issues of a crawler-based infrastructure.

While we were looking into Google, I was also looking at Lucene. Lucene has always interested me, because it isn't a typical open-source project. In my experience, most open-source projects are frameworks that have evolved. Take something like Struts. Before Struts, many people were rolling their own MVC layers on top of Servlets/JSPs. It made sense to not have to reinvent this wheel, so Struts came around.

Lucene is a different beast. It contains some really complicated low-level work, *not* just a nicely designed framework. I was really impressed that something of this quality was just put out there!

At first I was a bit disappointed with Lucene because I didn't really understand what it was ☺. Immediately I was looking for crawler functionality that would allow me to build an index just like ht://Dig was doing. At the time, LARM was in the Lucene Sandbox (and I have since heard of various other subprojects), but I found it strange that this wouldn't be built into the main distribution. It took me a day to realize that Lucene isn't a product that you just run. It is a top-notch search API that you can use to plug in to your system. Yes, you may have to write some code, but you also get great power and flexibility.

10.7.2 *High-level infrastructure*

When you look at building your search solution, you often find that the process is split into two main tasks: *building* an index, and *searching* that index. This is definitely the case with Lucene (and the only time when this isn't the case is if your search goes directly to the database).

We wanted to keep the search interface fairly simple, so the code that interacts from the system sees two main interfaces: IndexBuilder, and IndexSearch.

IndexBuilder

Any process that needs to build an index goes through the IndexBuilder (figure 10.7). This is a simple interface that provides two entry points to the indexing process. To do an incremental build and control how often to optimize the Lucene index as you add records, pass individual configuration settings to the class. To control the settings from an external configuration file, use a plan name. You will also see a main(..) method. We created this to allow for a command-line program to kick off a build process.

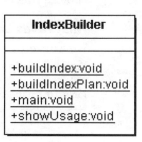

Figure 10.7
IndexBuilder

IndexSources

The IndexBuilder abstracts the details of Lucene, and the IndexSources that are used to create the index itself. As we will see in the next section, TheServerSide has various content that we wanted to be able to index, so a simple design is used where we can plug 'n play new index sources.

IndexSearch

The search interface is also kept very simple (see figure 10.8). A search is done via

```
IndexSearch11.search(String inputQuery, int
    resultsStart,
             int resultsCount);
```

For example, we look for the terms *EJB* and *WebLogic*, returning up to the first 10 results:

```
IndexSearch.search("EJB AND WebLogic", 0, 10);
```

Figure 10.8 IndexSearch

---

[11] Authors' note: Be careful not to confuse TheServerSide's IndexSearch class with Lucene's IndexSearcher class.

The query is built via the Lucene `QueryParser` (actually a subclass that we created, which you will see in detail later). This allows our users to input typical Google-esque queries. Once again, a `main()` method exists to allow for command-line searching of indexes.

10.7.3 *Building the index*

We have seen that the external interface to building our search index is the class `IndexBuilder`. Now we will discuss the index building process and the design choices that we made.

What fields should make up our index?

We wanted to create a fairly generic set of fields that our index would contain. We ended up with the fields shown in table 10.7.

Table 10.7   TheServerSide index field structure

Field	Lucene Type	Description
title	Field.Text	A short title of the content.
summary	Field.Text	A summary paragraph introducing the content.
fullcontents	Field.UnStored	The entire contents to index, but *not* store.
owner	Field.Keyword	The owner of the content (who wrote the post? who was the author of the article?).
category	Field.Keyword	The type of this content (is it a news item? an article?).
path	Field.Keyword	The unique path that points to this resource.
modifieddate	Field.Keyword	The modified date in Lucene format. Used for displaying the exact date of the content to the user.
createddate	Field.Keyword	The created date in Lucene format. Used for displaying the exact date of the content to the user.
modifieddate_range	Field.Keyword	Date as a `String` with the format YYYYMMDD. Used for date-range queries.
createddate_range	Field.Keyword	Date as a `String` with the format YYYYMMDD. Used for date-range queries.

We created a simple Java representation of this data, `SearchContentHolder`, which our API uses to pass this information around. It contains the modified and created dates as `java.util.Date`, and the full contents are stored as a `StringBuffer` rather than a `String`. This was refactored into our design because we found that some `IndexSources` contained a lot of data, and we didn't want to add to `Strings`.

What types of indexing?

Since the TSS content that we wanted to index is fairly large and a lot of it doesn't change, we wanted to have the concept of incremental indexing as well as a full indexing from scratch. To take care of this, we have an `incrementalDays` variable that is configured for the index process. If this value is set to 0 or less, then do a full index. If this is not the case, then content that is newer (created / modified) than `today - incrementalDays` should be indexed. In this case, instead of creating a new index, we simply delete the record (if it already exists) and insert the latest data into it.

How do you delete a record in Lucene again? We need the `org.apache.lucene.index.IndexReader`. The snippet that does the work is shown in listing 10.7.

Listing 10.7   Snippet from `IndexHolder` that deletes the entry from the index if it is already there

```
IndexReader reader = null;
try {
  this.close(); // closes the underlying index writer

  reader = IndexReader.open(SearchConfig.getIndexLocation());
  Term term = new Term("path", theHolder.getPath());
  reader.delete(term);
} catch (IOException e) {
  ... deal with exception ...
} finally {
  try { reader.close(); } catch (IOException e) { /* suck it up */ }
}

this.open(); // reopen the index writer
```

As you can see, we first close the `IndexWriter`, and then we open the index via the `IndexReader`. The path field is the ID that corresponds to this "to be indexed" entry. If it exists in the index, it will be deleted, and shortly after we will re-add the new index information.

What to index?

As TheServerSide has grown over time, we have the side effect of possessing content that lives in different sources. Our threaded discussions lie in the database, but our articles live in a file system. The Hard Core Tech Talks also sit on the file system but in a different manner than our articles.

We wanted to be able to plug in different sources to the index, so we created a simple `IndexSource` interface and a corresponding `Factory` class which returns all of the index sources to be indexed. The following code shows the simple `IndexSource` interface:

```
public interface IndexSource {
  public void addDocuments(IndexHolder holder);
}
```

There is just one method, `addDocuments()`, which an `IndexSource` has to implement. The `IndexBuilder` is charged with calling this method on each `Index-Source` and passing in an `IndexHolder`. The responsibility of the `IndexHolder` is in wrapping around the Lucene-specific search index (via Lucene's `org.apache.lucene.index.IndexWriter`). The `IndexSource` is responsible for taking this holder and adding records to it in the index process.

Let's look at an example of how an `IndexSource` does this by looking at the `ThreadIndexSource`.

ThreadIndexSource

This index source goes through the TSS database and indexes the various threads from all of our forums.[12] If we are doing an incremental build, then the results are simply limited by the SQL query that we issue to get the content.

When we get the data back from the database, we need to morph it into an instance of `SearchContentHolder`. If we don't have a summary, then we simply crop the body to a summary length governed by the configuration.

The main field that we search is `fullcontents`. To make sure that a user of the system finds what it wants, we make this field *not* only the body of a thread message, but rather a concatenation of the title of the message, the owner of the message, and then finally the message contents itself. You *could* try to use boolean queries to make sure that a search finds a good match, but we found it a lot simpler to put in a cheeky concatenation![13]

So, this should show how simple it is to create an `IndexSource`. We created sources for articles and tech talks (and in fact a couple of versions to handle an

---

[12] Authors' note: To clarify, the word *thread* here refers to a series of forum postings with a common subject.

[13] Authors' note: For more on querying multiple fields and this concatenation technique, see section 5.3.

upgrade in content management facilities). If someone wants us to search a new source, we create a new adapter, and we are in business.

How to tweak the ranking of records

When we hand the `IndexHolder` a `SearchContentHolder`, it does the work of adding it to the Lucene index. This is a fairly trivial task of taking the values from the object and adding them to a Lucene document:

```
doc.add(Field.UnStored("fullcontents", theHolder.getFullContents()));
doc.add(Field.Keyword("owner", theHolder.getOwner()));
```

There is one piece of logic that goes above and beyond munging the data to a Lucene-friendly manner. It is in this class that we calculate any boosts that we want to place on fields or the document itself. It turns out that we end up with the boosters shown in table 10.8.

Table 10.8 TheServerSide field boosts

Boost	Description
Title	A title should have more weight than something in the body of a message, so bump up this field booster.
Summary	A summary should also have more weight than the message body (although not as much as a title), so do the same here.
Category	Some categories are born more important than others. For example, we weight front-page threads and articles higher than the discussion forums.
Date boosts	Newer information is better, isn't it? We boost a document if it is new, and the boost decreases as time goes on.

The *date boost has been really important for us*. We have data that goes back for a long time and seemed to be returning old reports too often. The date-based booster trick has gotten around this, allowing for the newest content to bubble up.

The end result is that we now have a nice simple design that allows us to add new sources to our index with minimal development time!

10.7.4 *Searching the index*

Now we have an index. It is built from the various sources of information that we have and is just waiting for someone to search it.

Lucene made this very simple for us to whip up. The innards of searching are hidden behind the `IndexSearch` class, as mentioned in the high-level overview. The work is so simple that I can even paste it here:

```
public static SearchResults search(String inputQuery,
                      int resultsStart,
                      int resultsCount) throws SearchException {
  try {
    Searcher searcher = new
        IndexSearcher(SearchConfig.getIndexLocation());
    String[] fields = { "title", "fullcontents" };

    Hits hits = searcher.search(
                CustomQueryParser.parse(inputQuery, fields,
                                  new StandardAnalyzer()));

    SearchResults sr = new SearchResults(hits, resultsStart,
                                  resultsCount);
    searcher.close();
    return sr;
  } catch (...) {
    throw new SearchException(e);
  }
}
```

This method simply wraps around the Lucene `IndexSearcher` and in turn envelopes the results as our own `SearchResults`.

The only slightly different item to note is that we created out own simple `QueryParser` variant. The `CustomQueryParser` extends Lucene's and is built to allow a default search query to search both the `title` and `fullcontents` fields. It also disables the useful, yet expensive, wildcard and fuzzy queries. The last thing we want is for someone to do a bunch of queries such as `'a*'`, causing a lot of work in the Lucene engine. Our custom query parser is shown in listing 10.8.[14]

Listing 10.8   TheServerSide's custom query parser

```
public class CustomQueryParser extends QueryParser
{
  /**
   * Static parse method which will query both the title and
   * the fullcontents fields via a BooleanQuery
   */
  public static Query parse(String query, String[] fields,
                    Analyzer analyzer) throws ParseException {
    BooleanQuery bQuery = new BooleanQuery();

    for (int i = 0; i < fields.length; i++) {
      QueryParser parser = new CustomQueryParser(fields[i],
                                      analyzer);
```

---

[14] Authors' note: Refer to section 6.3.2 for an almost identical custom query parser and further discussion of subclassing `QueryParser`.

```
        Query q = parser.parse(query);
        bQuery.add(q, false, false);      ◁──┐  Combine queries,
    }                                          neither requiring nor
                                               prohibiting matches
    return bQuery;
}

public CustomQueryParser(String field, Analyzer analyzer) {
    super(field, analyzer);
}

final protected Query getWildcardQuery(String field, String term)
                                            throws ParseException {
    throw new ParseException("Wildcard Query not allowed.");
}

final protected Query getFuzzyQuery(String field, String term)
                                            throws ParseException {
    throw new ParseException("Fuzzy Query not allowed.");
}
}
```

That's all, folks. As you can see, it is fairly trivial to get the ball rolling on the search side of the equation.

10.7.5 *Configuration: one place to rule them all*

There have been settings in both the indexing process and search process that were crying out for abstraction. Where should we put the index location, the category lists, and the boost values, and register the index sources? We didn't want to have this in code, and since the configuration was hierarchical, we resorted to using XML.

Now, I don't know about you, but I am not a huge fan of the low-level APIs such as SAX and DOM (or even JDOM, DOM4j, and the like). In cases like this, we don't care about parsing at this level. I really just want my configuration information, and it would be perfect to have this information given to me as an object model. This is where tools such as Castor-XML, JIBX, JAXB, and Jakarta Commons Digester come in.

We opted for the Jakarta Digester in this case. We created the object model to hold the configuration that we needed, all behind the SearchConfig façade. This façade holds a Singleton object that held the configuration, as shown in listing 10.9.

Listing 10.9 Abstracting indexing and search configuration

```
/**
 * Wrap around a Singleton instance which holds a ConfigHolder
 * @return
 */
public synchronized static ConfigHolder getConfig() {
  if (ourConfig == null) {
    try {
      String configName = "/search-config.xml";
      File input = new File( PortalConfig.getSearchConfig() +
                            configName);
      File rules = new File( PortalConfig.getSearchConfig() +
                            "/digester-rules.xml" );

      Digester digester = DigesterLoader.createDigester(
                                          rules.toURL() );

      ourConfig = (ConfigHolder) digester.parse( input );
    } catch( ... ) {
      // ...
    }
  }

  return ourConfig;
}
```

This method tells the tale of Digester. It takes the XML configuration file (search-config.xml) and the rules for building the object model (digester-rules.xml) and throws them in a pot together, and you end up with the object model (ourConfig).

XML configuration file

The config file drives the index process and aids the search system. To register a particular index source, simply add an entry under the <index-source> element. Listing 10.10 shows an example of our configuration.

Listing 10.10 Sample search-config.xml file

```
<search-config>
  <!-- The path to where the search index is kept -->
  <index-location windows="/temp/tss-searchindex"
                  unix="/tss/searchindex" />

  <!-- Starting year of content which is indexed -->
  <beginning-year>2000</beginning-year>

  <!-- Information on search results -->
  <search-results results-per-page="10" />
```

```xml
<!-- Index Plan Configuration -->
<index-plan name="production-build">
  <optimize-frequency>400</optimize-frequency>
</index-plan>

<index-plan name="test-build">
  <optimize-frequency>0</optimize-frequency>
</index-plan>

<index-plan name="daily-incremental">
  <incremental-build>1</incremental-build>
  <optimize-frequency>0</optimize-frequency>
</index-plan>

<!-- Category Config Mapping -->
<categories>
  <category number="1" name="news" boost="1.3" />
  <category number="2" name="discussions" boost="0.6" />
  <category number="3" name="patterns"    boost="1.1" />
  <category number="4" name="reviews"     boost="1.08"/>
  <category number="5" name="articles"    boost="1.1" />
  <category number="6" name="talks"       boost="1.0" />
</categories>

<!-- Boost Value Configuration -->
<boost date-base-amount="1.0" date-boost-per-count="0.02"
       title="2.0" summary="1.4" />

<!-- List all of the Index Sources -->
<index-sources>
  <thread-index-source summary-length="300"
           class-name="com.portal.util.search.ThreadIndexSource">
    <excluded-forums>
      <forum>X</forum>
    </excluded-forums>
  </thread-index-source>

  <article-index-source
           class-name="com.portal.util.search.ArticleIndexSource"
           directory="web/tssdotcom/articles"
           category-name="articles"
           path-prefix="/articles/article.jsp?l="
           default-creation-date="today"
           default-modified-date="today" />

</index-sources>

</search-config>
```

If you peruse the file, you see that now we can tweak the way that the index is built via elements such as <boost>, the <categories>, and information in

`<index-sources>`. This flexibility allowed us to play with various boost settings until they felt right.

Digester Rules file

How does the Digester take the search-config.xml and know how to build the object model for us? This magic is done with a Digester Rules file. Here we tell the Digester what to do when it comes across a given tag.

Normally you will tell the engine to do something like this:

1   Create a new object `IndexPlan` when you find an `<index-plan>`.

2   Take the attribute values, and call set methods on the corresponding object (`category.setNumber(...)`, `category.setName(...)`, and so on).

Listing 10.11 shows a snippet of the rules that we employ.

Listing 10.11   A snippet of the digester-rules.xml

```xml
<?xml version="1.0"?>

<digester-rules>
  <!-- Top Level ConfigHolder Object -->
  <pattern value="search-config">
    <object-create-rule
        classname="com.portal.util.search.config.ConfigHolder" />
      <set-properties-rule/>
  </pattern>

  <!-- Search Results -->
  <pattern value="search-config/search-results">
    <set-properties-rule>
      <alias attr-name="results-per-page"
             prop-name="resultsPerPage" />
    </set-properties-rule>
  </pattern>

  <!-- Index Plan -->
  <pattern value="search-config/index-plan">
    <object-create-rule
              classname="com.portal.util.search.config.IndexPlan" />
    <bean-property-setter-rule pattern="incremental-build"
                               propertyname="incrementalBuild" />
    <bean-property-setter-rule pattern="optimize-frequency"
                               propertyname="optimizeFrequency" />
    <set-properties-rule/>
    <set-next-rule methodname="addIndexPlan" />
  </pattern>

... more rules here ...

</digester-rules>
```

All of the rules for the Digester are out of scope of this case study, but you can probably guess a lot from this snippet. For more information, visit http://jakarta.apache.org/commons/digester.[15]

So, thanks to another open-source tool, we were able to create a fairly simple yet powerful set of configuration rules for our particular search needs. We didn't have to use an XML configuration route, but it allows us to be flexible. If we were *really* good people, we would have refactored the system to allow for programmatic configuration. To do that nicely would be fairly trivial. We would have a configuration interface and use Dependency Injection (IoC) to allow the code to setup any implementation (one being the XML file builder, the other coming from manual coding).

10.7.6 Web tier: TheSeeeeeeeeeeeeeerverSide?

At this point we have a nice clean interface into building an index and searching on one. Since we need users to search the content via a web interface, the last item on the development list was to create the web layer hook into the search interface.

TheServerSide portal infrastructure uses a home-grown MVC web tier. It is home grown purely because it was developed before the likes of Struts, WebWork, or Tapestry. Our system has the notion of *actions* (or, as we call them, *assemblers*), so to create the web glue we had to

- Create a web action: SearchAssembler.java
- Create a web view: The search page and results

SearchAssembler web action

The web tier action is responsible for taking the input from the user, passing through to `IndexSearch.search(...)`, and packaging the results in a format ready for the view. There isn't anything at all interesting in this code. We take the search query input for the user and build the Lucene query, ready for the search infrastructure. What do I mean by "build the query"? Simply put, we add all of the query information given by the user into one Lucene query string.

For example, if the user typed **Lucene** in the search box, selected a date "after Jan 1 2003", and narrowed the search categories to "news", we would end up building

```
Lucene AND category:news AND modifieddate_range:[20040101 TO 20100101]
```

So our code contains small snippets such as

---

[15] Authors' note: Digester is also used for indexing XML documents in section 7.2.

```
if (dateRangeType.equals("before")) {
  querySB.append(
      " AND modifieddate_range:[19900101 TO " + dateRange + "]");
} else if (dateRangeType.equals("after")) {
  querySB.append(
      " AND modifieddate_range:[" + dateRange + " TO 20100101¹⁶]");
}
```

Search view

The view technology that we use is JSP (again, for legacy reasons). We use our MVC to make sure that Java code is kept out of the JSPs themselves. So, what we see in this code is basically just HTML with a couple of JSP tags here and there.

The one piece of real logic is when there are multiple results (see figure 10.9). Here we have to do some math to show the result pages, what page you are on,

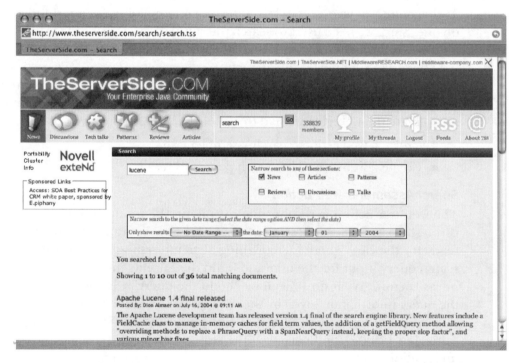

Figure 10.9 TheSeeeeeeeeeeeverSide

---

[16] Authors' note: Oh great, so we have a Y2010 issue on TSS. Dion probably thinks he won't be working there by then and someone else will have the pleasure of tracking down why searches don't work on January 2, 2010! ☺

and so on. This should look familiar to pagination in Google and the like. The only difference is that we always show the first page, because we have found that most of the time, page 1 is really what you want. This is where we could have really copied Google and placed *TheSeeeeeeeeeerverside* along the pages.

The web tier is clean and kept as thin as possible. We leverage the work done in the `IndexBuild` and `IndexSearch` high-level interfaces to Lucene.

10.7.7 *Summary*

You have seen all of the parts and pieces of TheServerSide search subsystem. We leveraged the power of Lucene, yet expose an abstracted search view. If we had to support another search system, then we could plug that in behind the scenes, and the users of the search packages wouldn't be affected.

Having said that, we don't see any reason to move away from Lucene. It has been a pleasure to work with and is one of the best pieces of open source software that I have personally ever worked with.

TheServerSide search used be a weak link on the site. Now it is a powerhouse. I am constantly using it as Editor, and now I manage to find exactly what I want.

Indexing our data is so fast that we don't even need to run the incremental build plan that we developed. At one point we mistakenly had an `Index-Writer.optimize()` call every time we added a document. When we relaxed that to run less frequently, we brought down the index time to a matter of seconds. It used to take a lot longer, even as long as 45 minutes.[17]

So to recap: We have gained relevance, speed, and power with this approach. We can tweak the way we index and search our content with little effort.

Thanks *so* much to the entire Lucene team.

10.8 *Conclusion*

It's us, Otis and Erik, back again. We personally have enjoyed reading these case studies. The techniques, tricks, and experiences provided by these case studies have factored back into our own knowledge and implicitly appear throughout this book. We left, for the most part, the original case study contributions intact as they were provided to us. This section gives us a chance to add our perspective.

Nutch, co-developed by Lucene's own creator Doug Cutting, is a phenomenal architecture designed for large server-farm scalability. Lucene itself has benefited

---

[17] Authors' note: Index optimization is covered in section 2.8.

from Doug's Nutch efforts. The Nutch analyzer is a clever alternative to avoid precision loss due to stop-word removal but keeping search speeds maximized.

The jGuru site search provides top-quality search results for Java terms. Lucene's own FAQ lives at jGuru. Give the site a try next time you have a Java-related question. It's often better than Google queries because of its domain-specific nature.

SearchBlox gives Lucene something it lacks: a user interface and manageability. Lucene itself is a low-level API that must be incorporated into applications by developers. Many times, folks are misled by Lucene's description and expect it to include the types of features SearchBlox provides.

LingPipe and orthographic variation—wow! We feel like we've just walked into the middle of a PhD-level linguistic analysis course. Bob Carpenter is a legendary figure in this space and a renowned author.

Michaels.com and TheServerSide show us that using Lucene doesn't require complex code, and being clever in how Lucene is incorporated yields nifty effects. Indexing hexadecimal RGB values and providing external indexing and searching configuration are two such examples of straightforward and demonstrably useful techniques.

We would again like to thank the contributors of these case studies for their time and their willingness to share what they've done for your benefit.

Installing Lucene

The Java version of Lucene is just another JAR file. Using Lucene's API in your code requires only this single JAR file on your build and runtime classpath. This appendix provides the specifics of where to obtain Lucene, how to work with the distribution contents, and how to build Lucene directly from its source code. If you're using a port of Lucene in a language other than Java, refer to chapter 9 and the documentation provided with the port. This appendix covers the Java version only.

A.1 *Binary installation*

To obtain the binary distribution of Lucene, follow these steps:

1   Download the latest binary Lucene release from the download area of the Jakarta web site: http://jakarta.apache.org. At the time of this writing, the latest version is 1.4.2; the subsequent steps assume this version. Download either the .zip or .tar.gz file, whichever format is most convenient for your environment.

2   Extract the binary file to the directory of your choice on your file system. The archive contains a top-level directory named lucene-1.4.2, so it's safe to extract to c:\ on Windows or your home directory on UNIX. On Windows, if you have WinZip handy, use it to open the .zip file and extract its contents to c:\. If you're on UNIX or using cygwin on Windows, unzip and untar (`tar zxvf lucene-1.4.2.tar.gz`) the .tar.gz file in your home directory.

3   Under the created lucene-1.4.2 directory, you'll find lucene-1.4.2.jar. This is the only file required to introduce Lucene into your applications. How you incorporate Lucene's JAR file into your application depends on your environment; there are numerous options. We recommend using Ant to build your application's code. Be sure your code is compiled against the Lucene JAR using the classpath options of the `<javac>` task.

4   Include Lucene's JAR file in your application's distribution appropriately. For example, a web application using Lucene would include lucene-1.4.2.jar in the WEB-INF/lib directory. For command-line applications, be sure Lucene is on the classpath when launching the JVM.

The binary distribution includes a substantial amount of documentation, including Javadocs. The root of the documentation is docs/index.html, which you can open in a web browser. Lucene's distribution also ships two demonstration applications. We apologize in advance for the crude state of these demos—they lack polish when it comes to ease of use—but the documentation (found in docs/demo.html) describes how to use them step by step; we also cover the basics of running them here.

A.2 *Running the command-line demo*

The command-line Lucene demo consists of two command-line programs: one that indexes a directory tree of files and another that provides a simple search interface. To run this demo, set your current working directory to the directory where the binary distribution was expanded. Next, run the IndexFiles program like this:

```
java -cp lucene-1.4.2.jar;lucene-demos-1.4.2.jar
⇒   org.apache.lucene.demo.IndexFiles docs

 .
 .
 .

adding docs/queryparsersyntax.html
adding docs/resources.html
adding docs/systemproperties.html
adding docs/whoweare.html
9454 total milliseconds
```

This command indexes the entire docs directory tree (339 files in our case) into an index stored in the index subdirectory of the location where you executed the command.

NOTE Literally every file in the docs directory tree is indexed, including .gif and .jpg files. None of the files are parsed; instead, each file is indexed by streaming its bytes into StandardAnalyzer.

To search the index just created, execute SearchFiles in this manner:

```
java -cp lucene-1.4.2.jar;lucene-demos-1.4.2.jar
            org.apache.lucene.demo.SearchFiles

Query: IndexSearcher AND QueryParser
Searching for: +indexsearcher +queryparser
10 total matching documents
0. docs/api/index-all.html
1. docs/api/allclasses-frame.html
2. docs/api/allclasses-noframe.html
3. docs/api/org/apache/lucene/search/class-use/Query.html
4. docs/api/overview-summary.html
5. docs/api/overview-tree.html
6. docs/demo2.html
```

```
7. docs/demo4.html
8. docs/api/org/apache/lucene/search/package-summary.html
9. docs/api/org/apache/lucene/search/package-tree.html
```

SearchFiles prompts interactively with Query:. QueryParser is used with Standard-Analyzer to create a Query. A maximum of 10 hits are shown at a time; if there are more, you can page through them. Press Ctrl-C to exit the program.

A.3 *Running the web application demo*

The web demo is slightly involved to set up and run properly. You need a web container; our instructions are for Tomcat 5. The docs/demo.html documentation provides detailed instructions for setting up and running the web application, but you can also follow the steps provided here.

The index used by the web application differs slightly from that in the command-line demo. First, it restricts itself to indexing only .html, .htm, and .txt files. Each file it processes (including .txt files) is parsed using a custom rudimentary HTML parser. To build the index initially, execute IndexHTML:

```
java -cp lucene-1.4.2.jar;lucene-demos-1.4.2.jar
  org.apache.lucene.demo.IndexHTML -create -index webindex docs


    .
    .
    .
adding docs/resources.html
adding docs/systemproperties.html
adding docs/whoweare.html
Optimizing index...
7220 total milliseconds
```

The -index webindex switch sets the location of the index directory. In a moment, you'll need the full path to this directory to configure the web application. The final docs argument to IndexHTML is the directory tree to index. The –create switch creates an index from scratch. Remove this switch to update the index with files that have been added or changed since the last time the index was built.

Next, deploy luceneweb.war (from the root directory of the extracted distribution) into CATALINA_HOME/webapps. Start Tomcat, wait for the container to complete the startup routine, and then edit CATALINA_HOME/webapps/lucene-web/configuration.jsp using a text editor (Tomcat should have expanded the .war file into a luceneweb directory automatically). Change the value of indexLocation appropriately, as in this example, specifying the absolute path to the index you built with IndexHTML:

```
String indexLocation =
    "/dev/LuceneInAction/install/lucene-1.4.2/webindex";
```

Now you're ready to try the web application. Visit http://localhost:8080/lucene-web in your web browser, and you should see "Welcome to the Lucene Template application..." (you can also change the header and footer text in configuration.jsp). If all is well with your configuration, searching for Lucene-specific words such as `"QueryParser AND Analyzer"` should list valid results based on Lucene's documentation.

You may try to click on one of the search results links and receive an error. `IndexHTML` indexes a `url` field, which in this case is a relative path of docs/.... To make the result links work properly, copy the `docs` directory from the Lucene distribution to CATALINA_HOME/webapps/luceneweb.

Yes, these steps are a bit more manual than they should be. Rest assured that improvements to Lucene's example applications are on our to-do list as soon as we're finished writing this book!

> **TIP** Cool hand Luke. Now that you've built two indexes, one for the command-line demo and the other for the web application demo, it's a perfect time to try Luke. See section 8.2 for details on using Luke. Point it at the index, and surf around a bit to get a feel for Luke and the contents of the index.

A.4 *Building from source*

Lucene's source code is freely and easily available from Apache Jakarta's CVS repository. The prerequisites to obtain and build Lucene from source are CVS client, Java Developer Kit (JDK), and Apache Ant. Follow these steps to build Lucene:

1 Check out the source code from Apache's CVS repository. Follow the instructions at the Jakarta web site (http://jakarta.apache.org) to access the repository using anonymous read-only access. This boils down to executing the following commands (from cygwin on Windows, or a UNIX shell):

```
cvs -d :pserver:anoncvs@cvs.apache.org:/home/cvspublic login
password: anoncvs

cvs -d :pserver:anoncvs@cvs.apache.org:/home/cvspublic
        checkout jakarta-lucene
```

2 Build Lucene with Ant. At the command prompt, set your current working directory to the directory where you checked out the Lucene CVS repository (C:\apache\jakarta-lucene, for example). Type `ant` at the command

line. Lucene's JAR will be compiled to the build subdirectory. The JAR filename is lucene-<*version*>.jar, where <*version*> depends on the current state of the code you obtained.

3   Run the unit tests. If the Ant build succeeds, next run `ant test` (add JUnit's JAR to ANT_HOME/lib if it isn't already there) and ensure that all of Lucene's unit tests pass.

Lucene uses JavaCC grammars for `StandardTokenizer`, `QueryParser`, and the demo `HTMLParser`. The already-compiled .java version of the .jj files exists in the CVS source code, so JavaCC isn't needed for compilation. However, if you wish to modify the parser grammars, you need JavaCC; you must also run the `ant javacc` target. You can find more details in the BUILD.txt file in the root directory of Lucene's CVS repository.

A.5 *Troubleshooting*

We'd rather not try to guess what kinds of issues you may run into as you follow the steps to install Lucene, build Lucene, or run the demos. Checking the FAQ, searching the archives of the lucene-user e-mail list, and using Lucene's issue-tracking system are good first steps when you have questions or issues. You'll find details at the Lucene web site: http://jakarta.apache.org/lucene.

B
Lucene index format

So far, we have treated the Lucene index more or less as a black box and have concerned ourselves only with its logical view. Although you don't need to understand index structure details in order to use Lucene, you may be curious about the "magic." Lucene's index structure is a case study in itself of highly efficient data structures and clever arrangement to maximize performance and minimize resource usage. You may see it as a purely technical achievement, or you can view it as a masterful work of art. There is something innately beautiful about representing rich structure in the most efficient manner possible. (Consider the information represented by fractal formulas or DNA as nature's proof.)

In this appendix, we'll look at the logical view of a Lucene index, where we've fed documents into Lucene and retrieved them during searches. Then, we'll expose the inner structure of Lucene's inverted index.

B.1 *Logical index view*

Let's first take a step back and start with a quick review of what you already know about Lucene's index. Consider figure B.1. From the perspective of a software developer using Lucene API, an index can be considered a black box represented by the abstract `Directory` class. When indexing, you create instances of the Lucene `Document` class and populate it with `Fields` that consist of name and value

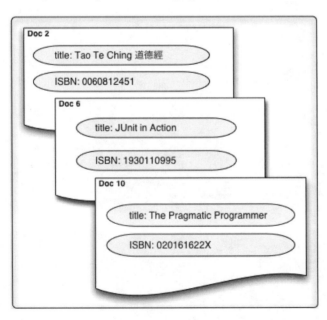

Figure B.1
The logical, black-box view
of a Lucene index

pairs. Such a `Document` is then indexed by passing it to `IndexWriter.addDocument` `(Document)`. When searching, you again use the abstract `Directory` class to represent the index. You pass that `Directory` to the `IndexSearcher` class and then find `Document`s that match a given query by passing search terms encapsulated in the `Query` object to one of `IndexSearcher`'s search methods. The results are matching `Document`s represented by the `Hits` object.

B.2 *About index structure*

When we described Lucene's `Directory` class in section 1.5, we pointed out that one of its concrete subclasses, `FSDirectory`, stores the index in a file-system directory. We have also used `Indexer`, a program for indexing text files, shown in listing 1.1. Recall that we specified several arguments when we invoked `Indexer` from the command line and that one of those arguments was the directory in which we wanted `Indexer` to create a Lucene index. What does that directory look like once `Indexer` is done running? What does it contain? In this section, we'll peek into a Lucene index and explain its structure.

Lucene supports two index structures: multifile indexes and compound indexes. The former is the original, older index structure; the latter was introduced in Lucene 1.3 and made the default in version 1.4. Let's look at each type of index structure, starting with multifile.

B.2.1 *Understanding the multifile index structure*

If you look at the index directory created by our `Indexer`, you'll see a number of files whose names may seem random at first. These are *index files*, and they look similar to those shown here:

```
-rw-rw-r--    1 otis     otis            4   Nov 22 22:43 deletable
-rw-rw-r--    1 otis     otis      1000000   Nov 22 22:43 _lfyc.f1
-rw-rw-r--    1 otis     otis      1000000   Nov 22 22:43 _lfyc.f2
-rw-rw-r--    1 otis     otis     31030502   Nov 22 22:28 _lfyc.fdt
-rw-rw-r--    1 otis     otis      8000000   Nov 22 22:28 _lfyc.fdx
-rw-rw-r--    1 otis     otis           16   Nov 22 22:28 _lfyc.fnm
-rw-rw-r--    1 otis     otis   1253701335   Nov 22 22:43 _lfyc.frq
-rw-rw-r--    1 otis     otis   1871279328   Nov 22 22:43 _lfyc.prx
-rw-rw-r--    1 otis     otis        14122   Nov 22 22:43 _lfyc.tii
-rw-rw-r--    1 otis     otis      1082950   Nov 22 22:43 _lfyc.tis
-rw-rw-r--    1 otis     otis           18   Nov 22 22:43 segments
```

Notice that some files share the same prefix. In this example index, a number of files start with the prefix *_lfyc*, followed by various extensions. This leads us to the notion of *segments*.

Index segments

A Lucene index consists of one or more segments, and each segment is made up of several index files. Index files that belong to the same segment share a common prefix and differ in the suffix. In the previous example index, the index consisted of a single segment whose files started with _lfyc:

The following example shows an index with two segments, _lfyc and _gabh:

```
-rw-rw-r--    1 otis      otis                4   Nov 22 22:43 deletable
-rw-rw-r--    1 otis      otis          1000000   Nov 22 22:43 _lfyc.f1
-rw-rw-r--    1 otis      otis          1000000   Nov 22 22:43 _lfyc.f2
-rw-rw-r--    1 otis      otis         31030502   Nov 22 22:28 _lfyc.fdt
-rw-rw-r--    1 otis      otis          8000000   Nov 22 22:28 _lfyc.fdx
-rw-rw-r--    1 otis      otis               16   Nov 22 22:28 _lfyc.fnm
-rw-rw-r--    1 otis      otis       1253701335   Nov 22 22:43 _lfyc.frq
-rw-rw-r--    1 otis      otis       1871279328   Nov 22 22:43 _lfyc.prx
-rw-rw-r--    1 otis      otis            14122   Nov 22 22:43 _lfyc.tii
-rw-rw-r--    1 otis      otis          1082950   Nov 22 22:43 _lfyc.tis
-rw-rw-r--    1 otis      otis          1000000   Nov 22 22:43 _gabh.f1
-rw-rw-r--    1 otis      otis          1000000   Nov 22 22:43 _gabh.f2
-rw-rw-r--    1 otis      otis         31030502   Nov 22 22:28 _gabh.fdt
-rw-rw-r--    1 otis      otis          8000000   Nov 22 22:28 _gabh.fdx
-rw-rw-r--    1 otis      otis               16   Nov 22 22:28 _gabh.fnm
-rw-rw-r--    1 otis      otis       1253701335   Nov 22 22:43 _gabh.frq
-rw-rw-r--    1 otis      otis       1871279328   Nov 22 22:43 _gabh.prx
-rw-rw-r--    1 otis      otis            14122   Nov 22 22:43 _gabh.tii
-rw-rw-r--    1 otis      otis          1082950   Nov 22 22:43 _gabh.tis
-rw-rw-r--    1 otis      otis               18   Nov 22 22:43 segments
```

You can think of a segment as a subindex, although each segment isn't a fully independent index.

As you can see in figure B.2, each segment contains one or more Lucene Documents, the same ones we add to the index with the addDocument(Document) method in the IndexWriter class. By now you may be wondering what function segments serve in a Lucene index; what follows is the answer to that question.

Incremental indexing

Using segments lets you quickly add new Documents to the index by adding them to newly created index segments and only periodically merging them with other, existing segments. This process makes additions efficient because it minimizes physical index modifications. Figure B.2 shows an index that holds 34 Documents. This figure shows an unoptimized index—it contains multiple segments. If this index were to be optimized using the default Lucene indexing parameters, all 34 of its documents would be merged in a single segment.

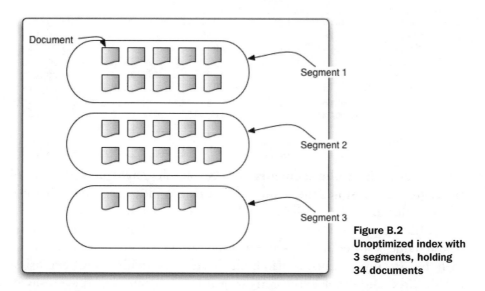

**Figure B.2
Unoptimized index with
3 segments, holding
34 documents**

One of Lucene's strengths is that it supports incremental indexing, which isn't something every IR library is capable of. Whereas some IR libraries need to reindex the whole corpus when new data is added to their index, Lucene does not. After a document has been added to an index, its content is immediately made searchable. In IR terminology, this important feature is called *incremental indexing*. The fact that Lucene supports incremental indexing makes Lucene suitable for environments that deal with large bodies of information where complete reindexing would be unwieldy.

Because new segments are created as new Documents are indexed, the number of segments, and hence index files, varies while indexing is in progress. Once an index is fully built, the number of index files and segments remains steady.

A closer look at index files

Each index file carries a certain type of information essential to Lucene. If any index file is modified or removed by anything other than Lucene itself, the index becomes corrupt, and the only option is a complete reindexing of the original data. On the other hand, you can add random files to a Lucene index directory without corrupting the index. For instance, if we add a file called random-document.txt to the index directory, as shown here, Lucene ignores that file, and the index doesn't become corrupt:

```
-rw-rw-r--    1 otis     otis           4   Nov 22 22:43 deletable
-rw-rw-r--    1 otis     otis     1000000   Nov 22 22:43 _1fyc.f1
```

```
-rw-rw-r--    1 otis    otis     1000000     Nov 22 22:43 _lfyc.f2
-rw-rw-r--    1 otis    otis    31030502     Nov 22 22:28 _lfyc.fdt
-rw-rw-r--    1 otis    otis     8000000     Nov 22 22:28 _lfyc.fdx
-rw-rw-r--    1 otis    otis          16     Nov 22 22:28 _lfyc.fnm
-rw-rw-r--    1 otis    otis  1253701335     Nov 22 22:43 _lfyc.frq
-rw-rw-r--    1 otis    otis  1871279328     Nov 22 22:43 _lfyc.prx
-rw-rw-r--    1 otis    otis       14122     Nov 22 22:43 _lfyc.tii
-rw-rw-r--    1 otis    otis     1082950     Nov 22 22:43 _lfyc.tis
-rw-rw-r--    1 otis    otis         128     Nov 23 12:34
⇒    random-document.txt
-rw-rw-r--    1 otis    otis          18     Nov 22 22:43 segments
```

The secret to this is the segments file. As you may have guessed from its name, the segments file stores the names of all existing index segments. Before accessing any files in the index directory, Lucene consults this file to figure out which index files to open and read. Our example index has a single segment, _lfyc, whose name is stored in this segments file, so Lucene knows to look only for files with the *_lfyc* prefix. Lucene also limits itself to files with known extensions, such as .fdt, .fdx, and other extensions shown in our example, so even saving a file with a segment prefix, such as _lfyc.txt, won't throw Lucene off. Of course, polluting an index directory with non-Lucene files is strongly discouraged.

The exact number of files that constitute a Lucene index and each segment varies from index to index and depends on the number of fields the index contains. However, every index contains a single segments file and a single deletable file. The latter file contains information about documents that have been marked for deletion. If you look back at the previous example, you'll notice two index files with a .f*N* extension, where *N* is a number. These files correspond to the indexed fields present in the indexed Documents. Recall that Indexer from listing 1.1 created Lucene Documents with two fields: a text contents field and a keyword filename field. Because this index contains two indexed fields, our index contains two files with the .f*N* extension. If this index had three indexed fields, a file named _lfyc.f3 would also be present in the index directory. By looking for index files with this extension, you can easily tell how many indexed fields an index has. Another interesting thing to note about these .f*N* files is their size, which reflects the number of Documents with that field. Now that you know this, you can tell that the previous index has 1,000,000 documents just by glancing at the files in the index directory.

Creating a multifile index

By now you should have a good grasp of the multifile index structure; but how do you use the API to instruct Lucene to create a multifile index and not the default compound-file index? Let's look back at our faithful `Indexer` from listing 1.1. In that listing, you'll spot the following:

```
IndexWriter writer = new IndexWriter(indexDir,
    new StandardAnalyzer(), true);
writer.setUseCompoundFile(false);
```

Because the compound-file index structure is the default, we disable it and switch to a multifile index by calling `setUseCompoundFile(false)` on an `IndexWriter` instance.

B.2.2 *Understanding the compound index structure*

When we described multifile indexes, we said that the number of index files depends on the number of indexed fields present in the index. We also mentioned that new segments are created as documents are added to an index; since a segment consists of a set of index files, this results in a variable and possibly large number of files in an index directory. Although the multifile index structure is straightforward and works for most scenarios, it isn't suitable for environments with large number of indexes, indexes with a large number of fields, and other environment where using Lucene results in a large number of index files.

Most, if not all, contemporary operating systems limit the number of files in the system that can be opened at one time. Recall that Lucene creates new segments as new documents are added, and every so often it merges them to reduce the number of index files. However, while the merge procedure is executing, the number of index files doubles. If Lucene is used in an environment with lots of indexes that are being searched or indexed simultaneously, it's possible to reach the limit of open files set by the operating system. This can also happen with a single Lucene index if the index isn't optimized or if other applications are running simultaneously and keeping many files open. Lucene's use of open file handles depends on the structure and state of an index. Later in the appendix, we present formulas for calculating the number of open files that Lucene will require for handling your indexes.

Compound index files

The only visible difference between the compound and multifile indexes is the contents of an index directory. Here's an example of a compound index:

```
-rw-rw-r--    1 otis    otis         418 Oct 12 22:13 _2.cfs
-rw-rw-r--    1 otis    otis           4 Oct 12 22:13 deletable
-rw-rw-r--    1 otis    otis          15 Oct 12 22:13 segments
```

Instead of having to open and read 10 files from the index, as in the multifile index, Lucene must open only two files when accessing this compound index, thereby consuming fewer system resources.[1] The compound index reduces the number of index files, but the concept of segments, documents, fields, and terms still applies. The difference is that a compound index contains a single .cfs file per segment, whereas each segment in a multifile index contains consists of seven different files. The compound structure encapsulates individual index files in a single .cfs file.

Creating a compound index

Because the compound index structure is the default, you don't have to do anything to specify it. However, if you like explicit code, you can call the setUse-Compound(boolean) method, passing it a true value:

```
IndexWriter writer = new IndexWriter(indexDir,
  new StandardAnalyzer(), true);
writer.setUseCompoundFile(true);
```

Pleasantly, you aren't locked into the multifile or compound format. After indexing, you can still convert from one format to another.

B.2.3 Converting from one index structure to the other

It's important to note that you can switch between the two described index structures at any point during indexing. All you have to do is call the IndexWriter's set-UseCompoundFiles(boolean) method at any time during indexing; the next time Lucene merges index segments, it will convert the index to whichever structure you specified.

Similarly, you can convert the structure of an existing index without adding more documents to it. For example, you may have a multifile index that you want to convert to a compound one, to reduce the number of open files used by Lucene. To do so, open your index with IndexWriter, specify the compound structure, optimize the index, and close it:

```
IndexWriter writer = new IndexWriter(indexDir,
  new StandardAnalyzer(), false);
writer.setUseCompoundFile(true);
writer.optimize();
writer.close();
```

---

[1] We don't count the deletable file because it doesn't have to be read during indexing or searching.

Note that the third `IndexWriter` parameter is `false` to ensure that the existing index isn't destroyed. We discussed optimizing indexes in section 2.8. Optimizing forces Lucene to merge index segments, thereby giving it a chance to write them in a new format specified via the `setUseCompoundFile(boolean)` method.

B.3 Choosing the index structure

Although switching between the two index structures is simple, you may want to know beforehand how many open files resources Lucene will use when accessing your index. If you're designing a system with multiple simultaneously indexed and searched indexes, you'll most definitely want to take out a pen and a piece of paper and do some simple math with us now.

B.3.1 Calculating the number of open files

Let's consider a multifile index first. A multifile index contains seven index files for each segment, an additional file for each indexed field per segment, and a single deletable and a single segments file for the whole index. Imagine a system that contains 100 Lucene indexes, each with 10 indexed fields. Also assume that these indexes aren't optimized and that each has nine segments that haven't been merged into a single segment yet, as is often the case during indexing. If all 100 indexes are open for searching at the same time, this will result in 15,300 open files. Here is how we got this number:

```
100 indexes * (9 segments per index *
    (7 files per segment + 10 files for indexed fields))
= 100 * 9 * 17
= 15300 open files
```

Although today's computers can usually handle this many open files, most come with a preconfigured limit that is much lower. In section 2.7.1, we discuss how to check and change this in some operating systems.

Next, let's consider the same 100 indexes, but this time using the compound structure. Only a single file with a .cfs extension is created per segment, in addition to a single deletable and a single segments file for the whole index. Therefore, if we use the compound index instead of the multifile one, the number of open files is reduced to 900:

```
100 indexes * (9 segments per index * (1 file per segment))
= 100 * 9 * 1
= 900 open files
```

The lesson here is that if you need to develop Lucene-based software that will run in environments with a large number of Lucene indexes with a number of indexed fields, you should consider using a compound index. Of course, you can use a compound index even if you're writing a simple application that deals with a single Lucene index.

B.3.2 *Comparing performance*

Performance is another factor you should consider when choosing the index structure. Some people have reported that creating an index with a compound structure is 5–10% slower than creating an equivalent multifile index; our indexing performance test, shown in listing B.1, confirms this. In this test, we create two parallel indexes with 25,000 artificially created documents each. In the `testTiming()` method, we time how long the indexing process takes for each type of index and assert that creation of the compound index takes more time than creation of its multifield cousin.

Listing B.1 Comparison of compound and multifile index performance

```
public class CompoundVersusMultiFileIndexTest extends TestCase {

    private Directory cDir;
    private Directory mDir;
    private Collection docs = loadDocuments(5000, 10);

    protected void setUp() throws IOException {
        String indexDir =
            System.getProperty("java.io.tmpdir", "tmp") +
            System.getProperty("file.separator") + "index-dir";

        String cIndexDir = indexDir + "-compound";
        String mIndexDir = indexDir + "-multi";
        (new File(cIndexDir)).delete();
        (new File(mIndexDir)).delete();

        cDir = FSDirectory.getDirectory(cIndexDir, true);
        mDir = FSDirectory.getDirectory(mIndexDir, true);
    }

    public void testTiming() throws IOException {
        long cTiming = timeIndexWriter(cDir, true);
        long mTiming = timeIndexWriter(mDir, false);

        assertTrue(cTiming > mTiming);          ❶ Compound timing greater
                                                   than multifile timing
        System.out.println("Compound Time : " + (cTiming) + " ms");
        System.out.println("Multi-file Time: " + (mTiming) + " ms");
    }
```

```
private long timeIndexWriter(Directory dir, boolean isCompound)
  throws IOException {
  long start = System.currentTimeMillis();
  addDocuments(dir, isCompound);
  long stop = System.currentTimeMillis();
  return (stop - start);
}

private void addDocuments(Directory dir, boolean isCompound)
  throws IOException {
  IndexWriter writer = new IndexWriter(dir, new SimpleAnalyzer(),
    true);
  writer.setUseCompoundFile(isCompound);

  // change to adjust performance of indexing with FSDirectory
  writer.mergeFactor = writer.mergeFactor;
  writer.maxMergeDocs = writer.maxMergeDocs;
  writer.minMergeDocs = writer.minMergeDocs;

  for (Iterator iter = docs.iterator(); iter.hasNext();) {
    Document doc = new Document();
    String word = (String) iter.next();
    doc.add(Field.Keyword("keyword", word));
    doc.add(Field.UnIndexed("unindexed", word));
    doc.add(Field.UnStored("unstored", word));
    doc.add(Field.Text("text", word));
    writer.addDocument(doc);
  }
  writer.optimize();
  writer.close();
}

private Collection loadDocuments(int numDocs, int wordsPerDoc) {
  Collection docs = new ArrayList(numDocs);
  for (int i = 0; i < numDocs; i++) {
    StringBuffer doc = new StringBuffer(wordsPerDoc);
    for (int j = 0; j < wordsPerDoc; j++) {
      doc.append("Bibamus ");
    }
    docs.add(doc.toString());
  }
  return docs;
}
}
```

❶ This test confirms that creating an index with the compound structure is somewhat slower than building a multifile index. Exactly how much slower varies
and depends on the number of fields, their length, the indexing parameters

used, and so on. For instance, you may be able to get the compound structure index to outperform the multifile index by adjusting some of the indexing parameters described in section 2.7.

Here's our advice: If you need to squeeze every bit of indexing performance out of Lucene, use the multifile index structure, but first try tuning compound structure indexing by manipulating the indexing parameters covered in section 2.7. This performance difference and the difference in the amount of system resources the two index structures use are their only notable differences. All Lucene's features work equally well with either type of index.

B.4   Inverted index

Lucene uses a well-known index structure called an *inverted index*. Quite simply, and probably unsurprisingly, an inverted index is an inside-out arrangement of documents such that terms take center stage. Each term refers to the documents that contain it. Let's dissect our sample book data index to get a deeper glimpse at the files in an index `Directory`.

Regardless of whether you're working with a `RAMDirectory`, an `FSDirectory`, or any other `Directory` implementation, the internal structure is a group of files. In a `RAMDirectory`, the files are virtual and live entirely within RAM. `FSDirectory` literally represents an index as a file-system directory, as described earlier in this appendix.

The compound file mode (added in Lucene 1.3) adds an additional twist regarding the files in a `Directory`. When an `IndexWriter` is set for compound file mode, the "files" are written to a single .cfs file, which alleviates the common issue of running out of file handles. See the section "Compound index files" in this appendix for more information on the compound file mode.

B.4.1   Inside the index

The Lucene index format is detailed in all its gory detail on the Lucene web site at http://jakarta.apache.org/lucene/docs/fileformats.html. It would be painful for us, and tedious for you, if we repeated this detailed information here. Rather, we have chosen to summarize the overall file structure using our sample book data as a concrete example.

Our summary glosses over most of the intricacies of data compression used in the actual data representations. This extrapolation is helpful in giving you a feel for the structure instead of getting caught up in the minutiae (which, again, are detailed on the Lucene web site).

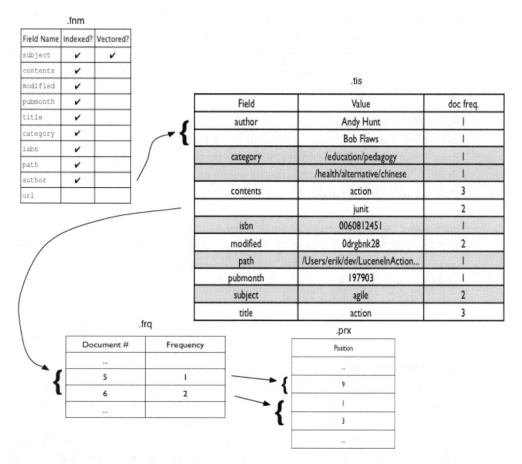

Figure B.3   Detailed look inside the Lucene index format

Figure B.3 represents a slice of our sample book index. The slice is of a single segment (in this case, we had an optimized index with only a single segment). A segment is given a unique filename prefix (_c in this case).

The following sections describe each of the files shown in figure B.3 in more detail.

Field names (.fnm)

The .fnm file contains all the field names used by documents in the associated segment. Each field is flagged to indicate whether it's indexed or vectored. The order of the field names in the .fnm file is determined during indexing and isn't necessarily alphabetical. The position of a field in the .fnm file is used to associate it with the normalization files (files with suffix .f[0–9]*). We don't delve into the normalization files here; refer to the Lucene web site for details.

In our sample index, only the `subject` field is vectored. The `url` field was added as a `Field.UnIndexed` field, which is neither indexed nor vectored. The .fnm file shown in figure B.4 is a complete view of the actual file.

Term dictionary (.tis)

All terms (tuples of field name and value) in a segment are stored in the .tis file. Terms are ordered first alphabetically by field name and then by value within a field. Each term entry contains its *document frequency:* the number of documents that contain this term within the segment.

Figure B.4 shows only a sampling of the terms in our index, one or more from each field. Note that the `url` field is missing because it was added as an `UnIndexed` field, which is stored only and not available as terms. Not shown is the .tii file, which is a cross-section of the .tis file designed to be kept in physical memory for random access to the .tis file. For each term in the .tis file, the .frq file contains entries for each document containing the term.

In our sample index, two books have the value "junit" in the `contents` field: *JUnit in Action* (document ID 6), and *Java Development with Ant* (document ID 5).

Term frequencies

Term frequencies in each document are listed in the .frq file. In our sample index, *Java Development with Ant* (document ID 5) has the value "junit" once in the `contents` field. *JUnit in Action* has the value "junit" twice, provided once by the title and once by the subject. Our `contents` field is an aggregation of title, subject, and author. The frequency of a term in a document factors into the score calculation (see section 3.3) and typically boosts a document's relevance for higher frequencies.

For each document listed in the .frq file, the positions (.prx) file contains entries for each occurrence of the term within a document.

Term positions

The .prx file lists the position of each term within a document. The position information is used when queries demand it, such as phrase queries and span queries. Position information for tokenized fields comes directly from the token position increments designated during analysis.

Figure B.4 shows three positions, for each occurrence of the term *junit*. The first occurrence is in document 5 (*Java Development with Ant*) in position 9. In the case of document 5, the field value (after analysis) is "java development ant apache jakarta ant build tool ***junit*** java development erik hatcher steve loughran". We used the `StandardAnalyzer`; thus stop words (*with* in *Java Development with Ant*, for example) are removed and aren't accounted for in positional information (see section 4.7.3 for more on stop word removal and positional information). Document 6, *JUnit in Action*, has a `contents` field containing the value "junit" twice, once in position 1 and again in position 3: "***junit*** action ***junit*** unit testing mock objects vincent massol ted husted".[2]

B.5 *Summary*

The rationale for the index structure is two-fold: maximum performance and minimum resource utilization. For example, if a field isn't indexed it's a very quick operation to dismiss it entirely from queries based on the indexed flag of the .fnm file. The .tii file, cached in RAM, allows for rapid random access into the term dictionary .tis file. Phrase and span queries need not look for positional information if the term itself isn't present. Streamlining the information most often needed, and minimizing the number of file accesses during searches is of critical concern. These are just some examples of how well thought out the index structure design was. If this sort of low-level optimization is of interest, please refer to the Lucene index file format details on the Lucene web site, where details we have glossed over here can be found.

---

[2] We're indebted to Luke, the fantastic index inspector, for allowing us to easily gather some of the data provided about the index structure.

Resources

Web search engines are your friends. Type **lucene** in your favorite search engine, and you'll find many interesting Lucene-related projects. Another good place to look is SourceForge; a search for **lucene** at SourceForge displays a number of open-source projects written on top of Lucene.

C.1 *Internationalization*

- Bray, Tim, "Characters vs. Bytes," http://www.tbray.org/ongoing/When/200x/2003/04/26/UTF
- Green, Dale, "Trail: Internationalization," http://java.sun.com/docs/books/tutorial/i18n/index.html
- Intertwingly, "Unicode and Weblogs," http://www.intertwingly.net/blog/1763.html
- Peterson, Erik, "Chinese Character Dictionary—Unicode Version", http://www.mandarintools.com/chardict_u8.html
- Spolsky, Joel, "The Absolute Minimum Every Software Developer Absolutely, Positively Must Know About Unicode and Character Sets (No Excuses!)," http://www.joelonsoftware.com/articles/Unicode.html

C.2 *Language detection*

- Apache Bug Database patch: language guesser contribution, http://issues.apache.org/bugzilla/show_bug.cgi?id=26763
- JTextCat 0.1, http://www.jedi.be/JTextCat/index.html
- NGramJ, http://ngramj.sourceforge.net/

C.3 *Term vectors*

- "How LSI Works," http://javelina.cet.middlebury.edu/lsa/out/lsa_explanation.htm
- "Latent Semantic Indexing (LSI)," http://www.cs.utk.edu/~lsi/
- Stata, Raymie, Krishna Bharat, and Farzin Maghoul, "The Term Vector Database: Fast Access to Indexing Terms for Web Pages," http://www9.org/w9cdrom/159/159.html

C.4 Lucene ports

- CLucene, http://www.sourceforge.net/projects/clucene/
- dotLucene, http://sourceforge.net/projects/dotlucene/
- Lupy, http://www.divmod.org/Home/Projects/Lupy/
- Plucene, http://search.cpan.org/dist/Plucene/
- PyLucene, http://pylucene.osafoundation.org/

C.5 Case studies

- Alias-i, http://www.alias-i.com/
- jGuru, http://www.jguru.com/
- Michaels, http://www.michaels.com/
- Nutch, http://www.nutch.org/
- SearchBlox Software, http://www.searchblox.com/
- TheServerSide.com, http://www.theserverside.com/
- XtraMind Technologies, http://www.xtramind.com/

C.6 Document parsers

- CyberNeko Tools for XNI, http://www.apache.org/~andyc/neko/doc/
- Digester, http://jakarta.apache.org/commons/digester/
- JTidy, http://sourceforge.net/projects/jtidy
- PDFBox, http://www.pdfbox.org/
- TextMining.org, http://www.textmining.org/
- Xerces2, http://xml.apache.org/xerces2-j/

C.7 Miscellaneous

- Calishain, Tara, and Rael Dornfest, *Google Hacks* (O'Reilly, 2003)
- Gilleland, Michael, "Levenshtein Distance, in Three Flavors," http://www.merriampark.com/ld.htm
- GNU Compiler for the Java (GCJ), http://gcc.gnu.org/java/
- Google search results for *Lucene*, http://www.google.com/search?q=lucene

- Jakarta Lucene, http://jakarta.apache.org/lucene
- Lucene Sandbox, http://jakarta.apache.org/lucene/docs/lucene-sandbox/
- SourceForge search results for *Lucene*, http://sourceforge.net/search?type_of_search=soft&words=lucene
- Suffix trees, http://sequence.rutgers.edu/st/
- SWIG, http://www.swig.org/

C.8 IR software

- dmoz results for *Information Retrieval*, http://dmoz.org/Computers/Software/Information_Retrieval/
- Egothor, http://www.egothor.org/
- Google Directory results for *Information Retrieval*, http://directory.google.com/Top/Computers/Software/Information_Retrieval/
- Harvest, http://www.sourceforge.net/projects/harvest/
- Harvest-NG, http://webharvest.sourceforge.net/ng/
- ht://Dig, http://www.htdig.org/
- Managing Gigabytes for Java (MG4J), http://mg4j.dsi.unimi.it/
- Namazu, http://www.namazu.org/
- Search Tools for Web Sites and Intranets, http://www.searchtools.com/
- SWISH++, http://homepage.mac.com/pauljlucas/software/swish/
- SWISH-E, http://swish-e.org/
- Verity, http://www.verity.com/
- Webglimpse, http://webglimpse.net
- Xapian, http://www.xapian.org/

C.9 Doug Cutting's publications

Doug's official online list of publications, from which this was derived, is available at http://lucene.sourceforge.net/publications.html.

C.9.1 Conference papers

- "An Interpreter for Phonological Rules," coauthored with J. Harrington, Proceedings of Institute of Acoustics Autumn Conference, November 1986

- "Information Theater versus Information Refinery," coauthored with J. Pedersen, P.-K. Halvorsen, and M. Withgott, AAAI Spring Symposium on Text-based Intelligent Systems, March 1990

- "Optimizations for Dynamic Inverted Index Maintenance," coauthored with J. Pedersen, Proceedings of SIGIR '90, September 1990

- "An Object-Oriented Architecture for Text Retrieval," coauthored with J. O. Pedersen and P.-K. Halvorsen, Proceedings of RIAO '91, April 1991

- "Snippet Search: a Single Phrase Approach to Text Access," coauthored with J. O. Pedersen and J. W. Tukey, Proceedings of the 1991 Joint Statistical Meetings, August 1991

- "A Practical Part-of-Speech Tagger," coauthored with J. Kupiec, J. Pedersen, and P. Sibun, Proceedings of the Third Conference on Applied Natural Language Processing, April 1992

- "Scatter/Gather: A Cluster-based Approach to Browsing Large Document Collections," coauthored with D. Karger, J. Pedersen, and J. Tukey, Proceedings of SIGIR '92, June 1992

- "Constant Interaction-Time Scatter/Gather Browsing of Very Large Document Collections," coauthored with D. Karger and J. Pedersen, Proceedings of SIGIR '93, June 1993

- "Porting a Part-of-Speech Tagger to Swedish," Nordic Datalingvistik Dagen 1993, Stockholm, June 1993

- "Space Optimizations for Total Ranking," coauthored with J. Pedersen, Proceedings of RIAO '97, Montreal, Quebec, June 1997

C.9.2 U.S. Patents

- 5,278,980: "Iterative technique for phrase query formation and an information retrieval system employing same," with J. Pedersen, P.-K. Halvorsen, J. Tukey, E. Bier, and D. Bobrow, filed August 1991

- 5,442,778: "Scatter-gather: a cluster-based method and apparatus for browsing large document collections," with J. Pedersen, D. Karger, and J. Tukey, filed November 1991

- 5,390,259: "Methods and apparatus for selecting semantically significant images in a document image without decoding image content," with M. Withgott, S. Bagley, D. Bloomberg, D. Huttenlocher, R. Kaplan, T. Cass, P.-K. Halvorsen, and R. Rao, filed November 1991

- 5,625,554 "Finite-state transduction of related word forms for text indexing and retrieval," with P.-K. Halvorsen, R.M. Kaplan, L. Karttunen, M. Kay, and J. Pedersen, filed July 1992

- 5,483,650 "Method of Constant Interaction-Time Clustering Applied to Document Browsing," with J. Pedersen and D. Karger, filed November 1992

- 5,384,703 "Method and apparatus for summarizing documents according to theme," with M. Withgott, filed July 1993

- 5,838,323 "Document summary computer system user interface," with D. Rose, J Bornstein, and J. Hatton, filed September 1995

- 5,867,164 "Interactive document summarization," with D. Rose, J. Bornstein, and J. Hatton, filed September 1995

- 5,870,740 "System and method for improving the ranking of information retrieval results for short queries," with D. Rose, filed September 1996

index